Parental Leave and Child Care

In the series
WOMEN IN THE POLITICAL ECONOMY,
edited by Ronnie J. Steinberg

Parental Leave and Child Care

Setting a Research and Policy Agenda

Edited by

Janet Shibley Hyde and
Marilyn J. Essex

Temple University Press ▪ *Philadelphia*

Temple University Press, Philadelphia 19122
Copyright © 1991 by Temple University. All rights reserved
Published 1991
Printed in the United States of America

The paper used in this publication meets the minimum
requirements of American National Standard for Information
Sciences—Permanence of Paper for Printed Library Materials,
ANSI Z39.48-1984 ∞

Library of Congress Cataloging-in-Publication Data

Parental leave and child care: setting a research and policy agenda/
edited by Janet Shibley Hyde and Marilyn J. Essex.
p. cm.—(Women in the political economy)
Includes bibliographical references.
ISBN 0-87722-732-2 (alk. paper)
1. Parental leave—United States. 2. Parental leave. 3. Child
care services—United States. 4. Child care services.
I. Hyde, Janet Shibley. II. Essex, Marilyn J. III. Series.
HD6065.5.U6P37 1990
362.7'12'0973—dc20   90-30258

Contents

v

Parental Leave and Child Care

Preface

PARENTAL LEAVE and child care are issues that have risen to prominence in recent years. At the national level, 1988 presidential candidates announced their intentions from the floors of day care centers, the Family and Medical Leave Act has received serious consideration in the U.S. Senate and House, and, as of this writing, the ABC Bill (Act for Better Child Care) has passed in the House of Representatives. In addition, in the last years of the 1980s, a number of states legislated some form of unpaid parental leave, and in many others such legislation is under consideration. The Ford Foundation saw these state trends as so important that it commissioned a study of four states with parental leave legislation; under the direction of Ellen Galinsky, the study will examine the actual experiences of employers and employees with the new laws.

Corporations and labor unions, too, are paying more attention to work and family issues. A 1989 labor contract for unionized employees of American Telephone & Telegraph featured substantial provisions for parental leave. The pharmaceutical firm of Johnson & Johnson has a glossy brochure, "Balancing Work and Family," that explains its flexible benefits plan, under which employees can choose from a variety of insurance plans and other benefits. J&J has family care leave (up to one year for male or female employees) at the time of birth or adoption, provides child care referral services, and, at the time of this writing, is building on-site child care centers at some of its larger facilities. Du Pont has a similar brochure entitled "Diversity: A Source of Strength," which discusses everything from affirmative action to child care.

In spite of this increased attention and concern however, relatively little progress has been made in most state and employer policies. As a result, families continue to experience stress from the competing demands of work and family responsibilities. We are currently faced with a pressing need for new parental leave and child care policy.

3

Women, especially those with young children, are significantly more likely to be in the workforce now. Whereas a third of mothers of children less than a year old were in the workforce in the late 1970s, over half are in the workforce today (see Chapter 1 by Sheila Kamerman). Yet current policies are not supportive of working mothers with infants; and they are even less supportive of fathers. Recent surveys of business and corporate policies show that many women lack sick leave coverage (which usually includes leave for pregnancy and childbirth-related disabilities) because they tend to work in small firms, where coverage is limited at best (see Chapter 11 by Eileen Trzcinski). Men, on the other hand, are more likely to have sick leave coverage, but not the broader parental leave coverage that would allow them to take time off around the births of their children. In fact, the majority of workers, both women and men, have no leave benefits that allow them to care for their infants beyond the protection available to some women while they are physically unable to work.

The State of Research

In part, parental leave and child care policy lags behind the needs of families because of the speed with which the workforce is changing. At the same time, there is little research knowledge on which to base sound policy decisions. There is considerable research on the effects of mothers' employment on children, for example, but much less on its effects on infants, and even less on its effects on women, men, and the family system. And, from the employer's point of view, very little is known about the effects of different parental leave and child care policies on work productivity and other business-related interests.

Although a large body of research has investigated the impact of mothers' employment on children's functioning and shown that they suffer neither emotional nor intellectual deprivation as a result (Hoffman, 1984), it has generally focused on school-aged children. When narrowed to the effects on infants, particularly in the first year, the findings are more sparse, complex, and contradictory. For example, because the quality of substitute child care is *thought* to have important effects on children's development, experts such as Edward Zigler (Zigler and Frank, 1988) advocate a six-month partially paid, voluntary infant-care leave. This may in fact be a good policy recommendation, but the research in this area is unclear.

The research on mothers' mental health during the post-partum period also shows contradictory results. Some research suggests that the tensions arising from trying to balance the multiple roles of mother, wife, and worker lead to depression, role strain, stress, and other health problems (see, for example, Cutrona and Troutman, 1986; Davidson and Robertson, 1985; Hock, Gnezda, and McBride, 1984). Other research shows that employed women are mentally and physically healthier than nonemployed women because multiple roles create more opportunities for self-esteem, status, and social identity (Baruch, Biener, and Barnett, 1987; Verbrugge, 1987). Furthermore, few studies have looked at mothers of infants in the first year. Research investigating the transition to parenthood, especially its effects on the marital relationship (Belsky, Lang, and Rovine 1985), shows a decline in the quality of marital life as the transition is made. These studies, however, have almost always ignored fathers.

Research on the effects of parental leave and child care benefits on employers is almost nonexistent, though many business organizations argue that a federally mandated policy would impose great difficulties on businesses, especially small ones. The U.S. Chamber of Commerce conducted a cost analysis of the proposed Family and Medical Leave Act (FMLA), concluding that it would cost American businesses $2.6 billion per year. This conclusion, in turn, was used to argue that undue costs to business, rather than benefits to families, should be the major consideration in assessing the FMLA. An important study by Roberta Spalter-Roth and Heidi Hartmann (see Chapter 3) provides a very different view of the economics of family leave.

The contributors to this volume explore themes that have previously received too little attention in either policy or research, recognizing the importance of considering all voices in the family unit—infants, mothers, and fathers; of allowing different sectors to speak to each other—business, labor, policymakers, and researchers; of acknowledging the different values and needs associated with cultural, ethnic, and social class diversity; and of bringing out a feminist analysis of these topics.

The seeds for this book were sown at a Wingspread Conference on parental leave and child care, conducted by the Women's Studies Research Center at the University of Wisconsin-Madison in September 1988. At that conference, we brought together representatives from business and labor as well as policymakers and researchers. Many of those who participated in the conference contributed chapters to this book. That core was then supplemented with other invited chapters.

Terminology

In the chapters that follow, "maternity leave" generally refers to a work leave granted a woman at the time of the birth of a child. The leave may begin in late pregnancy if the woman's health requires it, and may extend for some specified period for physical recovery. The key is that maternity leave is for mothers only and is meant to cover only the limited time of physical disability. It might alternatively be termed "pregnancy and childbirth disability leave." "Parental leave," on the other hand, is meant to be a gender-fair term, allowing fathers and mothers equal rights to work leave at the time of the birth or adoption of a child. It is an important concept because it is not gender-biased and because it suggests that fathers may or should want to contribute to the care of their infants. "Family leave" is still broader, referring to leaves from work for the purpose of caring for a newborn or adopted child or a sick family member (e.g., child, spouse, parent). The term "childrearing leave" is used to make the distinction between a leave due to physical disability at the time of childbirth (pregnancy and childbirth leave) and a later period of leave for the purpose of caring for the child.

J. S. H.
M. J. E.

REFERENCES

Baruch, Grace, Linda Biener, and Rosalind Barnett (1987). "Women and Gender in Research on Work and Family Stress." *American Psychologist* 42: 130–36.

Belsky, Jay, Mary E. Lang, and Michael Rovine (1985). "Stability and Change in Marriage Across the Transition to Parenthood: A Second Study." *Journal of Marriage and the Family* 47: 855–65.

Cutrona, C. E., and B. R. Troutman (1986). "Social Support, Infant Temperament, and Parenting Self-Efficacy: A Mediational Model of Postpartum Depression." *Child Development* 57: 1507–18.

Davidson, J., and E. Robertson (1985). "A Follow-Up Study of Postpartum Illness, 1946–1978." *Acta Psychiatrica Scandinavia* 71: 451–57.

Hock, Ellen, M. T. Gnezda, and S. L. McBride (1984). "Mothers of Infants: Attitudes Toward Employment and Motherhood Following Birth of the First Child." *Journal of Marriage and the Family* 46: 425–31.

Hoffman, L. W. (1984). "Maternal Employment and the Young Child." In Marion Perlmutter, ed., *Parent–Child Relations in Child Development: The Minnesota Symposia on Child Psychology*, Vol. 17. Hillsdale, N.J.: Erlbaum.

Verbrugge, L. M. (1987). "Role Responsibilities, Role Burdens and Physical Health." In F. J. Crosby, ed., *Spouse, Parent, Worker: On Gender and Multiple Roles*. New Haven: Yale University Press.

Zigler, Edward F., and Meryl Frank, eds. (1988). *The Parental Leave Crisis: Toward a National Policy*. New Haven: Yale University Press.

PART I

Overview

PART I

1 Parental Leave and Infant Care: U.S. and International Trends and Issues, 1978–1988

Sheila B. Kamerman

On October 31, 1978, President Jimmy Carter signed the Pregnancy Discrimination Act (PDA), Public Law 95-555. This act expanded the definition of sex discrimination in employment to include discrimination against women on the basis of pregnancy, childbirth, or related medical conditions, and stated that pregnancy and maternity should be treated—and thus implicitly defined—as temporary disabilities under employers' sickness, accident, and medical plans.

The result, as we all know, was that working women in firms with good disability and health insurance policies found that they were—or would be—covered for pregnancy and maternity as well. But the act did not require employers to establish such policies. There was no legislative mandate to provide sickness or disability benefits or even health insurance. Most employees, and thus most working women, did not have disability benefits, and therefore had neither job nor income protection at the time of childbirth as a matter of legislative entitlement.

Perhaps the most important immediate effect of this legislation was that it required the five states that had temporary disability insurance (TDI) programs (laws protecting workers against loss of income in case of short-term non-job-related medical disabilities) to cover working women at the time of pregnancy and childbirth as well. Expanding TDI coverage in this way assured close to one-quarter of the nation's female labor force of at least this minimal protection; overlapping, complementary, or supplementary provision through collective bargaining agreements or voluntary employee benefit plans brought coverage to about 40 percent of the female workforce.

Another important immediate benefit was that employers who provided health insurance for their employees were required by this legislation to include coverage for maternity care as well. A survey

11

carried out by the Health Insurance Association of America in 1982 found that 89 percent of employees with medical insurance under new policies had some form of maternity care benefits, compared with only 57 percent in 1977 (Gold and Kenney, 1985). In the intervening decade no additional states have legislated temporary disability insurance, although those that had TDI in place have made modest improvements in the protection they offered, extending coverage to more employees, raising the benefit levels (to keep pace with inflation or wage increases), and, in California, extending the duration of the benefit. Little has been established in the way of new "voluntary" paid disability or parenting policies, although labor union contracts have begun to include attention to this issue.

The result of these very limited developments is that short-term disability insurance coverage has remained about the same. Most working women still do not have income protection at the time of childbirth. Vacation and personal leave policies have remained stable as well. Surveys by the U.S. Department of Labor's Bureau of Labor Statistics (1980, 1981, 1982, 1983, 1984, 1985, 1986, 1987) indicate that there have been no increases in vacation and personal leave time. A few individual firms may have established more generous unpaid leave policies, but not more extensive paid leaves. A few large firms, confronted with the need to turn their maternity leave policies into parental leave policies, may have made their policies more restrictive. At best, more of the discretionary unpaid leave policies have now become formalized.

At the same time, the workforce is larger than ever before and more feminized. Making up 45 percent of the labor force, women are more important to the workplace than ever; and women—especially young married women—are more likely to be in the labor force than ever before.

In 1977, the year before the Pregnancy Discrimination Act was passed, 32 percent of mothers of children one year old and younger were in the workforce, including 31 percent of married mothers. In 1980, the rate for wives was 39 percent, already surpassing the rate for single mothers (38 percent). In 1987, for the first time, more than half of all mothers with children under age one were in the workforce. In 1988, the rate was 52 percent for married women and 51 percent for single mothers. In effect the labor force participation rate for women with children under age one had increased by almost 60 percent over the past decade, and by 33 percent since 1980. Now, more than half of all children have working mothers by the time they reach their first birthday.

The demand and need for maternity disability and parenting policies has increased enormously over the past decade. Although there has been some growth in the supply of infant care, it is far exceeded by the demand. Decent infant care is expensive, and some child development researchers have concerns about out-of-home group care for infants. Thus, a quick overview of the past decade would suggest that despite the dramatic rise in the demand for employment-related maternity/parenting leaves and benefits, employee policies remain inadequate, as does the supply of infant care services.

Reviewing the developments over the decade since the PDA was passed raises the following questions: What else, if anything, has been accomplished for working women at the time of pregnancy and childbirth? What are the implications of the limited nature of these achievements—despite the substantial increase in female labor force participation and attachment to the workforce? What should the policy agenda be for working women—and working men? What issues should be on the research agenda?

Post-PDA Decade: The Accomplishments and Failures

The Accomplishments

1. The media have now picked up the issue of maternity and parenting leaves. A dozen years ago, few people had heard of maternity leaves for working mothers—let alone parenting leaves. There was disbelief when the paid leave policies of many European countries were described. Now the topic is part of popular discussion as well as policy debate with regard to women, work and family, workplace and employment policy, and child/infant care. Magazines like *Business Week* carry lead stories featuring these issues (see, for example, the issue dated September 19, 1988). Unfortunately, the media often confuse family leave with medical disability leave, or fail to see the importance of medical leave, or fail to see the relationship between the two where maternity is concerned.

2. Maternity and parenting leaves are on the national political agenda, along with child care, in a way they have never been before. In the 1988 presidential campaign, both candidates listed "children's," "women's," and "family" issues as important, even if they did not provide the specific details that many of us wanted to hear.

3. Foundations have increased their attention to and support for research, information and experience sharing, and public education regarding maternity and parenting leave.

4. Private group health insurance policies for employees are now more likely to include maternity care, although it appears that fewer workers, and in particular fewer women, have health insurance coverage now than in 1980.

5. A federal Family and Medical Leave Act (or a Parental and Medical Leave Act) has been debated for several years after extensive hearings. For the third year in a row, a bill has been introduced in the 101st Congress. The proposal is very modest and unlikely to make a significant difference even if passed because it provides for no income while on leave, but it has important symbolic value.

The legislation proposed in the 101st Congress (the House and Senate bills were somewhat different) would require some employers with more than 50 employees to provide unpaid, job-protected medical and parental leaves to both male and female workers. An employee could take up to 10 weeks of unpaid "family" or "parental" leave during a 24-month period to care for a newborn, an adopted or foster child, or a seriously ill child, and up to 15 weeks of unpaid medical leave during a 12-month period if the employee had a serious health condition. Pre-existing health insurance would continue for the duration of the leave, and accrued leave and seniority would be protected.

6. In a landmark decision in 1987, the U.S. Supreme Court ruled that states may require employers to grant special job protection to employees who are physically unable to work because of pregnancy and childbirth. The Court upheld a California law requiring employers to grant up to four months of unpaid leave to women disabled at the time of maternity, even if similar leaves are not granted for other disabilities (*California Federal Savings and Loan Association* v. *Guerra*).

7. Finally, following this decision and the introduction of the proposed federal legislation, there has been growing action by several states to legislate *unpaid* parental leaves. In addition to California and Montana which had passed such laws earlier, and Rhode Island, whose TDI law provides job protection to all beneficiaries, the following states had special statutory provision concerning maternity or parenting leaves by the end of 1988:

- *Oregon* (1987) was the first state to pass a law requiring employers of 25 or more employees to grant an unpaid *parental leave* of up to 12 weeks following childbirth (longer for premature babies) or the adoption of a child younger than 6.
- *Minnesota* (1987) became the first state to require employers to offer a *parental leave* to both the mother and father of a newborn or adopted

child. Firms with 21 or more employees must offer up to 6 weeks of unpaid leave following childbirth or adoption, and the parents may go on leave at the same time or sequentially.

- *Rhode Island* (1987) passed a law providing up to 13 weeks of *family leave* in a two-year period to a working parent for the care of a newborn, an adopted child, or a seriously ill child. While the law does not provide for payment, the state TDI program pays benefits during the period of pregnancy and maternity disability. The law applies to employees in private firms with at least 50 employees, to those in municipal agencies with at least 30 employees, and to all employees of the state.

- *Iowa* (1987) provides for an unpaid *medical disability leave* due to pregnancy for up to 8 weeks for all employees in firms with at least 25 workers.

- *Tennessee* (1987) passed a law providing *female employees* in firms with at least 100 workers with up to 4 months of job-protected leave at the time of childbirth or adoption.

- *Maine* (1988) passed a law requiring that companies with at least 25 employees offer 8 consecutive weeks of unpaid *parental leave* after the birth or adoption of a child, or when a member of the immediate family becomes ill. Employees on leave will continue to be covered by health insurance but must pay the entire premium.

- *Wisconsin* (1988) passed a law requiring employers of 50 or more employees to provide *family leave* for the care of a newborn or newly adopted child or a seriously ill child, spouse, or parent, up to a maximum of 8 weeks in a 12-month period. If the leave is taken to care for a newborn or newly adopted child, the maximum leave period is 6 weeks. The maximum leave to care for a seriously ill family member is 2 weeks. Personal *medical (sickness) leave* can be taken for a maximum of 2 weeks in a 1-year period. In effect, a working mother could take off up to 8 weeks at the time of childbirth. Health insurance coverage must be continued while the employee is out on leave.

- *Massachusetts* (1988) passed a law requiring firms with at least 6 employees to give their *female employees* an 8-week job-protected leave at the time of childbirth or the adoption of a child under age 3.

- *Connecticut and Maryland* have laws that apply to state employees only; and *Hawaii, Illinois, Kansas, Ohio, New Hampshire, and Washington* are described as having regulations that provide for special job-protected leaves for certain employees.

- In 1989 about 20 other states had proposals with similar provisions before their legislatures.

The Failures

1. Since 1981, when we at Columbia University carried out the first national survey of employer's maternity and parenting policies (Kamerman, Kahn, and Kingston, 1983), there does not appear to

have been any significant increase in the percentage of women workers with paid maternity disability leaves. The findings of the National Council of Jewish Women survey (1987) suggest that coverage rates have remained stable during the intervening years. Moreover, there seems to be growing employer and supervisory pressure to shorten the "disability" period after childbirth from the 6 to 8 weeks that most doctors say is the minimum to 4 or 5 weeks.

2. Only two of the five states that have TDI in place have legislated job protection at the time of maternity as well.

3. Health insurance coverage of workers declined during the 1980s. There have been cutbacks, in particular, in dependents' coverage, meaning that women previously covered under their husbands' health insurance may no longer be covered now. Moreover, although 40 percent of all births in the United States are to women aged 18 to 24, in 1984 more than 25 percent of women this age had no health insurance coverage, private or public. (Of the women aged 25 to 29 who account for another 25 percent of all births, 15 percent had no such coverage).

4. It has been more than three years since the first congressional hearing on parental and disability leaves and since very modest parental and medical leave legislation was first introduced. We still do not have a federal law, and the proposed bills in 1988, 1989, and 1990 were watered-down versions of one that was very modest at the outset.

5. From the beginning, only *unpaid* leave has been considered in the Congress. Such a policy is of value only to the better-off, who can live on one salary for a while, or those very poor people who are willing—and able—to qualify for welfare. The working poor and many middle-class working parents would not be assured of any protection.

6. In New York State, Governor Mario Cuomo's 1988 Task Force on Work and Family, a large percentage of whose members were senior corporate executives, was not able to achieve consensus in support of the proposed federal legislation.

7. Many large firms that have policies comparable to or better than those proposed refuse to support the federal bill because they fear "breaking ranks"; and small and medium-sized firms insist that such a policy will bankrupt them or make them noncompetitive— despite the prevailing Canadian pattern of 4 months and the European pattern of 5 months paid leave and additional unpaid leave, and despite the example of Singapore, a newly industrializing country that is a competitor with the United States in certain industries

but can apparently afford an 8-week *paid* post-childbirth leave for working mothers.

8. High-flying professional and executive women who have "made it" into excellent positions in management or in law, accounting, or management-consulting firms find that despite relatively generous policies on paper, the "culture" of their firms frowns on taking full advantage of such policies.

9. A prestigious panel of social scientists, under the auspices of the National Research Council/National Academy of Science, issued a report (1990) supporting a federal policy mandating unpaid, job-protected parental leave; however, the panel could not obtain consensus regarding support for a policy of paid leave.

By way of contrast, what have been the cross-national trends during these same years?

Cross-National Trends

Major growth in labor force participation rates among married women with very young children occurred in the 1980s in the United States, Canada, Norway, and to a lesser extent Australia, France, Japan, and Singapore. Slight growth occurred in Denmark, Sweden, and Finland, but they already had rates of female labor force participation far higher than the United States (for example, 75 to 85 percent of women with pre-school-aged children are in the workforce, in contrast to a U.S. rate of about 57 percent). No significant growth occurred in countries such as Britain and West Germany—indeed, there may have been a slight decline in Germany.

Despite a decade of slow or no growth in social benefits, no cutbacks were carried out in any of these countries with regard to maternity and parenting benefits and leaves, and some significant improvements occurred instead. Table 1.1 provides a summary of the international situation. Within Europe, 5 months is the typical post-childbirth leave.

In the last decade, Denmark and Finland extended their paid maternity and parenting leaves and increased the part that fathers can take. The Danish paid leave was extended from 14 to 24 weeks, and the Finnish leave from 35 to 52 weeks. Sweden increased its paid leave from 9 months to 12, and then 15 months. Earlier, Sweden had established a right to part-time work until a child reaches the age of eight; during the 1980s, Finland established a similar policy. West Germany established a paid parental leave, at a very modest level, for up to one year, with the cash benefit for the last 6 months

TABLE 1.1
Paid Maternity/Parenting Leave Provisions in Selected Western Countries

Country	Date of Most Recent Information	Length of Leave	Available to Fathers	Supplementary Unpaid or Paid Parental Leave
Benefit Level at 100% of Earnings[a]				
Norway	1984	18 wks.	yes	yes
Austria	1987	16 wk. + 10 mon. at lower level		yes[b]
F.R. Germany	1987	14 wks.[c]	yes	15 mon. at flat rate[c]
Portugal	1984	3 mon.		yes
Netherlands	1984	12 wks.		
Sweden	1987	9 mon. + 3 mon. at flat rate[d]	yes	up to 3 more months 6-hr. workday until child is 8
Benefit Level at 90% of Earnings				
Denmark	1987	24 wks.	yes	yes
France	1990	16 wks.[c]		up to 2 yrs.
United Kingdom	1987	6 wks. unpaid + 12 wks. at flat rate		maternity leave
Benefit Level at 80% of Earnings				
Finland	1990	10½ mon.[d]	yes	2 yrs. at flat rate
Italy	1984	5 mon.		yes
Belgium	1984	14 wks.		
Ireland	1984	14 wks.		
Benefit Level at 75% of Earnings				
Spain	1984	14 wks.		
Israel	1984	12 wks.		
Benefit Level at 60% of Earnings				
Canada	1984	15 wks.[d]		
Benefit Level at 50% of Earnings				
Greece	1984	12 wks.		

Notes:
[a]Up to maximum covered under social security.
[b]Plus 2 years for low-income single mothers if they cannot find child care.
[c]The last 9 months are available on an income-tested basis.
[d]The benefit is taxable.

available on an income-tested basis. Several countries (including Finland, France, and Austria), have begun to develop supplementary childrearing policies that permit a parent, after the paid maternity or parenting leave, to take off a still longer period of job-protected time with some modest financial support. Most countries now include adoptive as well as biological parents, and most countries are moving toward including fathers, at least for some portion of the leave.

Summing Up: Toward a Policy and Research Agenda

The major accomplishments of the 1970s were the prohibition against firing pregnant workers or imposing an extended unpaid leave from the beginning of pregnancy; the definition of pregnancy and childbirth as "temporary disabilities" and the requirement that maternity be given "equal treatment" in employment policies with any other short-term physical disability; and the definition of discrimination at the time of pregnancy and childbirth as a form of sex discrimination, prohibited by law.

At the end of the 1980s there was still no federal legislation mandating unpaid, job-protected parenting and medical leaves at the time of childbirth, although close to half the states had moved toward such a policy. Thus far, the accomplishments have been modest and slow in coming.

The unfinished agenda for working women at the time of pregnancy and childbirth is substantial. The economic costs of offering some protection are modest. The General Accounting Office (GAO, 1987) found that an unpaid, 18-week parental leave policy for infants would cost American businesses no more than $340 million annually (less for a shorter leave; see GAO, 1988) and that a bill that covered adopted children, sick children, and medical leaves would cost only an additional $160 million annually, largely because of the cost of maintaining health insurance benefits while the worker was out on leave; the legislation introduced in 1989 (and again in 1990) would cost still less. The GAO reports (1987, 1988) concluded that there was no justification for the Chamber of Commerce estimates that a parental leave policy would cost businesses $2.6 billion to $16.2 billion a year. A Conference Board study should have reassured employers further. It found that "employers who contemplate the prospect of a national statute mandating paid maternity leave for women worry that the average benefit, the duration of leave, and the number of pregnancy claims could rise sharply in a baby boomlet. Their fears, however, appear to be ill founded" (Berman, 1987).

Pregnancy claims represented about 20 percent of all short-term disability claims in California in the early and middle 1980s and increased at a rate of only 1 percent a year during the first half of the decade. In New York, the percentage of claims has shown even slower growth, accounting for 8.5 percent of all claims in 1985, up from 6 percent in 1980. Nor are claims for pregnancy any more expensive than those for other short-term disabilities. In California, they represented about 15 percent of all short-term disability costs between 1980 and 1986; in New York, they accounted for about 13 percent; and in New Jersey, 17 percent. And some of these costs have to do with medical complications, which would have been covered in any case. The typical duration of maternity disability leave is about 10 to 11 weeks, only slightly longer than the typical nonmaternity disability (about 9 weeks). It is of some interest that the California and Rhode Island TDI is paid for completely by employee contributions (employers have the option of paying all or part but are not required to pay anything). In New Jersey, where financing is shared by employer and employee, TDI costs of 1 percent of wages (0.5 percent for each) constituted less than $120 per worker per year at the maximum level (about $60 for each) in 1988.

Up to now, the policy agenda for maternity/parenting leave has focused on getting federal legislation passed. Obviously, enacting a law requiring family (or parental) and medical leave is an essential next step. This would be a milestone even if the protection offered was very modest. Nonetheless, an agenda should be developed that goes beyond this. Legislative advocacy is needed at the state level to expand statutory parental leave policies; and advocacy efforts are needed, at both the federal and the state level, to legislate *paid* leaves as soon as possible. At the very least, stress should be placed on expanding the number of states with TDI laws, and these laws should be amended to include job protection.

Expanding health insurance coverage is a critical development as well; if mandatory group health insurance is not imposed on employers, then at least Medicaid coverage for all poor pregnant women should be mandated for all states.

Public education continues to be very important. A survey reported in *Public Opinion* in May/June 1987 indicated that the vast majority of Americans (89 percent) think that a federal law providing for unpaid maternity leave is a good idea; and a substantial majority (63 percent) believe that employers should be required to provide unpaid parental leave. But paid leave is still reported as being rejected by most Americans. One reason may be the way the question was posed: "Do you think it would be a good idea or a bad idea to enact a law that would require employers to give both mothers and fathers three months of leave at 75 percent pay following a birth or an adoption?" Instead, the researchers could have asked about requiring employers and employees to pay one-half of 1 percent of salary to provide for an insurance benefit that would cover about 60 to 70 percent of a wage earner's salary. It is essential to get the public to understand that paid leave at childbirth has value that goes beyond benefiting an individual worker, that TDI benefits all workers, including men who have heart attacks, strokes, or appendectomies, as well as pregnant women, and that such benefits are very inexpensive and paid for largely by the employees themselves.

Establishing unpaid medical and parental leave does not begin to satisfy the need for infant care; and even when (not *if*) paid leave becomes available, it will only affect the age at which infants are placed in care—it will not substitute for such care. Thus, continued advocacy for federal and state child care policies and programs is an essential part of any policy agenda in this field.

Among the factors driving the maternity and parenting leave debate now are the high costs of infant care; the desire to implement welfare reform by encouraging young women to enter the workforce even when their children are young and to remain in the workforce even after they give birth; and the continued conviction that the early months after birth are an important period for both child and parent. But most of all, what drives the debate is the continued and dramatic increase in the labor force participation rate of women with new babies, and this will not go away.

The Policy Agenda

The goal of any new policy agenda in this field should be to establish at least a floor of protection for all workers. The first target must be benefits for the low-wage, low-skilled women who are fungible in the labor market, have limited job options, and are under severe financial pressures. Most professional and executive women already have such benefits, but if they have not, such a policy will help them too. After the country establishes a minimum level of paid and unpaid leaves, more attention can be paid to issues having to do with women professionals, managers, and executives.

A proposed policy agenda with such an objective would include the following items:

- Federal parental and medical leave legislation, including coverage of small businesses (at least those with 15 or more employees)
- State TDI, with job protection, supplemented by unpaid but job-protected parental leave legislation
- Mandatory health insurance coverage

- Mandatory phasing in of a new parent's return to work by permitting part-time work for at least six months
- Expanding the supply of affordable infant care services of decent quality

Implicit in all of these proposals is an underlying theme: changing the culture of the workplace and of the society at large with the objective of enhancing the value placed on children and/or parenting.

A Proposed Research Agenda

Those who want to develop data that would be relevant to issues in the current debate or that might elaborate options for future action might consider the following:

- Analyze TDI costs and estimate what it would cost to establish TDI in the states that now lack such legislation.
- Analyze the experience of our neighbor to the north, Canada, where unemployment insurance is used to pay for 15 of the 17 weeks of the national job-protected maternity leave, and compare these results with the costs of using disability insurance as an instrument instead.
- Study why state TDI legislation passed initially in the 1940s and why there has been no increase in the states with such laws. What would it take to create an incentive for states to pass TDI?
- Compare the experiences of working women and their employers in companies with generous maternity/parenting policies and those without such policies in order to document the positive consequences, including, perhaps, productivity gains.
- Compare the costs of extended paid leaves with the costs of infant care.

Conclusion

The United States may be embarking on a "children's agenda" in the 1990s (Kamerman, 1989; Kamerman and Kahn, 1989). Such an agenda will have to pay attention to some broader policy issues as well as to the specifics addressed above. Among the major items on any child or family policy agenda would be child or family allowances, provided either as a direct cash benefit or a refundable tax credit; guaranteed minimum support for children in one-parent families where the living, noncustodial parent fails to pay support or pays it irregularly or at an inadequate level; housing allowances to help subsidize the high costs of housing for low- and moderate-income families with children; child health insurance; and child care services as well as paid, job-protected leaves for parents at the time of childbirth or adoption.

Maternity and parental leave policies constitute a modest component of such an agenda; nonetheless, if we cannot legislate such policies, we are unlikely to move ahead on the larger agenda.

REFERENCES

Berman, Melissa (1987). "What Do Women Get?" *Across the Board,* March.

General Accounting Office (1987). *Parental Leave: Estimated Costs of H.R. 925, Family and Medical Leave Act of 1987.* Washington, D.C.: GAO.

——— (1988). *Parental Leave: Estimated Costs of Revised Parental and Medical Leave Act.* Washington, D.C.: GAO. May 26 and September 27.

Gold, Rachel Benson, and Asta M. Kenney (1985). "Paying for Maternity Care," *Family Planning Perspectives* 17 (3):103–11.

Hayes, Cheryl D., John L. Palmer, and Martha J. Zaslow, eds. (1990). *Who Cares for Children?* Washington, D.C.: National Academy Press.

Kamerman, Sheila B. (1989). "Towards a Child Policy Decade." *Child Welfare* 68:371–90.

Kamerman, Sheila B., and Alfred J. Kahn (1989). "The Possibilities for Child and Family Policy: A Cross-National Perspective." In Frank J. Macchiarola and Alan Gartner, eds., *Caring for America's Children.* New York: Academy of Political Science.

Kamerman, Sheila B., Alfred J. Kahn, and Paul W. Kingston (1983). *Maternity Policies and Working Women.* New York: Columbia University Press.

National Council of Jewish Women (1987). *Medical and Family Leave.* New York: NCJW.

U.S. Department of Labor, Bureau of Labor Statistics (1980–). *Employee Benefits in Medium and Large Firms.* Washington, D.C.: Government Printing Office. Annual series beginning 1980.

2 | Childbirth and Maternal Employment: Data from a National Longitudinal Survey

Patricia Garrett, Sally Lubeck, and DeeAnn Wenk

> A young couple sit at the kitchen table, reviewing their fringe benefits and planning for the birth of their first child. They are concerned about when the woman will have to leave her job and how the family will manage without her paycheck.
>
> An expectant mother talks on the telephone, interviewing directors of day care centers. She is anxious to find one where a slot will open up at an opportune time and where her infant will receive good care.

Situations such as these are increasingly common in the United States. We would like to illuminate some of their characteristics by exploring the employment patterns of young women who are part of a large national sample, the Youth Cohort of the National Longitudinal Survey of Labor Market Experience. Our analysis focuses on their employment during the period immediately surrounding childbirth.

Some mothers in this sample have continuous work histories, while others drop out of the labor market before and especially after childbirth. After some time out, many return to work. Nationally, the labor force participation rates of mothers with infants increased from 30.9 to 49.8 percent between 1976 and 1986 (U.S. Bureau of the Census, 1987, p. 65). This trend is important because women with relatively uninterrupted employment patterns are prime targets for legislation concerning parental leave. That is, national, state, and corporate policies concerning parental leave are most salient to families in which women are employed at the time of conception and maintain consistent employment patterns thereafter. If a comprehensive policy of parental leave were implemented, women with rel-

24

atively unbroken work histories could qualify for a full range of benefits, including medical insurance, disability coverage, job protection, and wage replacement. Moreover, such legislation might encourage women to modify their work behavior, increasing or decreasing *time off* the job (i.e., leave) and decreasing *time out* of the labor market (i.e., resignation, followed by a period of unemployment).

It is difficult to anticipate how mothers' employment decisions would change if progressive parental leave legislation were implemented in the United States. Nevertheless, the current situation can be described. The most recent Census Bureau figures report that the majority of mothers whose infants were born during 1987 were employed before their child's first birthday (U.S. Bureau of the Census, 1988). Data from the National Longitudinal Survey (NLS), which will be presented in this paper, are consistent with these figures. Census Bureau and NLS data are mutually independent sources, and together they document the high maternal employment that creates the demand for infant day care. Many infants placed in extrafamilial care are very young, and this highlights the need for complementary parental leave and child care policies.

In this chapter we analyze a large, national sample and answer several questions. Who is employed 9 months before childbirth? Are ethnic differences important in predicting employment? Who drops out of the labor market after conception and before childbirth? How rapidly do new mothers resume employment? What explains the rate of return to employment after childbirth? Are ethnic differences important in predicting rate of return? What do these results mean for social policy?

The NLS Data

In 1979, members of the NLS Youth Cohort (some 12,000 men and women) were 14 to 21 years old. Interviews have occurred annually since then. The survey was originally designed to track young adults as they completed formal education and job training and entered regular employment. During this transition to adulthood, many respondents also formed new families. A Child Supplement was added to the interview schedule and administered in 1986 to the children of female members of the Youth Cohort. Information about the children and their mothers is available in the Merged Mother/Child NLS file. There are 5,876 children born to 3,322 mothers in the basic data set.

For this study, it was necessary to reduce the sample size to 4,634 by eliminating all children born before 1979. This was the year that the panel study began, and information about maternal employment was not available for pre-1979 births. Restricting the sample in this way effectively eliminates children born to the youngest and most poorly educated mothers, many of whom were ethnic minorities whose demographic characteristics put them at considerable disadvantage in terms of employment. If these mothers also gave birth after 1979, the younger children were included in the analysis.

The NLS was designed to ensure that economically disadvantaged and minority young adults would be well represented. This reflected a general understanding that poor and minority young people are likely to confront specific challenges as they enter the workforce and begin families. The NLS sample is sufficiently large and diverse to permit comparisons across ethnic groups. This is important because there are some significant ethnic differences in socioeconomic characteristics and employment patterns.

In this study, ethnicity is an interviewer-assigned category. Nearly one-third (29.0 percent) of the sample children were born to black mothers, and another substantial group (18.3 percent) were born to Hispanics. It was therefore possible to compare both ethnic groups with the remaining whites (52.6 percent).

Blacks and Hispanics experience numerous disadvantages in comparison with whites, but they are both similiar to and different from each other. In this study, consequently, the three groups are sometimes compared with each other, while at other times blacks are compared with nonblacks. Substantive concerns suggested which comparison was more relevant.

The proportion of female-headed households in the United States has increased from 7.2 percent in 1970 to 9.3 percent in 1986. A disproportionate number of these families are black or Hispanic (U.S. Bureau of the Census, 1987, p. 44). In the NLS sample, most children (67.1 percent) were born to married women, while a substantial minority (32.9 percent) were born to unmarried women. At the time of the child's birth, most white (82 percent) and Hispanic (73 percent) mothers were married. The spouse was present in the household at the time of the child's birth in 70 percent of the white and 61 percent of the Hispanic families. Black women were less likely to be married at the time of childbirth (37 percent) and less likely to have spouse present (28 percent). Ethnic differences in marital status and spouse presence are both statistically significant $(p < .001)$.

The proportion of children in the NLS data set who were born to unmarried mothers is substantially higher than national averages, partially because their mothers were young. In the recent past, approximately one-third of children in the United States were born to mothers aged 20 to 24 (U.S. Bureau of the Census, 1987, p. 60). The comparable figure for the NLS sample was almost double. White children were generally born to older mothers, while the mothers of black children tended to be younger. Hispanic children were intermediate between whites and blacks. Ethnic differences in maternal age at childbirth are statistically significant (p < .001).

The mothers in the NLS survey tend to be young and in the early stages of family formation. Most children in the sample (52 percent) were firstborn, and a substantial minority (33 percent) had one brother or sister. Black and Hispanic children were less likely than whites to be firstborn. During the interval between birth and mother's return to work, most children (69.2 percent) did not experience the birth of a sibling. Black children (34.9 percent) were the least likely and Hispanic children (41 percent) the most likely to see an additional birth before the mother returned to work.

Becoming a mother at a young age tends to disrupt education, which, in turn, has long-term negative consequences for occupational attainment and earnings. Most children in the sample were born to mothers with incomplete (41 percent) or completed (42 percent) high school educations. A few mothers had some college (13 percent) or had finished college (4 percent) at the time of the birth. Hispanic children were born to mothers with lower levels of formal education than black children. The mothers of white children had the highest levels of formal education. Ethnic differences in maternal education at the time of childbirth are statistically significant (p < .001).

Finally, income levels at the time of the child's birth varied dramatically by ethnic group. Average family income was substantially higher for whites ($18,092) than for Hispanics ($14,385) or blacks ($11,994). Average family income is depressed by the relatively low earnings of women. When attention is restricted to cases in which a spouse was present, the spouse's average income varied from $18,872 (whites) to $10,867 (blacks) and $10,340 (Hispanics).

Although they are poorly paid, women make substantial contributions to family budgets. For the United States as a whole, the median percentage of total family income contributed by wives with earnings was 27 percent in 1981. Contributions ranged from a high of 34 percent for blacks to a low of 26 percent for whites, with Hispanics intermediate (U.S. Department of Labor, Women's Bureau,

1983, p. 19). For the NLS sample, the comparable overall figure was 28 percent, which is similar to the national figure. The rank order of women's contribution by ethnic group, however, is radically different. In the NLS sample, white mothers contributed a slightly higher proportion of family income (29 percent) than blacks (26 percent) and Hispanics (25 percent), probably because minority mothers are, on the average, younger than white mothers.

These descriptive data suggest that income and family composition interact. Children in this sample born to white mothers enjoy, on the average, higher family incomes and paternal support, plus the protection that birth in wedlock affords. Their mothers are, on the average, older and better-educated. Children born to black mothers experience significantly lower levels of family income and paternal support, plus low levels of maternal marriage and spousal presence. Children born to Hispanic mothers are intermediate, in some respects similar to whites and in others similar to blacks.

The NLS sample is representative of children born between 1979 and 1986 to mothers who were 14 to 29 at the time of childbirth. Children born to young, less educated, economically disadvantaged, and minority mothers are overrepresented (Center for Human Resource Research, 1987). Consequently, many of the families represented in the NLS sample are likely to need support. It is, therefore, an ideal data set to use for exploring the general relationship between employment and child care for young mothers, considering alternative social policies, and identifying programs that might have negative consequences for poor and minority families. The NLS data document a familial context within which maternal employment around the time of childbirth can be explored.

Who Was Employed 9 Months Before Childbirth?

An extensive professional literature documents ethnic differences in employment. Less attention has been paid to ethnicity and maternal employment during the period immediately surrounding childbirth (Bumpass and Sweet, 1980; Mott and Shapiro, 1982; Shapiro and Mott, 1979; Tienda and Glass, 1985). It is critical to examine this period, however, because maternal leave policies will have a differential impact if ethnicity is related to pre-birth employment patterns.

In order to anticipate the consequences of social policy, several questions must be answered. What kinds of women were likely to be employed around the time of conception and, therefore, hypothetically eligible for coverage under an expanded parental leave policy in the United States? How were these women similar to and different from other expectant mothers? Specifically, is ethnicity an important dimension along which women who are/are not employed differ?

Characteristics of women in the NLS sample provide a preliminary answer to these questions. Overall, 54 percent of all children had mothers who were employed 9 months prior to childbirth. The rates were highest for whites (58 percent), followed by Hispanics (51 percent) and blacks (46 percent). Ethnic differences in initial levels of employment were statistically significant (p < .001). The demographic and socioeconomic characteristics of individuals who were and were not employed were analyzed using logistic regression (Agresti, 1984; Aldrich and Nelson, 1984).[1]

Substantively, the following relationships emerge, net of the effect of other variables in the model. Being black decreased the probability of employment, while having more education increased the likelihood that the mother was employed 9 months prior to childbirth. The presence of other adults in the household and a spouse with a relatively high income increased the likelihood of maternal employment, but marital status itself had no effect. Finally, the number of other children under five had a negative effect on employment. The mother's age at the child's birth had no effect. These relationships are fundamentally consistent with previous scholarship, most of which focused on employment prior to first births (Haggstrom, Waite, Kanouse, and Blaschke, 1984; McLaughlin, 1982; Mott and Shapiro, 1982; Waite, Haggstrom, and Kanouse, 1985).

The single most interesting result is that the year of the child's birth had a significant, positive effect on maternal employment. That is, between 1979 and 1986 and net of the influence of all other variables in the model, the probability of maternal employment increased. This finding is entirely consistent with Census Bureau reports of increased female labor force participation throughout the 1980s (Garrett and Lubeck, 1988; Hayghe, 1984, 1986; U.S. Bureau of the Census, 1987). It is striking, however, because it reinforces impressions that maternal employment changed fundamentally during the 1980s. That a longitudinal panel should corroborate cross-sectional data provides strong support for the interpretation that female employment increased during the last decade.

The analysis of what predicts employment at 9 months prior to childbirth has implications for the definition of a comprehensive maternal leave policy. If the NLS survey data are generalized to the nation, approximately half the expectant mothers in the United

States would not be covered by maternal leave policies if employment around the time of conception were the criterion for eligibility. Moreover, black women would be less likely than Hispanic or white women to meet this criterion. Such a maternity leave policy would inadvertently discriminate against blacks.

Do Mothers Drop Out of the Labor Market Before Childbirth?

In the absence of a comprehensive and national maternal leave policy, mothers in the United States who need to take time off are frequently compelled to exit the labor market.[2] Resigning a position is a serious step because it usually means the immediate loss not only of wages but also of fringe benefits. Medical coverage and disability insurance are especially important to expectant parents.

In the NLS sample, 54 percent of the children had mothers who were working 9 months prior to their birth. The week that individuals quit their jobs was graphed. The resulting curve sloped downward gradually, indicating that most women remained in the labor market during the early stages of pregnancy. Approximately half the prospective mothers had withdrawn from the labor market by 4 weeks prior to childbirth, but almost one-third remained economically active immediately prior to delivery.

Ethnic differences were not significant. The labor market exits of whites, blacks, and Hispanics were examined graphically, and no differences were observed. This means that although there were differences in the likelihood of employment, all ethnic groups, once employed, left jobs at about the same rate.

These employment levels are substantially higher than those Shapiro and Mott (1979) reported for mothers giving birth to a first child between 1968 and 1973. In their study, 80 percent of first-time mothers were employed at the beginning of their pregnancy. Their labor force participation rate dropped to 50 percent at 3 to 4 months before the birth and to 20 percent for whites and 40 percent for blacks just before the birth.

Another 6 percent of women in this study who had been employed at the time of conception quit their jobs after delivery. This means that a substantial minority (24 percent) of children had mothers with uninterrupted employment histories during the period immediately surrounding their birth. This permits a rough estimate of potential maternal leave coverage.

Approximately half of the children in this sample had mothers who were employed around the time of conception, one-fourth of whom had continuous employment histories. Considering only mothers who never resigned their positions, one can estimate that one-eighth (i.e., one-half of one-fourth) of the children in the sample had mothers who would probably have been covered by parental leave policies had international norms applied in their firm or state.

This provides a conservative estimate of potential eligibility for coverage under an enhanced parental leave policy. If progressive parental leave policies were implemented by firms and/or governments, mothers might modify their time-out behavior by remaining in the labor force and substituting time off (leave) for time out (resignation). Some women who quit their jobs would probably take maternal leave were this an option. Such a behavioral change would increase the proportion of mothers eligible for parental leave. Consequently, 12 percent would be a very conservative estimate of eligibility, defining the probable floor rather than the ceiling of the population affected by this social policy.

How Rapidly Do Mothers Resume Employment?

Most children whose mothers were employed around the time of conception returned to work during the first year of the child's life. Approximately 24 percent of these children had mothers who never resigned and, therefore, never technically left the labor market. Many probably negotiated some time off, but the NLS data set does not document how they combined vacation, sick, disability, and/or maternity leave to do so. It is likely that many new mothers were back on the job within 2 or 3 months post partum.

The NLS reports when mothers dropped out and reentered the labor market. Our analysis is restricted to those employed 9 months prior to childbirth. The proportion employed rose from 36 percent at 8 weeks after birth to 47 percent at 12 weeks to 60 percent at 26 weeks. The rate of reincorporation then slowed. Nevertheless, the vast majority (73 percent) of children whose mothers were employed around the time of conception had mothers who were back at work before their first birthday. Not all women who returned to work remained employed, a finding consistent with Shapiro and Mott (1979).

These data provide important insights into the current demand for infant day care. Women who take maternal leave or drop out of the labor market and then return to work must find care for extremely young children. The NLS data suggest that most are less than 6 months old, and many are younger than 2 months old. This puts the issue of child care for infants into a focus that can be related to parental leave policies.

Maternal leave in most countries covers eligible women for at least 8 weeks post partum (International Labour Office, 1984). The comparable figure for Europe is 20 weeks (see Chapter 1 by Sheila Kamerman). Applying the European standard to the current sample, at least half (55 percent) of the mothers employed at the time of conception would have been covered by parental leave policies. Moreover, mothers who were not employed around the time of conception, about half the total sample, would also not be covered by most international maternal leave policies. These figures permit one to estimate that approximately one-fourth of the children in the sample (i.e., one-half of one-half) had mothers who were employed during the period covered by paid parental leave in most European countries.

There are two principal reasons to believe that this estimate is conservative. Mothers in the NLS sample are relatively young and poorly educated. Older, better-educated first-time mothers with extensive work experience are likely to return to work more rapidly than those with different characteristics (O'Connell and Bloom, 1987). It is therefore likely that the NLS sample underestimates the proportions of mothers in the general population who would qualify for parental leave. It is also likely that if women were actually covered by legislation that guaranteed paid parental leave, some would increase their labor force attachment, responding to incentives to take time off from, rather than time out of, the labor market. Consequently, the behavior of the NLS mothers provides a very conservative estimate of eligibility for parental leave were international norms applicable in the United States.

What Explains the Rate of Return to Employment After Childbirth?

Some women return to work almost immediately after childbirth while others drop out of the labor market for longer periods. Differences in how rapidly mothers return to employment may be systematically related to their personal characteristics, household composition, and/or financial contribution to family income. To explore the effects of several factors simultaneously requires a multivariate statistical analysis. This technique allows one to evaluate the effects of specific variables after the influence of other variables in the model has been taken into account. One can determine whether an effect is statistically significant and how much change in the rate of return to employment is attributable to it. The return to work after childbirth is an event that occurs at different points in time for different individuals. The appropriate statistical technique to explore how several variables jointly influence rate of return is proportional hazards analysis.[3]

A model was developed to predict how rapidly mothers who had quit their jobs returned to employment during the first year after childbirth. The dependent variable was the number of weeks after childbirth the mother resumed employment. The predictors included personal, family, and economic characteristics. The overall model was statistically significant, so attention can focus on how much change in the rate of return to employment is attributable to statistically significant variables.

Taking time out prior to childbirth had a strong, negative influence on how rapidly mothers returned to employment after childbirth. Holding other variables in the model constant, the rate of return was nearly 64 percent lower for women who exited the labor force before childbirth than for those who worked throughout the pregnancy.

The birth of an additional child was also negatively associated with the return rate. Reasonably enough, women who had another child prior to labor market reentry returned 11 percent more slowly than others.

The fact that the mother's own mother worked is associated strongly and positively with her rate of return after childbirth. Women whose own mothers worked returned to employment 14 percent faster than others. A social-psychological explanation emphasizes maternal employment as a role model encouraging the daughter to remain economically active. A more structural explanation emphasizes the economic necessity of maternal employment, placing the daughter in a situation in which she too needs to work. It is not possible, or perhaps necessary, to choose between these alternative explanations. This finding, however, suggests promising directions for future research.

Ethnicity (i.e., being black rather than nonblack) is a statistically significant predictor of how quickly mothers return to employment. Being black is a strong predictor of not being employed at the time of conception, but it also has an important positive influence on how quickly women resume employment after childbirth. Controlling for other variables in the model, the rate of return for black women was 19 percent faster than that for others.

Family income was positively associated with returning to work, and it increased the rate of return 15 percent for each unit increase in logged income. Being married increased the rate of return 25 percent, while having other adults in the household increased the rate 62 percent. The effect of maternal education was positive, while maternal age at childbirth had a negative effect on how quickly women returned to employment. Finally, the proportion of income contributed by the mother had a positive and significant effect. Mothers earning all of the family income returned 60 percent more quickly than others. In summary, specific variables measuring some demographic characteristics of the mother, the composition of her household, and the nature of her financial contribution have statistically significant effects on how rapidly women return to work during the first year after childbirth.

It is noteworthy that the presence of other preschoolers in the household had no statistically significant effect on the rate of return to employment. Conventional wisdom suggests that mothers with several preschoolers are likely to dedicate themselves to childrearing, and census data report lower rates of labor force participation for women with young children (U.S. Bureau of the Census, 1987, p. 374). Recent scholarship, notably Glass (1988) and Spenner and Rosenfeld (1989), has found that the presence of other preschoolers does not necessarily depress female labor force participation. The demands of caregiving and the costs of child care may make it difficult for mothers with several children to work outside the home; on the other hand, mothers who have located care for an older preschooler may be familiar with the child care system and therefore successful in placing younger children. These interpretations are reasonable, but the statistically nonsignificant effect of other preschoolers in the NLS model does not favor any explanation. The relationship among household composition, maternal employment, and child care certainly requires further research.

What Are the Implications of This Research for Social Policy?

Analysis of the NLS data provides useful insights for the evaluation of policy alternatives. Women with different personal characteristics are not equally likely to work before childbirth, and the predictors of maternal employment reported in this paper are fundamentally consistent with other scholarship. Ethnicity is an important determinant of both maternal employment and labor market reentry. Ethnic differences were not found in the tendency to quit jobs before childbirth, but they were found in the rate of reentry into the labor force after childbirth. Who works at all is an important fact because it is a principal determinant of who can become eligible for maternal leave.

If maternal/parental leave were implemented in the United States, a critical issue would be coverage—that is, which jobs were covered for how long. A casual review of internatior.al legislation can overstate the impact of maternal leave policies because so many women work in categories excluded from coverage. Parental leave legislation that excluded small firms in the so-called competitive sector would inadvertently discriminate against poor families in general and ethnic minorities in particular because they are concentrated in jobs that are relatively unregulated. By contrast, policies that use expansive eligibility criteria would minimize negative consequences for disadvantaged families.

The structural bases for discriminatory effects will remain if parental leave policies are not accompanied by positive job-creation, training, and placement policies. Some regions are job-poor, and some individuals are unqualified for available positions. Data from the NLS, presented in this paper, document the importance of ethnicity and income for work behavior. Social policies encouraging expansive coverage, plus aggressive job creation and job training, would expand the population who can qualify for parental leave benefits. If policy initiatives are not comprehensive, ethnic minorities will clearly be at a disadvantage.

Alternative wage replacement policies also have differential consequences. Internationally, the wage replacement component of maternal leave is generally tied to the mother's salary, which permits mothers who earn relatively high wages to take leave without substantially reducing the family income. The floor is generally defined by a country's minimum wage. This is important because the very language of "wage replacement" makes it difficult to imagine a maternal leave policy that is redistributive.

A complementary policy of family allowances could encourage equity. Standard allowances that reflect the general costs of childbearing and -rearing could represent a substantial proportion of family income in poor households. Such a policy is often dismissed as "pro-natalist" because it encourages childbearing and facilitates child care by the mother. Often overlooked are its strong redistributive consequences. A basic, uniform family allowance provides proportionally greater financial assistance to poor than to moderate- and upper-income families. Similarly, if coverage were as universal as Social Security, this would benefit workers in stable and marginal jobs alike. Such policies, in conjunction with parental leave, would enhance equity by redistributing resources toward the bottom of the income scale.

If social policies supported parental leave during the earliest stages of infancy, the need for extraparental care of extremely young children might decline. The NLS data presented in this paper demonstrate that infants with working mothers are entering the child care system at extremely young ages—many by 2 months and most by 6 months. Paid parental leave would expand alternatives and permit some parents to take time off with less financial loss. It would not, however, eliminate the demand for infant care: some parents would still need infant care because the wage replacement was not adequate, and/or because the promotion clock kept ticking, and/or because the parent(s) preferred to resume employment shortly after childbirth. Under these circumstances, parental leave policies could supplement, but not replace, child care policies.

In conclusion, parental leave policies are critical intervening variables between parental choice and child outcomes because how employment and child care are reconciled fundamentally affects both parenting and early childhood socialization. Parental leave policies, by their absence as well as by their presence, have consequences. The overall import of comprehensive parental leave policies is to encourage labor force attachment by facilitating the transition to parenthood and the integration of work and family responsibilities. It is probable, however, that the absence of a coherent family policy in the United States negatively conditions the circumstances under which women, not to mention men, negotiate their absence from work during the period immediately surrounding childbirth. It is also probable that mothers and/or fathers would adjust the balance between time off a job and time out of the labor market if they were presented with economically viable alternatives. The behavior of the NLS women reported in this chapter provides a conservative estimate of coverage should maternal employment behavior remain the same and U.S. policies approximate the international norms.

NOTES

Acknowledgments. The research on which this chapter is based was supported by an Innovative Research Award from the Frank Porter Graham

Child Development Center to the first author and a National Institute of Child Health and Human Development (NICHD) traineeship (5T3224DO7168) to the third author. The order of authorship is alphabetical.

1. The results, not shown here, are available from Patricia Garrett, Frank Porter Graham Child Development Center, University of North Carolina at Chapel Hill, Chapel Hill, NC 27599-8040.

2. The logic of parental leave policies is to facilitate the reconciliation of employment responsibilities with the demands of parenting. The net effect is that *time off the job* is not necessarily *time out of the labor market*. This fundamental distinction, unfortunately, cannot be empirically sustained by the NLS data, since they give no specific information on provisions for parental/maternal leave. There is general information on employer-sponsored medical insurance, but no details are provided on coverage of dependents. A similar lack of specificity characterizes maternity benefits and disability insurance as it pertains to childbirth. Because of these limitations, the NLS data set does not permit us to apprehend how mothers mobilize benefits and take time off without resigning their jobs and exiting the labor market temporarily. This restricts empirical analysis to time-out behavior—that is, quitting and reentering the labor market. Women quit jobs for many reasons (Glass, 1988), childbirth among them.

3. Linear proportional hazards analysis is an appropriate way of analyzing longitudinal data to predict the occurrence and timing of an event. An individual can be considered at risk for experiencing the event until it actually occurs. As time passes, the number of individuals still at risk decreases by the number who have already experienced the event. The hazard function describes the risk of the event, given that the event (in this case, labor market reentry) has not yet occurred. The Betas associated with the hazards model can be interpreted like the unstandardized regression coefficients of ordinary least squares regression (Allison, 1984). The magnitude of each effect, net of the influence of other variables in the model, is reflected in the percentage change in the rate of return attributable to each unit change in the independent variables. The table reporting the linear proportional hazards analysis is available from Patricia Garrett (see n. 1 above).

REFERENCES

Agresti, Alan (1984). *Analysis of Ordinal Categorical Data*. New York: John Wiley.

Aldrich, John H., and Forrest D. Nelson (1984). *Linear Probability, Logit, and Probit Models*. Beverly Hills, Calif.: Sage Publications.

Allison, Paul (1984). *Event History Analysis: Regression for Longitudinal Event Data*. Beverly Hills, Calif.: Sage Publications.

Bumpass, Larry, and James Sweet (1980). "Patterns of Employment Before and After Childbirth." *Vital and Health Statistics Report.* Series 23, no. 4. Washington, D.C.: Government Printing Office.

Center for Human Resource Research (1987). *NLS Handbook, 1987: The National Longitudinal Surveys of Labor Market Experience.* Columbus: Ohio State University.

Garrett, Patricia, and Sally Lubeck (1988). "Family-Based Child Care: Implications for Social Policy." *Journal of Applied Social Science* 12(2):142–69.

Glass, Jennifer (1988). "Job Quits and Job Changes: The Effects of Young Women's Work Conditions and Family Factors." *Gender and Society* 2:228–40.

Haggstrom, Gus W., Linda J. Waite, David E. Kanouse, and Thomas J. Blaschke (1984). *Changes in the Lifestyles of New Parents.* Santa Monica, Calif.: Rand Corporation.

Hayghe, Howard (1984). "Working Mothers Reach Record Number in 1984." *Monthly Labor Review* 107:31–33.

——— (1986). "Rise in Mothers' Labor Force Activity Includes Those with Infants." *Monthly Labor Review* 109(2):43–45.

International Labour Office (1984). *Women at Work.* International Labour Office Global Survey, 1964–1984, no. 2. Geneva: ILO.

McLaughlin, Sara D. (1982). "Differential Pattern of Female Labor Force Participation Surrounding the First Birth." *Journal of Marriage and the Family* 44:407–20.

Mott, Frank L., and David Shapiro (1982). "Continuity of Work Attachment Among New Mothers." In F. L. Mott, ed., *The Employment Revolution: Young American Women in the 1970s.* Cambridge, Mass.: MIT Press.

O'Connell, Martin, and David E. Bloom (1987). *Juggling Jobs and Babies: America's Child Care Challenge.* Population Trends and Public Policy Pamphlet no. 12. Washington, D.C.: Population Reference Bureau.

Shapiro, David, and Frank L. Mott (1979). "Labor Supply Behavior of Prospective and New Mothers." *Demography* 16:199–208.

Spenner, Kenneth, and Rachael A. Rosenfeld (1989). "Women, Work, and Identities: An Event History Analysis." Duke University, Durham, N.C.

Tienda, Marta, and Jennifer Glass (1985). "Household Structure and Labor Force Participation of Black, Hispanic, and White Mothers." *Demography* 22:381–94.

U.S. Bureau of the Census (1987). *Statistical Abstract of the United States, 1988* (108th ed.) Washington, D.C.: Government Printing Office.

——— (1988). *Fertility of American Women: June 1987.* Current Population Reports, Series P-20, no. 427. Washington, D.C.: Government Printing Office.

U.S. Department of Labor, Women's Bureau (1983). *Time of Change: 1983 Handbook on Women Workers.* Bulletin no. 298. Washington, D.C.: Government Printing Office.

Waite, Linda J., Gus W. Haggstrom, and David E. Kanouse (1985). "Changes in the Employment Activities of New Parents." *American Sociological Review* 50:263–72.

PART II

Economic Issues

PART II

3

Science and Politics and the "Dual Vision" of Feminist Policy Research: The Example of Family and Medical Leave

Roberta M. Spalter-Roth and Heidi I. Hartmann

The Institute for Women's Policy Research (IWPR) is a feminist think tank devoted to conducting research on policy issues affecting women's lives and to developing networks between the research, policy, and advocacy communities. Given these goals, as its research staff we must, on the one hand, conduct policy research that meets the standards of the mainstream social sciences for validity, reliability, objectivity, and replicability. On the other hand, our work is influenced by the principles of feminist methodology and especially by its challenge to the rigid dichotomies between researcher and researched and between activists and truth seekers (see Cook and Fonow, 1986; Harding, 1987). In addition, like others of our generation, we have been schooled in both social sciences and social movements (Bookman and Morgen, 1988).[1]

We believe that the research that results from these two perspectives, despite some risks, provides a useful synthesis in these times. This synthesis of the political and the scientific is the "dual vision" of feminist policy research. In what follows, we will use the example of our cost–benefit study, *Unnecessary Losses: Costs to Americans of the Lack of Family and Medical Leave* (Spalter-Roth and Hartmann, 1986, 1990), to reflect critically on how the study came to be done, IWPR's methodological vision, and the concepts, methods, findings, and conclusions of the research itself.

The Context of Unnecessary Losses

The FMLA, the Question of Costs, and the Entry of IWPR

Currently, more than half of all mothers with children under age one are in the labor force. Approximately 64 percent of working women who bore children in 1985 returned to work within the year (Gainer, 1987). Although they are no longer full-time caretakers, women still do the major share of the work of caring for newborn babies, sick children, husbands, and elderly parents or in-laws. As more and more women combine work and taking care of dependents, the need for policies that allow women to balance these jobs has become more widespread.

Organizations representing these working women have increased their demands for national policies that move beyond the traditional wages and hours legislation that emerged from the Fair Labor Standards Act (FLSA) of 1938. Like the traditional standards, such "new labor standards" as the proposed Family and Medical Leave Act (FMLA) address a societal problem through a federally mandated minimum standard because voluntary corrective actions on the part of employers are viewed as inadequate. Like other federal labor standards, the FMLA attempts to mandate certain rights and benefits by requiring private employers to provide them and hence minimizes the costs to the federal government. Unlike the FLSA, whose coverage was primarily extended to male industrial workers (Palmer, 1988), the FMLA treats the "typical" worker as somebody who combines paid work with caring for family members.

The FMLA, which mandates job-protected leave for dependent care and a worker's own illness, was introduced as "no-cost" legislation that would promote the economic security and stability of families.[2] It quickly gained wide support from women's, labor, religious, and disability coalitions. It received widespread and largely favorable coverage in the press until the U.S. Chamber of Commerce activated its membership to lobby against the bill. According to Ann Radigan (1988) in her cogent study of the history of the legislation, "All the positive press coverage and good will toward the legislation finally succeeded in arousing the U.S. Chamber of Commerce, which had been following the parental leave issue in relative silence" (p. 20).

In addition to lobbying, the Chamber, through its economic policy division, undertook a cost analysis to show that the FMLA was not a no-cost bill. This study stated that the price tag for the FMLA would be approximately $16.2 billion, of which $9.4 billion would go to replace workers on leave, $1.24 billion to provide continued health insurance, and $5.5 billion to cover unspecified losses in productivity as a result of hiring untrained workers. The study assumed that replacements for covered workers would always be hired and would always be hired at a higher rate of pay, that no companies have existing leave policies, that firms of all sizes would be covered, and that there were no benefits to a leave policy that mandated that employers return experienced workes to their jobs (Shaine, 1987). (Later the Chamber revised its estimate substantially downward—to $2.6 billion.)

The Chamber concluded, based on this research, that the FMLA would put an undue burden on businesses and would lead to the failure of many small firms. The American Society of Personnel Administrators likewise warned that the act "will not help put America back on the road to competitiveness" but "will interfere with efforts to decrease costs and increase productivity" and will be "expensive and disruptive," especially for small businesses (Simpler, 1987).

The massive lobbying effort of organized business interests resulted in a shift of sympathies that radically altered the terms of the discourse. As businesses argued that they would be the victims of the policy, costs to business, rather than benefits to families, became the dominant language of the debate. The coalition supporting the FMLA needed to regain control of the costs and benefits rhetoric (Radigan, 1988). At this point Donna Lenhoff of the Women's Legal Defense Fund, one of the coalition leaders, came to Heidi Hartmann, the director of the newly formed IWPR. Referring to the 1987 testimony by T. Berry Brazelton, a well-known pediatrician and supporter of the FMLA, Lenhoff lamented that the only data available to the supporters of the FMLA were on child–parent bonding. Surely, she suggested, there must be costs to women and their families of not having leave. The coalition needed a single dollar amount that everyone could grab on to. Could IWPR do a study?

The Dual Vision of Feminist Policy Research

The resulting study, *Unnecessary Losses* (Spalter-Roth and Hartmann, 1988, 1990), funded by the Ford Foundation, was IWPR's first major research effort. As a policy research organization, IWPR has the task of producing valid and reliable social science research that assesses the efficacy of proposed policy solutions to social problems and that can stand up to the critical scrutiny of agencies such as the Office of Management and Budget (OMB).[3] As feminist researchers, in contrast, we must ask and answer such political ques-

tions as "Whose definition of a social problem is reflected in proposed policies?" and "To what extent do these policies treat women
not as productive citizens or workers, but rather as the social problem itself?" In short, we want to produce credible policy research
that can be used by those groups attempting to use the policy process to improve women's lives. The result of these two goals is a form
of policy research that incorporates our dual vision.

The dual vision is central to feminist theories of knowledge that
see historically oppressed groups as simultaneously holding both
dominant ideological and critical or oppositional views (Harding,
1987). For example, we use the dominant policy research paradigm
of welfare economics and its major tool, cost–benefit analysis, but we
filter it through a feminist prism that views the reproduction of gender, race, and class inequalities as a central feature of social life.

In the dominant welfare economics paradigm, the policy researcher is considered to be an objective expert working in the public interest as an advisor to policymakers. He is assumed to know all
the policy options and to be able to quantify the costs and benefits of
each. He will advise policymakers how and when the state should
intervene to correct "market failure" (Bobrow and Dryzak, 1987, p.
32). The state, like the policy researcher, is seen as a neutral arbitra-
tor that uses the results of cost–benefit analyses to moderate between interest groups and provide the greatest good for the greatest
number.

When we produce policy research, we accept the standpoint of
the objective expert using largely quantitative methods (rather than
in-depth interviewing or participant observation) to evaluate policy
options.[4] And we use the dominant paradigm of cost–benefit analysis when it is appropriate. Cost–benefit analysis, with its assumption
of the validity of monetary indicators that are usually divorced from
feelings, consciousness, and emotions, has been seen by its radical
critics as an expression of the dominant capitalist material values.
Nevertheless, we would argue that in a capitalist society, cost–benefit
analysis can provide a valid indicator of the gains and losses posed
by particular policy options to class, race, and gender groups.

Unlike mainstream policy analysts, however, we also follow the
principles of feminist research (Cook and Fonow, 1986). We view
research as political as well as scientific. We use our expert stance to
legitimate feminist ideas. Given our concern with gender, race, and
class inequalities and the resulting devaluation of women's work and
women's worth, we are critical of hegemonic views that see *only one*
public interest in cost–benefit analysis. We believe that state policy

frequently acts in the interests of dominant class, race, and gender groups, especially if grass-roots activists are denied access to policymaking. We want to carry out policy research that puts the interests of women—and policies' often uncounted costs and benefits to them—at the center of the analysis. We reject that part of the objectivity canon that distances the production of knowledge from its uses, and thus we apply a constituency test to see if research that we undertake will be of use to grass-roots and advocacy groups in defining and solving problems.

This dual vision is reflected in the concepts and methodology of our study of family and medical leave. *Unnecessary Losses* uses both the techniques of cost–benefit analysis and a feminist standpoint that centrally locates women's work in order to evaluate a proposed policy. In this case, we evaluate the benefits of the proposed policy by evaluating the costs of the current lack of policy.

The Research Study

Concepts and Method

Unnecessary Losses estimates the current costs in dollars to working women (and men), to taxpayers, and to society as a whole of three kinds of daily life-giving activities done by working adults: caring for newly arrived children; caring for oneself or a family member during illness; and caring for elderly parents. This third activity is measured and discussed in our full report, but because its analysis uses a somewhat different methodology, reasons of space prohibit its discussion here.

We are well aware that the costs of illness and dependent care to individuals and to society are not only economic. We limited our measures to costs in dollars, however, for both scientific and political reasons: first, because economic losses are verifiable quantitative measures; second, because the Chamber of Commerce used financial measures in its estimates of costs to businesses; and, third, because although much caring work is done out of love and duty, in a capitalist society revealing the monetary cost of an activity establishes its value.

Identifying Current and Proposed Costs and Benefits

When a person leaves employment temporarily because of the arrival of a child, the illness of a family member, or his or her own illness, there are economic costs for three groups: employers, workers, and society.

Employer Costs.   First, the employer must replace the worker either temporarily or permanently, or arrange for the work to be done in another way. Although recruiting, hiring, and training a new replacement worker cost something, these costs occur whether or not there is a parental or medical leave requirement. We contend that most of the costs to business that have been discussed as pertaining to parental and medical leave actually pertain to the unavoidable costs of having babies or being ill. Given that women will continue to have babies (at least until men can have them) and that workers will continue to get ill, employers must deal with their absence from work. Only the potential *additional* cost to employers of replacing temporarily rather than permanently is due to the requirements of leave legislation. The Ford Foundation program officer who handled our proposal encouraged us to look at actual costs to businesses as well as to workers, families, and taxpayers. We spent a considerable portion of the grant resources on this task, but in the end the lack of reliable data led us to decide to wait for the definitive report by the U.S. General Accounting Office (GAO). GAO (Gainer, 1989) estimated these costs to be relatively insignificant ($236 million) and by and large limited to the cost of maintaining workers' health insurance.

Worker Costs.   Second, there are costs to workers of the arrival of a child or their own illness. Some, such as the medical costs of birth (or illness) and wage loss, are not addressed by the proposed legislation (though the cost of health insurance is). Other costs that workers now bear, such as income losses that result from the increased length of time a returning worker is unemployed, or the lower relative wage at which she or he is reemployed elsewhere, when there is no right to return to a job, are addressed by the legislation and are measured in our study. Given our commitment to putting women's interests and policies' often uncounted costs (and benefits) to them at the center of research, these were the cost measures that most concerned us. Given our concern with race and class domination and the insensitivity of lumping together the categories "women" and "minorities," we disaggregate the costs to black women, white women, black men, and white men. As a result, we see both gender and race inequalities in our findings. Unfortunately, the data set we are using is not large enough to allow examination of costs for Hispanic or Asian American women and families.

Societal Costs.   Despite our belief that there is no single public interest, and our belief that the identification of who pays and who benefits is always problematic, we do look at the costs to society in general. We suggest that if workers experience more unemployment and wage loss without parental and medical leave, productivity is lost to the economy. Even if the employer finds an equally productive employee to replace an absent one, and so minimizes her or his individual loss, society still loses productivity because the original trained and skilled workers will have to find new jobs. Thus, the employer's action in terminating an ill or pregnant worker can be viewed as creating a cost to be borne by all of us, just as we all pay the price for one factory's pollution.

In addition to these economic costs of absence from work, there are financial costs borne specifically by taxpayers.

Taxpayer Costs. As a result of studies that show that welfare state policies frequently subsidize businesses at a cost to those who actually pay taxes (see, for example, Service Employees International Union, 1988), we also examine the financial costs to taxpayers. Taxpayers may pay for the lack of a federal policy and the resulting losses to workers of income and employment in the form of transfer payments such as unemployment insurance, Aid to Families with Dependent Children, general assistance, and food stamps. It is also worth noting here that both businesses and individuals are taxpayers.

Data and Methods

Our estimates of the current costs of parenting and illness rely on survey data gathered by the Institute for Social Research in its Panel Study of Income Dynamics (PSID). The PSID interviews a sample of nearly seven thousand households annually to provide information on their labor force participation, their employment and unemployment status, their hours on and off the job, earnings, other sources of income (including public transfer programs), and family size and other demographic information. The PSID is nationally representative, and the reliability of its income measures is considered to be high.

From a feminist perspective, however, PSID has two important methodological weaknesses. It treats respondents as the objects of research—they have no voice in defining the problems to be addressed or in using the outcomes—and the "head" of the household (the husband in a married-couple household) answers all questions for the wife as well as for other family members. (The persistent failure of the "head" to be available for interviewing generally means, however, that the wife, as proxy for the "head," responds to the interviewer's questions.) Not only does this technique result in problems of scientific reliability, but, politically, it muffles the voices of women. In general, more questions are asked about the activities of the "head" than about those of the wife or other family members. Of course, unmarried women are regarded as "heads" of their households, and they are the central informants in those cases.

Despite these weaknesses, the PSID is, to our knowledge, the only nationally representative survey to ask a question about parental leave, along with other income and demographic information that is useful in evaluating the outcomes of parenting and illness for workers, taxpayers, and society. In 1983–1984 questions about employee benefits included the following one about parental leave: "Would you/she (your wife or companion) get any leave (besides regular vacation time) from your (her) main job, if you (she) had a baby?" This is not an ideal question about parental leave, since it does not distinguish among parental leave, maternity leave, sick leave, or disability leave. Nonetheless, it is the kind of rough indicator that policy researchers often find themselves using.

Unnecessary Losses uses a quasi-experimental research design in which groups of individuals who experience an event are compared with a like group who did not have the experience. This kind of design attempts to appropriate the strengths of the rigorously controlled experimental design used in the natural sciences (Campbell and Stanley, 1966), and hence it is given a privileged methodological position in the social sciences (Sherif, 1987).

To evaluate the costs of parenting, we compare the economic circumstances of women under 41 who either had or did not have (or adopt) a baby and who were employed at least 600 hours in the year before the child's birth. We consider four points in time—the year prior to birth, the birth year, the first year after the birth, and the second year after the birth. (Women with births are those who had only one birth during the four-year period; the years in the sample used range from 1978–79 to 1983–84.) Because a question was asked about parental leave in the 1983–84 interviewing year, we are also able to compare the economic circumstances of those women who had (or adopted) babies and reported that they had some form of leave with those who had or adopted babies but reported having no such leave.

To evaluate the costs of illness, we used responses to the following question: "Did you miss any work in 1983 because you were sick? How much work did you miss?" and responses to an additional question about work missed as a result of the illness of other family members. We compare workers (both women and men) under age 55 who were not retired, who either experienced or did not experience more than 50 hours of absence from work because of illness (either their own or a family member's) in one year (out of the four-year period under examination), and who were employed for at least 600 hours in the year prior to this event. We chose the 50-hour figure because it was more than the average (40 hours) but still low enough that the sample size for the "ill" group would not be so small as to result in idiosyncratic findings.

Where we find differences in outcomes between those who experienced the events and those who did not, we interpret the net differences (that is, gross differences in outcomes net of differences in initial conditions) as being due to the events. For example, if the differences show that women who had a baby are significantly worse off during the years following a birth or adoption, compared with the year prior to the birth, when compared to women who did not have babies, the differences are interpreted as the costs of having (or adopting) a baby. The differences we report here are statistically significant—that is, they are unlikely to have occurred by chance. In all comparisons of this kind, the groups may differ for reasons other than the occurrence of the event being studied, and other unknown events may occur along with the event in question.

We look at several indicators to explore what "worse off" might mean, including annual work hours, unemployment hours, housework hours, hours out of the labor force, hourly wages, annual earnings, and income from public transfer programs. To provide estimates for all women or workers in the United States, we assume that the experiences of all workers are similar to those of the PSID sample, since the sample itself is representative of the U.S. population.

Findings

The Costs of Having a Baby

What do the data show? In the year before the birth, the earnings of women who (later) had babies looked very similar to the earnings of those who did not; those who had babies earned slightly more ($12,586 compared with $12,399 in 1986 dollars), even though they were somewhat younger (mid-twenties compared with early thirties). And there were no significant differences in "pre-birth" wage rates or annual hours of employment and unemployment between the two groups. They *did*, however, receive significantly less transfer in-

TABLE 3.1

Estimated Earnings Losses to Employed Women aged 41 or Under Who Gave Birth or Adopted a Baby Compared with Employed Women Who Did Not Have a Baby (1986 dollars)

	Earnings Lost for Births that Occurred	Earnings Loss per Woman	Earnings Losses for All Women Who Had Babies
This year		−3,232	−6,933,000,000
Last year		−5,993	−12,855,000,000
2 years ago		−5,204	−11,163,000,000
Total 3-year loss per woman		−14,429	
Current annual losses			−30,951,000,000

Interpretation: It costs American women more than $31 billion in earnings losses annually to have the next generation of workers and citizens.

Source: Institute for Women's Policy Research calculations. Earnings loss per woman is based on special tabulations from the 1979–1984 interview waves of the Panel Study of Income Dynamics, Institute for Social Research, University of Michigan. Earnings losses for all women are based on IWPR calculations and data from U.S. Bureau of the Census (1986), *Fertility of American Women: June 1985, Current Population Reports*, Series P-20, no. 406 (Washington, D.C.: Government Printing Office, June 1986), table 4, as adjusted by IWPR, which suggest that 2,145,000 employed women gave birth in 1985.

come than those women who did not give birth in the following year. In short, those who gave birth looked slightly better off financially in the pre-birth year than those who did not give birth.

In the year of the birth, however, their economic circumstances began to shift, and they became worse in the year after the birth. Annual earnings losses for the new mothers are substantial (see Table 3.1). In the year after the birth the losses were more than $5,000 compared with those women with no new baby. In addition, wage rates, hours of employment, and hours of unemployment differed significantly between the two groups of women by the year after birth. Those who had babies worked 745 fewer hours, and their wage rates were now $1.40 less per hour than those of women who did not give birth. Simultaneously, their hours of housework (*excluding* child care) and their receipt of public transfer income increased. New mothers went from receiving significantly less transfer income than those who did not give birth to receiving significantly more.

The second year after the birth, new mothers' annual earnings recover somewhat (because they are working somewhat more hours and experiencing fewer hours out of the labor force), but are still substantially below their pre-birth earnings. The hourly wage gap continues to increase in favor of those who did not give birth, and new mothers continue to do approximately four times as many hours of housework as they did in the pre-birth year. New mothers, somewhat better off in the pre-birth year than those who did not have a baby during this period, are worse off in the years after birth. It is likely that the losses continue beyond the second year.

When we generalize these individual losses to all employed women in the United States who gave birth in 1985 or the two prior years, the losses in earnings alone to American working women who have babies total nearly $31 billion annually.

Race Differences. The outcomes of having a baby are different for black women and men than for white women and men. As shown in Figure 3.1, black women who had babies had significantly lower annual earnings (approximately $1,600 less in 1986 dollars) in the pre-birth year than did white women who had babies; they also received a significantly lower hourly wage ($1.22 less per hour). In the birth year, the earnings difference and wage gap increased, possibly because black women were more likely to be unemployed and to work fewer hours. But in the two years following the birth, the earnings gap appears to be eliminated, as new black mothers earned $2,300 more in 1986 dollars than new white mothers. This increase in annual earnings is a result of the significantly higher number of hours black women worked (452 hours more in the year after birth, and 335 hours more in the second year after birth), but they also experienced more unemployment (they spent more time working or looking for work and less time out of the labor force). We suggest that their additional hours of work reflect the special needs of new black mothers to stay in the labor force and earn a living. These figures show that the right to job reinstatement after childbirth is especially crucial for black women, because it would likely reduce their earnings losses from unemployment. The right to job reinstatement would also reduce costs to taxpayers.

The right to job reinstatement appears even more critical for black women when we consider the income gap between black and white fathers in the years before and after birth. Black men are relatively disadvantaged in the labor market in general. The data show that relative to white fathers, the economic circumstances of black fathers get worse in the years following the birth or adoption of a child. Disparities in income between white and black fathers, who earned $25,201 and $20,215 (in 1986 dollars) respectively, are already significant in the pre-birth year. These disparities increase to more than $8,000 in the second year after birth. The data also show a significant increase in black fathers' unemployment rates com-

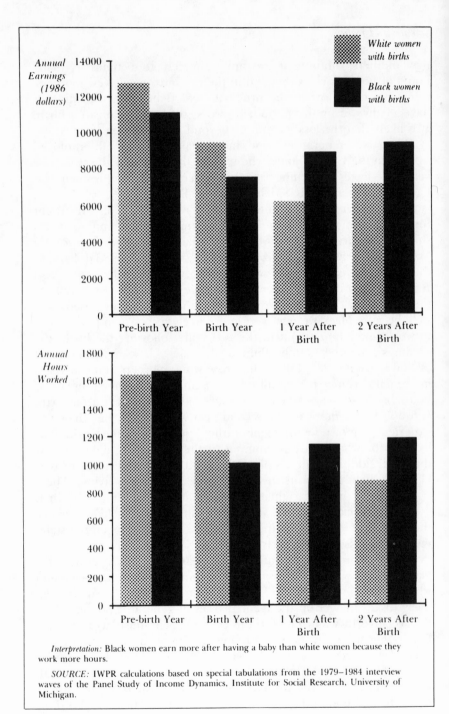

Interpretation: Black women earn more after having a baby than white women because they work more hours.

SOURCE: IWPR calculations based on special tabulations from the 1979–1984 interview waves of the Panel Study of Income Dynamics, Institute for Social Research, University of Michigan.

FIGURE 3.1 Earnings Before and After Birth: Black and White Women

pared with white fathers' in the years following the birth or adoption of a child. As a result of these losses, black women are less able than white women to rely on an increase in their spouse's income to rear a child should they want to. Having a birth increases sex role differentiation (as measured by earnings and labor market behavior) for whites but does not do so for blacks.

Gender Differences. When women who had babies are compared with men who had babies (or, to be more biologically, though not socially, correct, whose wives had babies), the differences in annual earnings between women and men, which are substantial in the year before the birth ($12,000 in men's favor), are magnified in the year of birth or adoption and in the two following years to almost $19,000 annually. The numbers that compare all working women who had babies with all men who had babies are very dramatic. Figure 3.2 uses two indicators, hourly wage rates and hours of housework, to illustrate that women bear a disproportionate share of the costs of having children. Between the year before the birth and two years after the birth, the wage gap between women's hourly wages and men's hourly wages increases by 60 percent. In addition, women's housework hours increase by 22 percent.

New parents, especially those who are married, may not experience income losses as a household; indeed, our data indicate that married white men who become fathers are able to increase their wages, and these gains may make up for wives' losses. Nonetheless, even when household income remains stable, economic equity between the sexes declines, women become the "natural" labor pool for marginalized jobs, and they become increasingly burdened with unpaid work as a result of having a baby. Researchers have shown that this uneven exchange has negative consequences for women's lifetime earnings and for their retirement and old age (see, for example, Reskin and Hartmann, 1986). Other researchers have shown that women's power within households, and especially their control over expenditures, is related to the portion of family income that they earn (see, for example, Pahl, 1989). Thus, women face the possibility of power losses within marriage along with the economic losses that result from childbirth.

As noted, these gender differences are more reflective of the experience of white women and men. The differences between black women and men stay relatively stable from the pre-birth through the post-birth years, with an annual earnings difference of about $8,000 (in 1986 dollars) and an hourly wage rate difference of about $3.00, both in black men's favor.

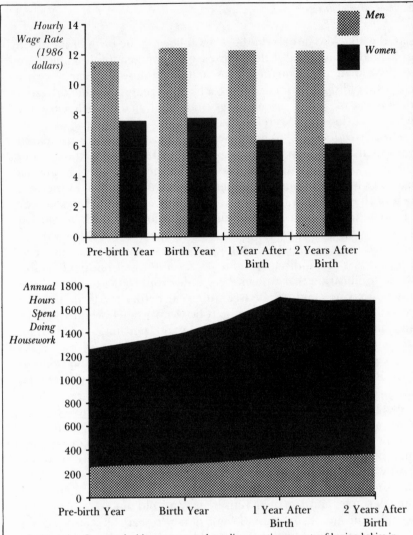

Interpretation: Compared with men, women bear disproportionate costs of having babies in lower hourly wage rates and more housework hours—not including child care.

SOURCE: IWPR calculations based on special tabulations from the 1979–1984 interview waves of the Panel Study of Income Dynamics, Institute for Social Research, University of Michigan.

FIGURE 3.2 Hourly Wage Rates and Housework Hours of Women and Men, Before and After Childbirth

The Costs of No Parental Leave

Costs to Women.   Data from the 1983–84 PSID interviews indicate that more than seven out of ten employed women report having some form of leave besides vacation. About one out of three women report that this leave is paid. The percentage of women who report having some leave (other than vacation time) available for the purpose of having a baby and caring for an infant seems high in light of other data (Trzcinski, 1988).

Fewer than half of all black men and about one-third of all white men report being entitled to leave other than vacation for the birth of a child. Male respondents (and especially white men) seem particularly confused as to whether they are entitled to leave, with high percentages answering "don't know."

Table 3.2 illustrates the costs in earnings losses of not having any form of maternity or parental leave for those women who give birth or adopt babies. Those new mothers who reported having no leave were in significantly worse economic circumstances in the pre-birth year than those women who reported having some form of leave. Those without leave earned $5,250 less because they worked approximately 150 fewer hours, because they experienced about 200 more hours of unemployment, and because they earned $2.65 less per hour, possibly as a result of holding jobs with few benefits in small, secondary-sector firms.

TABLE 3.2
Estimated Additional Earnings Losses of Not Having Leave to Employed Women Who Had Babies (1986 dollars)

Earnings Lost for Births that Occurred	Earnings Loss per Woman	Earnings Losses for All Women Without Leave
This year	− 631	−351,900,000
Last year	− 218	−121,500,000
2 years ago	− 239	−133,500,000
Total 3-year loss per woman	− 1,088	
Current annual losses		−606,900,000

Interpretation: Employed women who did not have some form of leave beyond vacation lost nearly $607 million in additional earnings annually when they returned to work after childbirth or adoption, compared with those women who had leave.

Source: Institute for Women's Policy Research calculations based on special tabulations from the 1979–1984 interview waves of the Panel Study of Income Dynamics, Institute for Social Research, University of Michigan. PSID data and the U.S. Bureau of the Census (1986), *Fertility of American Women: June 1985*, table 4, as adjusted by IWPR, suggest that 557,700 women who gave birth in 1985 did not have maternity or parental leave.

These women's relative economic circumstances continue to worsen in the years following the birth or adoption of a child, with greater losses in annual earnings, wages, and hours of work. Annual earnings losses are large for both groups of women (more than $2,000 every year), but the earnings disparities between the two groups widen to almost $5,900 in the year of birth and remain at about $5,500 in the two following years.

Part of this widening gap occurs because women who had no leave had a wage loss of an additional 76 cents per hour in the birth year (compared with the pre-birth year), followed by smaller additional losses in subsequent years. By the second post-birth year, they were still losing an additional 17 cents per hour compared with those women who did have some form of leave. Women without leave also experienced even more time on the official unemployment rolls, particularly in the year after the birth (no doubt reflecting the need to search for a job), and more hours out of the labor force (and off the unemployment rolls), a position sometimes termed "hidden unemployment." As noted, those *additional losses* occur because those without any form of leave experience more unemployment and lower wages (relative to those with some leave) when they return to work after childbirth.

Taxpayer and Societywide Costs. When these figures are generalized to estimate the annual costs to all employed women who gave birth without leave, as they are in Table 3.2, this loss totals almost

TABLE 3.3
Estimated Financial Cost to Taxpayers of Not Having Maternity or Parental Leave for Employed Women Who Had Babies (1986 dollars)

	Public Assistance Payments for Births that Occurred	Public Assistance Payments per Woman	Public Assistance Payments for All Women Without Leave
This year		− 80.75	−45,000,000
Last year		237.48	132,400,000
2 years ago		− 36.25	20,200,000
Total 3-year payments per woman		192.98	
Current annual cost			107,631,000

Interpretation: Employed women who gave birth and did not have any maternity or parental leave cost American taxpayers nearly $108 million in additional public assistance payments annually compared with women who had leave.

Source: Institute for Women's Policy Research calculations based on special tabulations from the 1979–1984 interview waves of the Panel Study of Income Dynamics, Institute for Social Research, University of Michigan. PSID data and U.S. Bureau of the Census (1986), *Fertility of American Women: June 1985*, table 4, as adjusted by IWPR, suggest that 557,700 employed women who gave birth in 1985 did not have maternity or parental leave.

$607 million.[5] Despite their substantially poorer circumstances, women without any form of maternity or parental leave received only $1.85 more in income assistance payments in the pre-birth year than did those with some form of leave. For reasons we cannot fully explain without further analysis, they received substantially less in income assistance payments in the birth year—despite their worsening economic circumstances—than those women who did have some form of parental leave. In the post-birth year, their relative public assistance income increased but then decreased again in the second post-birth year. (These fluctuations may have to do with changing eligibility to receive unemployment insurance benefits.) Overall, women without leave received nearly $200 more in income assistance, on average, than those who had leave.

When these additional costs are generalized to all U.S. working women who had babies but were not covered by some form of parental leave, the estimated total is nearly $108 million in additional income assistance costs borne by taxpayers, as shown in Table 3.3. The relatively *small* costs to taxpayers in additional income assistance payments, when compared with the costs to women in earnings losses, illustrate that women under the present arrangements are bearing a disproportionate share of the costs of having the next generation of citizens and workers.

These findings, although they probably underestimate the costs because they overestimate the proportion of women with leave, indicate that the effects of having or not having parental leave may actually be relatively small because of the overwhelming economic costs that women bear in having a baby. In the face of that cost, unpaid parental leave may represent a small ameliorative.

Costs of Illness

Thus far we have examined some of the costs to women and their families, to employers, and to society of childbirth. Now let us turn to the costs of illness. Workers under age 55 reported that they were off the job because of their own illness for 0.82 percent of a working week, or an average of four days, in survey year 1983–84. In addition, the average worker is off the job for one extra workday as a result of someone else's illness. Significantly, women lost fewer hours than did their male counterparts.

These data on time off the job indicate that U.S. workers, female or male, do not, on the average, take very much sick leave regardless of its availability. In any one year, a relatively small group of workers would benefit most from job guarantees for absence due to illness.

For convenience we will refer to those with more than 50 hours off the job as the "ill group" and those with 50 or fewer hours as the "well group," although this terminology is less than accurate because we include absence for the illness of others as well.

What do the results show? The most striking finding, as shown in Table 3.4, is that for the "ill" group, the losses in annual earnings *grow* in the two years following the one in which the worker took more than 50 hours off the job because of illness. These annual earnings losses stem from lower hourly wages, fewer hours worked, more hours unemployed, and more hours out of the labor force. Assuming that severe illness is limited to a relatively small group of the working population, our findings show that workers who experience lengthy illness experience significant economic losses in the form of lost wages, annual earnings, and hours of employment.

Gender Differences. In the year prior to illness, there were no significant differences in the economic conditions of the two groups of women, with the "well" group earning $13,522 and the "ill" group earning $13,476. Absence for illness resulted in substantial divergence in the economic circumstances of the two groups. In the absence year, those with more than 50 hours off the job earned $350 less, probably as a result of their significantly lower annual hours of work. Two years later those in the "ill" group were earning signifi-

TABLE 3.4
Estimated Earnings Losses to Workers Under Age 55 Who Were Off the Job for More Than 50 Hours Because of Illness, Compared with Workers Off the Job for Less Than 50 Hours (1986 dollars)

Earnings Lost from Absence Due to Illness that Occurred	Earnings Loss per Worker	Earnings Losses for All Workers with Absence
This year	−646	−13,479,000,000
Last year	−1,311	−27,372,000,000
2 years ago	−2,839	−59,268,000,000
Total 3-year loss per worker	−4,796	
Current annual losses		−100,119,000,000

Interpretation: Workers under age 55 lose $100 billion annually for above-average absence because of illness.

Source: Institute for Women's Policy Research calculations based on special tabulations from the 1979–1984 interview waves of the Panel Study of Income Dynamics, Institute for Social Research, University of Michigan. Based on the experience of the PSID sample, it is estimated that in 1985, 20,875,643 U.S. workers were out of the labor force for more than 50 hours because of illness.

cantly less ($2,000 a year), had significantly lower wages (86 cents less per hour), and suffered an additional 53 hours of unemployment and 88 hours out of the labor force. Whereas women's earnings losses from childbearing and -rearing seem to grow smaller over time, losses from absence due to illness seem to cumulate.

In contrast to the women's experience, there were significant differences in economic circumstances between the "ill" and the "well" groups of men in the year prior to absence. Men who were off the job for more than 50 hours in the absence year earned less than $27,000 (in 1986 dollars) the previous year, while the "well" group of men earned more than $29,000. These differences in earnings were magnified at an increasing rate in the post-absence years. During the following two years, the disparity in annual earnings almost trebled, and the male workers who had been absent for illness suffered more than 200 additional hours of unemployment and hours out of the labor force. As with women, these differences were magnified during the two years following the absence.

Race Differences. Black women had significantly lower earnings ($1,836 less in 1986 dollars) in the year prior to the illness than did white women who were ill. This disparity was primarily due to their significantly lower hourly wages ($1.20 less) and partly due to more hours of unemployment and fewer hours of work. In the absence year the income disparity continued to grow (though the wage gap partially closed). The most striking losses from which black women suffered as a result of illness were the increased hours of unemployment and increased hours out of the labor force. Two years after the illness, they were even worse off, with an additional 280 hours (6.7 weeks) of unemployment and 201 hours out of the labor force compared with white women.

Race exacerbates the economic costs of illness to men as it does to women. The $9,100 difference in annual earnings between black and white men in the year prior to illness increased by an additional 25 percent by two years after the illness as a result of an increasing disparity in hourly wages. In addition, the disparity between black and white men's unemployment hours and hours out of the labor force, which was insignificant in the year prior to illness, increased by over 450 hours, or more than 11 weeks. We suggest that the extremely high costs that black workers bear from increased hours of unemployment and hours out of the labor force are at least in part a result of the lack of rights to reemployment after illness.

Taxpayer and Societywide Costs. Decline in annual earnings, wage rates, and hours of employment may appear to be only an individual loss reflecting the reduced ability of a man or a woman to earn a decent living in the face of illness and subsequent job termination and unemployment. When aggregated and generalized to the entire population of U.S. workers under age 55, as it is in Table 3.4, the magnitude of the individual loss can be more fully appreciated. The estimated loss in earnings annually to U.S. workers who have been absent from work for more than 50 hours because of their own or a family member's illness (in the current year or in either of the two prior years) is $100 billion.

These lost dollars also represent the loss in productivity that occurs because trained and experienced workers are not at work. That a large part of this lost productivity may be caused by workers' lack of rights to return to their jobs after an illness is suggested by the fact that unemployment hours are 1.5 times greater for both women and men in the "ill" group compared with those who had no illness. These workers are looking for work and unable to find it, and their skills and abilities are going unused. In addition to the costs to workers and society, we estimate the annual cost to taxpayers to be nearly $8 billion. Workers who are absent for illness receive more income assistance than those who are not.

Conclusions

Our research supports the importance of family and medical leave for all workers. It shows that workers lose enormous amounts in earnings as a result of absences due to their own illness, others' illness, childbirth, or adoption. Not surprisingly, women bear a disproportionate share of these costs. Race differences are significant in both childbirth and illness because black workers suffer more unemployment and larger earnings losses as a result of these events. Our findings show further that taxpayers subsidize these costs, though at a relatively low proportion. The losses in earnings workers experience when they are absent for illness or family care are not fully made up by currently available sick pay, insurance benefits, or public income assistance programs. Gender and race inequalities in income are exacerbated by these events. The lack of job-protected leaves adds the costs of job termination (especially the cost of unemployment) to the already substantial costs of childbirth and illness.

From the findings in *Unnecessary Losses*, we conclude that currently proposed legislation would benefit workers, their families, taxpayers, and society because it would eliminate many, if not all, of these *added* losses. Because the FMLA provides for only unpaid leave, however, it would not fully eliminate the losses due to the events themselves.

Combining our own research with the GAO report (Gainer, 1987, 1989) on costs to business of the proposed legislation, we concluded that the costs of not having the legislation far outweighed the costs to business of implementing it. Under the FMLA, employers would be required to take on the costs of maintaining their employees' health insurance (if they carry it) and holding their jobs for them. This *is* a new cost to employers, but it is not, we concluded, a new economic cost to women, taxpayers, or society. The proposed legislation would simply *redistribute* some of the existing costs to employers and hence reduce some of the inequalities between workers and employers. In addition, we suggest that besides serving the public purpose of enhanced productivity, the proposed FMLA also serves a public purpose of decreasing unjustified inequities between women and men, between those with and without family responsibilities, between blacks and whites, and between the ill and the well. And, finally, we suggest that it serves a public purpose by encoding a new, progressive tendency to overcome gender-based definitions of adult work.

Unnecessary Losses was done with both advocacy groups and policymakers in mind. It assumed that dominant race, class, and gender relations are reflected in public policy (or the lack of it) *and* that because the state does mediate between interest groups, evidence can be used to sway policymakers to act in women's interests. It simultaneously used the dominant policy paradigm of welfare economics and its major method, cost–benefit analysis, *and* a feminist prism that put the costs to women at the center of the analysis.

As a result of applying the dual vision of feminist policy research, we believe that we were successful in providing the supporters of the proposed legislation with evidence to contest successfully the "cost to business" rhetoric. The study has been widely cited in the press and has become part of the received wisdom cited by policymakers in congressional committee reports and elsewhere. Although mainstream and feminist methods—science and politics—are often described as oppositional or contradictory, we would argue that current circumstances make this dual vision necessary for effective policy research. The use of mainstream policy research skills gives our work credibility, while our feminist standpoint encourages us to change the assumptions and the content of the debate.[6]

Unnecessary Losses is an example of the utility of the dual vision. But because it embodies two oppositional, if not contradictory, methodological views, this vision has its risks. First, although we were successful at contesting the rhetoric of this particular policy debate, feminist discourse is constrained and often silenced by more powerful mainstream ideologies (and resources). By putting *women's* rather than, for example, *families'* interests at the center, we risk losing the debate. Second, by using sophisticated quantitative techniques, we may make our research less accessible to the advocacy groups with whom we work and the women in whose interests we are working.[7] Finally, suppose the data had not turned out to show greater losses for those without some form of parental leave. Given our adherence to the canons of quantitative social science research, we would not have "cooked" the data. We might have explored other data sets or other models, but the time and money constraints of policy research would probably have prohibited this. We might have tried, possibly with some success, to convince coalition members that they needed to go back to the drawing board and redesign a leave policy that would show measurable effects. But we surely would have disappointed our constituency, which would probably have been less likely to risk working with us on another research study in the future. Our credibility as a feminist policy research think tank is based on our embracing these contradictions, but the uncertainties of research—under the tight time pressures of policymaking—result in many wide-eyed, sleepless nights for those cursed or blessed with the dual vision.

NOTES

1. Earlier feminist writers about feminist policy research, such as Jean Lipman-Blumen (1979), viewed researchers and activists as having contradictory interests—the researcher pursuing "truth" and the activist "change." The idea that these goals are frequently carried in the same person and, even if contradictory, can lead to a useful synthesis is seen in the work of later feminists, such as Ann Bookman and Sandra Morgen (1988).

2. Under the version of the bill reintroduced in the U.S. House of Representatives on February 2, 1989, the legislation would apply only to employees of businesses with 50 or more workers (although the number would drop to 35 after three years). Dependent care leaves would be limited to 10 weeks over two years, and medical leaves to 15 weeks per year. Employees would not be entitled to the leave until they had worked at a business for at least 20 hours per week for at least one year, and employers would be permitted to deny reinstatement to the highest-paid 10 percent of their employees. The version reintroduced in the U.S. Senate on the same day covers

firms with 20 or more employees, covers workers who have worked at least 17.5 hours per week for one year, and permits 13 weeks of medical leave. The GAO (Gainer, 1989) estimates that approximately 2 million workers (less than 2 percent of the employed workforce) would take advantage of the Senate version of the proposed legislation annually.

3. Currently, *Unnecessary Losses* and a further study on the effect of state-level leave policy on small business growth done by Roberta Spalter-Roth and John Willoughby (1988) for 9to5, National Association of Working Women, are being critically reviewed by the Special Studies Division of OMB. Given the Reagan and the Bush administrations' opposition to family and medical leave, we think it likely that OMB's fine-tooth combing of the studies' methods is less scientific than political.

4. In-depth interviewing and participant observation are, however, appropriate, if under-used, policy research tools in many circumstances—for example, for identifying needs that require policy solutions and for evaluating program or policy effectiveness.

5. Earnings losses in the birth year are more likely to be due to the absence of maternity or short-term disability leave, rather than the absence of parental leave. Thus, $255 million, the loss *excluding* the birth year, is an approximate estimate of loss due to not having parental leave alone, and $607 million is an approximate estimate of losses due to not having either maternity or parental leave.

6. The dual vision of feminist policy research may have as its founding mothers Jane Addams and the sociologists of Hull House, who wanted to combine scientific observation with ethical values and service to the community to produce a just and liberated society. This mode of analysis was regarded as feminine, "applied," and nonscientific by the men of the Chicago school of sociology, who were able to obtain institutional resources from the Rockefeller family to develop an "objective" social science. Despite their valuing of progressive social change as an outcome of research, the Hull House researchers believed in the scientific method as the way to find truth (see Deegan, 1988). As postmodernists, most feminist scholars no longer believe in any single truth but in many "subjugated knowledges" (a term coined by Teresa de Lauretis and cited in Harding, 1987, p. 188).

7. We are indebted for these two important points to Ronnie Steinberg in her role as discussant for a panel entitled "Gender Relevant Policy and Social Change," at the annual meetings of the Eastern Sociological Society, Baltimore, February 17, 1989.

REFERENCES

Bobrow, Davis B., and John S. Dryzak (1987). *Policy Analysis by Design.* Pittsburgh: University of Pittsburgh Press.

Bookman, Ann, and Sandra Morgen, eds. (1988). *Women and the Politics of Empowerment.* Philadelphia: Temple University Press.

Campbell, Donald T., and Julian C. Stanley (1966). *Experimental and Quasi-Experimental Designs for Research.* Chicago: Rand McNally.

Cook, Judith A., and Mary Margaret Fonow (1986). "Knowledge and Women's Interests: Issues of Epistemology and Methodology in Feminist Sociological Research." *Sociological Inquiry* 56(1): 2–29.

Deegan, Mary Jo (1988). *Jane Addams and the Men of the Chicago School.* New Brunswick, N.J.: Transaction Books.

Gainer, William J. (1987). "The U.S. General Accounting Office's Cost Estimate of S. 249, The Parental and Medical Leave Proposal." Testimony before the Subcommittee on Children, Families, Drugs, and Alcoholism of the U.S. Senate Committee on Labor and Human Resources, October. 29.

———(1989). "GAO's Cost Estimate of the Family and Medical Leave Act Proposal." Testimony before the Subcommittee on Children, Families, Drugs, and Alcoholism of the U.S. Senate Committee on Labor and Human Resources, February 2.

Harding, Sandra, ed. (1987). *Feminism and Methodology.* Bloomington: Indiana University Press.

Lipman-Blumen, Jean (1979). "The Dialectics Between Research and Social Policy: The Difficulties from a Research Perspective—Roshomon Part II." In Jean Lipman-Blumen and Jessie Bernard, eds., *Sex Roles and Social Policy.* London: Sage Publications in International Sociology.

Pahl, Jan (1989). *Money and Marriage.* London: Macmillan.

Palmer, Phyllis (1988). "Outside the Law: Domestic and Agricultural Workers' Exclusion Under the Fair Labor Standards Act." Paper presented at the panel entitled "The Fair Labor Standards Act After 50 Years" at the annual meeting of the Organization of American Historians, Reno, Nevada, March.

Radigan, Ann (1988). *Concept and Compromise: The Evolution of Family Leave Legislation in the U.S. Congress.* Washington, D.C.: Women's Research and Education Institute.

Reskin, Barbara F., and Heidi I. Hartmann (1986). *Women's Work, Men's Work: Sex Segregation on the Job.* Washington, D.C.: National Academy Press.

Service Employees International Union, Public Policy Department (1988). *The Hidden Story of Taxpayer Subsidies for Low-Wage Employment.* Washington, D.C.: SEIU.

Shaine, Frances (1987). Testimony of the U.S. Chamber of Commerce of the United States on S. 249, The Parental and Medical Leave Act of 1987, before the Subcommittee on Children, Families, Drugs, and Alcoholism of the U.S. Senate Committee on Labor and Human Resources, April 23.

Sherif, Carolyn Wood (1987). "Bias in Psychology." In Sandra Harding, ed., *Feminism and Methodology.* Bloomington: Indiana University Press.

Simpler, Cynthia (1987). Testimony on behalf of the American Society of Personnel Administrators on S. 249, The Parental and Medical Leave

Act of 1987, before the Subcommittee on Children, Families, Drugs, and Alcoholism of the U.S. Senate Committee on Labor and Human Resources, April 23.

Spalter-Roth, Roberta M., and Heidi I. Hartmann (1988). *Unnecessary Losses: Costs to Americans of the Lack of Family and Medical Leave, Executive Summary.* Washington, D.C.: Institute for Women's Policy Research.

——— (1990). *Unnecessary Losses: Costs to Americans of the Lack of Family and Medical Leave.* Washington, D.C.: Institute for Women's Policy Research.

Spalter-Roth, Roberta M., and John Willoughby (1988). *New Workforce Policies and the Small Business Sector: Is Parental Leave Good for Business? A Multivariate Analysis of Business Employment Growth.* Cleveland, Ohio: 9to5, National Association of Working Women.

Trzcinski, Eileen (1988). "Wage and Employment Effects of Mandated Leave Policy." Manuscript. Department of Economics, Cornell University, Ithaca, N.Y., 14853.

4 | Parenting Without Poverty: The Case for Funded Parental Leave

Ann Bookman

For the last six years the Congress of the United States and state legislatures across the country have considered bills aimed at providing the parents of newly born or adopted babies with a period of leave from employment. The movement to develop public policies and laws to support families during the period immediately following childbirth or adoption has generated an intense debate. Parental leave, which seems on the face of it to be a policy promoting babies and motherhood—if not apple pie—actually brings us face to face with some of the most controversial questions of our time. Is it desirable for women to be working outside the home? What value and importance do we place on the physical, social, and emotional care of children? Do institutions outside the home—particularly business and government—have a role to play in supporting the family? Parental leave policy, and family policy in general, is a contested domain. The discourse surrounding the development of family policy reveals both the depth of "traditional" family values and the vitality of a feminist movement that has catalyzed an expanded role for women in the workplace and new expectations for men's and women's roles in the family.

Many specific components of parental leave policy have been debated as various bills have come under public scrutiny: eligibility (how long must a person have been attached to the paid labor force in order to qualify?); length of leave (how long do babies and parents take to form a secure attachment to one another?); the extent of job protection and continuation of benefits; and options for structuring the leavetaker's return to full-time employment. But the most extensive debate by far concerns the issue of wage replacement. Should the provision of parental leave include pay or not? This is the question on which the opposing sides seem most deeply and irreconcilably divided.

66

In this chapter I will examine several issues in order to answer that basic question. First, I will explore current parental leave policies in other countries that provide wage replacement and the mechanisms they utilize to do this. Second, I will examine what currently exists in the United States in the way of paid parental leave, looking at the situation for those who work in different sectors of the economy. Third, I will present a case study of two Massachusetts legislative commissions that have proposed solutions to the problem of how to provide paid parental leave.

A Cross-Cultural Perspective on Parental Leave: What Do Other Countries Provide?

Investigating how the period immediately after childbirth is structured in other countries and cultures around the world provides two striking findings. First, in traditional pre-industrial cultures, we see a variety of well-defined, often extremely ritualized, systems of support for new mothers and fathers. In most cultures, this support system consists of female relatives, sometimes from the mother's side, sometimes from the father's, depending on kinship system and residency patterns. In societies that are relatively egalitarian, particularly hunting and gathering societies, there may be some participation from the husband or male relatives (Draper, 1975; Turnbull, 1961). In less egalitarian, sedentary agricultural societies, where there may be a fear of female pollution in the post-partum period, the support provided to new parents comes almost exclusively from women, including peers and/or women from the grandparental generation (Faithorn, 1975; Tanner, 1974). In many African agricultural societies, the child nurse (a child who performs child care) is common, and the new baby's siblings and/or cousins are involved (Whiting and Edwards, 1988; Whiting and Whiting, 1975). But whoever the helpers are, new parents are not left to fend for themselves. For a period after childbirth, food preparation, household chores and maintenance, agricultural work, or hunting and gathering are taken care of. These cultures ensure that both kin and nonkin members of the social group rally around to aid in the care and nurturance of the new baby and the new parents.

Second, the industrialized nations (both the highly industrialized countries and the so-called less-developed third world countries) present numerous examples of parental leave legislation, providing job security and, in many instances, wage replacement. There are now 119 countries around the world that provide either maternity leave or parental leave as a matter of national policy. The United States and South Africa are the only two industrialized countries that have no national parental leave policy. The work of Sheila Kamerman and her colleagues has been extremely useful in documenting what other nations deem necessary for the support of new parents and newly born children. Her first comparative study, with Alfred Kahn (1981), of France, Hungary, the Federal Republic of Germany, and the German Democratic Republic, was expanded to an eight-country study including Australia, Canada, England, Israel, and the United States (Kahn and Kamerman, 1983). Her comparative work was further updated in a review article for the recent volume on parental leave resulting from a Yale University Bush Center study panel (Kamerman, 1988). Kamerman states:

> Almost all industrialized countries provide maternity and/or parenting leaves and related cash benefits as statutory social insurance benefits, wherein pregnancy and maternity are defined as societal as well as individual risks that result in a temporary loss of income and, therefore, are subject to protection by social insurance. . . . Maternity and parenting benefits are modest social policies but they are an essential part of any country's family policy. (Kamerman, 1988, pp. 243–44)

In Western Europe, there are a variety of policies, some intended to encourage both mothers and fathers to be involved in infant caregiving (as in Sweden), others "parental" only in name and tending, in actuality, to encourage mothers, not fathers, to stay home (as in the Federal Republic of Germany).

The United Kingdom has three different programs for maternity leave, each of which includes a cash benefit. The benefits vary according to the length of time a woman has been attached to the paid labor force. A woman who has worked continuously for 6 months prior to delivery receives a maximum of 18 weeks of leave and a flat-rate weekly payment that in 1988 amounted to $52 for married women and $96 for single women. A woman who has worked two years full time (or five years part time) gets 90 percent of her earnings for 6 weeks and then the flat rate paid to women with shorter work histories for the remaining 12 weeks. The United Kingdom also provides a lump-sum payment to very poor families to help them obtain such necessities as clothing, diapers, medicine, and food for the new baby (Stoiber, 1989, p. 14).

The Federal Republic of Germany also has three parental leave programs: a required 8-week paid maternity leave for birth mothers, funded partly through an insurance fund and partly by the employer; a child-raising leave to permit one parent to stay home full time with a biological or adopted child, under which the parent is paid $360 a month and may work up to 18 hours a week for up to three years (Stoiber, 1989, p. 28); and a leave to care for sick children, amounting to 10 days per child per year for children under eight years old.

In Sweden, which became the first country to establish parental leave in 1974, there are five kinds of paid leave: a 12-week maternity leave (6 weeks before and 6 weeks after birth); a longer pregnancy leave, if medically required; a paternity leave that gives fathers 10 days off following the birth; a 9-month parental leave; and an extended parental leave of an additional 9 months. All of these leaves are paid—at a rate of 90 percent of the employee's usual earnings.

The mechanisms for financing these parental leaves vary. In the United Kingdom the administration of parental leave benefits was shifted from the public sector (the Department of Health and Social Services) to the private sector in 1986. National insurance taxes pay for both maternity/parental leave and unemployment claims. In the Federal Republic of Germany, wage replacement funds are drawn from two sources: an insurance fund and the mother's employer. The insurance funds come from a federal tax on the employer's annualized earnings and employee income, so that the employer is in fact shouldering most of the cost of providing leave. In Sweden, the leaves are paid for through a national social insurance system. This system is funded through payroll taxes (85 percent) and general revenues (15 percent) (Stoiber, 1989, p. 48). Women experiencing health problems related to pregnancy are supported through a sickness insurance system, which is an integral part of the overall social insurance system. Mothers and fathers in Sweden experience almost no loss of income in fulfilling their parental responsibilities to newborn, adopted, or sick children.

While it is true that these leave policies emerge from diverse historical and cultural conditions and have different and even conflicting objectives, what is striking to the American observer is that each country has managed to provide some job-protected leave for new parents (or mothers) *with pay*. And even though the scope of the benefits varies, it seems that employers are not overly burdened by these policies. As Susanne Stoiber comments in her excellent comparative analysis of the three European countries described above, "As long as the leave is kept within reasonable bounds, there is no evidence of harm to business" (Stoiber, 1989, p. 59).

Many Americans would argue that it does not make sense to look at countries whose economies conform to an advanced "welfare state" model. Yet examples of so-called less-developed countries with maternity or parental leave policies are also extensive. Currently 81 developing countries have devised policies that give women (or, less commonly, parents) a period of leave with pay both before and after childbirth. (Parental leaves became more common in the 1980s.) Considering that these nations have far fewer resources than either the United States or many other industrialized nations, it is a significant accomplishment and a boon to women in the paid labor force. As Peggy Pizzo points out (1988, p. 278), these third world policies have been adopted "in spite of staggering burdens caused by economic distress." The average gross national product (GNP) per capita in the United States is more than 53 times the average GNP per capita in most of the developing nations, particularly those in Africa and Asia, and still the resources have been found. Paid maternity leaves are financed by employers, a social security system, or some combination of the two. Examples of paid leave range from 30 days in Tunisia to 18 weeks in Cuba and Chile (Pizzo, 1988, p. 277). Countries providing paid nursing breaks when the mother returns to work include Algeria, Egypt, Costa Rica, the Dominican Republic, and Saudi Arabia (Pizzo, 1988, p. 278).

In sum, many countries, in both the "developed" and the "less-developed" sectors of the global economy, provide leave to mothers or parents following birth or adoption. While the length of job-protected leave and the degree of compensation provided during leave vary, the concept of maternity/parental leave goes hand in hand with the concept of wage replacement.

A Critical Perspective on Current U.S. Policy: What Do We Provide for New Parents?

New parents in the United States lack both the close-knit support systems of many traditional cultures *and* the state-provided protection and insurance mandated by many industrialized and "less-developed" nations. Before presenting data on what is currently available in the way of leave with pay in the United States, it is important to take a close look at the current economic situation of working parents to highlight the economic needs of these families. While it is well known that there has been a dramatic increase in the participation of women, particularly women who are mothers of young children, the income available to families with children is not as well known.

TABLE 4.1
Household Income for U.S. Families (1986)

	Households	
Annual Income	*Number*	*Percent*
Under $10,000	17,130	19.1
$10,000 to $20,000	19,157	21.4
$20,000 to $30,000	16,350	18.3
$30,000 to $40,000	13,167	14.7
$40,000 to $50,000	8,667	9.7
$50,000 and over	15,007	16.8
Total	89,479	100.0

Source: U.S. Bureau of the Census, *Current Population Reports*, Series. P-60, no. 157 (Washington, D.C.: Government Printing Office).

According to annual income data gathered by the U.S. Bureau of the Census for 1986, approximately 40 percent of American families live on $20,000 or less (Table 4.1).

Recent figures compiled by the U.S. Bureau of Labor Statistics help us to understand how household income varies by family type and race. Table 4.2 contains figures on median annual earnings for 1987.

With women contributing approximately one-third to one-half of family income in dual-earner households, and being the sole source of support in most female-headed households and in some families with two married adults, we can begin to appreciate the seriousness of depriving these families of any paid benefit in the period after childbirth or adoption. It is important to underscore the fact that the median income of white families is always higher than that of black families, no matter how many earners there are or what type of family it is. Therefore the lack of a cash benefit poses an even greater threat to the economic survival of black families.

TABLE 4.2
Median Annual Income by Family Type and Race (1987)

Family Type	*White*	*Black*
Married, dual-income	$38,896	$33,592
Married, only wife works	$12,012	$11,180
Families maintained by women	$16,798	$14,768

Looking at median income figures, however, obscures several
other dimensions of the problem faced by working families. For example, many two-parent working families are, in the words of David
Ellwood, "working poor." He states in *Poor Support: Poverty in the
American Family* (1988, p. 83), that 15 percent of two-parent families
with children are living in poverty—that is, they earn less than
$12,000 a year. He further states that "half of the poor children in
America are living in two-parent homes" (p. 85). Ellwood's data on
single-parent families are even more sobering. Approximately 50
percent of these families live in poverty and experience all of the
problems experienced by poor two-parent families—low wages, unemployment, lack of adequate medical benefits—to a much greater
extent. Currently 11.7 percent of all American households are fe-
male-headed/single-parent families and cannot afford any loss of income for even a short period.

So whether we are talking about the relatively comfortable situation of white dual-earner families or the extremely insecure situation
of minority, female-headed, and other working-poor families, it is
unclear whether an unpaid leave would be at all useful to the majority of working parents. The income provided by working mothers is
a vital and significant part of most families' survival. In a special
report issued by the Bureau of National Affairs in 1987, it was stated
that the enactment of the Family and Medical Leave Act (FMLA)
would have "very limited practical effect" because the leave it mandates is unpaid: "About 77% of women work in lower paying, non-
professional jobs, and likely would not be able to take [10–18] weeks
without pay" (Bureau of National Affairs, 1987, p. 5).

Another issue to be reckoned with in defining the economic profile of working families is the number of women working for small
businesses. As the economist Carolyn Shaw Bell states (1982, p. 213),
"More than three quarters of the establishments in the United States
have fewer than 10 employees," and women are disproportionately
represented in the workforces of small businesses, constituting a substantial majority in certain sectors, such as retail. Many parental
leave bills now pending, both before Congress and at the state level,
exempt the employers of small workforces (50 or fewer employees).
Thus, many working mothers will end up with no leave because
their employers will not be covered by most statutes now under legislative review.

As several other chapters in this book provide a good overview of
the laws that are now on the books and the policies of corporate
personnel/human resource departments, I will confine my review of

what is currently available to working parents to the issue of wage replacement. There are of course differences in the options available to people in different sectors (that is, public versus private) and with employers of different sizes (large, medium, and small).

The vast majority of leave plans (maternity and/or parental) offer an unpaid leave of absence. Some employers allow the leavetaker to use sick days, personal days, and/or vacation days to cover the period of childbearing and -rearing leave. Approximately 14 million government workers and 7 million workers in private industry are covered by sick pay insurance plans. These plans start three to seven days after the illness begins, last anywhere from 13 to 26 weeks, and give employees only 26 to 38 percent of their wage (Kamerman and Kahn, 1988, p. 54). Aside from the use of sick or personal days, two other mechanisms provide wage replacement at the time of childbirth; one is a state-mandated temporary disability insurance (TDI) system, and the other is an employer-provided TDI benefit system.

In 1978 the Pregnancy Discrimination Act was passed, requiring that an employee who became disabled because of pregnancy be treated the same way as an employee with any other kind of non-job-related temporary disability. While this was a positive step toward establishing the concept of paid maternity leave, it was not as far-reaching as many assume. It did not mandate that all employers *provide* TDI, but only that those who *already* provide it cover women disabled by pregnancy. As Kamerman and Kahn point out (1987, p. 56), many women work for firms with no TDI or other, comparable benefits: "Fewer than 40% of working women have income protection at the time of maternity that will permit them a six week leave without severe financial penalty."

The state-mandated TDI systems provide the most comprehensive form of nonexclusionary assistance. TDI now exists on a statewide basis in California, Hawaii, New Jersey, New York, and Rhode Island. Most states allow a maximum leave of 26 weeks, although in California the period is now up to 39 weeks. The benefit is usually offered with minimum and maximum caps and replaces approximately half of the wage of an average employee. Information on the main components of the TDI plans in four of the five TDI states is summarized in Table 4.3.

Two cases (fictional, but based on policies known to exist in particular companies in the states mentioned) illustrate the best and worst kinds of coverage now available to working parents. The options of Flora Lopez, an employee at a medium-sized (500 employees) high-tech company in California, are quite good. She lives

TABLE 4.3
Comparative Data on Four Statewide TDI Programs

Instituted	New York 1949	New Jersey 1948	Rhode Island 1942	California 1946
Employers covered	All employers of one or more employee on each of 30 working days; the state as an employer is exempt.	All employers with a minimum annual payroll of $1,000 and with one or more employees; the state as an employer was exempt until 1978.	All employers of one or more employees; the state is exempt (cities and towns can elect coverage).	All employers of one or more employees; the state is exempt, but in 1981 state employees were given the option to elect coverage.
Contributions	Employers and employees contribute. Employees pay .05% of the first $120, not to exceed $.60/week; employers make up the difference.	Employers and employees each contribute .05% of the first $10,700.	Employees contribute 1% of the first $12,000 (decreased from 1.2% in 1985).	Employees contribute .09% of the first $21,900 (rate can vary between .05% and 1.2%).
Benefits	50% of employee's average weekly wage, not to exceed $224/week and with a minimum of $20/week.	66% of employee's average weekly wage, not to exceed $200/week and with a minimum of $50/week.	60% of employee's average weekly wage plus benefits for dependent children, not to exceed $224/week with a minimum of $48/week.	Indexed quarterly, not to exceed $262/week with a minimum of $50/week; job security provided.
Duration	26 weeks	26 weeks	26 weeks	52 weeks
Permissible plans[a]	Employers can self-insure[b] or purchase plan benefits through the state or private insurance carriers.	Employers can use the state plan, purchase private insurance, or self-insure.[c]	Employers must use the state plan but can offer supplemental benefits.	Employers can use the state plan or provide a voluntary plan.[d]

Notes:
[a]All nonstate plans require state approval and regulation.
[b]The plan must offer benefits equal to or greater than state statutory benefits.
[c]Private and self-insured plans must be at least equal to the state plan.
[d]The voluntary plan must exceed the state plan's benefits in at least one area and must be approved by a majority of employees.

in a state with a TDI system, so that when she experienced complications 8 weeks before and for 14 weeks after a cesarean birth, she was covered under the California TDI program. Her company provides, in addition, an unpaid personal leave of up to 3 months with full job protection. It also allows women to come back on a part-time basis for a limited period of time because it has permanent part-time employees and a pool of temporary workers who provide back-up. So Flora Lopez was able to take a 2-month paid leave before her daughter was born, a 3-month paid leave after the birth, and an additional 3-month unpaid leave. When her daughter was 6 months old, she returned to her company to a job comparable (in content and wage level) to the one she held while she was pregnant, and worked part time for 2 more months while her daughter got used to family day care. Having made the transition into their new routines, Flora resumed full-time work and her daughter began full-time day care at 8 months of age.

Contrast the case of Flora Lopez with that of Betsy Clark, a retail worker in a small store (10 employees) in New Hampshire. Betsy also became disabled 2 months before her delivery, but as New Hampshire has no state-mandated TDI and her employer does not offer TDI insurance, she was out of work without pay before and after her pregnancy. Her employer allowed a 2-month unpaid, job-protected maternity leave, at the end of which she was expected to come back to work on a full-time basis. Thus, Betsy Clark lost 4 months of pay in order to take care of herself and her baby immediately before and after the baby's arrival. She had only 2 months to spend with her son at home and make arrangements for full-time day care to cover her own 9-to-5 job responsibilities. As infant care is very expensive, Betsy found that well over half of her wages were going to her day care provider, and she questioned whether the resumption of her job so soon after her son's birth was really worth it.

Finally I would like to describe the situation of a group of blue-collar women workers in Massachusetts, using some data I collected while doing a field study in an electronics factory in the Boston area (Bookman, 1977). The employer in this low-wage, nonunion facility, which I will call Digitex, offered no TDI and no maternity leave. In direct violation of the Massachusetts state law, which guarantees 8 weeks of unpaid leave, Digitex allowed women workers only to use a small number of sick days and vacation days for maternity leave. Men were not permitted any paternity leave except for the day of delivery. In a workforce with many recent immigrants from Portugal and the Azores, who had no savings and little seniority built up, the option of parental leave was virtually nonexistent.

The hardships this situation imposed on Digitex workers were enormous, and many women were faced with almost impossible choices. A number of women were forced to quit their jobs, although with few skills and limited command of English, they were afraid they would never find employment when they returned to the workforce. Others took part-time jobs or worked second or third shift, and the lack of quality infant day care forced many to choose providers with whom they were not happy. The lucky ones had relatives who could care for their newborns, but when they returned to work—at most 2 weeks after childbirth—they were extremely tired, and often despondent at being separated from their babies. The fatigue of working full time and then getting up two or three times a night meant that those who did return to work often ended up quitting a few weeks or months later.

In sum, the majority of working mothers and fathers in the United States do not have access to maternity/parental leave with wage replacement. The greatest strides have been taken by individual states that provide short-term disability plans, but, of course, these cover only biological mothers immediately before and after birth. They do not help to support biological fathers or adoptive parents who need and want time at home with newborn or adopted children. A 1981 survey conducted by Kamerman and Kahn showed that while 72 percent of employers provided some parental leave (about 50 percent offering 2 to 3 months), very few provide any pay once sick, vacation, and personal days have been used up. Large firms and those in the financial–banking industry have the most generous leaves in terms of time and money, while small firms in the retail and service sectors have the least generous ones. And working women are, of course, concentrated in the sectors with the least advantageous leave policies.

Developing Paid Parental Leave Legislation: The Massachusetts Experience

Over the last three years, the state legislature in Massachusetts has considered several bills designed to provide parental leave for working families and children in the commonwealth. Two of these bills were developed in statewide gubernatorial commissions composed of representatives from government, the academy, the business world, medicine, and so on. These commissions are of particular interest because the legislation they drafted includes provisions for wage replacement. The process whereby these provisions were included and the debates about these provisions illuminate both the possibilities and the constraints involved in providing parental leave with pay.

It should be stated from the outset that I was a "participant–observer" on both commissions. Wearing the hats of working mother, women's/children's rights advocate, and anthropologist, I served as an ad hoc member of the Special Gubernatorial Commission on Parenting Leave and as a gubernatorial appointee on the Temporary Disability and Dependent Care Leave Commission (see Gibson, 1989). The Commission on Parenting Leave, chaired by Representative Mary Jane Gibson (D-Belmont), was convened in the spring of 1986. It met for a year and solicited testimony from a diverse group of individuals and organizations in both public hearings and public meetings of the commission. The law on the books in Massachusetts when the commission began its work provided 8 weeks of job-protected, unpaid maternity leave. One of the lawyers on the commission commented at the outset that the leave was not only too short and without wage replacement provisions, but was probably in violation of the state's Equal Rights Amendment in that it was a provision for mothers only and offered nothing for fathers.

The commission held a series of briefings for its members in order to educate everyone on several dimensions of the issue: a briefing on child development and family welfare, a briefing on legal issues, a briefing with members of the business community and representatives of labor. These were extremely useful to the commissioners in putting together a draft piece of legislation. After these briefings, a public hearing was organized in September 1986 to solicit a broader range of opinion from working parents, community and women's rights activists, legislators, and others. From the end of September until December came an intensive period of commission meetings during which the bill was actually drafted. The commission considered a range of proposals on eligibility, length of leave, structuring the return to work, and continuation of benefits. The most extensive discussion, with the least agreement, concerned wage replacement. The strongest opposition came from the commission member representing the Associated Industries of Massachusetts (AIM) and contributing the business perspective to the commission. She was in the minority; the commission's child development experts, pediatricians, trade union representatives, and others involved in work/family counseling agreed that the Massachusetts bill should have a wage replacement component, even at the risk of alienating the business community.

The result of these deliberations was H.B. 5200, "An Act Estab-

lishing Parenting Leave." It provides 18 weeks of job-protected leave
to anyone who has worked at least 50 percent of what his or her
employer considers full-time hours for 3 consecutive months. The
leave for mothers and fathers of biological and adopted children can
be taken on a full-time or half-time basis for a period not to exceed
36 weeks. Anyone taking this leave is entitled to receive, from the
Parental Leave Wage Replacement Fund, the equivalent of 60 percent of her or his wages for 12 weeks. The amount of wage replacement received by any one individual cannot exceed 66 percent of the
average state weekly wage and cannot be less than the prevailing
minimum wage multiplied by the employee's average number of
hours worked per week during a defined base period. The wage
replacement can be prorated if leave is taken on a half-time basis.
The Parental Leave Wage Replacement Fund is to be funded exclusively by employee contributions at a rate of .025 percent of the employee's income through a payroll tax mechanism. All employees in
Massachusetts working at least half time would pay this tax.

At its first legislative hearings in April 1987, the bill met with
mixed reviews, especially in regard to its wage replacement provision. Members of the legislature's Commerce and Labor Committee,
which heard the bill, commented that the tax was unfair to those
workers who plan to remain childless or are past their childbearing
years. Advocates responded by stating that the money for the Parental Leave Wage Replacement Fund should be seen as comparable
to school taxes: people pay local taxes to support school systems regardless of whether they have school-aged children.

The business community's reaction was summarized in the next
day's issue of the conservative *Boston Herald*. Under the headline
"Uproar Over Maternity Plan: Longer Leave Too Costly," the article
quoted the president of a small business association who said that the
bill "puts us back in the ball park of being called Taxachusetts,"
would make some small businesses less competitive because they
would have to hire workers to fill empty posts while employees were
on leave, and would "hinder the economic revival" that was going on
at that time in Massachusetts. Representatives of organized labor
also had reservations. At the hearing, the president of the Massachusetts AFL–CIO expressed only qualified support for the bill because it did not require businesses to pay for the entire plan themselves.

The majority of commission members favored the bill's wage replacement plan as a "cost-sharing" model. Employees would pay an
average of $24.80 a year into the fund, while businesses would bear

TABLE 4.4
California TDI System

	1985	1986	1987
TDI claims paid	648,000	649,402	
Pregnancy claims paid:			
As % of all	19.7%	19.6%	15.7%
Number	127,428	127,088	130,395
Total paid for TDI claims	$1,168,537,000	$1,276,527,000	
Total paid for pregnancy claims:			
As % of all	15.6%	15.3%	15.5%
Amount	$185,600,000	$200,300,000	$218,110,674
Av. duration of all TDI claims	11.7 weeks	11.4 weeks	
Av. duration of pregnancy claims	10.2 weeks	10.9 weeks	
Contribution per employee per year	$96.08	$137.03	
Administration cost per year	$54,667,000	$60,302,000	$62,600,000[a]
Av. weekly benefit	$158.50	$162.40	$166.75
No. workers covered:			
Under state plan	9,057,000	9,307,300	
Under private plans	544,300	598,700	

Note:
[a]Estimated cost.

the cost of continuing benefits for the leavetaker and the costs of hiring and training replacement workers (Special Gubernatorial Commission, 1988). It was the majority opinion that these costs to both employers and employees were fairly minimal in view of the tremendous advantages to new parents and children of this type of leave policy. When this plan was being formulated, the commission considered a number of alternative funding schemes and mechanisms, in particular the TDI plans of Rhode Island, New Jersey, New York, California, and Hawaii. The experience of these states seemed very positive from a fiscal and a social policy perspective, but there was reluctance in the Commission on Parenting Leave to fully explore the TDI option for Massachusetts as it raised many issues related to non-pregnancy-connected disabilities that were well beyond the commission's mandate. So, recognizing the imperfection of the plan in H.B. 5200 and the importance of exploring the possibility of a statewide TDI system for Massachusetts, we proposed that a second commission be established to investigate both the feasibility of such a system and issues related to parental and other forms of dependent care leave.

The result was the establishment of the Temporary Disability and Dependent Care Leave Commission, also chaired by Representative Gibson. Its 14 members included more representatives from the business community, as the previous commission had been criticized for having too few. The TDI commission included representatives of AIM, the National Federation of Independent Business, the insurance industry, and labor, along with a member of the general public, cabinet secretaries from the executive branch, and state representatives and senators.

The commission held several meetings during the summer of 1988, during which people from the Conference Board in New York and the Bush Center at Yale University, and other experts on the current statewide TDI systems in other states, gave presentations. Two college interns assisted with in-depth telephone and survey research with the administrators of TDI benefits programs in New York, New Jersey, Rhode Island, and California.[1] Data were gathered for 1985–1987 on the total number of TDI claims paid, the number of pregnancy claims, and the totals paid for each (Tables 4.4–4.7), and on the duration of TDI and pregnancy claims, the employee contribution costs, administrative costs, the average weekly benefit, and the total number of workers covered under state (as opposed to private) plans. Using these data to develop cost estimates for a Massachusetts TDI system, the commission determined that the cost of providing a 50 to 66 percent wage replacement would run from $49.70 per year/per employee to $78.30 per year/per employee. This was calculated by multiplying the percentage of wage replacement by the average weekly wage and factoring in a range of leave durations and an estimated number of claimants. We also did cost estimates for parental leave using data collected by the Department of Public Health and the Department of Employment and Training (see Table 4.8).

The commission then considered various schemes for paying these costs, looking at a 100 percent employee pay-in model, a 100 percent employer pay-in model, and a model sharing costs equally between employers and employees. The third option was deemed the most equitable. When the bill-drafting stage of the commission's

TABLE 4.5
New Jersey TDI System

	1985	1986	1987
TDI claims paid	130,095	131,283	144,618
Pregnancy claims paid:			
As % of all	17%	17%	17%
Number[a]	22,100	22,300	24,600
Total paid for TDI claims	$176,300,000	$188,500,000	$211,200,000
Total paid for pregnancy claims:			
As % of all	16%	16%	16%
Amount[a]	$28,200,000	$30,200,000	$33,800,000
Av. duration of all TDI claims[a]	8.2 weeks		
Av. duration of pregnancy claims[a]	10.1 weeks		
Contribution per employee per year	$50.50	$53.50	$56.50
Administration cost per year	$15,200,000	$13,800,000	$16,700,000
Av. weekly benefit (approx.)	$153.00	$163.00	$169.00
No. workers covered:			
Under state plan	2,257,800	2,329,700	2,447,100
Under private plans	718,100	712,300	719,800

Note:
[a]Estimates based on a 1983–1984 study.

work began, there was more support among members for setting up a statewide TDI system than for setting up a dependent care leave plan that would cover parental leave and care of a seriously ill family member. Some members felt that dependent care leave would put too many burdens on business and would be ultimately harmful to the passage of the bill; others felt that a comprehensive bill covering a range of situations in which people need leave from employment, whether related to physical disabilities or to family responsibilities, would be more useful to the vast majority of working families today. The business and insurance representatives on the commission thought a statewide TDI system was unnecessary because some companies already have such plans and they perceived no demand for such a system from working people in the commonwealth. Further-

TABLE 4.6
Rhode Island TDI System

	1985	1986	1987
TDI			
claims paid	38,436	37,175	37,596
Pregnancy			
claims paid:			
As % of all	13%		
Number	4,997	NA	NA
Total paid for			
TDI claims	$34,895,041	$40,459,052	$48,963,022
Total paid for			
pregnancy claims:			
As % of all	11%	NA	NA
Amount	$3,972,853	NA	NA
Av. duration of			
all TDI claims	9.0 weeks	9.7 weeks	10.1 weeks
Av. duration of			
pregnancy claims	6.7 weeks	NA	NA
Contribution per			
employee per year	$106.02	$103.69	NA
Administration			
cost per year	$3,459,904	$3,747,975	$3,995,823
Av. weekly			
benefit	$122.53	$133.75	$153.70
No. workers covered:			
Under state plan	373,263	385,906	NA
Under private plans	0	0	0

more, they opposed the idea of government mandating such a policy for business. Opposition to any government regulation of the private sector surfaced over and over in testimony from business representatives at various hearings. However, this was a minority view on the commission.

In October and November the commission completed the drafting of H.B. 2191, "An Act Establishing Employment Leave Insurance." The Employment Leave Bill allows working men and women job-protected leave of up to 26 weeks during a temporary disability or illness or following an accident not related to work (those related to work are covered under worker's compensation). It also allows men and women up to 16 weeks of leave to care for a newborn or adopted baby or to care for a seriously ill family member. This type of leave insurance will expand the current forms of maternity leave, long-term disability insurance, and unemployment insurance by in-

TABLE 4.7
New York TDI System (State Plan Only)[a]

	1985	1986	1987
TDI			
claims paid	227,856	238,790	
Pregnancy			
claims paid:			
As % of all	29%		
Number	66,165		
Total paid for			
TDI claims	$218,372,375	$227,892,059	
Total paid for			
pregnancy claims:			
As % of all	33%		
Amount	$72,689,511		
Av. duration of			
all TDI claims	8.7 weeks	8.5 weeks	
Av. duration of			
pregnancy claims	8.9 weeks	9.2 weeks	
Contribution per			
employee per year	$49.00	$48.00	
Administration			
cost per year	$5,421,625	$6,125,945	
Av. benefit:			
Weekly	$110.60	$112.28	
Total	$958.38	$945.36	
No. workers covered:			
Under state plan	4,500,824	4,795,198	
Under private plans	NA	NA	

Note:
[a]Statistics on nonstate plan not available.

cluding all workers in Massachusetts who work at least half time, regardless of what their individual employers provide. The weekly benefit amount is set at 66 percent of the individual's average weekly wage, plus $25 for each dependent. The bill provides for the payment of benefits through a variety of plans (private, state, and so on) and calls for the administration of employment leave insurance under the existing Office of Industrial Accidents, rather than creating a new division in the state bureaucracy.

Both the Parental Leave Bill and the Employment Leave Bill had hearings in the spring 1989 legislative sessions and were referred to committee. The fact that neither bill was passed is not surprising in light of continued business opposition. This parallels the fate of a

TABLE 4.8
Cost Estimates on Parental Leave for Massachusetts, 1988

Wage Replacement Level		9 Weeks	12 Weeks	18 Weeks
Workers in employment statewide 3,188,000				
Av. weekly wage $430.69				
Claims (calculated at 30% live births claimed) 27,609[a]				
50% of salary	Av. pay-out per claim	$1,047	$1,395	$2,088
	Total cost, all claims	$28,895,855	$38,514,555	$57,647,592
	Av. pay-in per worker/year	$9.00	$12.08	$18.00
	Av. pay-in per worker/month	$0.75	$1.01	$1.51
60% of salary	Av. pay-out per claim	$1,279	$1,704	$2,556
	Total cost, all claims	$35,311,911	$47,045,736	$70,568,604
	Av. pay-in per worker/year	$11.08	$14.76	$22.14
	Av. pay-in per worker/month	$0.92	$1.23	$1.85
66% of salary	Av. pay-out per claim	$1,163	$1,548	$2,322
	Total cost, all claims	$32,109,267	$42,738,732	$64,108,098
	Av. pay-in per worker/year	$10.07	$13.41	$20.11
	Av. pay-in per worker/month	$0.84	$1.12	$1.68

Notes:

Where there is a 50% wage replacement, as in N.Y., experience shows that workers get an average of 27% of the N.Y. average weekly wage.

Where there is a 60% wage replacement, as in R.I., experience shows that workers get an average of 33% of the R.I. average weekly wage.

Where there is a 66% wage replacement, as in N.J., experience shows that workers get an average of 30% of the N.J. average weekly wage.

Chart assumes that 10% of fathers will claim parental leave and excludes administration cost of 7%.

[a]Estimate for 1988 based on percent increase in live births from 1980 to 1986.

much weaker and less comprehensive bill at the federal level, the Family and Medical Leave Act. Yet the Massachusetts bills provide models for the kind of family policy legislation that is desperately needed by working families in Massachusetts. The coalition supporting these two bills currently includes about 30 organizations. Because the Employment Leave Bill is intergenerational in its appeal, not only young parents but also the elderly and their various advocacy groups, chronically ill people, the Multiple Sclerosis Society, Alzheimer's support groups, and disabled rights groups are among its supporters.

However, the business community and their influential lobbyists at the State House remain unconvinced that this kind of legislation is in their interest. Until such time as family and child advocates and others can mount a grass-roots effort to persuade their local elected officials of the need for these bills, responding with facts and figures to the arguments raised by business leaders and organizations, Massachusetts will continue to be among those states that offer little in the way of real social support to working families.

Conclusion

While many argue in this book and elsewhere that parental leave is a necessary and long-overdue social policy for working parents and their children in the United States, I would extend that argument to say that it is only parental leave with pay that will make this policy a realistic option for most American workers. There are five major reasons we need a parental leave policy with wage replacement:

1. Without wage replacement, only middle- and upper-middle-class and predominantly white families will be able to take parental leave. Most families with newborn or adopted babies cannot afford to go for even 2 months, let alone 6, without income. The many low-income families in this country, which are disproportionately female-headed and families of color, will not be able to take advantage of leave unless there is wage replacement.

2. Without wage replacement many dual-earner middle-income families will fall into the low-income or poverty-line category during an unpaid leave. This set-back may take many months, even years, to recover from, putting the family and new baby at risk, not only economically but, because of increased stress, psychologically as well.

3. Without wage replacement many low-income or working-poor families will fall below the poverty line and be forced to rely on food stamps, Aid to Families with Dependent Children (AFDC), and

other forms of government assistance in order to survive. This is not only costly to the government, but an insult to those who work hard at their jobs.

4. Without wage replacement it is unlikely that men will take advantage of parental leave. If there were a serious desire to promote paternal involvement in infant or early childhood care, it is unlikely that a policy without pay would even be proposed. It is striking that in Sweden, the country with the greatest philosophical commitment to equality between the sexes in the workplace and the home, virtually no income is lost during parental leave.

5. Without wage replacement we are putting many children at risk in terms of nutrition, housing, health care, and other needs. Again, the infants already at greatest risk, from low-income, predominantly minority families, will suffer the most.

Balancing work and family is never easy, and funding solutions to this problem is an even more challenging task in this period of rising federal (and some state) deficits. The first thing called for, I believe, is the establishment of a national TDI system of the sort that exists on the state level in California, Hawaii, New Jersey, New York, and Rhode Island. This system would cover any disability birth mothers experience before and after childbirth, and male and female workers who experience other short-term, non-job-related disabilities. The United States already has a national insurance system for job-related disabilities—worker's compensation; why not have a parallel and complementary system for non-job-related disabilities? This would provide roughly 6 to 12 weeks of paid leave for birth mothers. In addition, we need to establish a national family leave system that would pay wage compensation to the parent (male or female) who stays home with a child on a full-time or part-time basis (not less than 20 hours a week). This could be administered by a national or state-based apparatus, and could be funded through employee contributions, employer contributions, contributions from government, or some combination of two or all three. Such a program would be tantamount to a paid leave for biological mothers and fathers and adoptive parents. Benefits could vary in terms of amount of time off (6 months, a year, or more), extent of paid employment allowed while collecting, and so on. Future research on wage replacement must consider what kinds of public–private partnerships could be formed to fund these systems. Since virtually all sectors of our society—children, parents, schools, employers, communities—will benefit from having infants receive parental care following birth or adoption, why not have all these sectors contribute to the financing of parental leave?

One public–private partnership that has met with some success is the Boston Compact, a joint venture between the public school system in the city of Boston, which is trying to improve the quality of high school education and the number of teenagers who complete it, and Boston-area employers, who need workers and hope that the high schools will provide them with an adequately educated and skilled workforce. The partnership based on their complementary needs helps graduates of the Boston public school system find gainful employment in their hometown after graduation. While some recent commentary on the Compact (Snyder, 1988) states that the employers have done more on their side (that is, providing jobs) than the school system has done on its side (that is, providing a quality high school education), the partnership suggests exciting possibilities for those of us concerned about the caregiving and educational environments children experience not only in high school, but at the very beginning of life. Perhaps our major social and economic institutions, like schools and businesses, need to invest in potential students and potential workers much earlier in the life cycle to ensure that children grow into adults who are capable of learning and working to their fullest capabilities.

Government, local, state, or federal, also has an important role to play in developing new initiatives in the area of parental leave and other family policies. Governments can be a catalytic force in setting up commissions that bring together a broad range of experts to develop legislation, and they can provide the administrative structures to implement new pieces of legislation and, over time, assess their effectiveness. The extent to which federal and state dollars can be utilized to fund new programs will, of course, depend on the economic climate, but it is always possible for elected officials to use their positions to encourage business to respond to the needs of working families. Former governor Thomas H. Kean has written persuasively on this point, both commending and criticizing business:

> New Jersey, in fact, is home to some progressive corporate giants and smaller business ventures that have helped reduce the pressures on working parents to choose between career growth and having a family. But while many companies have been responsive to the nature of the changing workforce, industry still has a long way to go before company policies accommodate all women's professional and personal needs. (Kean, 1988, p. 339)

Those of us involved in the shaping of parental leave policy must think about what kinds of partnerships and compacts we can build to support the care of our youngest citizens. We must be imaginative and at the same time fiscally hard-nosed, and, most important, our social policies must address the situation of families with the greatest economic need, who are disproportionately minority families. We must not fall back on the idea that we cannot afford parental leave with wage replacement, but instead think creatively about how to link families, schools, government, and business in providing the funds that new parents and new babies deserve for a healthy start in life.

NOTES

Acknowledgments. I first want to thank Representative Mary Jane Gibson, chair of both legislative commissions described in this chapter, for her inspiring leadership in the area of family policy. She is the kind of elected official who makes citizens believe that our government is truly of, by, and for the people. Her compassion for the struggles of working parents, her commitment to making a better world for our children, and her gift as facilitator of groups containing both those who agree with her and those who disagree are all unparalleled. I also want to thank and credit the outstanding work of two members of Representative Gibson's legislative staff, Mary Shannon and Nancy May. Finally, I am grateful to Dr. Paula Rayman, director of the Program on Work/Family Relations and Social Policy at the Stone Center of Wellesley College, for her long-term support of my research on parental leave and her insightful comments on the draft version of this chapter.

1. I want to give credit and special thanks to Kim Glickman, intern in the Governor's Office on Women's Issues, and Anson Chiou, intern in the Executive Office of Labor. Their work was indispensable to the Temporary Disability Commission, and I am grateful to them for preparing Tables 4.2–4.6.

REFERENCES

Bell, Carolyn Shaw (1982). "Small Employers, Work, and Community." In Sheila Kamerman and Cheryl Hayes, eds., *Families That Work: Children in a Changing World.* Washington, D.C.: National Academy Press.

Bookman, Ann (1977). "The Political Socialization of Women and Immigrant Workers: A Case Study of Unionization in the Electronics Industry." Ph.D. dissertation, Harvard University.

Bureau of National Affairs (1987). *Pregnancy and Employment Handbook.* Washington, D.C.: BNA.

Draper, Patricia (1975). "!Kung Women: Contrasts in Sexual Egalitarianism in Foraging and Sedentary Contexts." In Rayna R. Reiter, ed., *Toward an Anthropology of Women*. New York: Monthly Review Press.

Ellwood, David (1988). *Poor Support: Poverty in the American Family*. New York: Basic Books.

Faithorn, Elizabeth (1975). "The Concept of Pollution Among the Kafe of the Papua New Guinea Highlands." In Rayna R. Reiter, ed., *Toward an Anthropology of Women*. New York: Monthly Review Press.

Gibson, Mary Jane (1990). "Employment Leave: Foundation for Family Policy." *New England Journal of Public Policy* 6(1).

Kahn, Alfred J., and Sheila B. Kamerman (1983). *Income Transfers for Families with Children: An Eight-Country Study*. Philadelphia: Temple University Press.

Kamerman, Sheila B. (1988). "Maternity and Parenting Benefits: An International Overview." In Edward F. Zigler and Meryl Frank, eds., *The Parental Leave Crisis: Toward a National Policy*. New Haven: Yale University Press.

Kamerman, Sheila B., and Alfred J. Kahn (1981). *Child Care, Family Benefits, and Working Parents: A Study in Comparative Policy*. New York: Columbia University Press.

——— (1987). *The Responsive Workplace: Employers and a Changing Labor Force*. New York: Columbia University Press.

Kean, Thomas H. (1988). "The State's Role in the Implementation of Infant Care Leave." In Edward F. Zigler and Meryl Frank, eds., *The Parental Leave Crisis: Toward a National Policy*. New Haven: Yale University Press.

Pizzo, Peggy (1988). "Uncertain Harvest: Maternity Leave Policies in Developing Nations." In Edward F. Zigler and Meryl Frank, eds., *The Parental Leave Crisis: Toward a National Policy*. New Haven: Yale University Press.

Snyder, Sarah (1988). "Business to Schools: We Want Results." *Boston Globe*, October 25.

Special Gubernatorial Commission on Parenting Leave (1988). *Special Interim Report of the Special Commission Relative to Providing Parental Leave*. March 23. Boston: State House Library.

Stoiber, Susanne A. (1989). *Parental Leave and "Woman's Place": The Implications and Impact of Three European Approaches to Family Policy*. Washington, D.C.: Women's Research and Education Institute.

Tanner, Nancy (1974). "Matrifocality in Indonesia and Africa and Among Black Americans." In Michelle Zimbalist Rosaldo and Louise Lamphere, eds., *Women, Culture, and Society*. Stanford, Calif.: Stanford University Press.

Turnbull, Colin (1961). *The Forest People*. New York: Simon and Schuster.

Whiting, Beatrice Blyth, and Carolyn Pope Edwards (1988). *Children of Different Worlds: The Formation of Social Behavior*. Cambridge: Harvard University Press.

Whiting, John, and Beatrice Whiting (1975). *Children of Six Cultures: A Psycho-Cultural Analysis*. Cambridge: Harvard University Press.

PART III

Legal Issues

5 | Legal Aspects of Parental Leave: At the Crossroads

Susan Deller Ross

We are at a crossroads, faced with a choice between several different legal models for providing parental and related forms of leave, each with quite different consequences for men and women workers and their families. If we go down one path, we support an egalitarian division of labor at home and in the workplace by giving fathers as well as mothers the right to a guaranteed leave from work to care for newborn children. If we go down another path, we give only women that right and thus reinforce the traditional sex-based division of labor: the division between the stay-at-home Mom and the breadwinner Dad, or, in the newest version of that division, the part-time, low-earning, low-status Mom and the more than full-time, higher-earning, higher-status Dad.

We face other paths and other consequences as well. For example, should leaves be provided to workers who are unable to work for medical reasons? Should parental leave for the care of newborns be expanded to allow for the care of sick children, or even for the care of other family members? In order to explore those paths and consequences more fully, however, we must retrace our steps to see what brought us to this intersection. That leads us to the historical setting for the fights currently being waged over pregnancy, parental, medical, and family leave, followed by an analysis of the various state and federal models for providing leave—including models based on pregnancy disability, on medical need, on parental duties, and on broader family obligations. I shall conclude by urging adoption of the most comprehensive form of leave, that required for both medical need and for the obligation to care for many different family members. Only that approach sets the stage for the integration and transformation of work and family life that the feminist revolution seeks.

The History

As women entered the labor market in ever increasing numbers in the late 1960s and 1970s,[1] they found themselves faced with a Catch-22 when they decided to have babies. On the one hand, employers frequently fired pregnant women or forced them to take long, unpaid leaves of absence, starting as early as the fourth month of pregnancy and continuing months past the birth of their children. While most women were fully capable of working up to childbirth and of resuming work 6 to 8 weeks after it, employers forced them off the job under the pretense that the pregnant woman or new mother was incapable of working during the entire pregnancy and for months afterward.[2] On the other hand, when these women workers were actually incapacitated from working because they had to go to the hospital for childbirth or were recuperating from childbirth, employers had a contradictory theory. Women giving birth were not disabled from working after all, they declared; pregnancy and childbirth were just normal conditions. Therefore, women giving birth could be denied the disability and medical benefits to which other hospitalized workers were entitled under company fringe benefit plans.[3]

Women caught in this double bind began suing on both issues under the Constitution and Title VII of the 1964 Civil Rights Act,[4] seeking both the right to work when they were able to and the right to paid fringe benefits other workers received when they were not capable of working.[5] Soon the Equal Employment Opportunity Commission—the federal agency charged with enforcing Title VII's ban on sex discrimination in employment—leaped into the fray. In 1972 it issued regulations on the subject of pregnancy and childbirth.[6] Its theory was simple and confronted the double bind head on. Insofar as pregnant workers and new mothers were actually disabled from working by pregnancy complications, childbirth, and the post-partum recovery, they were entitled to the same fringe benefits received by other workers needing medical attention—generally, payments under health insurance programs to cover doctor and hospital bills, and money under paid sick leave programs or temporary disability insurance (TDI) plans to cover wage loss when they were unable to work.[7] Insofar as they were able to work during pregnancy and the post-partum period, they were to be allowed to continue in paid employment.[8]

The EEOC regulations were based on classic antidiscrimination legal concepts. In particular, they rested on a comparison. Employer treatment of male workers provided the standard measurement. Insofar as male workers had generous fringe benefit programs, the EEOC approach resulted in upgrading the fringe benefits of pregnant workers. But where male workers had sparse benefits, the standard left pregnant women equally badly off.

The practical result of the EEOC approach was that in most medium to large firms, pregnant workers gained substantially. These employers tended to have generous fringe benefit plans, so pregnant women working for them ended up with comprehensive coverage for medical bills running easily into thousands of dollars per pregnancy. Women also gained paid sick leave for childbirth and the post-partum period, which typically continued a woman's salary for 6 to 8 weeks after childbirth and guaranteed a return to her job.[9] But many employers—often smaller companies—did not provide such generous fringe benefits, and some claimed not to provide any sick leave at all, not even an unpaid sick leave.[10] Under the EEOC's theory, a pregnant woman working for such an employer could be legally fired when she needed to take time off for childbirth, as long as the employer could prove that men with medical problems that prevented them from working were also fired in such circumstances.

Although the Supreme Court rejected the EEOC approach in 1976 in the famous *General Electric Company* v. *Gilbert* decision,[11] Congress quickly repudiated the Court. In 1978 it passed the Pregnancy Discrimination Act, which essentially reinstated the EEOC approach.[12] By this time, too, a number of states had copied the federal approach, requiring that women disabled by pregnancy and childbirth be treated the same as other disabled workers, and that women not so disabled be treated as other able workers.[13] But a few states adopted a different approach. Rather than equal treatment, these states created a special leave for one category of disabled workers: those women disabled by pregnancy, childbirth, and related medical conditions. Under these laws, employers could not fire such women, at least so long as their disability did not last more than a certain period of time (ranging from a "reasonable" time to 8 weeks to 4 months).[14] The theory of those who fought for these laws was rather like that of the Supreme Court in the *Gilbert* case, though with a more favorable twist for the women involved. Both saw pregnancy as unique. This had led the Court to decide that pregnancy-related disabilities were not comparable to other disabilities and could therefore be excluded from disability insurance and paid sick leave programs without causing sex discrimination problems.[15] The proponents of special leaves for pregnant workers agreed that pregnancy disabilities were not comparable to other disabilities, but concluded that disabled pregnant workers could therefore receive a special, unpaid leave of absence to protect their jobs without creating sex discrimination problems.[16]

With the Pregnancy Discrimination Act (PDA) on the books, employers in two of the "special leave" states—Montana and California—saw a chance to get rid of the statutorily mandated unpaid leaves of absence for disabled pregnant women. In two different lawsuits, they asserted that the special leave discriminated against disabled male workers, and that the PDA required that the state laws be invalidated.[17] Feminists split on how to resolve the controversy. One group (the "equal-treatment" feminists) fought for the core PDA principle of equal treatment for all disabled workers, and therefore agreed with the employers about the conflict with the PDA. Unlike the employers, however, these feminists would have extended the statutory leave to all disabled workers rather than getting rid of it for pregnant workers as the employers wanted to do.[18] The other feminist group (the "special-treatment" feminists) focused for comparison purposes, not on the PDA disability principle but on the parenting role. Men did not have to lose their jobs on becoming a parent; women should not have to either, they argued.[19] Therefore, they concluded, there was no conflict with the PDA, and the California law was permissible as drafted. In early 1987, the Supreme Court resolved the controversy in the California case (*California Federal Savings and Loan Association* v. *Guerra*, or *Cal Fed*).[20] It decided that the PDA was designed only to prevent discrimination *against* pregnant women, not to prevent discrimination in their favor. Ignoring the disability comparison, it chose the parenting comparison, ruling that California law allowed "women, as well as men, to have families without losing their jobs."[21] But it also emphasized the limited nature of the California law—and, in particular, the fact that it was "narrowly drawn to cover only the period of *actual physical disability* on account of pregnancy, childbirth, or related medical conditions" (emphasis in original).[22] The Court concluded:

> Accordingly, unlike the protective labor legislation prevalent earlier in this century, [the California law] does not reflect archaic or stereotypical notions about pregnancy and the abilities of pregnant workers. A statute based on such stereotypical assumptions would, of course, be inconsistent with Title VII's goal of equal employment opportunity.[23]

The Court was alluding here to an argument of the equal-treatment feminists. They had urged extension of the unpaid leave to all disabled workers rather than supporting a female-only statute because they feared the effects of female-only legislation.[24] Earlier in the century, many states had enacted laws limiting women's hours on the theory that women workers needed special protection so they could get home to their families and fulfill their home duties. But the laws also protected women right out of desirable jobs that male workers got instead; so once Title VII was enacted, women workers had used Title VII to get the jobs and get rid of the state laws.[25] The equal-treatment feminist group feared the same kind of impact from the new female-only pregnancy leave laws. If employers had to give a special leave only to women, they reasoned, employers might prefer to hire men instead. They worried also that if positive pregnancy-based laws were found legal, then a precedent would be set allowing negative pregnancy-based laws as well.[26]

But the Court rejected these arguments, reasoning that as long as the special pregnancy leave laws were disability-based, they did not stereotype pregnant women. In theory, then, there was now nothing to prevent many more states from passing mandatory leave laws based on the California model of a special, women-only, pregnancy disability leave. After all, the Court had given the green light to narrowly drawn women-only statutes.

However, that did not happen. For while the *Cal Fed* case was working its way up through the courts, the equal-treatment feminist groups had begun working at the federal level on a new model for providing leaves—one that incorporated both the disability *and* the parenting perspectives, and did so on a gender-neutral basis. This model went through various incarnations but eventually became known as the Family and Medical Leave Act.[27] The act's medical leave section was designed to give all disabled workers—including women disabled by pregnancy, childbirth, and related medical conditions—an unpaid leave of absence.[28] Under this provision, employers could not fire any worker who was forced to stop work for medical reasons, as long as the leave lasted less than 26 weeks. (The original version was 26 weeks in any one-year period; by April 1990, it had been shortened to 15 weeks on the House side and 13 weeks on the Senate side.)[29] The family leave section provided an unpaid leave to all workers—male or female—who wanted time off to care for newborns or newly adopted children, as well as time to care for seriously ill children.[30] The leave could also be used for the care of seriously ill parents.[31] The family leave would originally have been for 18 weeks in a two-year period, and by 1990 was for 10 weeks.[32] As with the medical leave, this provision effectively prevented employers from firing workers who decided to take time off for these purposes.[33] In the case of women giving birth, the FMLA approach assumed that the typical woman would receive 6 to 8 weeks of medical leave for childbirth and the post-partum recovery period, and that this leave would be a *paid* leave under PDA principles whenever the employer had paid sick leave or TDI plans for other disabled employees. After using the medical leave, the new mother could then take an additional 18 weeks (10 weeks, in early 1990) of unpaid family leave.[34] Thus, even under the versions of the FMLA pending in 1990, mothers giving birth could get a total of 16 to 18 weeks off, using both forms of leave to which they are entitled. Fathers and adoptive parents of both sexes could not take the medical leave, since they are not medically affected by childbirth, but they could take the 10-week family leave.

Because this new model was pending in Congress by the time the Court issued its *Cal Fed* decision, states that were motivated by the Court's decision to pass new mandatory leave legislation had two models to choose from: the California female-only model and the federal gender-neutral model of a combined medical and family leave. The new model made an enormous difference. Prior to the *Cal Fed* decision, 9 states had laws or regulations providing for a female-only leave.[35] Between the *Cal Fed* decision on January 13, 1987, and June 1989, 14 more states enacted legislation, but only 3 adopted the female-only California approach (Iowa, Louisiana, and Tennessee).[36] Of the remaining 11 states, 3 passed pared-down versions of the FMLA (Connecticut, Maine, and Wisconsin), 3 passed parental leave laws (Minnesota, Oregon, and Rhode Island), 2 passed laws allowing the use of accrued sick leave for parental or family obligations (South Carolina and Washington), and 3 passed laws providing leaves for adoptive parents (Colorado, Missouri, and New York).[37] All 11 laws were applicable to both men and women. That leaves four basic models for providing leaves—in shorthand, the California female-only pregnancy disability approach, and the three gender-neutral approaches of the FMLA, the pared-down FMLA, and parental leave. (The sick leave and adoptive parent approach are too limited in application to merit being considered as models but have some interesting features.) With this background, we can now turn to a more extensive analysis of each of these models, and of their advantages and disadvantages.

Advantages and Disadvantages of the Different Models

The female-only pregnancy disability approach is still that of the largest number of state mandatory leave laws. The major advantage to this approach is that it is the cheapest way to ensure that pregnant women will not lose their jobs when they have a baby. However, it is the cheapest way because it helps no other workers, not even women with other medical problems, and therein lies a major disadvantage. Even more significant is the exclusion of fathers from the new parenting process. The California leave is theoretically available to women only for childbirth and the post-partum disability period—typically 6 to 8 weeks—with a 4-month cap for those women whose disability lasts longer than the 6- to 8-week norm. However, the rumor is that, in practice, California employers typically give women the full 4 months.[38] If so, California women get a combined medical and child care leave lasting 4 months, while a California man who wants to spend even one day caring for his newborn child can be fired for doing so. If we exclude men from the experience of caring for newborns, are we not reinforcing the norms that drive them ever more into seeking fulfillment at work? And if men put their major emotional energies into work, does that not increase the pressure on their wives to play the most significant role at home? One can see the vicious cycle this creates.

Some of the other female-only statutes go one step further than California by spelling out that the leave is not necessarily disability-related. The pre–*Cal Fed* Massachusetts law, for example, provides 8 weeks of leave to women for childbirth or for the adoption of a child under three, while male adoptive parents receive no leave. The Massachusetts regulations also specify that women giving birth get the full 8 weeks even if they are not disabled for part of this time;[39] the nondisabled biological father gets no such entitlement. Similarly, the post–*Cal Fed* Tennessee female-only statute provides a 4-month leave for pregnancy, childbirth, and nursing, with no reference at all to disability.[40] Fathers who want to bottle-feed their babies or just spend time with them get no help from the statute. Incidentally, both of these laws—and several other female-only laws and regulations—violate the *Cal Fed* ruling that female-only leaves must be limited to the disability period in order to comply with the PDA, but they are still on the books, creating substantial discrimination against fathers in apparent violation of both Title VII and the Constitution.[41]

Another problem with the California model is that it contains provisions that discriminate *against* pregnant workers. This was apparently the compromise wrung from the legislature by employers in exchange for the special leave. Small employers (those with 5 to 14 employees) are specifically authorized to exclude pregnancy coverage from medical insurance, to cap paid disability benefits at 6 weeks, and to exclude pregnant women from training programs if they cannot finish the training program at least 3 months prior to their due date.[42] It was these provisions that led equal-treatment feminists to fear that preferential pregnancy laws could easily boomerang into negative pregnancy laws. And, indeed, Louisiana passed a law in 1987 that copied all these provisions directly from the California law and extended them to employers large enough to be covered by Title VII and the PDA.[43] While the extension to Title VII employers is flatly illegal, Louisiana's law is still on the books, and one would not be surprised to find at least some Louisiana employers cheerfully complying with a law that allows them (albeit in violation of federal law) to exclude health insurance for pregnant workers from their insurance plans, among other discriminatory measures.[44]

Yet another concern about the female-only statutes is their narrow focus even for women. The obsessive concern with pregnancy and childbirth seems to have made legislators forget that women have a wide range of other medical conditions. Employers who refuse to provide any sick leave, paid or unpaid, will fire a woman for a broken leg, an appendectomy, or a serious heart condition just as readily as for childbirth. It does this woman's children little good to preserve her job when she has a baby, only to let her employer fire her when she is hospitalized for some other serious medical condition.[45] The same is true, of course, for fathers. Firing workers with serious medical conditions seems even worse when one realizes that, in contrast to parental leave, workers do not choose to take medical leave. If the condition is serious enough, such an employee simply cannot go to work.

Nor does the second form of state law being passed now—the pure parental leave legislation—address this problem. Minnesota, Oregon, and Rhode Island are all in this category, providing leaves of 6, 12, and 13 weeks respectively for the care of newborns or newly adopted children. (Rhode Island adds leave for the care of children on the edge of death or with a very serious medical problem, such as an organ transplant or limb amputation.).[46] The major advantage of this approach is that leave is available to both fathers and mothers, thus avoiding the reinforcement of traditional sex roles fostered by the California-type statute. However, while parental leave is an important step forward, it entirely ignores the plight of seriously ill workers—male or female—forced off the job by employers with no medical leave policies. There is one exception. The 12- and 13-week provisions do allow a de facto medical leave for disabled pregnant workers only, combined with a short parental leave, and Minnesota's 6-week leave likewise effectively gives the pregnant woman a medical leave, with no additional parental leave, since the typical disability period after childbirth is 6 to 8 weeks.[47]

That suggests yet another problem with the pure parental leave legislation. To understand it, one must recall that a major advance under the PDA was that women gained 6 to 8 weeks of *paid* leave time for the childbirth recuperation period, wherever employers had general paid sick leave programs for other workers, whether through accrued sick leave or TDI plans. Parental leave passed by itself, without an accompanying medical leave, may lead some employers to give mothers the new *unpaid* parental leave instead of the old *paid* sick leave. This might especially be the case when the length of the parental leave is the same as the length of the typical paid sick leave, as in Minnesota. And while this practice would clearly violate Title VII and the PDA, how many women will realize that, or have the resources to bring a lawsuit to stop it? One remedy might be to add provisions to the parental leave laws subjecting employers who try to do this to some significant deterrent—perhaps an award of treble back wages and attorney's fees to the woman who brings a successful lawsuit against such an employer. This might be enough money to give women an economic incentive to sue and employers an incentive not to violate the PDA provision that sick leave and temporary disability plans must cover pregnancy-related disability to the same extent as other conditions. However, the best remedy would be to enact laws providing a medical leave *as well as* a parental leave, thus ensuring that employers and employees alike realize that women need the former for childbirth and the typical 6-week recuperation period, and the latter for the post-recuperation period when the only purpose of the leave is to care for the newborn.

Close analysis of the parental leave laws now on the books reveals other problems as well. The Oregon statute contains restrictions that foster traditional sex roles in the family and discriminate against two-earner couples. And each of the statutes contains restrictions that seriously hamper their usefulness to families in need.

A unique feature of the Oregon law makes the 12-week leave a combined maximum for both parents, not an individual parent entitlement. Moreover, an employer may deny leave to one parent while the other parent is taking the leave.[48] In contrast, both Minnesota and Rhode Island give their respective 6-week and 13-week leaves to the individual parent. Thus, to maximize parental time with the newborn or newly adopted child in these states, both the mother and the father will have to take the leave (yielding a total of up to 12 or 26 weeks of leave during which one parent or the other can care for the infant). Under Oregon's combined entitlement, a family seeking the maximum parenting time with the newborn can allow the mother alone to be the parent on leave and still get the entire 12 weeks. The provision thereby reinforces all the societal pressures that discourage fathers from taking an active role in caring for newborns.

Oregon's unique feature allowing employers to deny simultaneous father–mother leaves plays a similar, though narrower, role. Even a traditional father might be willing—indeed, eager—to spend a few days home caring for the baby when mother and baby both arrive home from the hospital, and the mother is most in need of recuperation time and help with the infant. A father's care in these early days might cement his bond with the baby and give him a powerful incentive to take parental leave later on when the mother has recovered physically and can go back to work. But his employer can deny even these few days of leave to the father on the ground that the mother is on parental leave. Since she will always be on leave in the early days after childbirth, the father's employer has an automatic out—and an easy way to pressure the father not to become too involved with his baby.

The Oregon statute also discriminates against fathers in two-earner families, since in situations where the mother does not work outside the home, the father is guaranteed the full 12 weeks of leave. Where both spouses are in the paid workforce, however, the father will in most cases be forced to sacrifice at least part of his parental leave in order to allow his wife to take time off for recuperation.

Restrictions reducing the flexibility of the leave are found in each state. Minnesota requires that parental leave begin within 6 weeks of birth or adoption.[49] In situations where the newborn is hospitalized for some time after birth, say for 8 weeks, neither parent will be able to take advantage of the guaranteed parental leave once the child arrives at home, because the leave did not start within the 6-week period. Oregon has a similar provision, with a similar effect. Its law allows the parental leave to be taken only in the period from birth until a newborn is 12 weeks old or a premature infant reaches a developmental age of 12 weeks, or until 12 weeks from the day the adoptive parents take custody of their child.[50] Oregon also limits use of the parental leave for adoptive parents to those adopting children aged 5 or under (Minnesota's leave covers the adoption of any child, while Rhode Island covers adoptions of children through age 16).[51] Finally, Rhode Island extends its parental leave from the care of newborn or newly adopted children to the care of seriously ill children, but undermines that purpose by the extremely narrow definition of serious illness (the child must be virtually at the brink of death) and by its requirement that the 13 weeks of leave be "consecutive work weeks in a two-year period."[52] A parent who takes only 6 weeks of parental leave to care for a newborn will not be able to use the remaining 7 weeks to care for even a dying child one year later because of the "consecutive work week" requirement.

Thus, on balance, while the parental leave model offers an improvement over the female-only pregnancy disability model by allowing both mothers and fathers to care for infants, it too has significant disadvantages. It fails to provide medical leave to workers who can now be fired for illness, and Oregon's version makes it easy to leave fathers out of the parenting process. Moreover, all versions now on the books reflect a narrow, timid, and rigid approach to the problems of working parents. Many families needing leave time for young or sick children will simply not qualify under these restrictive laws.

Finally, we come to the states following the FMLA model—namely, Connecticut, Maine, and Wisconsin. These states take a major step beyond the parental leave model, since they do provide medical leaves in addition to parenting leaves.[53] They also provide a genuine family leave, extending the concept of a parenting leave beyond the care of newborns and newly adopted children (but not foster children) to the care of seriously ill children, parents, or spouses.[54] Indeed, in reaching spouses, they are more comprehensive than the federal model.[55] In other respects, however, they are sharply narrower. Wisconsin, for example, offers a medical leave of a mere 2 weeks and a family leave of the same amount of time for the purpose of caring for a seriously ill child, spouse, or parent. Only for the care of a newborn or newly adopted child does a parent get 6 weeks of family leave.[56] Although 2 weeks of medical leave is better than none, this provision has the same potential as a no-medical-leave policy to lead to a cutback in paid medical leave; that is, employers may be tempted to give only 2 weeks of paid leave to new mothers, rather than the 6 to 8 weeks required under the PDA standard.

Maine is not much better. It provides a grand total of only 8 weeks of "family medical leave" for all these purposes.[57] Moreover, its requirement that the leave consist of consecutive work weeks seems to imply that a worker could not take a medical leave of, for example, 2 weeks early in the year for himself or herself, and then an additional 6 weeks to care for a seriously ill child later in the year. Maine's definition of "seriously ill" is also far more stringent than the federal standard. It requires that the sick family member be in imminent danger of death, face hospitalization for something like an organ transplant or limb amputation, or suffer from a condition requiring constant in-home care.[58] The federal standard, in contrast, requires only that a child or parent have a condition requiring continuing treatment or supervision by a doctor, nurse, or other "health care provider."[59]

In comparison, Connecticut's law is generous and comprehensive, providing for 24 weeks of leave in a two-year period for medical leave, and another 24 weeks for family leave.[60] Although it is limited to state employees, the actual operation of this plan should be closely studied as a possible model for other states. Such studies will be made somewhat easier by the fact that the law specifically requires periodic reporting by state agencies on their experience with these leaves of absence.[61]

That brings us back to the federal FMLA model. The federal FMLA has some significant strengths that should be discussed—strengths derived from its equal-treatment approach to the problems of both medical disability and parenting. First, it goes farther than any other model in recognizing workers' dual roles in the family and in the workplace. It helps to set the stage for a more complete integration of fathers at home by allowing them substantial time off to care for seriously ill children and their own parents as well as for newborns. And by giving fathers the right to do so, it takes pressure off mothers to be Super Mom and do all these tasks, thus setting the stage for women to be more completely integrated into the workforce. It ensures that workers will not be fired because of their own medical condition, thus preventing the economic collapse of families when a sick wage earner also loses a job. And because the FMLA provides medical leave that equal numbers of men and women will take, and family leave that a significant number of men will take,[62] it also eliminates the incentive that special-treatment, female-only, state laws give employers not to hire women. Similarly, it has no pregnancy-based provisions, and hence no potential for encouraging the use of negative pregnancy-based classifications like those in California's and Louisiana's laws; at the same time, it provides comprehensive leave for medically disabled women (either while pregnant or while recuperating from childbirth), and leave to care for newborns once the mothers have recuperated.

Another important provision of the FMLA that is ignored in most state statutes is the availability of family leave on a reduced-hours basis and medical leave on an intermittent basis.[63] Both provisions are designed to help lower-income workers by giving them at least part-time pay while they take part-time leave. The FMLA allows the employee to take the total amount of family leave on a "reduced" (or part-time) leave schedule if the employer agrees, thereby conceivably converting a 10-week full-time leave to a 20-week part-time leave. Such a provision is desirable for most employers as well as employees. An employee who cannot afford to take a substantial period of time off from work without pay may be able to do so on a part-time basis, while an employer may often prefer to keep an experienced employee on a part-time basis rather than hire a full-time temporary replacement. Another way in which the FMLA attempts to accommodate more fully the needs of the employer and the employee is by allowing medical leave and family leave for the care of a seriously ill son, daughter, or parent to be taken intermittently when medically necessary, up to the maximum amount of time. This leave could be used for periodic but short visits to the doctor: for example, for prenatal care or chemotherapy. (Only two state laws address these part-time options. Wisconsin permits family leave on a part-time basis and medical leave when it is "medically necessary" without the employer's permission, being in the first respect more progressive than the federal model.[64] Minnesota allows the employee—with the employer's agreement—to return to work part time during its parental leave period, but the statutory language implies that the 6-week leave cannot thereby be stretched out to a 12-week total.)[65]

For all these strengths, the FMLA also has significant defects. Under relentless pressure from the small business community, it had already been scaled back significantly by early 1990, and Congress was still negotiating as this book went to press. The cutback in the number of weeks of leave has already been noted.[66] Another major concession was the decrease in the number of covered employers. While the early 1990 Senate version still covered those employers with 20 or more employees, the House side started at 50, and then expanded coverage to employers of 35 or more after three years.[67] Only about 40 percent of all employees would be covered by the House version in these first three years, after adjusting for the effect of even further concessions. These include provisions that allow employers to deny leaves to highly paid "key employees" (the top 10 percent by pay) and to those who have not worked for the employer for at least one year.[68] A major gap in the original design was the fact that the leave was unpaid. That was at least balanced by a provision allowing the disability and parental leaves (as they were then called) to be taken on a part-time basis, leaving the worker with part-time pay, and another provision establishing a commission to study ways of providing paid leave and propose legislation for doing so.[69] By 1990, the part-time family leave had been made contingent on employer approval, and even the study had been scaled back to a study of "policies."[70]

Incidentally, two other post–*Cal Fed* state laws set up an interesting mechanism for providing some *paid* family leave. Washington State allows employees to use their own accrued paid sick leave to care for an ill child.[71] South Carolina allows state employees to use up to five days a year of their paid sick leave for the care of members of their broadly defined "immediate family."[72] While these laws are limited in their present form, combining them to allow all employees to use all their accrued sick leave for the care of ill members of the immediate family would provide a way of getting at least some paid family leave in the immediate future in other states. In this same vein, at least one state (Missouri) has allowed state employees paid adoption parental leaves by permitting use of the employee's accrued sick and annual leave for the care of newly adopted children. However, this leave is available only to "the person who is primarily responsible for furnishing the care and nurture of the child."[73] Apparently, the legislators could not conceive of the possibility that parents might act as equals in this domain, and did not care that such a provision will prevent many fathers from playing more than a minor role at home.

Conclusion

This completes our survey of the available federal and state models from which legislators in the 1990s can choose. Of all these models, the FMLA represents the biggest improvement over early attempts to deal with problems at the intersection of work and family caused by the enormous influx of women into the paid labor market. It reflects substantial movement away from a women-only legislative position that reinforces traditional sex roles to a gender-neutral solution that lays the foundation for a more egalitarian relationship at home and at work. The effort to enact the FMLA shows that the country is beginning to grapple with the changed demographics of work and family life.

Some cautionary notes must be struck, however. The FMLA has not yet been enacted. Many of the state laws reveal a real paucity of imagination and an unfortunate lack of concern for changing sex roles and the needs of families with two parents in the paid workforce. At the end of the twentieth century, many employers are vigorously opposing the FMLA model—in effect, fighting for the right to fire seriously ill workers and force parents back on the job within a few weeks after the birth of a child. They are refusing even to study the concept of paid leaves, even though there are available models (such as the state TDI programs) that could be used to provide universal paid medical and family leaves in ways that would cost employers little or nothing.[74] Clearly, it will be many more years before we have achieved a genuine accommodation between work and family life, one that actually encourages employees to attend to family needs by continuing their pay while they do so, in the belief that both the family and employment spheres will thereby be strengthened. But at least we have begun to work toward that goal.

NOTES

Acknowledgments. Special thanks to Taraneh Maghamé, Peter James Curtin, and Laura A. Ng, students at Georgetown University Law Center, for their research and editorial assistance.

1. In 1964, when Congress enacted the Civil Rights Act outlawing sex-based employment discrimination, 38.7 percent of all women were in the nation's labor force; the percentage jumped to 51.6 percent of all women by 1980 (U.S. Department of Labor, Women's Bureau (1983), *Time of Change: 1983 Handbook on Women Workers* p. 9). The increase was particularly dramatic for women of childbearing age. As the Labor Department reported in 1983 (ibid., p. 7), "Since the mid-1960's, the greatest labor force increases for women have occurred among those under age 45. Currently, more than two-thirds of the women in their twenties, and slightly less—about 65 percent—of those in their thirties and forties, are in the labor force."

2. See, for example, *Cleveland Board of Education* v. *La Fleur*, 414 U.S. 632, 641, 648 (1974), the legal decision in which the Supreme Court invalidated the forced-leave policies of two school boards. In each instance, the board justified its policy in part on the theory that pregnant or postpartum teachers were physically unfit for long periods of time—in one case, from 5 months before birth to 3 months after. For an example of an employer policy of firing pregnant workers, see *Mitchell* v. *Board of Trustees of Pickens County*, 599 F.2d 582, 584 n. 1 (4th Cir. 1979) (school policy required that pregnant teachers notify the principal of their pregnancy, and that their contracts be terminated at least 3 months prior to childbirth).

Doctors, however, have determined that women with uncomplicated pregnancies are not disabled from working until "near the termination of pregnancy, during labor, delivery, and the puerperium," and that the disability period generally lasts about 6 to 8 weeks after labor and childbirth. See American College of Obstetricians and Gynecologists (1974), "Policy Statement on Pregnancy-Related Disabilities" (March 2), quoted in *Geduldig* v. *Aiello*, 417 U.S. 484, 500 n. 4 (1974) (dissenting opinion of Justice Brennan).

3. See, for example, *General Electric Company* v. *Gilbert*, 429 U.S. 125 (1976). The Supreme Court ruled in that case that there was no illegal sex discrimination in a GE disability insurance plan that granted benefits of 60 percent of pay to workers who were disabled from working by sickness or accidents, but denied these same benefits to women for disabilities arising from pregnancy. Like the employer, the Court was influenced in part by its view that pregnancy is "significantly different from the typical covered disease or disability. The District Court found that it is not a 'disease' at all, and is often a voluntarily undertaken and desired condition" (p. 136). For a similar disparity in the coverage of health insurance plans, see *Nashville Gas Co.* v. *Satty*, 434 U.S. 136, 138 n. 1 (1977) (health insurance plan paid lower hospitalization benefits for pregnancy than for other medical conditions).

4. 42 U.S.C. §2000e et seq. (1982).

5. See the cases cited in nn. 2 and 3 above and in Wendy W. Williams' comprehensive analysis (1985): "Equality's Riddle: Pregnancy and the Equal Treatment/Special Treatment Debate," *New York University Review of Law and Social Change* 13: 325, 344 n. 77, 356–57 n. 125, 358 n. 127, 375 n. 196.

6. 29 C.F.R. §1604.10 (1973).

7. The 1972 guidelines dealing with this issue stated, "Disabilities caused or contributed to by pregnancy, miscarriage, abortion, childbirth, and recovery therefrom, are for all job-related purposes temporary disabilities and shall be treated as such under any health or temporary disability insurance or sick leave plan available in connection with employment. Written and unwritten employment policies and practices involving matters such as the commencement and duration of leave, the availability of extensions, the accrual of seniority and other benefits and privileges, reinstatement, and payment under any health or temporary disability insurance or sick leave plan, formal or informal, shall be applied to disability due to pregnancy or childbirth on the same terms and conditions as they are applied to other temporary disabilities." 29 C.F.R. §1604.10(b) (1973).

8. The guidelines relating to the pregnant woman's right to continued employment when able to work stated, "A written or unwritten employment policy or practice which excludes from employment applicants or employees because of pregnancy is in prima facie violation of Title VII." 29 C.F.R. §1604.10(a) (1973). See also 29 C.F.R. §1604.2(b)(1) (1973) (invalidating state laws that prohibited women from working for fixed periods of time before and after childbirth).

9. See Sheila B. Kamerman, Alfred J. Kahn, and Paul W. Kingston (1983), *Maternity Policies and Working Women*, pp. 47–76; Personnel Policies Forum (1983), "Policies on Leave from Work," pp. 22–24.

Illustrations of the increase in benefits caused by the EEOC approach are found by examining the experience of the five states with laws requiring temporary disability insurance benefits for workers. All but one of those states originally denied or limited benefits for pregnant workers. See CAL. UNEMP. INS. CODE §2626 (Deering 1971); N.J. STAT. ANN. §43:21–29 (West 1962); N.Y. WORK. COMP. LAW §205 (McKinney 1965); and R.I. GEN. LAWS §28–41–8 (1979); but see HAW. REV. STAT. §392–21 (1976). After Congress passed the Pregnancy Discrimination Act (PDA) of 1978, incorporating the EEOC approach (see text below), pregnant women's benefits were raised to the level of other workers'. See, for example, N.J. STAT. ANN. §43:21–29 (West Supp. 1988); *United States* v. *Rhode Island Department of Employment Security*, 619 F.Supp. 509 (D. R.I. 1985) (awarding back pay and interest to approximately 9,000 women in the state who had been given lower benefits for pregnancy-related disabilities than other workers received for all other disabilities; the back pay covered the time from the effective date of the PDA until the date the Rhode Island legislature finally brought the state program into compliance with it, through R.I. Gen. Laws §28–41–8 (1986), effective July 5, 1981). In the Rhode Island case, the state ultimately identified 8,727 women who had received pregnancy-related disability benefits in the two-year period in question. The state reviewed all of these claims and sent 5,045 women checks for back pay and interest in a total amount of $2,128,696, determined that it could not locate 226 women, and determined that the rest had not been paid less than other workers. Telephone interview with Vincent F. Calitri, administrator of the Temporary Disability Insurance Program, State of Rhode Island, June 7, 1989.

10. Employers in both California and Montana have claimed to have such policies. See *California Federal Savings and Loan Association* v. *Guerra*, 479 U.S. 272, 278, and 278 n. 8 (1987); *Miller–Wohl Co., Inc.*, v. Commissioner of Labor and Industry, 515 F.Supp. 1264, 1265 (D. Mont. 1981), vacated on other grounds, 685 F.2d 1088 (9th Cir. 1982); *Miller–Wohl Co., Inc.*, v. Commissioner of Labor and Industry, 692 P.2d 1243, 1250 (Mont. 1984), vacated and remanded, 479 U.S. 1050 (1987), judgment reinstated and cause remanded, 744 P.2d 871, 874 (Mont. 1987).

11. See n. 3 above.

12. Pregnancy Discrimination Act of 1978, Public Law 95–555, 92 Stat. 2076 (1978), codified in part as 42 U.S.C. §2000e(k)(1982) (amending Title VII of the 1964 Civil Rights Act, 42 U.S.C. §2000e et seq.). The act provided that "The terms 'because of sex' or 'on the basis of sex' include, but are not limited to, because of or on the basis of pregnancy, childbirth, or related medical conditions; and women affected by pregnancy, childbirth, or related medical conditions shall be treated the same for all employment-related purposes, including receipt of benefits under fringe benefit programs, as other persons not so affected but *similar in their ability or inability to work*" (emphasis added). The second clause effectively required that pregnant women who were able to work should be treated like other able workers (like persons who are "similar in their ability . . . to work"); that is, that they should be allowed to work while pregnant as long as they were physically able to do so.

It also required that a pregnant woman who was unable to work (e.g., a woman in labor) should be treated like other disabled workers (or like persons who are "similar in their . . . inability to work"); that is, she should receive the fringe benefits designed for other medically disabled workers.

13. HAW. REV. STAT. §378-1 (1985) (enacted in 1977, using the PDA language set forth in n. 12 above; but see Hawaii Department of Labor and Industrial Relations Administrative Rules adopting the special leave approach in 1982, n. 14 below); MD. ANN. CODE art. 49B, §17 (Michie 1986) (enacted in 1977 and stating that employer policies on "matters such as the commencement and duration of leave, . . . and payment under any health or temporary disability insurance or sick leave plan . . . shall be applied to disability due to pregnancy or childbirth on the same terms and conditions as they are applied to other temporary disabilities," which is language taken from the EEOC guidelines; see n. 7 above); MINN. STAT. ANN. §363.03(1)5 (West Supp. 1989) (enacted in 1977 and using the second clause of the PDA language set forth in n. 12 above); OR. REV. STAT. §569.029 (1987) (enacted in 1977 and using the PDA language set forth in n. 12 above).

In addition to state statutes incorporating the EEOC approach, a number of state agencies interpreted state laws prohibiting sex-based discrimination in employment to reach the same result: 3 COLO. CODE REGS. Sec. 708–1, §80.8 (1982) (*State Sex Discrimination Guidelines*, issued in 1977); IOWA ADMIN. CODE r. 240–3.10(601A) (1980) (adopted in 1978 and possibly superseded by IOWA CODE ANN. §601A.6(2)e, which adopted the special leave approach in 1987; see n. 14 below); 8B Lab. Rel. Rep. 455:1094 (BNA 1988) (Michigan Civil Rights Commission, *Interpretive Guidelines* §A(6), adopted in 1973); 8B Lab. Rel. Rep. 459:558 (BNA 1988) (Oklahoma Human Rights Commission, *Guidelines on Employment Discrimination* §VI(I), adopted in 1973); 16 PA. CODE §41.101–4 (1981) (adopted in 1975); 8B Lab. Rel. Rep. 457:1276–77 (BNA 1988) (Rhode Island Commission for Human Rights, *Sex Discrimination Guidelines* §7, adopted in 1973); S.D. ADMIN. R. 20:03:09:12 (1986) (employment policies and practices to be "applied to pregnancy and childbirth on the same terms and conditions as they are applied to other temporary disabilities," but with a specific exception for insurance, adopted in 1976); 8B Lab. Rel. Rep. 457:3307–10 (BNA 1988) (Wisconsin Department of Industry, Labor and Human Relations, *Guidelines Relating to Pregnancy and Childbirth*, adopted in 1975 and spelling out through questions and answers an EEOC-type approach).

Some states adopted the EEOC approach by statute in the years *after* the passage of the PDA. D.C. CODE ANN. §1–2505 (Michie Supp. 1986) (PDA-type provision, added in 1985); KY. REV. STAT. ANN. §344.030(6) (Michie/Bobbs-Merrill 1983) (PDA provision, added in 1980); ME. REV. STAT. ANN. tit. 5, §4572–A(1–4) (West Supp. 1988) (unlawful "to treat a pregnant woman who is able to work in a different manner from other persons who are able to work" or "to treat a pregnant woman who is not able to work because of a disability or illness resulting from pregnancy in a different manner from other employees who are not able to work because of other disabilities or illnesses"; with a specific proviso that no special benefits for pregnant women are required if such benefits are not also provided to "other employees," enacted in 1979); NEB. REV. STAT. §§48–1102(10), 48–1111(2) (reissued 1988) (PDA provisions added in 1986 and 1984); NEV. REV. STAT. §608 (Supp. 1987) (pregnant female employees entitled to same sickness and disability leaves as other employees receive for their medical conditions, to be used "before and after childbirth, miscarriage or other natural resolution of [the] pregnancy," added in 1987); OHIO REV. CODE ANN. §4112.01(B) (Baldwin 1988) (PDA provision, added in 1979; but see, in n. 14 below, the Ohio Civil Rights Commission regulations adopting the special leave approach in 1977); R.I. GEN. LAWS §28–5–6(9) (Michie Supp. 1988) (PDA provision, added in 1988, supporting the guidelines already in use by the Rhode Island Commission for Human Rights); S.C. CODE ANN. §1–13–30(1) (rev. 1986) (PDA provision, added in 1979); TEX. REV. CIV. STAT. ANN. art. 5221K, §1–04(c) (Vernon 1987) (PDA provision, enacted in 1983); VA. CODE ANN. §2.1–716 (Michie 1987) (prohibits any practice that violates Title VII of the 1964 Civil Rights Act, thus incorporating the PDA; enacted in 1987); WIS. STAT. ANN. §111.36(c) (West 1988) (partial PDA language enacted in 1981, supplementing the previously existing state *Guidelines Relating to Pregnancy and Childbirth*).

A few other states have adopted the EEOC approach by regulation in the post-PDA years. 8A Lab. Rel. Rep. 453:2764 (BNA 1988) (rules regarding pregnancy, childbirth, and childbearing issued jointly in 1985 by the Illinois Department of Human Rights and the Human Rights Commission as part of the rules on sex discrimination); MO. CODE REGS. tit. 8, §60–340(16) (Supp. 1988) (adopted in 1980); TENN. COMP. R. & REGS. ch. 1500–1–.11(2) (1979) (adopting EEOC sex discrimination guidelines in 1978, including the pregnancy guidelines; in 1988, however, the state passed a special leave statute: see n. 14 below).

New York and Nevada have also issued such regulations, but their dates of enactment are unclear. 8B Lab. Rel. Rep. 455:2351 (BNA 1988) (*Nevada Equal Rights Commission Guidelines* §6, adopting EEOC sex discrimination guidelines, supplemented by NEV. REV. STAT. §608); 8B Lab. Rel. Rep. 455:3159 (BNA 1988) (New York State Division of Human Rights, *Rulings on Inquiries* §12(A), (C), using some of the EEOC's regulations on pregnancy discrimination).

14. CAL. GOV'T CODE ANN. §12945(b)2 (West 1980) (right to take unpaid leave for the period during which the "female employee is disabled on account of pregnancy, childbirth, or related medical condition," up to a maximum period of 4 months, enacted in September 1978); CONN. GEN. STAT. ANN. §46a–60(a)7 (West 1986) (right to a "reasonable leave of absence for disability resulting from her pregnancy," enacted in 1973); MASS. GEN. LAWS ANN. chs. 149, §105D, 151B, §4(11A) (West 1982) (employer shall give female who has completed probationary term 8 weeks "maternity leave" for the purpose of "giving birth or for adopting a child under three years of age"; unlawful discrimination to fail to comply with requirement or to deny

female state employees vacation credit for such leave, enacted in 1972); MONT. CODE ANN. §49–2–310(2) (1987) (employer may not refuse to grant a pregnant woman "a reasonable leave of absence for such pregnancy," enacted in 1975); P.R. LAWS ANN. tit. 29, §467 (Equity 1985) (pregnant workers entitled to leave at half-pay for 4 weeks before and 4 weeks after childbirth, or 1 week before and up to 7 weeks after, with unpaid extension of up to 12 additional weeks for post-natal complications if they prevent the woman from working; enacted in 1947 and amended in 1969 and 1975).

Other states achieved the same result through agency regulations interpreting state fair employment practice statutes. KAN. ADMIN. REGS. 21–32–6(d) (1978) ("childbearing must be considered by the employer to be a justification for a leave of absence for female employees for a reasonable period of time," adopted in 1975); OHIO ADMIN. CODE §4112–5–05(G)2 (1980) (employer policy of "insufficient or no maternity leave" that causes termination of employees temporarily disabled by pregnancy is "unlawful sex discrimination," adopted in 1977); WASH. ADMIN. CODE §162–30–020(5) (1977) (employer must provide leave "for the period of time that she is sick or temporarily disabled because of pregnancy or childbirth," unless insufficient or no-leave policy is "justified by business necessity").

After passage of the PDA, three more states passed laws requiring special leaves for pregnant women. IOWA CODE ANN. §601A.6(2)e (West 1988) (pregnant employee entitled to "a leave of absence if the leave of absence is for the period that the employee is disabled because of the employee's pregnancy, childbirth, or related medical conditions, or for eight weeks, whichever is less"; provision added in 1987 despite contrary Iowa regulations, see n. 13 above); LA. REV. STAT. ANN. §23:1008B(2) (West Supp. 1989) (1987 provision adopting the California model); TENN. CODE ANN. §4–21–408(a) (Michie Supp. 1989) (a 1988 law providing female employees with up to 4 months of "maternity leave" for "pregnancy, childbirth and nursing the infant").

In addition, Hawaii and New Hampshire have post-PDA special leave *regulations*. 8B Lab. Rel. Rep. 453:2328–29 (BNA 1988) (*Hawaii Department of Labor and Industrial Relations Administrative Rules* §12–23–58(a): "Disability due to and resulting from pregnancy, childbirth, or other related medical conditions shall be considered by the employer to be justification for a leave, with or without pay, by the female employee for a reasonable period of time," with reasonable time to be "determined by the employee's physician, with regard for [her] physical condition and the job requirements"; these regulations were adopted effective November 15, 1982, while the state statute enacting the equal-treatment approach passed in 1977, see n. 13 above); N.H. CODE ADMIN. R. HUM. 402.03(a) (1984) (a 1982 provision that "employer shall permit a female employee to take leave of absence for the period of temporary physical disability resulting from pregnancy, childbirth or related medical conditions"; job to be held for her "unless business necessity makes this impossible or unreasonable").

15. See n. 3 above.

16. Wendy Williams has analyzed the philosophical and practical differences in the approaches of the "equal-treatment" and "special-treatment" advocates: see her discussion ("Equality's Riddle," 1985, pp. 366–69) of two "special-treatment" articles arguing in support of special pregnancy leaves: Linda J. Krieger and Patricia N. Cooney (1983), "The Miller–Wohl Controversy: Equal Treatment, Positive Action and the Meaning of Women's Equality," *Golden Gate University Law Review* 13:513; "Note: Sexual Equality Under the Pregnancy Discrimination Act" (1983), *Columbia Law Review* 83: 690.

17. See the cases cited in n. 10 above.

18. Brief *amici curiae* of the National Organization for Women; NOW Legal Defense and Education Fund; National Bar Association Women Lawyers' Division, Washington Area Chapter; National Women's Law Center; Women's Law Project; and Women's Legal Defense Fund in Support of Neither Party; pp. 3–4, 7–11, 19–31, *California Federal Savings & Loan Association* v. *Guerra*, 472 U.S. 272 (1987) (No. 85–494) (*Cal Fed*). Brief *amici curiae* of the American Civil Liberties Union; League of Women Voters of the United States; League of Women Voters of California; National Women's Political Caucus; and the Coal Employment Project; pp. 9–10, 48–64, *Cal Fed* (No. 85–494).

19. Brief *amici curiae* of Coalition for Reproductive Equality in the Workplace; International Ladies Garment Workers Union, AFL-CIO; Planned Parenthood Federation of America, Inc.; California School Employees Association; American Federation of State, County and Municipal Employees, District Council 36; California Federation of Teachers; Coalition of Labor Union Women, Los Angeles Chapter; Union of Food and Commercial Workers, Local 770; Utility Workers Union of America, AFL-CIO, Local 132; Orange County Central Labor Council; American Association of University Women, California State Division; Women For; Los Angeles City Commission on the Status of Women; Comision Femenil De Los Angeles; American Jewish Congress—Pacific Southwest Region; Mexican American Bar Association of Los Angeles County; Hispanic Women's Council; Lawyers Club of San Diego; Women Lawyers of Alameda County; Women Lawyers of San Luis Obispo County; Inland Counties Women at Law; Queen's Bench; Los Angeles Feminist Legal Scholars; and 17 named individuals; pp. 2–5, 7, 12–14, 22, 36–38, 53, *Cal Fed* (No. 85–494); brief *amici curiae* of Equal Rights Advocates, California Teachers' Association, Northwest Women's Law Center, San Francisco Women Lawyers' Alliance; pp. 5–7, *Cal Fed* (No. 85–494).

20. 479 U.S. 272 (1987).

21. Ibid., p. 289.

22. Ibid., p. 290.

23. Ibid. See also the Court's point that "a State could not mandate special treatment of pregnant workers based on stereotypes or generalizations about their needs and abilities" (p. 285, n. 17). Similarly, Justice Stevens noted in his concurring opinion that "I do not read the Court's opinion as

holding that Title VII presents no limitations whatsoever on beneficial treatment of pregnancy. . . . the Court . . . points out that there are limitations on what an employer can do, even when affording 'preferential' treatment to pregnancy" (p. 294, n. 3).

24. These arguments were spelled out in several briefs to the Court in both the *Cal Fed* case and the related Montana *Miller–Wohl* cases, n. 10 above.

25. See generally Barbara Allen Babcock, Ann E. Freedman, Eleanor Holmes Norton, and Susan Deller Ross (1975), *Sex Discrimination and the Law: Causes and Remedies*, pp. 19–53, 247–78, for the history, philosophy, and effects of such laws. The leading court decision in striking down such laws at the request of a woman worker is *Rosenfeld* v. *Southern Pacific Co.*, 444 F.2d 1219 (9th Cir. 1971); see also the cases cited in Babcock et al. (1975, pp. 269–71).

26. See American Civil Liberties Union brief, pp. 6–7, 8–9, 11–23, *cited* n. 18 above; National Organization for Women brief, pp. 14–17, *cited* n. 18 above.

27. The bill began life as the Parental and Disability Act of 1985, H.R. 2020, 99th Cong., 2d Sess. (1985) (introduced by Representative Patricia Schroeder on April 4, 1985). In 1986, it became the Parental and Medical Leave Act, introduced as H.R. 4300, 99th Cong., 2d Sess. (1986) by Representatives William Clay and Shroeder (March 4, 1986) and as S. 2278, 99th Cong., 2d Sess. (1986) by Senator Christopher Dodd (April 9, 1986); 1987 saw its reintroduciton by the same chief sponsors as the Family and Medical Leave Act, H.R. 925, 100th Cong., 1st Sess. (1987) (February 3, 1987), and S. 249, 100th Cong., 1st Sess. (January 6, 1987).

On February 2, 1989, it was reintroduced as H.R. 770, 101st Cong., 1st Sess. (1989) (Congressional Quarterly's Washington Alert Service, BILL-TEXT data base, 101st Cong.), with Representative Marge Roukema added as a chief sponsor. On the Senate side, it became S. 345, 101st Cong., 1st Sess. (1989) (BILLTEXT database, 101st Cong.), and was also introduced on February 2, 1989. H.R. 770, as marked up by the House Committee on Education and Labor, is printed in H.R. REP. No. 101–28, 101st Cong., 1st Sess., pt. 1, pp. 42–55 (1989), which also details the act's legislative history, pp. 2–5. S. 345, as reported out by the Senate Committee on Labor and Human Resources, is printed in S. REP. No. 101–77, 101st Cong., 1st Sess., pp. 2–21 (1989).

Throughout this chapter, all references are to the versions pending as of April 30, 1990, unless otherwise noted. On the House side, the version cited is the marked-up bill printed in H.R. REP. No. 101–28. On the Senate side, the version cited is the initial bill, S. 345, which is virtually identical to the bill reported out by the Senate Committee.

All of these efforts began with a meeting convened by the chief sponsor of the California legislation, who had since become a member of the Congress. Representative Howard Berman, California Assemblywoman Maxine Waters, and Janis Berman met with Donna Lenhoff, Director for Legal

Policies and Programs of the Women's Legal Defense Fund, Diann Rust-Tierney of the National Women's Law Center, and Professor Wendy Williams, of Georgetown University Law Center concerning Representative Berman's proposal to enact similar legislation on the federal level. After discussion, it was agreed that a gender-neutral formulation would be better. Other outside groups subsequently became involved with the effort to shape the legislation, including the Women's Rights Project of the American Civil Liberties Union and the Women's Law and Public Policy Fellowship Program at Georgetown University Law Center, whose fellows participated by conducting extensive background research and analysis. (The author participated in these early efforts and is director of the above-mentioned Fellowship Program. She was also Co-Chair of the Campaign to End Discrimination Against Pregnant Workers (the coalition that worked for passage of the PDA), worked on the early EEOC pregnancy guidelines, and litigated or wrote *amici curiae* briefs in a number of pregnancy discrimination cases, including the *Cal Fed* case and the *Rhode Island* case cited in n. 9 above).

28. The bill provides that "Any eligible employee who, because of a serious health condition, becomes unable to perform the functions of such employee's position, shall be entitled . . . to temporary medical leave. Such entitlement shall continue for as long as the employee is unable to perform such functions, except that it shall not exceed 15 workweeks during any 12-month period." H.R. 770 (see n. 27 above, §104(a)(1) (1989).

The House Report (cited in n. 27 above) states (p. 23): "The purpose of this provision is to help provide reasonable job security to workers faced with serious health problems, including pregnancy and childbirth." The report also notes (p. 30): "Examples of serious health conditions include . . . ongoing pregnancy, miscarriages, complications or illnesses related to pregnancy, such as severe morning sickness, the need for prenatal care, childbirth, and recovery from childbirth. All of these conditions meet the general test that either the underlying health condition or the treatment for it requires that the employee be absent from work on a recurring basis or for more than a few days for treatment or recovery. They also involve either inpatient care or continuing treatment or supervision by a health care provider, and frequently involve both."

29. See H.R. 2020, cited in n. 27 above, at §102(a); S. 345, cited in n. 27 above, at §104(a)(2). See n. 28 above for the text of the 15-week provision in H.R. 770. The ban on firing is contained in the language requiring that the employee returning from either medical or family leave is entitled "to be restored by the employer to the position of employment held by the employee when the leave commenced, or . . . to be restored to an equivalent position with equivalent employment benefits, pay, and other terms and conditions of employment." H.R. 770, cited in n. 27 above, at §106(a)(16); see also S. 345, §106(a)(1).

30. H.R. 770, cited in n. 27 above, at §103(a) provides, "An eligible employee shall be entitled . . . to 10 workweeks of family leave during any 24-month period—(A) because of the birth of a son or daughter of the em-

ployee, (B) because of the placement of a son or daughter with the employee for adoption or foster care, or (C) in order to care for the employee's son, daughter, or parent who has a serious health condition." See also S. 345, cited in n. 27 above, at §103(a)(1).

31. See n. 30 above. The House Report, cited in n. 27 above, at p. 28, clarifies that the leave is "to care for a parent of any age who, because of a serious mental or physical condition, is unable to care for his or her own basic hygienic or nutritional needs or safety."

32. See n. 30 above. H.R. 2020, cited in n. 27 above, at §103(a)(1), contained the 18-week family leave.

33. See n. 29 above.

34. In discussing the section 103(a) family leave and the section 104(a) medical leave, the House Report cited in n. 27 above states (pp. 26–27) that the family leave provision permits a father and mother to take leave "at the same time, on an overlapping basis, or sequentially. . . . In the case of a newborn child it permits a mother to take leave under section 103 after having taken childbirth related medical leave under section 104."

35. California, Connecticut, Massachusetts, and Montana had passed statutes, while Hawaii, Kansas, New Hampshire, Ohio, and Washington had state regulations. Puerto Rico also enacted legislation in 1947. See n. 14 above for the legal citations.

36. See n. 14 above for the citations to and summaries of the special leave provisions in the Iowa, Louisiana, and Tennessee statutes.

37. The pared-down FMLA statutes include: CONN. GEN. STAT. ANN. §§5–248a, 5–248b (West Supp. 1989) (enacted May 20, 1987); ME. REV. STAT. ANN. tit. 26, §§843–49 (West 1988) (enacted 1987; effective August 4, 1988, and repealed by its own terms effective July 1, 1990, with review of the law's provisions and effectiveness by the joint standing committee on labor of the legislation by March 15, 1990); WIS. STAT. ANN. §§103.10, 108.04(1)(b)1, 108.04(1)(b)3, 111.91(2)(f), 230.35(2), 230.35(2m), 632.897 (6), 893.96 (West Supp. 1988) (enacted 1987; effective April 26, 1988).

The parental leave statutes are: MINN. STAT. ANN. §§181.940–181.944 (West Supp. 1989) (enacted 1987); OR. REV. STAT. ANN. §§659.360–659.370 (Butterworth 1989) (enacted 1987); R.I. GEN. LAWS §§28–48–1 to –9 (Michie Supp. 1988) (enacted 1987).

The accrued sick leave statutes are: S.C. CODE ANN. §8–11–40 (Law. Coop. 1986 & Supp. 1988) (enacted 1987; effective May 1, 1987); WASH. REV. CODE ANN. §§49.12.270–.295 (West Supp. 1989) (enacted 1988; effective September 1, 1988).

The adoptive parent statutes are: COLO. REV. STAT. §§19–5–211(1.5) (Bradford Supp. 1988) (enacted 1988); MO. ANN. STAT. §105.271 (Vernon Supp. 1989) (enacted 1987); N.Y. LABOR LAW §201–C (McKinney Supp. 1989) (enacted 1987; effective October 4, 1987).

In addition to these post–*Cal Fed* statutes, Delaware and Minnesota passed similar laws giving leave entitlements to adoptive parents in 1984 and

1983 respectively. DEL. CODE ANN. tit. 29, §5116 (Michie Supp. 1988); MINN. STAT. ANN. §181.92 (West Supp. 1989).

In the post–*Cal Fed* period, states have also continued to pass laws based on the EEOC equal-treatment approach. These statutes are not discussed in the text because they do not create a new entitlement to a leave regardless of an employer's actions, but instead require only that employers extend to pregnant workers leave rights that the employers already give to other employees. See n. 13 above for citations to the 1987 Nevada statute, the 1988 Rhode Island law, and the 1987 Virginia statute, which take this approach.

38. This observation is not based on hard data, but rather on information from a California attorney active in the employment discrimination field who has talked to California employers about the subject. Given the lack of data, it would make an interesting research project.

39. MASS. REGS. CODE tit. 804, §8.01(3) (1986). The regulation provides that "if a disability caused or contributed to by childbirth and recovery therefrom is less than eight weeks duration or if a temporary leave policy of an employer would result in a maternity leave of less than eight weeks, a female employee who meets the requirements [of the Massachusetts Maternity Leave Law] shall be entitled to an eight week maternity leave."

40. See n. 14 above.

41. In addition to violating the Supreme Court's explicit prescription in *Cal Fed*, 479 U.S. at 285 n. 17, 290, and 294 n. 3, the state laws also appear to run afoul of the Supreme Court's decision in *Weinberger* v. *Wiesenfield*, 420 U.S. 636 (1975) (equal protection violation to award mothers, but not fathers, Social Security "mother's" benefits to care for young children whose other parent has died). Men in these states would have very strong grounds to bring lawsuits seeking the same leave rights for themselves as women receive, just as Stephen Wiesenfield did. See n. 14 above for summaries of the remaining provisions that appear to have facial violations of the *Cal Fed* ruling (Montana, Puerto Rico, and Kansas).

42. CAL. GOV'T CODE ANN. §12945(b)(1) and (a) (West 1980) ("Nothing in this section shall be construed to require an employer to provide his or her employees with health insurance coverage for the medical costs of pregnancy, childbirth, or related medical conditions"); ("no employer shall be required to provide a female employee disability leave on account of normal pregnancy, childbirth, or related medical condition for a period exceeding six weeks"); and (an employer may not, because of a woman's "pregnancy, childbirth, or related medical condition . . . refuse to select her for a training program leading to promotion, *provided she is able to complete the training program at least three months prior to the anticipated date of departure for her pregnancy leave*") (emphasis added).

Other features of the California law also discriminated against pregnant workers in companies with a labor force of 5 to 14 workers. A ban on pregnancy-based discrimination in *hiring* that was in the first version of the proposed legislation (AB 1960, introduced in May 1977) was subsequently deleted after employers protested that they should not have to hire pregnant women [Sen. Comm. Bill File (Ind. Rel. Comm.)], leaving such employers free to refuse to hire pregnant women on the basis of their pregnancy. The 4-month leave is a *maximum*, so that women disabled for *more* than 4 months by complications of pregnancy and childbirth can receive less than other workers where the employer allows others workers longer leaves. Finally, the law requires pregnant workers to give notice of the commencement and duration of the leave even if no other worker with predictable disabilities is subject to such a requirement. CAL. GOV'T CODE §12945(b)(2) (West 1980).

43. See n. 14 above. The California law included a provision rendering it "inapplicable to any employer subject to Title VII of the federal Civil Rights Act of 1964," CAL. GOV'T CODE §12945(e) (West 1980). Thus, the California provision that discriminated against pregnant workers applied only to employers of 5 to 14 workers (California law covers employers of five or more employees, while Title VII coverage starts at 15 employees). In contrast, Louisiana law applies to employers of 26 or more—that is, to employers within the reach of Title VII's coverage. ("The provisions of this Section shall not be applicable to an employer having twenty-five or fewer employees." LA. REV. STAT. ANN. §23:1008B (West Supp. 1989).)

44. Any Louisiana women who are denied health insurance benefits for pregnancy and childbirth, and pregnancy-related disability benefits for disability extending beyond 6 weeks, or who are excluded from training programs because of their pregnancy could, of course, sue their employers under Title VII. Nevertheless, it is rather remarkable that 10 years after passage of the PDA, a state should pass a law purporting to authorize employers to violate the PDA, and requiring as a practical matter that women employees go to federal court to resolve this problem.

The Puerto Rico and Iowa statutes (see n. 14 above) have similar problems. Puerto Rico provides half pay for women on leave, which could be *less* than the full pay employers frequently provide to workers on paid sick leave. Iowa caps the leave period at 8 weeks, even if the woman is disabled for a longer time. In contrast, Congress specifically defeated an amendment to the PDA proposed by Senator Orrin Hatch that would have capped disability benefits at 6 weeks. 123 CONG. REC. 29, 650–65 (1977).

45. This has particular meaning for the author, since her mother was hospitalized for months with endocarditis and meningitis when she was a young child.

46. See n. 37 above. The Rhode Island provision allows parental leave to be used for the care of a "seriously ill child," defined as "a child under the age of 18 who by reason of an accident, disease or condition (1) is in imminent danger of death or (2) faces hospitalization involving an organ transplant, limb amputation or such other procedure of similar severity as shall be determined through regulation." R.I. GEN. LAWS §§28–48–1(d), (e) (Michie Supp. 1988).

Illinois has adopted a similar provision, but it is a regulation, it applies only to state employees, and it provides merely a right to "*request* a childcare leave," not an entitlement to the leave. ILL. ADMIN. CODE tit. 80 §§420.645 (1988) (emphasis added).

47. Indeed, the statute provides that "the length of leave provided by [this act] may be reduced by any period of paid parental or disability leave, but not accrued sick leave, provided by the employer." MINN. STAT. ANN §181.943 (West Supp. 1989). This provision appears to mean that if the woman's employer provides wage replacement for sick days through a TDI plan, which will ordinarily cover the 6 to 8 weeks after childbirth, the Minnesota statute gives her no parental leave at all; the 6-week parental leave is simply subtracted from the 6-week paid disability leave she ordinarily receives, leaving zero new parental leave days. Inexplicably, where the employer does not use TDI to cover wage loss, but instead merely continues a worker's salary through an accrued sick leave system, the woman will be allowed to add the unpaid parental leave onto the paid sick leave, thus genuinely extending the time off she can acquire. Oregon's similar provision is even worse, allowing the employer to force "the employee seeking parental leave to utilize *any* accrued leave during the parental leave." OR. REV. STAT. ANN. §659.360(3) (Butterworth 1989) (emphasis added). Rhode Island has no such provision; thus, its parental leave is a genuine addition to existing employee leave rights.

48. The Oregon law provides that "The employer is not required to grant to an employee parental leave which would allow the employee and the other parent of the child, if also employed, parental leave totaling more than [the 12-week period commencing at a child's birth or adoption] nor to grant to an employee parental leave for any period of time in which the child's other parent is also taking parental leave from employment." OR. REV. STAT. ANN. §659.360(2) (Butterworth 1989).

49. The law states, "The leave may *begin not more than six weeks after the birth* or adoption." MINN. STAT. ANN. §181.941(2) (West Supp. 1989) (emphasis added).

50. The Oregon provision states that an employer may not deny a parental leave for "[a]ll or part of the time between the birth of that employee's infant and the time the infant reaches 12 weeks of age, or, in the case of a premature infant, until the infant has reached the developmental stage equivalent to 12 weeks as determined by an attending physician; or . . . [a]ll or part of the 12-week period following the date an adoptive parent takes physical custody of a newly adopted child under six years of age." OR. REV. STAT. ANN. §659.360(1)(a), (b) (Butterworth 1989).

51. See n. 50 above for the Oregon provision. Minnesota provides that "An employer must grant an unpaid leave of absence to an employee who has been employed by the employer for at least 12 months and who is a natural or adoptive parent in conjunction with the birth or adoption of a child." MINN. STAT. ANN. §181.941(1) (West Supp. 1989). Rhode Island defines "'[p]arental leave'" as "leave by reason of . . . the placement of a child

sixteen (16) years of age or less with an employee in connection with the adoption of such child by the employee." R.I. GEN. LAWS §28–48–1(d) (Michie Supp. 1988).

52. See n. 46 above for the definition of serious illness. The other provision states, "Every employee who has been employed by the same employer for twelve (12) consecutive months shall be entitled, upon advance notice to his or her employer, to thirteen (13) consecutive work weeks of parental leave in any two (2) calendar years." R.I. GEN. LAWS §28–48–2(a) (Michie Supp. 1988).

53. CONN. GEN. STAT. ANN. §5–248a(a)(2) (West Supp. 1989) (state employees entitled to "a maximum of twenty-four weeks of medical leave of absence within any two-year period upon the serious illness of such employee"); ME. REV. STAT. ANN. tit. 26, §§843(4), 844(1) (West 1988) (employees entitled to "up to 8 consecutive work weeks of family medical leave in any 2 years," for, among other purposes, the "[s]erious illness of the employee"); WIS. STAT. ANN. §103.10(4) (West Supp. 1988) ("employee who has a serious health condition which makes the employee unable to perform his or her employment duties" entitled to no more than "2 weeks of medical leave during a 12-month period" for "the period during which he or she is unable to perform those duties").

54. CONN. GEN. STAT. ANN. §5–248a(a)(1) (West Supp. 1989) (state employees entitled to "[a] maximum of twenty-four weeks of family leave of absence within any two-year period upon the birth or adoption of a child of such employee, or upon the serious illness of a child, spouse or parent of such employee"); ME. REV. STAT. ANN. tit. 26, §§843(4), 844(1) (West Supp. 1988) (the 8-week family medical leave may also be used for "[t]he birth of the employee's child; . . . [t]he placement of a child 16 years of age or less with the employee in connection with the adoption of the child by the employee; or . . . [a] child, parent or spouse with a serious illness"); WIS. STAT. ANN. §103.10(3) (West Supp. 1988) (in a 12-month period, employees entitled to: (1) a maximum of 6 weeks leave for birth or adoption, "if the leave begins within sixteen weeks of the child's birth" or placement; (2) a maximum of 2 weeks "[t]o care for the employe's child, spouse or parent, if the child, spouse or parent has a serious health condition"; and (3) a combined maximum of 8 weeks for leave taken for any combination of the above reasons).

55. Both the pending House and Senate bills provide leave only "to care for the employee's son, daughter, or parent who has a serious health condition." H.R. 770, cited in n. 27 above, at §103(a)(1)(c); S. 345, cited in n. 27 above, at §103(a)(1)(c). However, the federal bills do allow family leave "because of the placement of a son or daughter with the employee for adoption *or foster care*," and "son or daughter" is specifically defined to include a "foster child." H.R. 770 §§103(a)(1)(B), 101(11); S. 345 §§103(a)(1)(B), 102(12) (emphasis added).

56. See n. 54 above.

57. See n. 53 and 54 above.

58. ME. REV. STAT. ANN. tit. 26, §843(5) (West 1988) ("'[s]erious illness' means an accident, disease or condition that . . . [p]oses imminent danger of death; . . . [r]equires hospitalization involving an organ transplant, limb amputation or other procedure of similar severity; or . . . [a]ny mental or physical condition that requires constant in-home care.").

59. The House bill defines "'serious health condition'" as "an illness, injury, impairment, or physical or mental conditions [*sic*] which involves—(A) inpatient care in a hospital, hospice, or residential health care facility, or (B) continuing treatment or continuing supervision by a health care provider." H.R. 770, cited in n. 27 above, at §101(10); see also S. 345, cited in n. 27 above, at §102(11). "'Health care provider'" is in turn defined as "any person licensed under Federal, State, or local law to provide health care services, or . . . any other person determined by the Secretary [of Labor] to be capable of providing health care services." H.R. 770, §101(7); S. 345, §102(6). Connecticut's and Wisconsin's definitions of serious illness are virtually identical to the proposed federal definition. CONN. GEN. STAT. ANN. §5–248a(c) (West Supp. 1989); WIS. STAT. ANN. §103.10(1)(g) (West Supp. 1988).

60. See n. 53, 54, and 59 above.

61. CONN. GEN. STAT. ANN. §§5–248a(f), 5–248b (West Supp. 1989) ("commissioner of administrative services" to report annually starting July 1, 1989, to General Assembly "on the extent of use by permanent employees of leaves of absence . . . in the preceding twelve-month period, and the impact of such use on state employment"; state agencies to report periodically to the state commissioner on "their current experience with leaves of absence.").

62. The report of the House Committee on Education and Labor stated "Recent studies provided to the Committee indicate that men and women are out on medical leave approximately equally. Men workers experience an average of 4.9 days of work loss due to illness or injury per year, while women workers experience 5.1 days per year." H.R. REP. No. 101–28, 101st Cong., 1st Sess., pt. 1 (1989), p. 15. There are no reported data on male use of parental or family leave in the United States, but Sweden has a generous system of paid parental leaves, with reported data on its use by men. Although women still use it more than men, male use has steadily increased. By 1983, 25 percent of fathers used it in the first 6 months after birth, for an average of 1 month, and 30 percent used it in the second 6 months for an average of 10 days. Male use of the leave for the care of sick children was even higher, with 200,000 fathers and 270,000 mothers using it for this purpose in 1983, for the same average amount of time by each sex. Soren Kindlund, "Family Policy in Sweden" (1984), paper presented at a seminar entitled "The Working Family: Perspectives and Prospects in the U.S., Canada, and Sweden," co-sponsored by the Swedish Information Service and the Swedish embassies in Ottawa and Washington, D.C., May, Washington, D.C., p. 6, cited in Williams, "Equality's Riddle" (1985, p. 378 n. 213).

63. The House and Senate bills have slightly different versions. H.R. 770

allows intermittent leave when it is medically necessary for either the worker (medical leave) or the ill family member (family leave); however, this is an absolute right for the worker's own serious health condition, but contingent on employer approval when it is a family member who needs care. H.R. 770, cited in n. 27 above, at §§103(a)(3), 104(a)(2). On the Senate side, it is always the employee's right to take intermittent leave for these purposes, without employer approval. S. 345, cited in n. 27 above, at §§103(a)(3), 104(a)(3).

Both bills allow use of family leave on a reduced-leave basis, but only with employer approval. H.R. 770, §103(b); S. 345, §103(b). ("Upon agreement between the employer and the employee, leave under this section may be taken on a reduced leave schedule, however, such reduced leave schedule shall not result in a reduction in the total amount of leave to which the employee is entitled").

64. WIS. STAT. ANN. §103.10(3)(d), (4)(c) (West Supp. 1988) ("employee may take family leave as partial absence from employment"; "employee may schedule medical leave as medically necessary").

65. MINN. STAT. ANN. §181.942(3) (West Supp. 1989) ("employee, by agreement with the employer, may return to work part time during the leave period without forfeiting the right to return to employment at the end of the leave period").

66. See nn. 29 and 32 above.

67. S. 345, cited in n. 27 above, at §102(4) ("employer" covers "any person engaged in commerce or in any industry or activity affecting commerce who employs 20 or more employees at any one worksite for each working day during each of 20 or more calendar work weeks in the current or preceding calendar year"); H.R. 770, cited in n. 27 above, at §101(5)(A) ("50 or more employees" in the "3-year period beginning after the effective date of this title," and "35 or more employees" thereafter). The earliest versions of the bills reached the smallest employers. H.R. 2020, introduced on April 4, 1985, covered employers of "one or more employees," cited in n. 27 above, at §101(3); and H.R. 4300, introduced on March 4, 1986, covered employers of "five or more," cited in n. 27 above, at §102(3)(A).

68. H.R. REP. 101–28, cited in n. 27 above, at 24. The report notes: "The exemption of employers with less than 50 employee [sic] means that 95% of all employers are excluded from the coverage of the bill and 44 percent of all employees are exempted. An exemption of employers with less than 35 employees excludes 92 percent of all employers."

The key-employee provision is found only in the House bill, H.R. 770, cited in n. 27 above, at §106(b)(2), and does set some limits on employers' use of it. To be denied a leave, the key employee must be salaried and "among the . . . highest paid 10 percent of employees, or . . . 5 highest paid employees, whichever is greater." The employer must also find that denying the leave is "necessary to prevent substantial and grievous economic injury to the employer's operations," and so notify the employee on leave; only if the employee then decides not to return can he or she be fired. H.R. 770, §106(b)(1). The one-year service requirement is found in both bills. H.R.

770, §101(3)(A); S. 345, cited in n. 27 above, at 102(A). The original bill, H.R. 2020, contained none of these provisions.

69. H.R. 2020, cited in n. 27 above, tit. II (entitled a "Commission to Recommend Means to Provide Salary Replacement for Employees Taking Parental and Disability Leaves").

70. See n. 63 above. H.R. 770, cited in n. 27 above, at tit. III, is now entitled simply "Commission on Family and Medical Leave," and the commission is no longer specifically directed to study and recommend ways to provide for paid leaves, although the language is broad enough to allow that result. (Commission to study "existing and proposed policies relating to family leave and temporary medical leave." H.R. 770, §302(1)(A).)

71. WASH. REV. CODE ANN. §49.12.270 (West Supp. 1989) ("An employer shall allow an employee to use the employee's accrued sick leave to care for a child of the employee under the age of eighteen with a health condition that requires treatment or supervision.").

72. S.C. CODE ANN. §8–11–40 (Law. Co-op. 1986 & Supp. 1988) ("'immediate family' means a spouse, children, mother, father, a spouse's mother and father, legal guardian, a spouse's legal guardian, and grandchildren if the grandchild resides with the employee, and the employee is the primary caretaker of the grandchild"). The provision grants state employees 15 days of paid sick leave per year, which can accrue to a maximum of 180 days, so the 5-day limit on use for family care purposes leaves many more days of leave potentially untapped.

73. Mo. ANN. STAT. §105.271(2) (Vernon Supp. 1989). The leave is for the "purposes of arranging for the adopted child's placement or caring for the child after placement." See §105.271(1). It is also keyed to the leave granted "biological parents," as are the adoptive leaves provided by the Colorado and New York statutes. COLO. REV. STAT. §19–5–211(1.5) (Bradford Supp. 1988) ("employer who permits paternity or maternity time off for biological parents following the birth of a child shall, upon request, make such time off available to individuals adopting a child"; "any other benefits provided . . . such as job guarantee or pay, shall be available to both adoptive and biological parents on an equal basis"); N.Y. Labor Law §201–c(1) (McKinney Supp. 1989) (adoptive parents "entitled to the same leave upon the same terms" as the leave given employees upon the birth of their children). It may sometimes be hard to know what an "equal basis" is for adoptive parents. Should their employment rights be compared to those of the woman giving birth who has medical problems and therefore frequently gets paid sick leave, or to the father who has no medical problem and therefore will typically get at most a short, unpaid, parental leave?

74. CAL. UNEMP. INS. CODE §§2601–3272 (West 1986 & Supp. 1989); HAW. REV. STAT. §§392–1 to –101 (1985 & Supp. 1988); N.J. STAT. ANN. §§43:21–25 to –56 (West 1962 & Supp. 1988); N.Y. WORK. COMP. LAW §§200–242 (McKinney 1965 & Supp. 1989); R.I. GEN. LAWS §§28–39–1 to – 41–33 (Michie 1986 & Supp. 1988). Some of these programs are funded entirely through a small tax on employees. For example, California requires

employees to contribute a tax varying from 0.1 to 1.2 percent of their salary, with the tax not applying to salaries above a defined maximum amount (after January 1, 1991, $32,429). CAL. UNEMP. INS. CODE §§984, 985, 2655, 2901 (West 1986 & Supp. 1990).

REFERENCES

American College of Obstetricians and Gynecologists (1974). "Policy Statement on Pregnancy-Related Disabilities." March 2.

Babcock, Barbara Allen, Ann E. Freedman, Eleanor Holmes Norton, and Susan Deller Ross (1975). *Sex Discrimination and the Law: Causes and Remedies.* Boston: Little, Brown.

Kamerman, Sheila B., Alfred J. Kahn, and Paul W. Kingston (1983). *Maternity Policies and Working Women.* New York: Columbia University Press.

Kindlund, Soren (1984). "Family Policy in Sweden." Paper presented at a seminar entitled "The Working Family: Perspectives and Prospects in the United States, Canada, and Sweden." Co-sponsored by the Swedish Information Service and the Swedish embassies in Ottawa and Washington, D.C. May, Washington, D.C.

Krieger, Linda J., and Patricia N. Cooney (1983). "The Miller–Wohl Controversy: Equal Treatment, Positive Action and the Meaning of Women's Equality." *Golden Gate University Law Review* 13: 513–72.

"Note: Sexual Equality Under the Pregnancy Discrimination Act" (1983). *Columbia University Law Review* 83: 690–726.

Personnel Policies Forum (1983). "Policies on Leave from Work." PPF Survey no. 136. Washington, D.C.: Bureau of National Affairs, Inc. June.

U.S. Department of Labor, Women's Bureau (1983). *Time of Change: 1983 Handbook on Women Workers.* Bulletin no. 298. Washington, D.C.: Government Printing Office.

Williams, Wendy W. (1985). "Equality's Riddle: Pregnancy and the Equal Treatment/Special Treatment Debate." *New York University Review of Law and Social Change* 13: 325–80.

6 | Legal Aspects of Child Care: The Policy Debate Over the Appropriate Amount of Public Responsibility

Lucinda M. Finley

The problem of child care for working parents is currently receiving prominent media and political attention. During the 100th Congress, members introduced more than a hundred bills that would affect child care (Reisman, 1989). Persistent clamor for Congress and state legislatures to do something in response to the growing need creates the impression that at present the law has little involvement with or impact on the provision or financing of child care services.

In one sense this impression could hardly be farther from the truth. Virtually every substantive area of the law touches on child care.[1] For example, constitutional law may control whether regulatory schemes can exempt some types of services, or whether the government can support church-related child care centers.[2] Tax law, both federal and state, figures prominently, through deductions and credits, in helping individuals and businesses afford child care services. Equal employment opportunity laws, including state parental leave and maternity leave legislation, can shape what employers offer workers, especially mothers, to help them rear their children and retain their jobs. Other labor laws, such as state unemployment compensation schemes, can affect whether someone who is out of work because of child care problems receives any income replacement. Another labor law, the federal Fair Labor Standards Act (FLSA), can bring the minimum wage/maximum hour requirements to bear on some kinds of child care providers. Federal welfare laws, such as Aid to Families with Dependent Children (AFDC), and Title XX of the Social Security Act, the Social Services Block Grant program, affect the availability of child care for low-income women. Corporate and other business laws will affect the form of business operation for child care centers, while zoning and land use laws determine whether child care facilities can be located in certain areas. And, finally, there are state regulatory laws, including education laws, that set licensing standards and operating requirements for child care facilities (see generally Grubb, 1985; Murray, 1985).

The federal government's principal support of child care costs comes through tax law, as a form of indirect subsidization. In addition to personal deduction allowances for dependents, which can be considered a form of indirect child care subsidy, section 44A of the Internal Revenue Code (26 U.S.C. §44A)[3] provides for a tax credit for "household and dependent care services necessary for gainful employment." The amount of credit a taxpayer may take is based on the taxpayer's adjusted gross income; those with a lower income may take a greater percentage of expenses as a credit than higher-income taxpayers. There is also a limit on the maximum dollar amount of expenses against which the percentage credit may be taken. Expenses that qualify for the credit include child care costs and the costs of nursery school and private kindergartens. If the child care is provided in a center caring for seven or more children, the center must be in compliance with all state and local regulations. Expenses that do not qualify include the cost of private education after kindergarten, and the costs of transporting a child from home to child care (Murray, 1985). This tax credit program represents by far the largest amount of the federal government's financial contribution to child care, with a value of over $3 billion of tax revenue foregone in 1985, and $4 billion in 1988 (Besharov, 1989, p. 509; Divine-Hawkins and Livingston, 1985, p. 250). But it is an indirect subsidy that does nothing to increase the supply of child care services. And while the cumulative value in terms of revenue foregone to the government may be significant, the amount of tax credit that any one family can take (up to $720 for one child and $1,440 for two children)[4] is far below the actual costs of child care. Moreover, since the credit is not refundable, those who owe little or no taxes will receive no benefit from the credit.

Federal tax law also subsidizes child care by allowing employers to implement Dependent Care Assistance Plans (DCAPs), a form of cafeteria plan for employee benefits. Under these plans employees can elect to have child care costs deducted from their pay, with the deducted amount not counting as taxable income to the employee. In the 1986 Tax Reform Act, however, Congress curtailed cafeteria plans by adding restrictions and reducing the maximum amounts of income that could be sheltered. Perhaps because of continued uncertainty about how Congress and the Internal Revenue Service will treat cafeteria plans in the future, DCAPs have not been widely adopted by employers. This method of reducing taxable income provides the greatest relative benefit to higher-income taxpayers (Murray, 1985, p. 294).

The tax code allows employers to deduct as business expenses certain costs associated with providing child care services to employees. The code also allows favorable depreciation and an investment tax credit for the capital expenses of establishing child care programs (Divine-Hawkins and Livingston, 1985, p. 250). The incentives provided by favorable tax treatment are the principal way in which federal law interacts with employers. These incentives remain the most salient reason some employers do set up various forms of child care assistance for their employees (Kamerman and Kahn, 1987).

Programs providing financial assistance for low-income families are the other principal means by which federal law affects child care services. Title XX of the Social Security Act, now part of the Social Services Block Grant program (42 U.S.C. §602(a)(8)(iii)), provides grants to states for a variety of social service programs. Most states use part of their Title XX grants to subsidize child care for low-income children by buying spaces in day care centers or family day care homes. Under federal law, any center receiving Title XX subsidies must comply with all state regulatory requirements. Thus, many family day care centers, which go largely unregulated, cannot receive Title XX subsidies. Yet family day care, in which a person (usually a woman) takes a few children into her own home, is the day care arrangement most accessible to low-income families (Murray, 1985, pp. 284–87). Federal law also subsidizes child care expenses under the AFDC program for recipients of this form of welfare grant. Child care costs of up to $160 per month per child are considered an allowable work expense, and thus are deducted from, or "disregarded" as part of, a welfare recipient's income in determining the amount of the AFDC award (42 U.S.C. §602(a)). The "child care expense disregard" is based on a recognition that in order to work and thus reduce their financial dependence on welfare, welfare recipients are going to have to obtain child care. The form the assistance takes reflects the same philosophy as the tax credit: people should be free to determine their own arrangements for their children and purchase them on the "free market" (Murray, 1985, p. 295). This child care expense disregard is of limited use to low-income people, however. The maximum amount disregarded is far below the cost of most forms of child care. In addition, AFDC recipients must first pay for child care out of their own limited funds and then be reimbursed through their monthly welfare grant. This arrangement forces poor families to weigh child care against other necessities such as food, shelter, clothing, and transportation.

There are currently few federal laws or regulations concerned with the quality of child care services.[5] In 1985, in response to sensational revelations of sexual abuse in child care programs, Congress passed the Model Child Care Standards Act (Public Law 98-473). This act directed the Department of Health and Human Services to draft model minimum standards for child care. But the department's response was to issue "regulatory options" that were little more than a compilation of the variations in existing state regulations (Grubb, 1985, pp. 318–19, Phillips, 1986). Since 1985, federal law does require that programs receiving federal training funds under Title XX have procedures for checking the background, employment history, and criminal record for child abuse of applicants for jobs (Grubb, 1985, p. 319).

Licensing standards and regulatory oversight of the quality and safety of child care centers thus remain the province of state law. State statutes vary widely in terms of operating standards such as space requirements, staffing ratios, and staff training, and in terms of the kinds of centers regulated: proprietary, not-for-profit, family day care centers, or all forms of care arrangements. Another source of variation is whether centers are regulated as schools by educational authorities, or are specially regulated, or are lumped in with nursing homes, foster care, and other custodial care programs. (For a survey of the variety of state licensing schemes and litigation that has arisen under them as to whether certain kinds of centers can or should be regulated by school authorities as opposed to social service or health authorities, see Grubb, 1985, pp. 320–34).

Programs that receive public subsidies are the most heavily regulated. In terms of the reach of state regulatory statutes, however, the most vexing issue seems to be whether and how to regulate family-based day care. It is estimated that while state regulations effectively reach 95 percent of center-based caregivers, whether nonprofit or proprietary, the same percentage of family-based caregivers escape regulation (Sale, 1984, pp. 21–22). Family day care occurs in providers' homes, raising issues of privacy and freedom from government interference. It is also widespread, with each home caring for only a few children. Many providers think of themselves as "helping out" rather than running a business (Kamerman, 1985, pp. 268–69).

For these reasons family day care is exceedingly difficult to regulate effectively. Several states require only that family day care homes register with the state, and parents are expected to enforce compliance with health and safety standards. Child care that occurs in the parents' home, by a paid caretaker other than the parents, is, of course, even more difficult, practically and philosophically, to regulate. Although the care providers are legally employees of the parents, few employers of domestic workers bother to comply with labor laws such as Social Security and unemployment tax withholding requirements.

The purpose and detail of state regulatory schemes also vary widely. Some states have detailed codes. Others have program "guidelines," or goals, which are often expressed as educational and developmental aspirations. Most states, however, do have regulatory standards that establish minimum requirements for physical space, staff–child ratios, staff training and qualifications, parental involvement, and equipment (Grubb, 1985, p. 328). Child care experts agree that criteria such as space, staff ratios, and staff training are the most significant factors in determining the quality of a child care program, and are thus the most important areas for minimum standards (Morgan, 1984). The wide variations permitted from state to state are therefore cause for concern, especially with the rise of nationwide for-profit child care chains. Chains such as Kinder Care operate their programs differently in different states, tailoring such features as space, equipment, and the size and training of staff to the minimum requirements of each state's law, rather than to some uniform criteria for quality service (Lewin, 1989).

State tax law also has an impact on child care services. More than half the states provide their own tax credits to parents, linked to the federal income tax credit. The tax codes of a handful of states also provide credits to companies that establish child care assistance programs for employees, and generous tax deductions for child care providers to alleviate their operation costs (Trost, 1988). For example, Connecticut offers businesses a 50 percent tax credit, up to $1 million, for the costs of subsidizing employee child care expenses. It also offers a 40 percent credit to offset the expenses of planning, renovating, or acquiring a licensed, nonprofit child care center (Clark, 1987, p. 849). The use of state tax codes to provide employers with incentives to establish child care programs or subsidies appears to be a largely untapped but promising resource.

Another innovative use of state and local law to encourage the creation of more child care services involves land use ordinances. In

1985 San Francisco enacted a land use ordinance, revising the city planning code, to require office developers either to provide space in their projects for child care centers or to pay a fee to a citywide fund used to establish affordable day care (Caplan, 1987). This sort of requirement, known as a child care linkage law, is now being considered by several other communities. On the state level Maryland has a linkage law requiring space for child care facilities in state buildings (Maryland Family Law Code Ann. §§5-586–89 (1988)), and a statewide child care linkage bill passed the Massachusetts House of Representatives in the 1988 legislative session (Hanlon, 1989).[6] Seattle allows developers who include free space for child care in new buildings more square footage than otherwise allowed under city planning ordinances, and other localities have required developers to subsidize child care centers in order to get permission to build commercial complexes (Trost, 1988).

Yet despite the panoply of laws that touch on child care services, in many important ways the law does not sufficiently address the problems parents face trying to fit workplace demands with the necessities of parenting. Nor does the law adequately address the needs of those who provide child care to these parents. The existing laws are often a contradictory maze. For example, state licensing requirements might conflict with local zoning laws (Morgan, 1984, p. 165); state licensing requirements, and efforts to enforce standards, are quite variable; different enforcement agencies, such as fire, building, and health and welfare departments, all have regulatory authority over day care centers; and a program that one court sees as custodial (so that its cost represents a tax deduction for the parents) may look to another court like an educational program subject to the Fair Labor Standards Act.[7] There is a pressing need for unification or coordination of the requirements in each state (Grubb, 1985, pp. 323–24).

In addition to the conflicts and confusion in existing laws, another reason the legal system has not yet adequately responded to the child care crisis is that the laws either run at cross purposes to or fail to respond to the two key (and related) factors that contribute to the perception of a crisis: availability and affordability of quality care. While tax laws provide some financial relief to parents and some incentives for employers to create various forms of assistance, the tax credits help only those who can already find and afford child care. Moreover, they primarily benefit the middle and upper classes.[8] Title XX federal grants to states are only useful to those low-income mothers who can find an opening in a subsidized program. In some states the number of low-income children on the waiting list almost equals the number of low-income children being served (Clark, 1987, p. 839). And under the Reagan administration, in 1981, Title XX funding was cut by 21 percent (Clark, p. 840). By 1985, 22 states, without adjusting for inflation, and 35 states, adjusting for inflation, were spending less on child care than they were spending in 1981 (Blank & Wilkins, 1985, p. 7). The conflicting maze of licensing requirements makes opening and operating a day care center an increasingly expensive proposition, and some would-be providers are deterred from entering the business by the legal hurdles, including liability insurance, and the extremely high start-up costs (Ingrassia, 1988).

There is a growing public clamor, and a consensus is emerging among politicians—even some conservative public officials previously hostile to governmental involvement in "private family matters"—that government and employers need to do more to address the availability and affordability of child care.[9] Whatever form it takes, this "doing more" will unavoidably bring the law more directly and deeply into child care. The legal involvement could take the form of comprehensive federal legislation, or state or local legislative initiatives. It could comprise amendments to federal and state tax codes. Thus, it is necessary for policymakers and advocates squarely to address the fundamental policy issues that historically have colored and shaped, and continue to shape, the debate over the proper role for government and the law in providing, funding, and regulating child care. One's stance on these policy questions will influence one's support for different forms and degrees of legislative intervention.

The Underlying Policy Debates

The key policy debate shaping legal responses to the child care problem is a variant of what has come to be known in the language of feminist legal theory as the public–private split. In this terminology "private" refers to the realm of the family and to notions of individual responsibility and free choice. "Public" can mean either the government or the world of the marketplace and employers, both contrasted with the supposedly purely private sanctity of the family (Finley, 1986; Olsen, 1983). This debate engages us in the following disputes. Is child care a public responsibility of government? Or does a direct governmental role involve undesirable and feared intrusion into the private realm of the family, parental responsibility, and free choice? Is child care a public responsibility of employers, a necessary service and benefit to be provided workers to assist their employment? Or are the workplace and the family separate spheres, such that people with children must find their own way to fit the personal demands of parenthood in with the schedules and expectations of employment, just as people must manage other personal aspects of their lives that are of no concern to employers? If child care is a public responsibility, is it primarily the responsibility of government or employers?

The answer to this last question will be partly determined by another policy debate: what is the principal justification for child care assistance by either the government or employers? Is child care primarily something that helps parents maintain employment, as envisioned by the Internal Revenue Code? Or is the primary purpose of child care services to provide care, education, nutrition, and socialization for children, as envisioned by the federal Head Start program? Or are both purposes inextricably linked, dual needs that policymakers and providers must keep equally in sight? A view of child care as primarily a service directed at parental employment obviously points to advocating that employers assume a greater share of the responsibility for addressing the need. Employers would be deemed to have primary responsibility even though responding to the needs of employed people has also long been an important concern of the federal government, as evidenced by minimum wage, occupational safety, pension protection, and equal employment opportunity laws. If, on the other hand, child care is regarded as primarily a matter of child development, safety, and education, that points to greater involvement by government, especially local governmental bodies such as school and child welfare authorities. The position that parental employment assistance and child development are equally important suggests that a partnership between government and employers is the answer. In such a partnership government would provide assistance and services that go beyond and reach more people than whatever services employers can provide, but governmental policy would not ignore incentives or requirements for employers to respond to child care needs.

Related to the issue of how great a responsibility for child care employers should be expected to bear are policy questions stemming from the close connection between equal employment opportunities for women and the availability and affordability of child care. Problems in accommodating their primary responsiblity for childrearing with the structures of the workplace are a principal barrier to obtaining, advancing in, and retaining employment for women. Is it helpful to the effort to produce a more responsible and effective role by both government and employers to characterize child care as a woman's employment issue? If child care is understood as a crucial equality issue for women, do equal opportunity laws offer an overlooked basis for pressuring employers to do more? For which group of women is child care an equal employment issue? Women currently on welfare and trying to break into the workforce? Women with young children who are already employed? The largely female, and poorly compensated, workers who provide the care to children of other workers? Are the interests of these groups of women—consumers and providers of child care—ineluctably in conflict?

A consensus that there should be some public responsibility for making child care services more available and affordable does seem to be emerging among the American working public, women's organizations, children's organizations, labor leaders, and politicians. Thus, the policy debate will become focused on the form that the governmental response should take. What level of government should bear major responsibility—federal, state, or local? Should the government respond directly or indirectly; should its primary role be that of provider, or funder and subsidizer, or regulator? Should subsidies be direct (grants) or indirect (tax credits or deductions)? Should, and how could, government address an often ignored or hidden form of public subsidization of child care services—namely, the poverty-level wages earned by many workers in the child care system? What are the effects of the various forms of governmental intervention on availability of child care, on its affordability, on individual choices and parental liberty, on the operation of the market?

Policymakers, legislators, and legal advocates concerned with child care must carefully ponder all of these issues. It is these latter questions that are currently the subject of intense debate in Congress, as the House and the Senate move on child care bills of sharply differing philosophies.

Justifying and Evaluating the Responsibility of Government and Employers

Crossing the Great Public–Private Divide

Many people in the United States hold a nostalgic and deeply entrenched commitment to the ideology that childrearing is the quintessential private activity and as such should be sacrosanct from governmental intervention. Many who adhere to this ideology fear that any family-oriented action by government is but a toe in the door of pervasive public oversight of what should be private matters. Another prominent but anachronistic American ideology exalts the family with a breadwinner father and a mother who works inside the home caring for the children. This family form is posited not only as traditional and numerically dominant but also as preferred. Not co-incidentally, this family form is also the most consistent with long-standing and slowly eroding gender role ideologies.

The ideological commitment to the traditional family seems to trump the hostility to government intervention, in a curious way. Government policies that promote the male breadwinner/female hearth-tender family are rarely decried as interventionist. Rather, such policies are either ignored or regarded as simply recognizing the "natural order." For example, during the Progressive Era the mother's pension program of the U.S. Children's Bureau, which gave government grants to poor women so that they could stay at home with their children rather than obtain outside employment, did not meet strong objections citing interference in the private family realm (Grubb and Lazerson, 1982, p. 25). Similarly, the income tax system treats the single-wage-earner family more favorably than dual-income married couples and tends to disallow as "personal" (not business-related) many of the expenses families incur when the wife works outside the home (Blumberg, 1971; Wolfman, 1984). The cornerstones of the Social Security system—old age survivor's and disability insurance—are also structured around the assumption that families consist of working fathers and dependent wives in stable marriages. For example, survivor's benefits were available to nondivorced widows, based on the earnings and Social Security tax payments of the deceased husband. Divorced women could not receive survivor's benefits from their former husband, no matter how long they had been married; widowers received survivor's benefits only if they were actually dependent on the deceased wife. In the case of *Califano* v. *Goldfarb*,[10] the Supreme Court found this scheme of gender distinctions to constitute unconstitutional sex discrimination. The case of *Weinberger* v. *Wiesenfeld*[11] struck down another provision assuming women's dependency—a program known as the mother's benefits program. Insurance benefits were not available to surviving widowers with children, even when the father had actually been dependent on the wife's earnings and was the principal caretaker of the children. Surviving widows caring for children, however, were automatically entitled to insurance benefits. Despite Supreme Court decisions eliminating many of the more obvious penalties exacted by the Social Security Act on families who did not fit the traditional model, the presumption of women's dependency still infects the act. Thus, this hallowed facet of federal policy continues to treat women who work outside the home to support their families less favorably (Abromowitz, 1988, pp. 253–66; Kay, 1988, pp. 218–21).

On the other hand, government policies that seem designed to assist those who do not fit the traditional family ideal are frequently castigated as intervention in people's choices about their families. This condemnation occurs even when the assistance is intended to help overcome barriers erected by other systems, such as the value structure of most workplaces, that are built around the fading traditional family. For example, contrast the heated debate over the wisdom of the proposed federal Family and Medical Leave Act (FMLA) and the issue of whether government should help provide child care with the absence of calls for revamping the tax code or the Social Security Act because they favor one family form over others.

Another prominent ideological feature of the perceived dichotomy between public and private is the defense of the family as a realm of personal freedom and private choice. Having children is understood as a private choice and a private responsibility—and thus a private problem. Government should not tell people what they can and cannot do with or for their children. Indeed, many of the key cases establishing the constitutional right to privacy involved challenges to state efforts to exercise authority in the realm of the family and childrearing.[12] This ideology is fraught with contradiction, however, for under the notion of *parens patriae* (literally, "father of his country"), we also look to the state to provide for the welfare of children, to prevent their abuse, to require their education, and to regulate their labor.[13]

Despite the frequent acceptance of state power over children's welfare, the intertwined ideologies of the separation between public and private and the worship of the traditional family create suspicion about a prominent or direct federal role in providing or paying for child care. As one commentator has expressed it, "The tension between public and private responsibility for children has persisted throughout this century, and has played a role in every effort to regulate day care since the progressive era" (Grubb, 1985, p. 309). Thus, although he previously supported day care for poor women, in 1971 President Richard Nixon vetoed the Comprehensive Preschool Education and Child Day Care Act (H. R. 13520, 91st Cong.,

85 Stat. 866, September 24, 1971), which authorized publicly supported child care programs open to all parents. His asserted
grounds for the veto were that day care weakens families and that a
"family-centered" (i.e., "private") approach was preferable to "com-
munal" (i.e., "public") approaches to childrearing (Grubb, 1985, p.
316). Senator Walter Mondale, the vocal sponsor of a child care bill ·
in the early 1970s, was widely denounced at the time as an enemy of
traditional values and the nuclear family, and his bill soon died (Roberts, 1989).

A similar ambivalence surrounds the issue of the employer's role
in providing child care assistance.

For example, reminiscent of the "big brother" concerns about
federal involvement in child care are some commentators' fears that
employers providing child care will paternalistically assume greater
and greater direction over employees' private lives, fostering an un-
healthy dependency on corporate welfare (Kamerman and Kahn,
1987, pp. 189, 296–97).

The ideology of the family as a private realm of personal choice
and responsibility anchors the idea that work and family are two
separate realms of human activity. Under this view, what goes on in
each realm does not concern the other. Thus, employers have not
been expected to provide benefits or work schedules that take into
account such family matters as childbearing, childrearing, and the
care of ill dependents. The difficulty encountered by the primary
caretaking parent in simultaneously meeting work demands and
children's needs is attributed to personal choices made by that parent, and not to the structures and expectations of the workplace.
Employers' responses to these facts of life are regarded as "accommodations," or as "special treatment"—terminology that carries the
connotation of generous gifts, rather than essential components of a
humane and socially responsible workplace (Finley, 1986). It was not
so long ago that employers routinely and legally fired women when
they became pregnant, or refused to hire married women or women
with young children. Rather than being controversial, these actions
were regarded by employers and women alike as recognizing the
natural division between work and family and the natural place of
women within the family realm (Finley, 1986).

The structure of the workplace remains geared to the assumption that the typical worker is a man who has a wife at home to tend
to all the necessities of maintaining a home and rearing children.
For example, the starting and finishing hours of the normal workday are not geared to the opening times of schools, or shops and

services, or day care centers. Performance expectations, especially in white-collar and professional jobs, often include dedication to the job to the exclusion of family concerns. A committed, and thus promotable, worker is expected to be ready and able to work evenings and weekends, and to travel at a moment's notice (Fisk, 1986). The benefits that employers offer are far more likely to be tailored to the worker as an individual, or as a merely economic provider for a family, rather than as a reproducer, nurturer, and caretaker (see Kamerman and Kahn, 1987, for a survey of such benefits). Indeed, one legal scholar has characterized the values and structure of the workplace as fundamentally hostile to working mothers (Frug, 1979).

Prior to the late 1980s, child care was an important issue to employers only during World War II, when women had to work in the factories to replace the men who were off to war. Stimulated by the federal Lanham Act (Public Law 77-137, Title II, §201), which gave federal matching funds for day care centers, many employers sponsored on-site nurseries to care for the children of their female employees. These centers closed when the war ended and the men resumed their "rightful place" in the factories (Grubb, 1985, p. 312; Kamerman and Kahn, 1987, p. 190).

Judicial decisions also reflect the ideology that work and family are such separate realms that employers bear no responsiblity for the job consequences of employees' "private" childbearing choices. For example, in 1976, in *General Electric* v. *Gilbert*,[14] the Supreme Court held that an employer's failure to cover pregnancy under its disability insurance plan was not discriminatory, even though all temporary disabilities that could visit men were covered. The Court reasoned that pregnancy was unique and, unlike other reasons people might temporarily be unable to work, a voluntary condition. The Court's focus on the "voluntariness" of childbearing expresses the idea that there is no connection between the workplace and female workers' status as mothers. More recently, in 1987, in *Wimberly* v. *Labor and Industrial Relations Commission of Missouri*,[15] the Supreme Court held that a woman who was out of work because her employer did not offer job-protected maternity leave was ineligible for unemployment compensation. The state statute examined by the Court rendered all employees who left work "voluntarily" for no reason attributable to the employer ineligible for unemployment compensation. The Court reasoned that the application of this statute to women who were out of work because of pregnancy was not forbidden discrimination based on pregnancy, since all workers who left work for non-job-related reasons were treated the same. The Court failed to address the fact that the only reason Sharon Wimberly was out of work was that her employer did not hold her job for her while she was on maternity leave. That the Court did not even regard the lack of job-protected maternity leave as salient reflects the entrenched nature of the assumption that workplace structures and policies are completely unrelated to the choices, options, and consequences of childbearing and childrearing.

Pressure generated by the dramatic recent changes in the demographics of the workforce is changing these attitudes about public and private responsibility. Recitation of the changes in women's participation in the workforce in the past 10 to 15 years has become a standard litany in discussions of child care, yet they bear repeating here. Women now constitute approximately 45 percent of the workforce. Well over half of all women with children under 18, and 54 percent of women with children under 6, are working outside the home. It is becoming more and more likely that women will return to and remain in the workforce after bearing children. Approximately 20 percent of the workforce—men and women—have preschool-aged children (Kamerman and Kahn, 1988, p. 12). These statistics do not even reflect the women who would like to obtain employment but cannot because of the lack of child care. Nor do they measure mothers who are trying to juggle the time demands of education and training programs with the responsibilities of childrearing. These trends have made the need for expanded and affordable child care for working parents a pressing practical issue. Practical need often leads people to look to the government or to employers for help, despite ideological commitments to private choice and private responsibility.

Another factor contributing to the growing acceptance of some public responsibility for child care is the increasing presence of the state and the legal system in childrearing decisions. The idea that the family is a private realm guarded from legal intervention is now largely a myth. Increased legal scrutiny of parenting has come about in part because of growing awareness of child abuse. The impact of the mushrooming drug problem on younger and younger victims, either because of violence or addicted parents or acquired immune deficiency syndrome (AIDS), and the increased presence of families with young children among the homeless population, are also bringing more legal intervention in families. The legal apparatus that intervenes in the family through abuse or neglect proceedings, or through the welfare system, primarily affects poor families. But legal judgments about parenting are also reaching across the class spec-

trum in the form of divorce proceedings and custody decrees. Iron-
ically, while the spurt in divorces has involved the law more heavily
in scrutinizing how families conduct themselves and in making judgments about parental fitness, it has also led to more single-parent
families. The growth in such families has, in turn, increased both the
need for child care and the calls for more governmental involvement.

Enhanced knowledge about childhood development and socialization has produced awareness about the connection between quality
child care when children are young and the prevention of abuse,
delinquency, dropping out, and poverty later. This connection has
become one of the principal justifications for a governmental role in
providing child care assistance.[16] States have found that every dollar
spent on quality programs for young children leads to many more
social service dollars saved later (Clark, 1987, p. 851).

But the reasons government should help to *provide* child care services, and not just help make them more affordable for those who
can already buy them, run deeper than just breaking the cycle of
poverty and abuse. Children are more than their parents' treasured
possessions—they are a vital public resource. They are the future
generations of workers, producers, consumers, entrepreneurs, scientists, researchers, teachers, and parents. Widely available quality
child care that offers development, nutrition, socialization, and affection, along with custodial services, presents an opportunity to increase the capacities and health of the future adult population.
Thus, the arguments for government involvement in child care can
be quite similar to the arguments for a public role in education.
And, as understanding about child development and the learning
capacities of young children is augmented, the notion that public
education need not or cannot start until a certain age becomes out-
moded.

Government in the United States addresses virtually every important social need, free market rhetoric notwithstanding: education,
transportation, communication, public safety, defense, food quality
and availability, and housing safety, availability, and cost. Quality,
safety, and availability of child care certainly deserve to be on this
list. A public response is warranted because the need exceeds the
resources of the private market, largely because of the limited ability
of many parents to pay for quality care and the limited benefit structure of the employment market.

Inequities in the private market also justify a role for government. After all, concerns about equality led to significant govern-

ment intervention in the employment standards of the private market. If the private market of child care providers is left completely alone by government, the present tendency toward a two-tier child care system will be exacerbated. Higher-quality care plays down the purely custodial role and puts greater emphasis on learning and development, on smaller staff–child ratios, and on professionally trained staff. Yet such care costs much more than more custodial arrangements, such as family day care. High-quality day care centers are fast becoming available only to middle- and upper-middle-class parents, or to the few low-income parents able to get their children off waiting lists and into places subsidized by Title XX. While family day care arrangements currently are used by a majority of those who need child care, studies reveal that most parents would prefer to enroll their children in child care centers with a developmental component if more places were available and they could afford to do so (Grubb, 1985; Murray, 1985). Without governmental activity to increase the supply and subsidize the cost of quality day care, we may be faced with "yuppie day care" for already socially advantaged children, and custodial day care for the socially disadvantaged. Such a situation promises to increase the already troubling gaps in opportunity that contribute to so many societal problems.

Since the quality of care provided in day care centers is determined by factors that are susceptible to regulation, such as group size, physical space, staff–child ratios, and staff qualifications (Murray, 1985, p. 287), there is strong justification for a governmental role in setting minimum standards. There would appear to be no reason why minimum quality standards should vary from state to state. A federal role in standard setting may be necessary to ensure adherence to quality minimums. Another justification for a public role in standard setting is that the ability of parents to make active and in-depth assessments is practically limited. A parent already struggling with the delicate balancing act between work expectations and family responsibilities has little time to research child development guidelines, to visit numerous centers, to review staff members' educational backgrounds, to interview staff, to inspect physical plants, and to observe several group sessions. Although many parents might want to be this actively involved, most have to choose child care on the basis of the convenience, for them, of the cost, location, hours, and ages of children served (Browne, 1985).

But what about the concern that an increased governmental role, particularly at the federal level,[17] in setting quality standards for child care services will unduly interfere with parents' private rights and choices? It seems a curious and tenuous leap from the government's ensuring a greater supply of a service many people want to the government's compelling people who do not want that service to use it. Just as private schools and private mail and delivery services flourish and innovate in the face of government-run systems, so, too, non-government-supported day care arrangements, such as domestic help in the child's home or family day care in a provider's home, are likely to survive and prosper. After all, many parents will still prefer these forms to regulated and subsidized centers or schools. Where there is a demand, there is likely to be a market.

For those who are concerned about preserving and defending that vanishing breed, the "traditional" family, fear of government support for child care seems especially misplaced. Increased availability of child care is not the reason this family form is in decline. While it is no doubt true that some of the "ideal" mothers who do not work are at home because of the lack of child care, this arrangement cannot confidently be proclaimed their true or natural choice. If a governmental response to the need for child care results in more women working outside the home, the availability of day care will hardly be the only factor. Economic and psychic need, ambition, intelligence, curiosity, and desire for social stimulation will all play a role in their decisions to work.

It may be true, however, that greater governmental involvement in child development by subsidizing and setting standards for child care will lead to greater governmental scrutiny of parents. The incorporation into parental termination or custody proceedings of "best interests of the child" standards from the child psychology and development professions has brought more legal oversight of parenting. Similarly, government-set child care quality standards might subtly influence legal "good parent" criteria. This kind of involvement can have a positive impact, however. It can increase awareness of how to spot abuse, and it can cause parents who need help to get it sooner. It can also get parents more involved in the healthy development of their children, to the benefit of the whole family system, as has happened through the Head Start program (Miller, 1987). Those who are concerned that a governmental role in providing child care might lead to excessive governmental intrusion into people's homes and childrearing preferences can look to the ideology of privacy and nonintervention itself as a source of solace. The strength of this ideology, and the constitutional liberties built upon it, will serve as an important check on controversial actions. The constitutional rights of parents will survive public assistance for child care.

All of the above justifications for public responsibility for child care are directed at the needs and interests of children and society. The employment-related needs of parents are also a fertile source of arguments in support of expanded governmental responsibility. In a market society such as ours, work is crucial to economic survival and to self-image. A supply of workers is also vital to the continuation of the economy. For these dual reasons of individual and market need, the government, both federal and state, has often stepped in to support and encourage work, and to ease its dislocations. Thus, we have minimum wage and maximum hour laws, workers' compensation laws, equal employment opportunity laws, equal pay laws, an unemployment compensation system, pension laws, disability insurance laws in some states, and, in a growing number of states, maternity and parental leave laws. An affordable and adequate supply of child care services is becoming just as necessary for the facilitation and support of work, given current demographics, as adequate pay, injury compensation, pension protection, and equal opportunity.

Just as the incapacities or imperfections of the private market necessitated a public response to these other needs, market inadequacies also compel public assistance for child care. Throughout the country millions of parents and children need child care services. But at any individual workplace only a minority of workers need it at any one time. Moreover, the individual need is not sustained throughout the work career, since children grow up and the school system assumes a greater role. Consequently, many employers do not feel great pressure to elevate the provision of child care services to a high place on their benefits agenda (Kamerman and Kahn, 1987). Some employers who have directly provided child care services for their employees have found that the need does not remain large and ongoing enough to warrant the expense; small and medium-sized employers find child care services especially hard to justify economically (Kamerman and Kahn, 1987, p. 216). The trend in employer assistance is toward information and referral services, limited financial assistance, or reserving places in existing programs. Employers are moving away from taking actions to increase the supply of child care services (Kamerman and Kahn, 1987, pp. 191–206). Thus, the need for an increased supply of affordable child care services is not likely to be addressed satisfactorily if left to the private sector alone. Yet employers certainly have a major role to play. Inducements to employers to expand the assistance offered to employees should be an important component of any public policy response to the child care problem.

The arguments advanced to justify action by employers usually rely on market rationales, such as increased productivity, reduced absenteeism, and greater loyalty from the workforce (Browne, 1985). There is currently little evidence, however, that employer child care benefits actually have a direct impact on productivity. If studies do not bear out a measurable correlation, appeals to economic interest will prove of limited usefulness in persuading employers to assume more responsibility for child care. Nor is the desperate need of many employees, especially women, for workplace policies that are responsive to their family roles likely to be a sufficient inducement to employers. As we have noted, the assumption that family responsibilities are a private matter with no connection to the workplace runs too deep. Justifications for increased employer responsibility must directly confront this assumption by addressing the ways in which workplace structures, policies, or lack of policies are every bit as responsible for the problems confronting workers as the workers' "private" and "voluntary" childbearing choices.

The workplace and the family are not two separate realms, but rather intertwined parts of people's lives (Finley, 1986; Taub, 1985). What happens in people's families can have a great impact on their opportunities and satisfaction at work. Expectations and policies at work can make it more or less difficult for a person to manage the dual responsibilities of parent and employee. For example, once employers stopped firing women for becoming pregnant, and started covering pregnancy under disability plans and offering limited maternity leave, most women started returning to work to enjoy productive careers after childbearing. This disproved the formerly fashionable argument that it was "natural" for women to stop work, and that their cessation of work had nothing to do with employer attitudes and policies.

The same connection exists between employer policies and child care. Women who work for employers who provide parental leave, flexible scheduling, and child care assistance, and who allow sick leave time to be used when a dependent is ill, will find that having children presents far fewer barriers to successful participation and advancement in the workforce than will women who work for unresponsive employers. None of the structures of the workplace are natural or inevitable. Rather, they are dictated by employer choices and values, and by assumptions about gender roles and the relationship between family and work. These structures, such as the eight-hour day and five-day week, have been feasible for employers only because "the family structure provided the services necessary to make the [male] labor available. The real cost of employing a worker who has children includes the cost of hiring someone to care for the children so that the parent–worker is free to devote his or her services elsewhere. Child care is a cost of producing that employers have avoided paying until recently. [Their avoidance] is unfair to women, who continue to bear a disproportionate amount of the cost" (Fisk, 1986, p. 96). Because employer-created structures are a large part of the problem that makes child care such a pressing need, employers must be part of the solution.

Keeping the Needs of Both Children and Parents in Sight

The reasons government and employers must take a large measure of public responsibility for child care are based on both the developmental needs of children and the employment needs of parents. Neither set of needs should crowd out the other in the policy debates or in legal responses. Policymakers need to be aware that certain initiatives respond more to one need than to the other, and should take care to see that both are addressed by any comprehensive legislative response to the child care problem. Thus, policies that use the tax system to provide financial relief to parents and to provide incentives to employers are incomplete because they do little to address the quality and supply issues that are important to the developmental needs of children. Similarly, regulations that rely solely on social service financing agencies, or that lump child care providers in with foster homes or state custodial institutions and fail to bring in educational authorities, may put too much emphasis on custodial concerns to the detriment of educational and developmental opportunities. Legislative responses to child care should clearly state that child care services relate both to children's developmental needs and to the needs of the labor market. Drafters should look to eliminate inconsistencies between various regulatory schemes that demand that child care services be either solely custodial or totally educational.

Expanding Employment Opportunities for Women

The justifications advanced above for increased employer responsibility suggest that the workplace's persistent lack of responsiveness to family needs presents significant employment opportunity barriers for women, because they still shoulder far greater responsibility for childrearing than men. Indeed, the U.S. Commission on Civil Rights (1981) identified the connection between child care and employment barriers for women as a crucial and relatively overlooked policy issue. The commission called for increased use of existing equal employment opportunity legislation to address the absence of child care policies. Other scholars have asserted that child care services may be at least as important for achieving workplace equality for women as equal pay, affirmative action, punishment of sexual harassment, and maternity leave (Fisk, 1986; Frug, 1979; Kamerman, 1985).

Difficulties in obtaining child care may prevent women from taking advantage of educational opportunities and training programs to enhance their employment prospects. Child care requirements can also prevent women from changing jobs or accepting promotions that require longer hours, overtime, evening or weekend work, or travel. The cost of child care can also discourage women from getting off welfare and into employment. Child care problems may also cause women to take excessive sick days because they must stay home when the child is sick, or repeatedly to come in late because child care is unavailable or hard to get to. The absences and latenesses are held against the workers and may lead to discharge, discipline, lack of promotion, or poor references. And women have been denied unemployment compensation because they have refused to accept "suitable work," even though their refusal was due to child care problems: either they could not find child care, or the job was too far from child care, or the shift times conflicted with parenting duties (Pearce, 1985). Moreover, many women "choose" to work part time because of child care responsibilities, even though part-time work usually offers low pay and few benefits and contributes to the disadvantaged economic status of women.

. Given these numerous ways that lack of adequate child care can adversely affect women's employment opportunities, it is curious that it has not been the subject of much equal employment litigation. Nor has it, until recently, been a priority for feminist organizations. Sheila Kamerman has asserted that the lack of leadership and initiative by women's organizations is a major reason no significant child care legislation emerged from the federal or state governments in the 1980s (Kamerman, 1985, p. 260).

The women's movement has tended to focus its energies on employment issues that treat women as individual competitors with men, rather than as people embedded in family networks that situate them in relation to the labor market quite differently from men. The legal framework of equality has also been much more suited to this individualistic and nonstructural emphasis (Dowd, 1989; Finley, 1986). The legal vision of equality assumes white men as the norm

against which other groups are measured, and thus it defines inequalities as those practices that treat groups such as women differently from white men when the women are otherwise similarly situated.

Many legal activists in the women's movement have been particularly reluctant to argue for structural changes in the workplace,
such as maternity leave, necessitated by the fact that women are differently situated in society from men because of their reproductive
and childrearing roles. The fear, not unfounded, is that any arguments that women are different from men will always wind up being
used to justify women's disadvantaged position (Williams, 1985). But
the danger that women will be penalized for acknowledgment of
their different needs in the workplace is likely to be reduced by two
factors: an increased understanding of the connection between
workplace family policies (or lack thereof) and women's employment
opportunities; and the growing awareness among lawyers, judges,
and policymakers of the male bias that permeates the "sameness"
vision of equality.[18] Perhaps the organized women's movement's recent embrace of child care and parental leave as legislative priorities
stems from the realization that arguments that "women are just like
men and need no different policies" are of limited usefulness in confronting the current pressing employment needs of women.

Still, some caution that it is not helpful to characterize child care
as a women's issue. They argue that employers, because of persistent
male bias and the marginal roles of most women workers, are likely
to dismiss as unimportant anything styled as a need solely of women
workers. Women's employment issues have rarely achieved the legislative attention that men's (i.e., human) employment needs have.
Moreover, there is some concern that responses tailored to women,
such as lengthy periods of childrearing leave, will only reinforce
pressure on women to stay home and withdraw from the workforce
while their children are young. A woman-focused argument might
entrench sexist societal attitudes that women are naturally better
suited to be, and thus should be, primarily responsible for child care
(Fisk, 1986, p. 106; Williams, 1985, p. 377). No doubt some who are
eager to push women down the "mommy track" subscribe to these
views.

Child care is one of those issues that simultaneously have a lot to
do with gender and transcend gender (Dowd, 1989). Certainly more
workplace responsiveness to family life and expanded availability of
child care will benefit men and women workers, fathers as well as
mothers. But since men have not been disadvantaged in the employ-

ment market by their family roles, child care, while important for both men and women, is an *equal* employment opportunity issue only for women. Seeing it this way does not mean we have to lose sight of and never mention the benefits to men and children. Addressing the particular employment-related needs of women does not mean that policies such as childrearing leaves should be available only to women. In order to minimize the danger of playing into traditional notions about women's role, we must propose and implement gender-neutral solutions to the child care problem. In addition, we must justify these solutions not only with arguments about women's needs, but also by making constant reference to the interconnection between work and family and the consequent necessity of restructuring workplaces. As Nancy Dowd has said:

> Legislation must be carefully examined to ensure that it does not perpetuate a stunted male role of father solely as breadwinner; that it does not reconstruct a subservient, undervalued, dominated female role; and that it does not require a male-headed, male-dominant, or male-female dual-parent family as the essential form. . . . it is not simply a matter of adding women to work and men to family, or integrating the values of each sphere to reflect the other, but requires rethinking and changing work and family and their relationship to each other. (Dowd, 1989, pp. 170–71)

An advantage of emphasizing the connection between child care and women's equal employment opportunity in policy debates is that strategies and responses *in addition to* tax relief and government subsidization will be called for. The full dimensions of the problem—its public and private impacts—can be addressed more comprehensively. Another advantage of thinking of child care as a women's equal employment issue is that a broader spectrum of women may benefit. The lowest-paid and least skilled women workers are likely to suffer the greatest disadvantage from the lack of workplace responsiveness to child care: they can least afford quality child care, and they work in the least flexible and forgiving jobs. Keeping the needs of these women in mind will lead to a consideration of policy initiatives other than the ones that currently predominate. As Sheila Kamerman has written, the focus "on increasing consumer subsidies through the tax system or through incentives for employers to subsidize employees' child care service purchases certainly adds to the amount and diversity of supply, but it still does not assure quantitative adequacy, quality, or equal access to all parents desiring and needing care and is probably least helpful to the lowest-paid workers" (Kamerman, 1985, p. 260).

Legislative responses addressing the equal employment aspects of child care could include the following: States or the federal government could adopt laws, similar to maternity and parental leave legislation, requiring employers to provide all workers, including part-time workers, with a certain amount of sick leave, and specifying that sick leave can be used by both female and male employees when a dependent is ill. Congress could significantly increase the amount of the child care expense disregard under AFDC; Congress and states could require all employers or educational institutions that receive government funds or contracts to provide certain kinds of assistance with child care as a condition of receiving the public funds. Just as Title VII was amended by the Pregnancy Discrimination Act of 1978 and many states' equal employment laws were also amended to prohibit employment discrimination on the basis of pregnancy, equal employment opportunity statutes could be amended to ban discrimination against women or men on the basis of parental role or childrearing responsibilities. Such an amendment should also specify that workplace structures, requirements, policies, or lack of policies that have a disparate impact on workers with principal childrearing responsibilities constitute discrimination. Proposals to fund parental leave, by, for example, using the Social Security or unemployment tax or disability insurance systems, should be elevated to the top of the policy agenda. As long as leave is unfunded, it will not really be a viable option for low-income or single parents. So unfunded leave perpetuates the disparate impact of present workplace structures for the groups that most need relief.

The suggestion that Title VII should be amended is necessitated by recent court decisions that have seriously undermined the usefulness of discrimination law for reaching structural employment barriers. In 1971 the U.S. Supreme Court ruled in *Griggs* v. *Duke Power Co.*[19] that racially neutral employment policies with a disparate impact on the work opportunities of protected groups could be set aside as a form of employment discrimination. In the same year the Court ruled in *Phillips* v. *Martin Marietta Corp.*[20] that an employer's refusal to hire women, but not men, with small children violated Title VII. Such a policy could be deemed nondiscriminatory only if the employer met the heavy burden of proving that women's conflicting family obligations were so much more relevant to women's job performance than to men's that lack of such responsibilities could amount to "a bona fide occupational qualification reasonably necessary to the normal operation" of the business.

Picking up on the implications of these rulings, in 1979 legal scholar Mary Joe Frug offered a compelling argument that workplace structures, expectations, and lack of policies amounted to labor market hostility to working mothers and could be considered a form of disparate-impact discrimination (Frug, 1979). In another promising legal event of the late 1970s, the U.S. Court of Appeals for the Ninth Circuit ruled, in the case of *De La Cruz v. Tormey*,[21] that the plaintiffs could proceed with their suit alleging that lack of child care facilities at a community college deprived the women plaintiffs of equal educational opportunities guaranteed by Title IX of the Education Act. The plaintiffs, young low-income mothers seeking an education to improve their job prospects, had asserted that the discrimination was intentional. The community college district officials had actively opposed all efforts of students and community groups to establish child care facilities. They had also denied college space for child care cooperatives, and had turned down money from the state board of education to fund off-campus child care centers. While the court did not rule on the merits of the complaint, its action overturning the dismissal of the case by a lower court paved the way for an eventual settlement that brought child care facilities to the district (Maloney, 1981; Murray, 1985, p. 274). In 1983 another promising ruling was issued. In *Abraham v. Graphic Arts International Union*,[22] the U.S. Court of Appeals for the District of Columbia ruled that an employer's failure to have a sick leave policy for temporary and part-time workers doomed women who became pregnant to certain termination and thus constituted disparate-impact discrimination on the basis of pregnancy.

The gist of an employment discrimination case seeking to require an employer to provide child care assistance would be that the employer's policies (such as those covering overtime, travel, promotion, hiring, or restrictive leave) impose adverse job consequences on women because of their gender role as primary childrearers, but do not disadvantage fathers. The theory supporting such a case would be that gender roles that "place primary child care responsibilities upon women, combined with a labor system premised on the male norm of an employee who does not have significant child care responsibilities, cause women more than men to suffer a variety of adverse employment consequences" (Fisk, 1986, p. 98).

This litigation theory has rarely been tried, and cases subsequent to *De La Cruz* have rarely been successful. For example, in *Gifford v. Atchison, Topeka and Santa Fe Railway*,[23] the same court that had decided *De La Cruz*, although refusing to grant the plaintiff relief because her case was not timely, stated that a woman's challenge to an employer's requirement that she travel as part of her job could have gotten relief because the union and the company had adopted the travel policy knowing that it would disadvantage women. But a year later, in *Giocoechea* v. *Mountain States Telephone and Telegraph Co.*,[24] the same court ruled that the plaintiff's theory that the employer's travel requirement adversely impacted on women with childrearing responsibilities did *not* state a claim under Title VII, because the employer had shown that the travel requirement bore a "manifest relationship" to her job. The travel policy therefore was justified by business necessity. In another case brought against a telephone company, yet another court rejected a woman's challenge to a travel requirement as sex discrimination, ruling that the woman had voluntarily declined the proferred promotion because of her personal situation, namely that she had five children to care for and thus did not want a job requiring travel.[25]

The "voluntariness" argument rests on the view that the choices women make are free, unfettered, and personal, rather than attributable to the failure of employers' policies to take childrearing responsibilities into account. Thus, this view rejects the essential theory of a Title VII case in these circumstances. The same understanding of "personal choice" colored the outcome of the *Wimberly* unemployment insurance case, discussed previously. These courts failed to comprehend how women's choices to conform to societal expectations about their mothering role are socially constructed and thus not "free" in a meaningful sense (Finley, 1987).

The meaning of women's choices and their connection to employer policies were hotly contested in *Equal Employment Opportunity Commission* v. *Sears Roebuck and Co.*[26] Feminist historians Alice Kessler-Harris and Rosalind Rosenberg were retained as experts by opposite sides and were pitted against each other in arguing whether the absence of women in highly paid commissioned sales positions at Sears was attributable to discrimination by Sears or to the personal choices and preferences of women. Sears argued that it had tried mightily to find women for these jobs, but that women did not want them because their childrearing roles were incompatible with the jobs' financial risks, long hours, and occasional travel. Kessler-Harris emphasized the ways that employer policies and job structures have shaped or dictated women's "choices." Rosenberg, on the other hand, scrutinized women rather than employers, arguing that throughout history women have willingly sacrificed employment opportunities because of their families and female values. Both the district court and the Court of Appeals accepted Rosenberg's testimony and ruled that women's choices, rather than Sears' policies, were responsible for the lack of women in commissioned sales jobs—a position predicated upon a wholesale acceptance of the public–private dichotomy. The *Sears* case has closed the door on many hopes for using Title VII to overcome those structural barriers to women's employment built upon the assumption that workers do not have principal childrearing responsibility (Eichner, 1988).

A further blow to the prospects for using Title VII occurred during the spring 1989 Supreme Court session. The Court issued a decision all but overruling its venerable decision in *Griggs* that neutral policies with a disparate impact could constitute discrimination. In *Griggs* the Court had ruled that the employer must proffer a reason for the policy that amounted to a business necessity. In *Antonio* v. *Ward Cove Packing Co.*[27] however, the Court ruled that the employer need only suggest some plausible business reason for the policy. The employees then had the virtually insurmountable task of proving that the business connection was not legitimate. Given the wide leeway courts have traditionally given to employers to decide what is and is not in their business interest, *Ward Cove Packing* may make disparate-impact cases impossible to win unless Congress acts to overrule the Court's interpretation of Title VII.

Another barrier to using Title VII is that women burdened by lack of child care must often challenge the *absence* of an employer policy, rather than a specific practice. *Abraham* remains one of the few cases permitting a challenge to the lack of any employer response to a need. Courts are much better able to grasp the discriminatory effects of what is there than of what is not. The difficulty of getting courts to impose affirmative obligations on employers, when added to the likelihood that any employment consequences faced by women will be attributed to their own choices rather than to employer policies, suggests that the prospects are dim for using the courts to prod employers to respond to the child care crisis and its adverse impact on women workers.

The limited comprehension of the effects of what is not provided is not due only to flawed vision on the part of judges. Title VII and other antidiscrimination laws are, by their very design, inadequate instruments for forcing structural change. Litigation is far better suited to telling employers what they may *not* do, or how they have to change discrete practices, than to making employers institute fundamental changes in the assumptions, values, and practices that dictate the structure of the workplace (Dowd, 1989). Thus, without specific statutory action focusing on the connection between work and family, and on how ignoring this connection can adversely affect women's employment opportunities, discrimination litigation will remain an inadequate tool.

Efforts to comprehend child care as a women's equal employment issue must not focus only on the women who need to consume child care to advance their employment. The workers in the child care system, who are and will remain overwhelmingly women, must not be ignored. Given the general devaluation of women's work and caretaking and nurturing skills in our society, it is difficult for child care workers to earn much more than poverty-level wages. The people who look after our cars, our pets, and our gardens earn far more than the people who tend what is supposed to be our most precious resource, our children. The low wages offered child care workers contribute to extremely high staff turnover, which decreases the quality of care. The women who provide family day care may be even more exploited as workers than the women who work in child care centers; many providers, as noted above, see family day care not as work or a business, but as a way of helping out or bringing in a bit of extra money (Kamerman, 1985, pp. 268–69). They are beyond the reach of minimum wage laws and of Social Security and unemployment insurance laws, and they receive no benefits such as pensions or paid vacations or health insurance.

To address these concerns, legislative efforts should not ignore child care workers. Government could increase enforcement efforts to ensure that child care operators are adhering to the minimum wage laws. As part of the operating standards for child care centers, government could require not only certain levels of staff training, but adequate benefits. Increased government subsidies for child care services could be earmarked for salary support and staff training. The federal government could require parents who seek to claim tax credits for care provided in their home to certify that they are making required Social Security and unemployment contributions for their employee. And government might consider requiring family day care providers to operate as a part of a system of providers, with a central organizer who would be deemed their employer and thus responsible for Social Security and unemployment contributions, tax withholding, and benefits.

Concern about the adequacy of wages for child care workers also suggests that the educational approach to child care should be stressed. For example, if government either lowered the age at which children are required to attend school or brought child care under the umbrella of schools, child care workers would likely be considered professional teachers, would be members of teachers' unions, and would receive teachers' salaries and benefits (Liebman, 1989, p. 362).

Affordable care and adequate salaries do not have to be in conflict. Indeed, the need to reduce the possibility of conflict between groups of vulnerable women is an important argument for government subsidization of child care services, which can help ensure more equal access to quality care while reducing the financial pressures that cause centers to keep wages low.

Choosing Between Tax Relief and Direct Subsidies

Now that a consensus seems to have formed in the United States that the government should respond to the great need for child care, the debate has become crystallized around what form the response should take. Two competing bills are presently working their way through Congress. The House bill is supported by the Bush administration and preferred by most self-styled conservatives. The Senate version is known largely as the Democratic bill, although it is supported by conservatives such as Senator Orrin Hatch, a Republican. The positions being staked out essentially depend on views about the appropriate level of governmental responsibility for family matters and the degree of "privacy" to be accorded the family and parenting.

The bill that as of this writing has passed the Senate, the Act for Better Child Care (S. 5, 101st Cong., 1st Sess.), popularly known as the ABC Bill, primarily takes the subsidization and regulation route. The bill, whose principal sponsor is Senator Christopher Dodd (D-Conn.), authorizes federal expenditures to help states establish and expand child care facilities, to train staff, and to subsidize the cost of care for more low- and middle-income families. States must use some of their funds to provide weekend and evening care. The bill also calls for the development of federal quality, health, and safety regulations for subsidized day care centers, supplanting the maze of conflicting state requirements with uniform federal minimums that "reflect the median standards for all States." The bill was modified from its 1988 version, in response to the concerns of church supporters, to allow subsidies for day care based in churches. The estimated amount of the direct federal support for child care called for by this bill is $2.5 billion per year.

Not surprisingly, conservative interests opposed generally to governmental involvement in matters they consider private are opposed to this bill. President Bush, despite pronouncements during his campaign that child care was an urgent national priority, has threatened to veto any bill providing for direct federal subsidies for child care. He espouses the philosophy that by providing direct funds and imposing standards the government is butting into an essentially private domestic decision (Trost, 1988).

The president and others who adhere to the ideology of private responsibility are more sympathetic to a bill recently voted out of the House Ways and Means Committee. Although the eventual cost to the treasury of this bill might be higher than that of the Senate bill—up to $5 billion, largely in tax revenue foregone, is the newspaper estimate (Roberts, 1989)—the federal support is indirect, taking the form of expanded tax credits for low-income taxpayers. The House bill would also change present tax law by making the credit refundable, which means that low-income workers whose tax liability was reduced below zero would receive the unused credit as a tax refund. The House bill also calls for allocating a modest amount, in comparison with the Senate bill, to help states provide child care facilities—$400 million per year for grants to the states. The bill does not envision a federal role in setting uniform quality standards for subsidized care.

The tax credit route chosen by the House bill and preferred by President Bush reflects the ideology of private choice because it would provide financial assistance for whatever arrangements parents prefer for their children. Although its expanded and refundable credits for low-income taxpayers would help such taxpayers, the reality is that approaches using the tax system have the greatest marginal benefit to higher-income people. And the tax credit approach does little to address the problems of availability and affordability. Tax credits are of little use to people who cannot find care arrangements, or who cannot afford, even with some after-the-fact tax relief, the level of care that they would prefer.

Once one accepts any arguments for public responsibility in addressing the need, tailoring the policy response to the ideology of private market and private choice becomes incoherent. Using the tax system may be indirect government support, but it is still involving the government. And people may have to tailor their choices around what qualifies for a tax credit just as much as they may have their choices affected by what is available and what it costs. The tax relief route essentially reinforces the status quo, and therein may lie its strongest appeal to conservatives. It leaves parents to the vagaries of the existing range of services; it perpetuates inequities in access to higher-quality services; it does not reduce the actual out-of-pocket cost of care; it does not alter the current state of conflicting or over-lapping or inadequate state quality standards; it does not reduce regulatory overlap or conflict; it does not address the training or compensation of child care providers. Because it is precisely these aspects of the status quo that contribute to the sense that there is a problem calling for a public response, the response of additional tax relief is wholly inadequate. While the Senate bill will certainly not cure the lack of widely available and equally affordable high-quality care, it is far more of a step in that direction than further tinkering with the tax system.

Left unaddressed by both bills are the problems of children's educational needs, greater employer responsibility and accommodation, and the availability of services for ill children and for infants. A more visionary and comprehensive bill introduced by Representative Augustus Hawkins (D-Calif.), the Child Development and Education Act of 1989 (H.R. 3, 101st Cong., 1st Sess.), would do more to address all the needs than either bill being acted on. This bill would greatly expand Head Start, would provide for widespread school-based child care, and would support services providing infant and toddler care. It would set income eligibility levels for subsidized care, and then would set sliding-fee scales. The federal funds would go mostly to local education agencies, and thus would place principal responsibility for child care squarely within the educational system. Perhaps recognizing that such an extensive level of public involvement in child care would be extremely controversial, Representative Hawkins says that he has introduced the bill to encourage discussion of needs and alternatives not presently addressed in the other legislation. But as more comprehensive proposals such as this one work their way into the discussion, political tolerance for an extensive public role using the in-place and accepted educational system will no doubt increase.

Conclusion

The ongoing tension in the United States between the need for public responsibility for the welfare and care of children and the ideology of private choice in family matters limits the range of immediately possible legislative responses to the pressing need for expanded child care services. Nevertheless, policymakers, wherever they come out on the public–private debate, must be sensitive to every proposal's impact on availability, quality, and affordability. As we have seen, proposals for addressing the need through tax relief do the least to respond to the full dimensions of the problem. It is also important to encourage a greater role for employers, so as to advance the goal of equal employment opportunity for women, and to start restructuring the workplace to reduce the stressful conflict between people's lives as workers and as family members.

NOTES

Acknowledgments. I would like to acknowledge with gratitude the able research assistance of Erin Ringham, J.D. candidate at the State University of New York at Buffalo School of Law.

1. The phrases "child care" and "day care" will be used to refer to care of children performed by people other than the parents, whether the nonparental care is performed in the child's home, in the caretaker's home, or in a profit or nonprofit center.

2. For a full analysis of this issue, which will not be treated in this chapter, see Boothby, 1989; Whitehead, 1989.

3. The tax code had previously allowed a limited deduction for child care expenses. As a deduction from income, rather than credit against taxes owed, the former provision could be used only by itemizers, and it provided a relatively greater benefit to those with higher marginal tax rates (Wolfman, 1984, pp. 156–60).

4. Using House Ways and Means Committee data, Douglas Besharov estimates that in 1988 approximately 9.6 million families will claim tax credits, with an average credit of $419 (1989, p. 509). The average cost of center-based child care, on the other hand, ranges from $2,000 to $3,000 per child per year (Reisman, 1989, p. 474).

5. For a history of federal standard-setting efforts, see Grubb, 1985, pp. 312–19.

6. To assist legislators interested in having linkage laws in their localities, the Harvard Legislative Research Bureau has drafted a proposed model child care linkage law. The text appears in the *Harvard Journal on Legislation* 26 (1989):667–73.

7. Compare *U.S. Department of Labor* v. *Elledge*, 614 F.2d 247 (10th Cir. 1980) (court found program for working parents' children to be a "preschool" subject to the requirements of the FLSA), with *Marshall* v. *Rosemount, Inc.*, 584 F.2d 319 (9th Cir. 1978) (court reached opposite conclusion, finding that a day care center was not a preschool under the FLSA); and *San Francisco Infant School* v. *Commissioner*, 69 T.C. 957 (1978) (tax court denied tax-exempt status to day care program because it was not an "educational program"), with *Zoltan* v. *Commissioner*, 79 T.C. 490 (1982) (tax court found that cost of sending children to a summer camp that had many activities

qualified for dependent care tax crédit because camp program primarily facilitated parents' employment and was not an educational program). For purposes of the dependent care tax credit, the tax code was amended in 1984 to focus on the adults' purpose in using the program (whether care is obtained to allow adult to be employed) rather than on the program's content as educational or custodial. See 26 U.S.C.A. §501(k) (West Supp. 1985). The educational versus custodial distinction still governs the applicability of the FLSA, however, and can therefore affect the level of legal protection afforded child care workers.

8. Besharov reports that in 1985 close to half of the tax benefits went to families whose income was above the national median. Less than 1 percent went to families with adjusted gross incomes of less than $10,000, and 13 percent of the benefits went to families with incomes below $15,000. The recent tax reform legislation will exacerbate these distributional effects because fewer low-income families will owe taxes and thus fewer will be able to use a nonrefundable tax credit (Besharov, 1989, pp. 509–10).

9. The changing position of Senator Orrin Hatch (R-Utah) provides a good barometer of the political status of government-aided child care. In 1984 Hatch stated categorically that "the Federal Government should not be in the business of providing day care or even assuring that it is available." In 1987 he introduced the Child Care Services Improvement Act, stating that "greater leadership by the Federal Government is needed to address the [child care] issue" (Reisman, 1989, p. 473). In 1989 Senator Hatch was a cosponsor, with liberal Senator Christopher Dodd (D-Conn.), of the ABC Bill, Act for Better Child Care Services, which calls for federal subsidization and regulation of child care services.

The grass-roots strength of the sentiment that government—and thus the law—must do more in this area has caught some by surprise. In a survey recently conducted by over 20 national magazines asking readers about their family needs, the response rate was unprecedented for surveys of this kind, and a startling 80 percent of respondents thought that the president and Congress were not paying sufficient attention to child care. Seventy-four percent responded that family matters such as child care and parental leave should be a *top* priority for Congress and the president (Ogintz, 1989).

10. 430 U.S. 199 (1977).

11. 420 U.S. 636 (1975).

12. The public educational system has been one locus of constitutional struggle between parents and the state. In *Meyer* v. *Nebraska*, 262 U.S. 390 (1923), the Supreme Court struck down a law that prohibited nonpublic schools from teaching foreign languages before the eighth grade. In *Pierce* v. *Society of Sisters*, 268 U.S. 510 (1925), the Court invalidated a law requiring all children to attend public schools. The Court expressed the view that the state had no power to "standardize its children"; nor were children to be regarded as "the mere creatures of the state" (p. 535). These laws were deemed to violate the right to liberty, which included the right "to marry, establish a home, and bring up children" (*Meyer*, p. 399). The liberty rights

of parents included the right to "direct the upbringing and education of children under their control" (*Pierce*, pp. 534–35).

Meyer and *Pierce* were later invoked by the Supreme Court to support the right of procreative privacy in cases such as *Griswold* v. *Connecticut*, 381 U.S. 479 (1965), and *Eisenstadt* v. *Baird*, 405 U.S. 438 (1972) (finding a right of access to contraceptives).

13. Contrast with the right-to-privacy cases the judicial pronouncements of the reach of *parens patriae* authority, which in English common law refers to the power of the king: "Every statute which is designed to give protection, care, and training to children, as a needed substitute for parental authority and performance of parental duty, is but a recognition of the duty of the state, as the legitimate guardian and protector of children where other guardianship fails" (*Wisconsin Industrial School for Girls* v. *Clark County*, 103 Wis. 391, 79 N.W. 422, 427 (1899)).

"The state's authority over children's activities is broader than over like actions of adults. . . . A democratic society rests, for its continuance, upon the healthy, well-rounded growth of young people into full maturity as citizens, with all that implies. . . . It is too late now to doubt that legislation appropriately designed to reach such evils [the corruption of children; child labor] is within the state's police power, [even] against the parent's claim to control of the child" (*Prince* v. *Massachusetts*, 321 U.S. 158, 168–69 (1944)). In the latter case, the Supreme Court upheld a state law barring child labor against a challenge brought by parents whose child helped them distribute religious handbills.

14. 429 U.S. 125 (1976).

15. 479 U.S. 511, 107 S. Ct. 821 (1987).

16. An example is the federal Head Start program, whose demonstrated success helped keep it viable during the Reagan administration when other federal family and social service programs were cut drastically (Miller, 1987).

17. Those who are leery of government involvement in private matters are usually even more suspicious of the federal government than of state and local governments. This may be partly attributable to the antipathy, generated by our federalist tradition, to the idea of a large central government. It may also be due to concerns that the central government will be more bureaucratic and less responsive to people's concerns and rights because of its size and remoteness from daily lives.

18. This has been a persistent theme of feminist legal scholarship, frequently emphasized at professional conferences. An indication that at least some judges are starting to be aware of the bias can be found in Justice Thurgood Marshall's opinion for the majority of the Supreme Court in the case upholding California's maternity leave law, *California Federal Savings and Loan Association* v. *Guerra*, 479 U.S. 272 (1987).

19. 401 U.S. 424 (1971).

20. 400 U.S. 542 (1971).

21. 582 F.2d 45 (9th Cir. 1978), cert. denied, 441 U.S. 965 (1979).

22. 660 F.2d 811 (D.C. Cir. 1981).
23. 685 F.2d 1149 (9th Cir. 1982).
24. 700 F.2d 559 (9th Cir. 1983).
25. *Chapman* v. *Pacific Telephone and Telegraph Co.*, 456 F.Supp. 65 (1978).
26. 628 F. Supp. 1264 (N.D. Ill. 1986), affirmed 839 F.2d 302 (7th Cir. 1988).
27. 57 U.S.L.W. 4583 (June 1989).

REFERENCES

Abromowitz, Mimi (1988). *Regulating the Lives of Women*. Boston: South End Press.

Besharov, Douglas (1989). "Fixing the Child Care Credit: Hidden Policies Lead to Regressive Policies." *Harvard Journal on Legislation* 26:505–15.

Blank, Helen, and Amy Wilkins (1985). *Child Care: Whose Priority? A State Child Care Fact Book*. Washington, D.C.: Children's Defense Fund.

Blumberg, Grace (1971). "Sexism in the Code: A Comparative Study of Income Taxation of Working Wives and Mothers." *Buffalo Law Review* 21:49–98.

Boothby, Lee (1989). "The Establishment and Free Exercise Clauses and Their Impact on National Child Care Legislation." *Harvard Journal on Legislation* 26:549–63.

Browne, Angela C. (1985). "The Market Sphere: Private Responses to the Need for Day Care." *Child Welfare* 64:367–81.

Caplan, Emily (1987). "Child Care Land Use Ordinances: Providing Working Parents with Needed Day Care Facilities." *University of Pennsylvania Law Review* 135:1591–621.

Children's Defense Fund (1988). *State Child Care Fact Book*. Washington, D.C.: CDF.

Clark, Christine (1987). "Corporate Employee Child Care: Encouraging Business to Respond to a Crisis." *Florida State University Law Review* 15:839–63.

Divine-Hawkins, Patricia, and Dodie Livingston (1985). "Preface to the Federal Role in Child Care." *Santa Clara Law Review* 25:247–59.

Dowd, Nancy (1989). "Work and Family: The Gender Paradox and the Limitations of Discrimination Analysis in Restructuring the Workplace." *Harvard Civil Rights and Civil Liberties Law Review* 24:79–172.

Eichner, Maxine (1988). "Getting Women Work That Isn't Women's Work: Challenging Gender Bias in the Workplace Under Title VII." *Yale Law Journal* 97:1397–417.

Finley, Lucinda M. (1986). "Transcending Equality Theory: A Way Out of the Maternity and the Workplace Debate." *Columbia Law Review* 86:1118–82.

———— (1987). "Choice, Freedom, and Community: Elusive Issues in the Search for Gender Justice." *Yale Law Journal* 96:914–43.

Fisk, Catherine (1986). "Employer Provided Childcare Under Title VII." *Berkeley Women's Law Journal* 2:89–138.

Frug, Mary Joe (1979). "Securing Job Equality for Women: Labor Market Hostility to Working Mothers." *Boston University Law Review* 59:55–103.

Grubb, Erica (1985). "Day Care Regulation: Legal and Policy Issues." *Santa Clara Law Review* 25:303–74.

Grubb, W. Norton, and Marvin Lazerson (1982). *Broken Promises: How Americans Fail Their Children.* New York: Basic Books.

Hanlon, Natalie (1989). "Child Care Linkage: Addressing Child Care Needs Through Land Use Planning." *Harvard Journal on Legislation* 26:591–662.

Ingrassia, L. (1988). "Day Care Business Lures Entrepreneurs." *Wall Street Journal,* June 3.

Kamerman, Sheila B. (1985). "Child Care Services: An Issue for Gender Equity and Women's Solidarity." *Child Welfare* 64:259–70.

Kamerman, Sheila B., and Alfred J. Kahn (1987). *The Responsive Workplace: Employers and a Changing Labor Force.* New York: Columbia University Press.

Kay, Herma Hill (1988). *Text, Cases, and Materials on Sex-Based Discrimination* (3d ed.). St. Paul, Minn.: West.

Lewin, Tamar (1989) "Small Tots, Big Biz." *New York Times Magazine,* January 29, p. 30.

Liebman, Lance (1989). "Evaluating Child Care Legislation: Program Structures and Political Consequences." *Harvard Journal on Legislation* 26: 357–90.

Maloney, C.M. (1981). "Title IX, Disparate Impact, and Child Care." *University of Colorado Law Review* 52:271–95.

Miller, Laura (1987). "Head Start: A Moving Target." *Yale Law and Policy Review* 5:322–44.

Morgan, Gwen (1984). "Change through Regulation." In James Greenman and Robert Fuqua, eds., *Making Day Care Better.* New York: Teachers College Press.

Murray, Kathleen (1985). "Child Care and the Law." *Santa Clara Law Review* 25:261–302.

Ogintz, Eileen (1989). "Child Care Survey Reveals a Surprising Consensus." *Buffalo News,* July 10.

Olsen, Frances (1983). "The Family and the Market: A Study of Ideology and Legal Reform." *Harvard Law Review* 96:1497–578.

Pearce, Deborah (1985). "Toil and Trouble: Women Workers and Unemployment Compensation." *Signs* 10: 439.

Phillips, Deborah (1986). "The Federal Model Child Care Standards Act of 1985: Step in the Right Direction or Hollow Gesture?" *American Journal of Orthopsychiatry* 56(1):56–64.

Reisman, Barbara (1989). "The Economics of Child Care: Its Importance in Federal Legislation." *Harvard Journal on Legislation* 26:473.

Roberts, Stephen (1989). "Child Care Bills Pour In and Obstacles Arise." *New York Times*, February 14.

Sale, S. G. (1984). "Family Day Care Homes." In James Greenman and Robert Fuqua, eds., *Making Day Care Better*. New York: Teachers College Press.

Taub, Nadine (1985). "From Parenting Leaves to Nurturing Leaves." *New York University Review of Law and Social Change* 13:381.

Trost, C. (1988). " . . . While States, Cities, and Businesses Find Ways to Fulfill a Growing Need." *Wall Street Journal*, May 6.

U.S. Commission on Civil Rights (1981) *Child Care and Equal Opportunity for Women*. Clearinghouse Publication no. 67. Washington, D.C.: Government Printing Office.

Whitehead, John W. (1989). "Accommodation and Equal Treatment of Religion: Federal Funding of Religiously Affiliated Child Care Facilities." *Harvard Journal on Legislation* 26: 573–90.

Williams, Wendy W. (1985). "Equality's Riddle: Pregnancy and the Equal Treatment/Special Treatment Debate." *New York University Review of Law and Social Change* 13:325–80.

Wolfman, Brian. (1984). "Child Care, Work, and the Federal Income Tax." *American Journal of Tax Policy* 3:153–93.

PART IV

Perspectives on Work and Society

7 | Family Leave: The Need for a New Minimum Standard

Ellen Bravo

In the 1930s, the excesses of the industrial revolution in the United States resulted in the creation of certain minimum standards to protect workers from abuse. These included the minimum wage, unemployment compensation, and Social Security—a very important provision, because the change in work patterns meant that elderly people for the most part no longer lived within an extended family and needed some means to support themselves when they were too old to work.

Today, additional changes in family and work patterns have led to the need for *new* minimum standards. Ward and June Cleaver may be recycled on television, but they are disappearing from the neighborhood. Currently 57 percent of women with children under six are in the workforce—up from 19 percent in 1960. While the number of working women has doubled since 1940, the number of working mothers has increased tenfold. It was their wages that kept family income from falling a full 18 percent between 1973 and 1986 (U.S. Congress, Joint Economic Committee, 1986).

The question is, who takes care of the caretaker's daughter (or son or husband or elderly parent) when the caretaker is busy on the job? Workers have responsibilities at home as well as at work, but many businesses have not kept pace with the change in family realities.

Rather than acknowledge the problem, the nation's largest representative of business interests, the Chamber of Commerce, has organized a massive lobbying effort in opposition to proposed family leave legislation. Chamber representatives do not challenge family leave as a good management practice, in the way they dispute the rationale behind pay equity, for example. Instead, they object to the practice's being *mandated*. Their arguments boil down to opposition to the very idea of regulation.

For those who debate the subject, certain themes emerge over

165

and over—sometimes in sophisticated arguments, sometimes much less subtly from a furious employer in the audience. But whatever the form, these views share certain erroneous assumptions.

1. "Government mandates for family leave interfere with the protected negotiations between employer and employees."

Representatives of the Chamber of Commerce frequently use this argument in debates. Most workers, however, do not engage in negotiations with their employers over wages and benefits. Fewer than one in five workers is in a union; 87 percent of all female workers have no collective bargaining agreement. Requesting leave is very different from having power to negotiate for leave. Most women have little or no power on the job.

The notion that all employees freely choose the terms of their employment has an interesting history. In the late 1800s and early 1900s, local laws restricting the work week to 40 hours were struck down on the grounds that such restrictions interfered with the employee's freedom of contract, the "right to purchase or to sell labor" protected by the Fourteenth Amendment to the Constitution (*Lochner* v. *New York*, 198 U.S. 45 (1905)). Not until passage of the Fair Labor Standards Act in 1938, which established a 40-hour work week and the minimum wage, was this interpretation repudiated. What workers do because they have to is hardly the same as what they are "willing" to do.

Workers who are covered by collective bargaining can negotiate benefits far more substantial than those mandated by a minimum government standard (see Chapter 8 by Carolyn York). However, in recognition of the fact that most workers lack bargaining power, and that even those who engage in negotiations need a floor from which to proceed, a national minimum standard is necessary.

2. "All employers set wages and benefits according to productivity or other appropriate measures."

Unfortunately, many examples exist of companies that could well afford to grant unpaid leave but do not. According to a 1986 study by Catalyst, an independent research firm based in New York, only half the large and medium-sized companies offer unpaid family leave with a job guarantee (76 percent of the largest firms offer such leaves). Only a third allow employees to use sick days or personal leave to care for a sick child. Fewer than one out of five offers leave for adoption.

These are the statistics. Consider some of the people behind the numbers:

- Brenda returned to her job after a short unpaid leave, only to find that she had been given a different position at $1 per hour less pay and with evening hours. No bus goes to Brenda's house late at night, and she had no car.
- Sandra's 85-year-old father in Connecticut had two heart attacks. The family told her to come home from Wisconsin. When Sandra asked for a one-week unpaid leave, her boss refused. Instead, he told her she could take two days off if her father died, with a third day for travel.
- Lorena's baby was born with a birth defect. At the end of her 6-week leave, she still had not found a child care provider who could deal with the disability. The company refused her request for a longer leave. Later, when the baby required weekly physical therapy sessions that could only be scheduled during working hours, Lorena's supervisor tried to make her take a personal leave—which would have meant losing her health insurance.
- Denise worked 9 years at a company that had no family leave policy. When she took time off for her first baby, she was terminated, but she was allowed to reapply and be rehired later—as a new hire. Eventually she became pregnant again. This time she needed a medical leave because of problems during the pregnancy. However, the company granted medical leave only to employees with at least 2 years' seniority. Even though Denise had worked at this company nearly 11 years, she did not have enough seniority to qualify for medical leave and was terminated again.

We like to think that business leaders are enlightened about social relations and respond accordingly. But sometimes they are sadly out of tune. At a Harvard seminar for high-ranking executives, participants were asked what percentage of the workforce corresponds to the "traditional" family, with Dad at work and Mom at home. They responded with percentages ranging from 40 to 70, whereas the real figure is less than 12 percent (9to5, 1988b).

As the Economic Policy Council of the United Nations Association of the United States noted in its landmark report, *Work and Family in the United States: A Policy Initiative* (1985): "Our national interest will best be served if we can enable working parents to concentrate on their jobs without neglecting their families. We can no longer leave to chance an area of policy so primary to our country's social and economic fabric."

3. "Many employees will abuse whatever leave they are given."

Of course, some employees do take advantage of available leave. But the United States now has a body of experience on this issue, thanks to the companies and states where some sort of parental leave has been instituted. Studies show that people take *less* leave than allowed, sometimes at great personal risk (Kamerman, Kahn, and Kingston, 1983).

Again, personal anecdotes flesh out the numbers:

- Lila was permitted to take as much time as she needed to return from maternity leave. But because the leave was unpaid and her husband was laid off, Lila returned to work after only 2 weeks. A month later she suffered a herniated disk, a permanent injury that caused her to miss additional work.
- Sophie had a heart attack and was advised to stay off work for 3 months. Her boss agreed. But Sophie knew that the office was short-handed and returned 4 weeks early out of loyalty to the company. When she described her situation to 35 people during a workshop, four others chimed in with similar examples.

4. "Government mandates deny employers flexibility and take away freedom."

At a forum on family leave in Racine, Wisconsin, an executive from a large manufacturing firm argued that passage of family leave legislation would mean that his company could no longer give generous paid leaves. They would now have to restrict their benefits, he argued, to the much lower requirements of the law. The *minimum required* by law, however, is never the same as the *maximum allowed*. Firms still have enormous flexibility in offering, or negotiating, more generous leave. The legislation establishes a floor—not a ceiling.

Business's record on voluntary provision of family leave has been less than sterling. Until 1978 many firms routinely fired women for being pregnant, or denied them paid medical benefits and/or the right to return to work. When the Supreme Court examined the issue in 1976 (*General Electric Company* v. *Gilbert*, 429 U.S. 125 (1976)), the Justices ruled that treating pregnant women differently does not constitute discrimination because pregnancy has nothing to do with sex. Even Congress knew something was wrong with that argument; they overruled the Court by passing the Pregnancy Discrimination Act (PDA) in 1978.

This law is limited to companies that already have disability policies. Only 40 percent of all working women are covered by such plans (Kamerman, Kahn, and Kingston, 1983). When the Chamber of Commerce asserts that high percentages of large and medium-sized businesses offer maternity leave, it is actually citing companies that are complying with the mandate of the PDA. Since these firms have disability policies, they must treat pregnancy the same as other disabilities. Their policies are not, in the main, examples of voluntary practices.

Not all business owners have followed the lead of the national Chamber of Commerce. Robert Weisenberg (1987), owner of Effective Management Systems, testified in favor of state and national legislation. Although Weisenberg described himself as "sympathetic to the argument that we should carefully restrict those areas in which government controls the day-to-day operations of a business," he sees family leave legislation as falling within "that limited category of basic employee rights that must be guaranteed for everyone."

5. "Mandated family leave will be too expensive and will destroy small businesses."

None of the women described above worked in very small businesses. Most small business owners know their employees personally; it is hard to imagine many of them denying leave to visit a dying father.

But representatives of small businesses have joined forces with the Chamber of Commerce in lobbying against family leave legislation. They argue that they simply cannot afford to replace certain key employees. And they cannot—which is why a reasonable family leave policy makes good business sense. Refusing an employee leave is what forces businesses to replace workers on a permanent basis.

One study estimates the cost of hiring and training a new employee to be 93 percent of the first year's salary (Bradley, 1987). The cost is less to small businesses, but still significant. The cost of implementing unpaid family leave, on the other hand, is not much at all, according to a report by the General Accounting Office (Gainer, 1987). The study says that many employers cope with family leave the same way they deal with vacations: by shifting workloads or hiring less expensive temporary employees. While there is some loss in productivity, employers save on recruitment costs by retaining experienced and trained people. The only new cost involved is providing health insurance to those on leave.

In addition, there is now hard evidence showing that family leave does not hurt small businesses' growth. In a recent report, 9to5, National Association of Working Women, compared seven states with parental leave policies, most of them in effect since the 1970s, with the seven states rated as having the most pro-business climate (9to5, 1988a). Both groups of states experienced employment growth, but the rates of growth (measured through a multi-regression analysis) were *21 percent higher* in parental leave states. Employment growth was higher in businesses of all sizes in the parental leave states studied. Jobs in firms with fewer than 20 employees, for instance, grew 32 percent in parental leave states, compared with 22 percent in "pro-business" states. In firms with fewer than 50 employees, jobs grew 36 percent in parental leave states, compared with 27 percent in pro-business states. In short, family leave does not inhibit employment growth.

Another interesting study poses the cost question in a different form: what does it currently cost society *not* to provide family leave? Economists Roberta Spalter-Roth and Heidi Hartmann (1988, 1990; and see Chapter 3 in this volume) estimate that figure to be $363 million a year in reduced earning power and public assistance programs.

Despite wildly exaggerated cost estimates by the Chamber of Commerce, a number of business representatives have commented on the cost savings to their companies of implementing family leave policies. The director of employee benefits for Southern New England Telecommunications told a congressional committee (Kardos, 1986): "In the long run we save money. We've invested a lot of training and experience in these people. We want them to stay."

Fortune magazine gave Merck and Company top marks for its "ability to attract, develop and keep talented people" (Chapman, 1987). Merck has a wide range of programs to balance work and family life, including 6 weeks paid maternity leave; up to 18 months unpaid child care leave with full medical benefits; on-site child care; financial support for several nearby child care centers; and flextime.

The workforce at HBO in New York City is more than half female. To retain experienced, skilled employees, the firm uses flexible benefits such as 12 weeks additional unpaid leave after paid maternity leave and 1 week paid paternity leave. Shelly Fischel, vice president for human resources, says, "Many of the women who return to work after giving birth do *better* at their jobs than they did before" (Sweeney and Nussbaum, 1989).

6. "Family leave will lead to discrimination."

A woman business owner at a conference hosted by the Wisconsin Business and Professional Women's group argued that if family leave were extended to small businesses, she would choose to hire a 45-year-old woman rather than a young woman with children. To choose personnel by age, however, is discriminatory and against the law. Moreover, the 45-year-old may well need leave to care for an elderly parent or a personal illness. No employee is a thoroughly "safe bet."

Although there are business owners who discriminate, statistics show no rise in unemployment for women in states with family leave laws (Rosenthal, 1987).

7. "Other countries that provide leave are stagnating. They don't have buoyant job creation like the United States."

Economists disagree sharply over how successful job creation has been in the United States, given that more than half the new jobs developed since 1982 are part-time or temporary, many offering lower pay and few or no benefits. Of the 37 million Americans with no health insurance, two-thirds are employed. Few would argue that Japan's economy is stagnating, yet that country has 12 weeks paid maternity leave. Closer to home, Canada's economy is also doing well, and Canadians have 17 to 41 weeks leave, with 60 percent pay for 15 of those weeks (Gladstone, Williams, and Belous, 1985).

8. "Mandated leave will cause chaos and be impossible to administer."

Consider this similar argument:

> [This bill] would create chaos in business never yet known to us. . . . It sets an all-time high in crackpot legislation. Let me make it very clear that I am not opposed to the social theory. . . . No decent American citizen can take exception to this attitude. What I do take exception to is any approach to a solution of this problem which is utterly impractical and in operation would be much more destructive than constructive to the very purposes which it is designed to serve.

These objections will sound familiar to anyone involved in the current debate on family leave. However, the author is actually U.S. Representative Lamneck arguing more than 50 years ago (November 1937) against proposed laws to abolish child labor and establish a minimum wage.

9. "I already give leave for vacation and medical. I can't give it for all these frivolous things, too."

Already more than half of all mothers of infants under the age of one are in the workforce. By the year 2000, 75 percent of mothers of children under age six will be employed (Hofferth and Phillips, 1987). Along with these figures, consider that more than 12 percent of today's population is age 65 or older. Combining work and care for young or elderly dependents is becoming a necessity—not a frill—for most Americans.

- When Jean's mother died, her boss considered her grief a frill. He told her the best remedy was to get right back to work—and offered her a drug to make her feel better. She insisted on taking some unpaid time off, which he reluctantly agreed to. But when Jean returned to work, she was let go.

- Chris was adopted into his first real family at the age of 12. His only regret was that his new mom had to put the kids to bed at eight o'clock every night so she could go to work. The adoption agency required her to be home the first 6 months, but her job would not release her.

10. "This is just the first step. Next thing you know we'll have 20 weeks paid vacation."

Opponents typically exaggerate what the other side really wants. Proponents of family leave want a minimum standard, by which we mean a *floor*, not a ceiling—and not a cellar. "Minimum" does not equal optimal or even good, but it must be *realistic* and *survivable*. Similarly, when the minimum wage was established, it was not intended to be a subsistence amount but, as Franklin Delano Roosevelt put it, "a fair day's pay for a fair day's work."

The minimum has to take into account the needs of the child and the needs of the parents. Allowing only 6 weeks for childbirth, for example, addresses the minimum *medical* recovery time necessary for a new mother, but not the needs of the newborn infant or the emotional needs of the parents. Such a meager leave also ignores the realities of adoption, since it is not uncommon for agencies to require one parent to be at home for 6 months.

The minimum also has to include time off for sick dependents, both children and elderly parents. Conflicts between work and family are not limited to parents of newborns. According to a 1980 Gallup poll, worry about sick children is the second greatest concern for working parents after child care.

A growing worry for many employees is the illness of an elderly parent. Today more than 12 percent of the population is over 65. Even when Medicaid pays the bills, it does not wipe the brow. According to a 1982 National Long-Term Care Study, at least 11 percent of caregivers of elderly parents quit a job because of the pressures of balancing that care with work.

How long should employees be able to take off to care for a sick family member? Here the standard has to allow for situations that are not typical but also not uncommon. Most people will have to deal with a serious illness only once or twice in their working careers, but should it happen, they may need a substantial amount of leave.

Proposed federal and most state measures have called only for unpaid leave. Under those conditions, lack of resources would effectively deny leave to many individuals. Even though a job guarantee without pay is better than no pay *and* no job, a minimum family leave standard should include some wage replacement plan. Five states currently have temporary disability insurance; most of them have had such a program in place since the 1940s (Schwartz, 1988). The success of these plans should be studied, along with the Canadian model, which utilizes the unemployment insurance fund.

Provisions for family leave can include tax breaks for small businesses that cannot easily afford any increase in costs, however small. But the legislation ultimately cannot exclude one-third or more of all employees because they happen to work in smaller firms. Nor can it tell certain people that they will not be able to exercise their right to family leave because they are too "key" to the business.

It is also not acceptable for family leave to mean a trade-off with health or child care benefits. Cafeteria plans can be a good arrangement, but certain things should be guaranteed to all workers. It simply cannot be considered a "fringe benefit" to have both a family and a job.

In order to make family leave a reality, we also need changes in roles within the family. It is no accident that the expression "working fathers" is not part of our vocabulary; the concept does not exist in our culture. Education is needed, but the greatest educator is a role model. Our nation will have more men sharing responsibilities in the home when men are no longer punished for being good fathers and good sons. We cannot change ideas on a large scale without changing reality.

For a start, we need changes in corporate culture. Too many women are forced out of a firm for lack of "team spirit" because they suggested that the manager not have emergency meetings at 5:15 when the child care center closes at 5:30. Instead of talking about the "mommy track" (Kingson, 1988), where mothers who choose to combine work and family become second-class members of the organization, we need to define a "human track" that *admires* those who make time for interests other than work and actively recruits top managers from among their ranks.

In summary, there is broad agreement that family leave is valuable to employees, to families, and to business. The issue is whether or not to *guarantee* that this policy will be extended to all employees. Until all workers really have the freedom to contract, we need a minimum standard of protection.

Family leave legislation recognizes employees' lack of bargaining power and takes action to correct abuses. Instead of spending effort and money on lobbying against the provision, business leaders need to acknowledge that some in their ranks are guilty of abuse—even if they do not agree on how many—and that these practices have to be stopped. Employer and employee representatives can then cooperatively figure out ways to assist newer and more struggling businesses to provide family-sensitive policies.

REFERENCES

Bradley, Barbara (1987). "Is Maternity Leave Too Costly for Employers?" *Christian Science Monitor*, February 2.

Catalyst (1986). "Report on a National Study of Parental Leaves." New York: Catalyst.

Chapman, Fern Schumer (1987). "Executive Guilt: Who's Taking Care of the Children?" *Fortune*, February 16.

Economic Policy Council of the United Nations Association of the United States of America (1985). *Work and Family in the United States: A Policy Initiative*. New York: UNA.

Gainer, William J. (1987). "Estimated Costs of HR 925, the Family and Medical Leave Act of 1987." Testimony before the Subcommittee on Labor–Management Relations, of the House Committee on Education and Labor. Washington, D.C.: General Accounting Office. November.

Gallup (1980). *American Families 1980: Report Submitted to the White House Conference on Families*. Princeton, N.J.: Gallup Organization.

Gladstone, Leslie W., Jennifer D. Williams, and Richard S. Belous (1985). *Maternity and Parental Leave Policies: A Comparative Analysis*. Washington, D.C.: Library of Congress, Congressional Research Service.

Hofferth, Sandra, and Deborah Phillips (1987). "Child Care in the United States, 1970 to 1995." *Journal of Marriage and the Family* 49: 559–71.

Kamerman, Sheila B., Alfred J. Kahn, and Paul W. Kingston (1983). *Maternity Policies and Working Women*. New York: Columbia University Press.

Kardos, Jeanne (1986). Testimony on the Parental and Medical Leave Act of 1986. Joint hearing before the Subcommittee on Labor–Management Relations and the Subcommittee on Labor Standards of the Committee on Education and Labor. September 9.

Kingson, Jennifer A. (1988). "Female Lawyers Stuck in the 'Mommy Track.'" *New York Times*, August.

9to5, National Association of Working Women (1988a). *New Workforce Policies and the Small Business Sector: Is Parental Leave Good for Business? A Multivariate Analysis of Business Employment Growth*. Cleveland, Ohio: 9to5.

——— (1988b). *Profile of Working Women*. Cleveland, Ohio: 9to5.

Rosenthal, Hannah (1987). Testimony before the Wisconsin Senate Committee on Agriculture, Health and Human Services on Wisconsin Family and Medical Leave Act, August 25.

Schwartz, William (1988). Panel on State Government. Wingspread Conference on Parental Leave and Child Care, Racine, Wis., September 16.

Spalter-Roth, Roberta M., and Heidi I. Hartmann (1988). *Unnecessary Losses: Costs to Americans of the Lack of Family and Medical Leave, Executive Summary.* Washington, D.C.: Institute for Women's Policy Research.

—— (1990). *Unnecessary Losses: Costs to Americans of the Lack of Family and Medical Leave.* Washington, D.C.: Institute for Women's Policy Research.

Sweeney, John, and Karen Nussbaum (1989). *Solutions for the New Workforce: Policies for a New Social Contract.* Cabin John, Md.: Seven Locks Press.

U.S. Congress, Joint Economic Committee (1986). "Working Mothers Are Preserving Family Living Standards." Washington, D.C.: Government Printing Office. September 9.

Weisenberg, Robert (1987). Testimony before the Senate Committee on Agriculture, Health and Human Services, September 23.

8 | The Labor Movement's Role in Parental Leave and Child Care

Carolyn York

Parental leave and child care are at the top of many unions' current bargaining and legislative agendas. Labor's interest in the family, however, is not a new trend. In fact, the family has always been a key concern of working people and their unions. The Fair Labor Standards Act of 1938 (establishing a minimum wage and the 40-hour work week) and the Social Security Act of 1935 are among labor's greatest victories: both protect the family economically and physically and provide workers with the time they need to sustain their families.

Labor's current efforts to address work and family concerns should be viewed as an expansion of this history, rather than a dramatic policy shift. A number of factors account for unions' increasing support for working women's issues: the rapid entrance of women into the labor force and into unions, the impact of the women's movement on society at large and specifically on union women, the gradual growth of women's committees within unions and the movement of women into union leadership positions, and the emergence in 1974 of the Coalition of Labor Union Women (CLUW). From its founding, CLUW has maintained a close relationship with the women's movement and has worked to connect women and labor, taking on issues ranging from parental leave and child care to pay equity and sexual harassment (Balser, 1987). All of these factors spurred unions to make child care and parental leave bargaining priorities. By focusing primarily on the achievements of the Service Employees International Union (SEIU), this paper will illustrate labor's bargaining gains in the areas of parental leave and child care and suggest directions that labor activities may take in the future.

Parental Leave

Bargaining Trends

When workers become parents or have a child who falls ill, many are forced to make a choice that no person should have to make—their job or their family. SEIU and 9to5, the National Association of Working Women, have compiled several examples of the tragic consequences when employees are denied leave (Sweeney and Nussbaum, 1989).

Robin McCabe, a hospital technician in Seattle, pregnant with her second child, requested 11 weeks of maternity leave. Her leave was approved by her supervisors, but when she reported back to work, her job was gone.

James Callor requested a week off from work to stay with his six-year-old daughter while she was dying of cancer. His employer, a large mining company in Utah, turned him down.

Unions have responded to the needs of working parents in two ways: by bargaining vigorously for parental leave and by pushing for federal legislation that would establish a national minimum standard for parental leave. A parental leave policy that includes a job guarantee is crucial for all parents, but it is most important for low-income women, who, like all women, must take some time off for childbirth but cannot risk losing their jobs. Paid leave ensures that parents at all income levels can take advantage of the full leave period.

At the bargaining table, unions generally begin by winning the most basic benefit: a period of job-guaranteed unpaid (disability) leave for new mothers. In subsequent negotiations they may push to lengthen the leave and to cover fathers and adoptive parents, in instances where they were not originally covered. Unions also work for paid benefits during leave so that new parents can keep their medical and life insurance coverage at no additional cost during this critical period. Lastly, some unions have been successful in winning *paid* parental leave.

How successful has labor been at winning parental leave at the bargaining table? According to several recent surveys, progress has been quite remarkable. A study by the National Council of Jewish Women found that unionized workers are more likely than nonunion employees to receive leaves: 55 percent of the union members in this survey had the right to job-protected leaves of 8 or more weeks, while only 33 percent of nonunion workers enjoyed this benefit (Bond, 1987).

In another survey (1987a), SEIU examined the parental leave provisions in 19 of its largest public sector contracts (covering 60 percent—or 271,000—of the 450,000 American public service workers whom SEIU represents in federal, state, and local government) and 119 private sector contracts (covering half of the private sector workers they represent). In the public sector, SEIU found:

- Almost all contracts (representing 84 percent of public employees in the survey) provide 6 months or more job-guaranteed leave.
- Nearly all contracts continue health benefits during a leave of absence. In about half of the contracts surveyed, employers continue to pay the health premiums while an employee is on leave. In the other half, employees may continue their coverage by paying the premiums at the group rate.
- Eleven of the 19 contracts surveyed offer adoption leave.

SEIU's largest public sector contract, covering 80,000 California state employees, provides up to one year of unpaid leave for new mothers and fathers, including adoptive parents (State of California, 1987).

Some of SEIU's public sector contracts go even farther. For instance, in the Sacramento, California public schools, SEIU members have won up to two years of parental leave, and SEIU Local 285 in Boston provides parents with the option of returning to work part time for one year after parental leave (City of Boston, 1987).

A similar survey of public sector contracts by the American Federation of State, County, and Municipal Employees (AFSCME) corroborated SEIU's findings. AFSCME looked at 85 contracts covering 755,000 state and local government employees and found that 635,000, or 84 percent of the total, are eligible for parental leaves of up to or exceeding 6 months (AFSCME, 1988).

In the private sector, where SEIU represents over 400,000 workers in predominantly low-wage jobs, the union has encountered much stronger employer resistance. Nevertheless, the survey indicates significant progress. Nearly two out of three of the private sector contracts (64 percent, covering 74 percent of the private sector workers surveyed) provide 3 months or more job-guaranteed leave. However, fewer than half (45 percent, covering 70 percent of the private sector workers surveyed) continue health benefits during the leave period.

In analyzing the survey results, SEIU found that the best family leave provisions are contained in private sector contracts where a large number of employers are organized across an industry so that all companies must play by the same rules. In these instances, even very small employers can afford to raise their standards for family leave (SEIU, 1987a).

For example, in New York City, SEIU Local 32B–32J's master contract sets the standard for over 60,000 janitors and building service workers employed by thousands of different companies. The union has won up to 12 months of parental leave for its members with full job guarantees and seniority rights (Service Employers Association, 1987). SEIU's master nursing home contract in New York provides up to 10 months of unpaid leave with a full job guarantee for new parents (Greater New York Health Care Facilities Association, 1987).

Likewise, the International Ladies Garment Workers Union (ILGWU) scored a major parental leave victory in its 1988 negotiations with the apparel industry. In negotiations covering 38 manufacturers of women's outerwear in the Northeast, the union won 6 months of unpaid leave for either parent upon the birth or adoption of a child. At the end of the leave, the employee is entitled to return to a comparable job with the same company. The ILGWU has continued its push for parental leave by winning leave provisions in contracts covering garment workers in Chicago, St. Louis, and San Francisco.

However, there is no doubt that winning parental leave worksite by worksite in the private sector is a battle. It is extremely difficult to establish workplace standards when unions must bargain unit by unit in industries in which workers have not yet won many basic benefits. All too often, working people are forced to choose between job-protected leave and another essential benefit such as basic health insurance coverage.

From the union perspective, it is imperative that the United States join the rest of the industrialized world and establish minimum standards for family leave that protect all workers. To reach this goal, SEIU placed the Family and Medical Leave Act (FMLA) at the top of its legislative agenda in the last congressional session. Although the bill, even as originally introduced, provides only a minimum standard of job-guaranteed unpaid leave, the union views it as an urgently needed first step (Sweeney, 1987).

Directions for the Future

Parental leave, like all work and family issues, will continue to grow in importance at the bargaining table. The commitment of unions to these issues can be seen in the Communications Workers of America's (CWA) announcement that family issues would be a top priority in 1989 negotiations covering 600,000 telecommunications workers and in the union's subsequent success in winning a work and family benefits package in the AT&T contract. "We intend to redefine these kinds of family issues as workers' issues, which directly impact on the future competitiveness of our industries and our nation," CWA president Morton Bahr stated (Labor Relations Week, 1988).

In contracts that do not yet provide parental leave, winning a minimum standard will be the first item of business. In contracts that already contain such a provision, the focus will shift to improving that leave in a variety of ways.

One growing trend is toward flexibility in leave provisions. The term "family leave" is replacing the narrower concept of parental leave to acknowledge that a family's need for short-term leave may extend well beyond the initial period after the birth or adoption of a child. Employees, for example, must often care for ill children, spouses, and parents. Unions have tackled this issue by winning the right for employees to use all or a portion of their sick leave for family illness, and by bargaining for short-term leaves of absence for employees who need to care for ill family members.

Increasingly, leave policies are defined more broadly to meet the needs of employees in a wide variety of situations. An example of this trend is the leave-of-absence language in SEIU Local 134's contract with Brown University. Brown employees may take up to 12 months of unpaid leave for a specified reason such as family illness, study, or travel (Brown University, 1988). Personal days, which can be used to take care of any personal needs, will also be pursued more vigorously at the bargaining table.

Perhaps the most important trend, however, will be toward establishing paid leave. One model for partially paid leave is offered by short-term temporary disability insurance (TDI). Employers who offer TDI programs, including those in states where TDI is required, must treat pregnancy disability as they would treat any other disability, and provide partially paid leave to new mothers for the period of time that they are disabled. Therefore, negotiating a short-term disability plan in workplaces where one does not already exist is an excellent first step toward establishing paid parental leave.

Another model is the Canadian program that offers partially paid maternity leave through their national unemployment insurance program. By supplementing these benefits at the bargaining table, SEIU's Canadian local unions have been able to win up to 17 weeks of leave with 95 percent pay (SEIU Research Department, 1988).

While pushing for a national policy, some unions have already made progress toward winning paid leave at the bargaining table. For example, SEIU/District 925's contract with Beacon Press in Boston provides 8 weeks of fully paid leave (Beacon Press, 1988).

Unions will continue to explore these and other options for paid leave in order to establish parental leave provisions that all workers, regardless of income, can take full advantage of.

Child Care

Bargaining Trends

The themes of the child care crisis are becoming a familiar refrain: supply is too little; cost is too high; and quality is too low. As with parental leave, unions are combining bargaining and legislative strategies to address these problems.

Employers have been slow to agree to workers' demands, primarily because of the cost involved in providing child care benefits. For example, it took SEIU Local 399 ten years of bargaining supported by extensive grass-roots lobbying to win a very modest demand: a child care resource and referral program at Kaiser Permanente in Los Angeles. Yet unions have established a significant number of child care benefits. In a recent survey of union child care initiatives, SEIU found over 50 examples of union-sponsored programs involving 14 labor unions and covering 23 states (SEIU Public Policy Department, 1988).

SEIU local unions alone account for 16—or 30 percent—of the child care programs. Service sector unions with large female memberships—such as SEIU, AFSCME, and CWA—led the list in SEIU's survey, but many industrial unions, including the United Auto Workers and the Steelworkers, have also made significant strides in winning child care.

Union child care activities run the gamut from resource and referral services, on-site child care centers, child care subsidies, afterschool programs, sick child programs, and a large number of dependent care assistance plans. Many of the union programs began with a joint labor–management committee to address child care needs. Examples of these types of programs are discussed below.

Resource and Referral Programs. Resource and referral programs are often a first step in child care negotiations. These programs are relatively inexpensive and therefore relatively easy to win at the bar-

gaining table, and they provide members with an important service—help in finding child care. The best resource and referral programs also address the issue of quality by maintaining up-to-date
files with parent evaluations of providers and by making periodic
inspections of the programs on the referral list.

In negotiations with South Central Bell, CWA members in Tennessee negotiated an employer-paid child care referral service. By
calling a toll-free number, an employee can now talk to consultants
who help determine his or her child care needs, answer questions,
and provide up-to-date information about child care vacancies in the
employee's area (SEIU Public Policy Department, 1988). Another resource and referral program, the Metropolitan Washington, D.C.,
Child Care Network, was originally established in negotiations between the Bureau of National Affairs, a private sector publishing
company, and the Newspaper Guild. The service is now funded by a
number of area businesses and the Council of Governments and receives over 31,000 calls a year (SEIU Public Policy Department,
1988).

Employer Subsidies.   The biggest drawback of resource and referral services is that they do not help parents with their greatest need:
paying for child care. To begin to address this problem, some unions
have bargained for employer subsidies. At the *Village Voice* newspaper in New York, District 65 of the UAW won contract language
specifying that the employer will pay $500 a year for each family's
child care expenses (SEIU Public Policy Department, 1988). In
Maine, AFSCME negotiated contract language providing annual
payments of $500 for families with an adjusted gross income of less
than $25,000 in the previous year (SEIU Public Policy Department,
1988).

On-Site Child Care Programs.   Despite the expense and complexity
of establishing child care programs at worksites, a number of unions
have been successful in bargaining for on-site child care centers.
These centers provide double benefits to working parents by adding
to the supply of child care in the community and, if partially subsidized by the employer, by offering an affordable child care option.

One example of this approach is at Boston City Hospital, where
SEIU Local 285 established an on-site center in 1982. The center,
which cares for infants and toddlers up to age two and a half, was
the product of a joint labor–management committee. The hospital
provides rent-free space, maintenance, and utilities, and fees are
based on a sliding scale (SEIU Public Policy Department, 1988).

The Garment Industry Day Care Center in New York's Chinatown is perhaps the best-known product of labor's involvement in child care. Established after a persistent, well-organized campaign by the ILGWU, the center is jointly funded by the city and by a consortium that includes the Greater Blouse, Skirt and Undergarment Association, Local 23/25 of the ILGWU, and some individual garment manufacturers. The center currently serves 80 children from ages two to five. Parents are charged on a sliding scale, with many paying no more than $10 per week, and three union members sit on the 13-person governing board (SEIU Public Policy Department, 1988).

Before- and After-School Care. Some local unions have found that their members' greatest child care need is for before- and after-school care for school-aged children. SEIU Local 715 has successfully responded to this need at three school districts in Santa Clara County, California, through collaboration with local school districts, the YWCA, and the county. The centers are located in under-utilized school buildings, and the YWCA runs the programs. The centers also provide a full-day program during school vacations (SEIU Public Policy Department, 1988).

Sick Child Care. Because most child care providers will not accept children when they are ill—even mildly ill with a cold or an earache—parents must miss work whenever a child gets sick, unless they can afford to pay someone to care for him or her. Generally, fees for sick child care come on top of regular child care expenses, which must be paid even if a child is absent.

SEIU Local 616 and Alameda County, California, set up an innovative project to help employees with temporary or unanticipated child care needs, such as sick child care. The county committed $120,000 for the 8-month project, in addition to administrative and evaluation costs. Under the program, employees are reimbursed for 75 percent of their emergency child care expenses (SEIU Public Policy Department, 1988).

Dependent Care Assistance Plans. Undoubtedly the most frequently negotiated child care benefit is a Dependent Care Assistance Plan (DCAP). Using a DCAP, parents may set aside up to $5,000 per year in a pre-tax account to pay for child care expenses. Because DCAPs cost little, if anything, to an employer, unions have been quite successful in winning them at the bargaining table.

One example of this approach is in the International Brotherhood of Electrical Workers' contract with New York State Electric and Gas Corporation. The IBEW and the company negotiated a voucher system that allows employees to set aside pre-tax dollars for child care expenses. Under the system, an employee determines his or her child care costs (not to exceed the federal limit of $5,000) for the year, and that amount is withheld through payroll deductions and converted into vouchers. The vouchers may be used to pay any licensed day care center, a family home, or an in-home sitter (SEIU Public Policy Department, 1988).

Directions for the Future

Despite significant gains at the bargaining table, bargaining alone cannot solve the child care crisis in this country. SEIU believes that federal and state action is urgently needed to ensure high-quality, affordable child care for all American families. In *Who's Minding the Children* (SEIU, 1987b), the union states, "A first step is to increase federal child care funding and to pass child care legislation designed to increase the supply, quality, and affordability of child care." Subsidies—whether through the tax system or through vouchers— should be available to all families that need them, including low-income working parents, parents in job training or school programs, and parents who are seeking employment. However, with the passage of the welfare reform law, Congress moved in the opposite direction by limiting tax breaks for child care expenses covered under the Family Support Act of 1988.

SEIU and a number of other labor unions have been active in the Alliance for Better Child Care, which pushed for the Act for Better Child Care (the ABC Bill). As originally introduced, the ABC Bill provided that states had to spend at least 75 percent of the funds received under the bill to assist parents in purchasing child care. Of equal importance, the bill would have established federal standards in key areas affecting the quality of child care: staff–child ratios, health and safety requirements, and staff qualifications, training, and background for day care centers; health and safety requirements, a minimum age for caregivers, and maximum number of children and infants per caregiver for family day care.

Another important component of the debate is the impact of providers' wages on the quality of care. The low wages earned by child care providers—averaging $9,464 for workers in centers and $4,732 for home day care providers in 1986—produce high turnover rates, forcing children constantly to adjust to new providers. Furthermore, these below-poverty-level salaries make it difficult to hire staff with specialized training (Child Care Employee News, 1987). Salaries must be raised to compensate employees fairly for the skills and responsibilities that their job requires. As our society addresses the child care crisis, the labor movement cannot forget the workers whose livelihood is to care for children. Affordability and quality concerns will continue to clash—with quality often forced to take a back seat—until government assumes responsibility for developing a comprehensive child care system.

REFERENCES

American Federation of State, County, and Municipal Employees (1988). *Leading the Way: Parental Leave Arrangements in AFSCME Contracts*. Washington, D.C.: AFSCME.

Balser, Diane (1987). *Sisterhood and Solidarity: Feminism and Labor in Modern Times*. Boston: South End Press.

Beacon Press and SEIU District 925. (1988). Contract. Boston.

Bond, James T. (1987). Statement of James T. Bond, Director, National Council of Jewish Women, Center for the Child, Submitted to Subcommittees on Labor–Management Relations and on Labor Standards of the U. S. House of Representatives Committee on Education and Labor, March 12.

Brown University and SEIU Local 134, Library Unit (1988). Contract. Providence, Rhode Island.

Child Care Employee News (1987). "Child Care Workers: A Precious Resource." *Child Care Employee News*, Spring/Fall, p. 1.

City of Boston and SEIU Local 285 (1987). Technical–Clerical Agreement. Boston.

Labor Relations Week (1988). "Family Issues Will Top CWA's Agenda in 1989 Contract Talks." *Labor Relations Week*, August 3, p. 765.

Greater New York Health Care Facilities Association, Inc., and SEIU Local 144, Hotel, Hospital, Nursing Home and Allied Service Employees Union (1987). Agreement. New York.

Service Employees International Union (1987a). *SEIU Survey of Parental Leave Policies in Low-Wage Service Industries: Some Progress, Not Far Enough*. Washington, D.C.: SEIU.

—— (1987b). *Who's Minding the Children?* Washington, D.C.: SEIU.

—— Public Policy Department (1988). *Summary of Union Child Care Activities*. Washington, D.C.: SEIU. September.

—— Research Department (1988). *Settlements Report: First Half 1988*. Washington, D.C.: SEIU. May.

Service Employers Association and SEIU Local 32B–32J (1987). Agreement. New York.

State of California and California State Employees Association, SEIU Local 1000 (1987). Agreement. Sacramento.

Sweeney, John J. (1987). Testimony of Service Employees International Union on H. R. 925, the Parental and Medical Leave Act of 1987, Be-

186 PERSPECTIVES ON WORK AND SOCIETY

fore the Labor–Management Relations Subcommittee of the U.S. House of Representatives Committee on Education and Labor.

Sweeney, John J., and Karen Nussbaum (1989). *Solutions for the New Workforce: Policies for a New Social Contract*. Cabin John, Md.: Seven Locks Press.

9 | The Wisconsin Family and Medical Leaves Act: States Resolving the Conflict Between Parenthood and Livelihood

John R. Plewa

When the family leave bill was introduced in Wisconsin, there were those who asked why we had done so, considering that family leave was already under discussion in the U.S. Congress. My answer was that if there is one thing I have learned in my 16 years as a state legislator, it is never to wait for Congress to act.

Today, Congress seems to face an institutional crisis. Talented members of Congress are leaving it because they can no longer stand the frustration. Congress seems in perpetual stalemate, working all year on budgets that it cannot pass. Leadership seems unable to lead. So it should not be surprising that Congress has stalled on family leave as it has on other major issues.

While the institutional crisis has mounted in Congress, state legislatures have become better at dealing with tough issues than ever before. The willingness and ability of state legislatures to deal with family leave is a function of three factors: professionalism, demographics, and local political tradition.

Legislatures have increasingly become full-time bodies dominated by professional politicians backed up by professional staffs. In Wisconsin, we have attorneys who draft our bills, more attorneys who review those bills, fiscal analysts who tell us how much they will cost, and personal staffs who help us get legislation passed. State legislators now have time and resources, practically equal to those available to members of Congress, to tackle large, complex issues.

Another factor is demographics. On average, Wisconsin state legislators are 10 years younger than members of Congress. State legislators are more likely than their national counterparts to be part of the "sandwich generation"—the generation faced with meeting the needs not only of children, but of parents who are living longer.

Younger state legislators are more likely to understand the need for two incomes and the strain two jobs place on young families. Our leadership is younger as well. In Wisconsin, both the assembly speaker and the senate majority leader are in their early forties, far younger than their congressional counterparts.

Another important demographic difference is the increased role played by women in state legislatures. Women make up about 20 percent of the Wisconsin legislature, but only 5 percent of Congress. Some of the key players in the Wisconsin family leave debate were Republican women lawmakers, who helped persuade our conservative governor to accept a compromise despite his strong reservations about the concept.

Finally, it is important to remember the unique political history and heritage of each state and how it influences policymaking. The Louisiana of Huey Long is far different from the Minnesota of Hubert Humphrey.

Wisconsin's political heritage was shaped by the Progressive Movement led by Robert La Follette in the early part of this century. That movement was so successful that Theodore Roosevelt once called Wisconsin "a laboratory for wise experimental legislation to secure the social and political betterment of the people as a whole."

We are used to being first, not waiting for Congress to act. This is especially true on workers' rights issues. Wisconsin was the first state to put a worker's compensation law into operation (1911), the first to enact unemployment compensation (1931), and among the first to pass a minimum wage law (1913).

For these reasons, state legislators have come to recognize that the baby boom generation is confronted with a cruel Hobson's choice. For most of us, the economics of family life demand two incomes—not one income for the basics and one for the luxuries, not one career to support the family and one for personal fulfillment, but two incomes just to achieve the American Dream of a home and a better future for our children. We are like Alice in Wonderland—it takes all the running we can do to stay in the same place.

And while we run so hard, our children still need us. The economy may have changed; our children have not.

It is not so much that we should not be forced to choose between our jobs and our children, because that choice does not really exist. Most of us need both. The challenge for policymakers is to find ways to ease the friction between the two, to balance the demands of a career and the public good of raising healthy children.

Many public policy proposals aimed at the problems of the modern family represent a quiet revolution in the way we think about work and family. The traditional belief in the United States is that one's career is "public" and raising children is "private." I want to suggest that just the opposite is true, or at least that career and child-rearing are equally public.

What could be more public than shaping a new generation? When our jobs force us to steal time from our children, we are robbing everyone's future. On the other hand, our careers are more personal. If we botch them, it may have a devastating impact on us, but if we fail in raising our children it jeopardizes the future. Imagine an entire generation of young adults who have been deprived of the attention of their parents, who have not been sufficiently nurtured, and who have not had ample opportunity to absorb values, to learn to tell right from wrong.

If it is in the public interest to raise healthy children, then it is surely government's role to facilitate childrearing—not to interfere with the prerogatives of the parents or to meddle within the family, but to protect the family unit from outside forces that threaten it.

For years, protecting the family has been defined in terms of what some policymakers were against. If you were pro-family, then you were expected to be *against* abortion and *against* pornography and possibly even *against* gay rights. Traditionally, pro-family policymakers have ignored the more fundamental threats to family life based in an economic system that is demanding more of us for a smaller reward. Let me hasten to add that I am not questioning the sincerity of those who call themselves pro-family. I only want to point out that those of us who have long considered ourselves pro-family badly need to cast our policies in more positive terms. Family leave legislation is undeniably pro-family, and yet it does not fight change, but rather attempts to meet new challenges created by a changing economy.

Today, only 7 percent of Wisconsin families are traditional in the sense that the father works for a paycheck and the mother works inside the home caring for children. There has been perhaps no greater revolution in either family life or our economy in the last 20 years than that of women working in great numbers outside the home. Today, fully 60 percent of mothers with children under three years old are in the workforce.

Women work for a variety of reasons, but for the purposes of this discussion I would like to focus on the economic forces that bring women into the workforce. Two of the most basic elements of the American Dream are a house and a better future for our children. The price of both has risen dramatically faster than our ability to pay for them. In 1949, it took just 14 percent of the average 30-year-old man's income to buy the average house. Today, the average 30-year-old man spends 44 percent of his income on the average house. Clearly, one income does not stretch as far as once it did.

The cost of higher education, which is generally recognized as the ticket to a better future, has outpaced our ability to pay for it as well. The cost of a year at college increased at a rate greater than inflation every year in the 1980s, and it is expected to continue to do so through the end of the century.

So, whatever other motives women may have in entering the workforce, the economics of the American Dream are a powerful catalyst. And it is a poignant paradox. Mothers work because they love their children and want them to grow up in good neighborhoods and go to college. Yet the very fact of working limits the most precious resource mothers, or fathers, can give to their children—their time.

This is the challenge: to fashion policies that keep the American Dream alive and the American family intact. It is no longer enough for those who think of themselves as pro-family to be against change; they must be *for* policies that recognize the more difficult environment for families and work to make things better.

The Wisconsin Family and Medical Leaves Act is one of a series of bills introduced in the states and at the federal level to protect the jobs of workers who need to take time off to care for their families. To my knowledge, no state has a permanent law as comprehensive as Wisconsin's.

What we have accomplished in Wisconsin is to enact complete family protection. Our law not only allows time away from a job for both mothers and fathers to care for a newborn or newly adopted child, but also allows time for the care of a seriously ill child, spouse, or parent or for the worker's own serious illness. The Wisconsin law is intergenerational; that is, it recognizes the other side of the two-earner dilemma. Our parents become more frail and need their children more just when those children have less time.

People over 85 are the fastest-growing segment of the elderly population. New technologies keep increasingly frail individuals alive, and deemphasis of institutionalization places more of the care burden on family members. Again, the impact of more women in the workforce is profoundly felt. Daughters have been the traditional caregivers for their elderly parents. Of all care provided to the elderly, 25 percent is provided by daughters. (An even larger share, 36 percent, is provided by spouses, who are also covered in Wisconsin.)

The Wisconsin law is not perfect. It only covers employers of 50 or more, which excludes one-third of the workforce in my state. It limits leave for care of seriously ill family members to 2 weeks, although I know from personal experience that it can take at least that long to place a family member in a good nursing home. It limits parental leave to 6 weeks, when child development experts recommend close parental contact for at least the first 18 weeks of life. And its definition of a "serious illness" as a disabling condition requiring at least outpatient care may be too restrictive. Perhaps most important, leaves are unpaid, limiting the law's utility for low-income workers. (It should be pointed out, however, that the law does give employees the option of using paid vacation, sick leave, or paid leave of any other kind during a protected leave period.) The law can and will be improved. The important thing is that the foundation is there. The principle is established in law that employees have a right to a job-protected family leave. Now that we have laid the foundation, we can build on it.

The movement for family and medical leave in this country marks both a fundamental change in how we view family and work and a reverence for traditional family values. It is a pro-family expression that talks about what we are for, not what we are against. Most of all, it recognizes that in an increasingly difficult and challenging environment, our families have a right to survive.

10 The Place of Caregiving Work in Contemporary Societies

Deanne Bonnar

> Motherhood is no longer a synonym for bland, unthinking goodness, nor does it designate the guardian of an irrelevant domestic backwater, or an untouchable area of sanctity. Motherhood is a political battleground, a contested area for control of women's bodies, of the fortunes of families, of the obligations of community support, of the constraints on choice.
>
> (Keohane, Rosaldo, and Gelpi, 1982)

The Invisibility of Caregiving as Work

Many people today are concerned that personal caregiving work, particularly child care, is being pushed to the margins of parents' available time and energy, and that the failure to provide for it may have serious consequences for all of us. However, enlarging the place for this vital human work will take more than tinkering with policy. It will require fundamental shifts in our world view and conscious struggle by people to redefine the terms of our collective life.

The forces that have made caregiving, and particularly parenting, undervalued work done at the margins of one's time are complex, but two streams deserve initial attention. The most significant influence is the development of industrialization and wage economies whose definition of work is centered on the production and servicing of goods. The second influence is feminist theory. While less powerful an influence than industrialization, an early stage of feminist theory reinforced the dominant belief that what happened in the domestic sphere was trivial and much less valuable than activity in the public arena.

But all societies must have systems for both the production and care of the material basis of life and the reproduction and care of human life. In most cultures the production and care of the material basis of life have been done by both males and females, but the reproduction and physical care of people has been almost exclusively a female activity. The definition of work, especially in industrialized Eurocentric cultures, has focused almost exclusively on the production and care of goods. Human care has been looked at as love, duty, or biological destiny, but not as work. Rarely has it entitled the women engaged in caregiving to direct access to economic resources. This has left women as a class in a position of economic disadvantage and made them especially vulnerable when they do not live in male-based households.

A United Nations group found that women are one-third of the world's formal labor force and do four-fifths of all informal work, but receive only 10 percent of the world's income and own less than 1 percent of the world's property (Leghorn and Parker, 1981, p. 14). The fact that a woman's labor, though long and arduous, routinely leaves her poor has received remarkably little attention, but it is a worldwide phenomenon. Until recently, socialists and feminists were the only two groups that made any systematic attempts to address this issue. Both groups concluded that economic and social equality for women would occur through their entrance into the market sector. Neither group paid much attention to the work that was occurring in the domestic sector. When it was looked at, both feminists and socialist theorists predicted that it would be collectivized or purchased in the marketplace and that household labor would wither away (Engels, 1972; Gilman, 1966). In early stages of the current feminist movement, feminists uncritically adopted the dominant view that housework was boring, trivial, and not real work. Feminists shunned it in favor of employment, which was seen as more important, more challenging, and more rewarding. Many women with families who entered market employment in the 1960s and 1970s learned what some women—especially minority and poor women, who had long held "jobs" in addition to being mothers—had known for a long time: paid employment does not make homemaking labor disappear, but instead compresses it into the hours employed men usually counted as leisure. Most employed women, far from feeling liberated, now felt that they held two jobs. Current investigators into women's work hours find that for employed married women in 1980, the workday is longer than it was for their grandmothers. Joann Vanek reports that whereas nonemployed married women work 56 hours a week, employed wives 71 hours, and employed mothers of young children 80 hours, their husbands average 65 hours (1980, p. 277). And although there has been a reduction in the amount of housework done by employed women, for mothers with young children the reduction does not compress domestic labor below 30 hours. Mystified by the demands of the work that remains in the household and burdened by dual workloads, feminists have turned their attention to household work.

The Housework Label

In 1974 Ann Oakley broke new ground within sociology by publishing *The Sociology of Housework*. Others followed suit. Some efforts, like *All Work and No Pay*, by Wendy Edmond and the Wages for Housework Collective (1975), focus on the drudgery and slave/servant aspects of housework. Others, like *Homemakers: The Forgotten Workers*, by Rae André, argue that "housework is not demeaning in and of itself, but only under certain social and economic conditions. It is not demeaning, but it is demeaned" (1981, p. 182).

The literature on homemaking as work has been augmented by an unlikely ally—the insurance industry. Insurance companies have examined the economic value of a homemaker to a family. By looking at the component parts and assessing them at current market averages, the industry has claimed that a homemaker's work is worth between $10 thousand and $40 thousand a year (Burr, 1981; Edmunds, 1978). Merely listing the multitude of tasks that homemakers do has challenged the notion that a homemaker does not work.

Yet welcome as the studies of homemakers as workers are, many of them trivialize domestic sector work by defining it as a collection of rationalized tasks. There is a marked tendency in many studies to look at homemaking as a series of physical jobs—cooking, laundry, cleaning—and to ignore the human care, with its intellectual, managerial, and psychological components, which is actually the most demanding aspect of the work. Thus, one sees "cook" listed repeatedly in studies, but rarely "judge," "negotiator," "family historian," "accountant," "philosopher," "lobbyist," "lawyer," "spiritual guide," "policewoman," "healer," or even "counselor." Yet women who are caring for children, even under the most limiting of circumstances, perform these functions routinely.

Caregiving as the Focus

Work in the domestic sector is almost inevitably assumed to absorb little of women's mental and psychic energy. But when feeding children is examined, for example, the complexity of the task is revealed. Providing meals involves not only the purchase and preparation of food but multiple decisions about what to purchase, how to prepare it, and when to serve it. These decisions are built on stores of information about food prices, nutritional content, tastes, schedules of household members, ethnic traditions, cooking techniques, and perhaps medical requirements. The failure to see the absorptive level of work in the domestic sector arises, it appears, from focusing on housework, rather than parenting or caregiving, as the primary work done in the home. Caregiving work, defined as work that involves the supervision and care of another person who needs personal assistance in order to sustain life, is highly absorptive work. "Housework" refers to the care given to things. Housework done in the process of raising children or providing other caretaking can be complex, time-consuming, and arduous, but it is the human care that is truly absorptive and most likely to impinge on the selection of market work. Housework is a vital and demanding part of the caregiving, but it is the human care that sets the basis for and organizes the demands. Caregiving is not a part of the housework; housework is a part of the process of human care. This distinction is frequently overlooked by feminists, theorists, and policymakers. Early feminists and others were not wrong to call for enabling women to do work other than housework, but in their eagerness to eschew housework, they almost literally threw out the baby with the bathwater. Meanwhile, investigators who say housework is not demeaning often fail to clarify its importance. Caregiving should be the focus. Caregiving work, whether raising children or enabling disabled or frail adults to maintain themselves, is not a minor pursuit. It is more gratifying to some people and a greater social contribution than many types of work in the market sector.

The Requirements of Human Care

Nurture is work that the market sector has a hard time organizing on a rationalized basis. Economies of scale, which seem fundamental to industrialized enterprises, prove to be antithetical to the nurturance that is fundamental to the caregiving process. Production line systems may provide meals, but not necessarily sustenance. Teams of people can come through residences and clean them, but there are reasons that teams of people should not take over the care of dependent others. It matters little if tables are dusted by different people every week, but it matters a lot if children's caregivers are repeatedly changed. It matters little if laundry is done by one person or a dozen, but it matters a lot if an ailing or confused person is cared for by 20 different people in a week, as happens frequently in nursing homes. Caring for people and caring for things are not comparable activities. Because they go on in the household together, we have confused their separate requirements and their vastly different value.

Households in which there are people who need caregiving—whether they are children, chronically ill or disabled adults, or frail elderly people—require management. For many caregivers this unacknowledged management work uses a great deal of energy. Innumerable mothers who have taken on outside employment and have succeeded in sharing household tasks with their mates still feel oppressed by the work at home and have a difficult time articulating the problem. In addition to the physical work, employed mothers struggle with the responsibility for thinking out, planning, and organizing the elements of parenting. It is common to hear, "He does a lot more than he used to, but I'm still the responsible person." Thus, even if the father takes the child to buy shoes, in most instances it is the mother who watches the growth of the child's feet, selects a shoe store that matches the family budget or the child's particular footwear needs, and makes the timing decisions. In addition, she is likely to maintain responsibility for the purchase if her mate is somehow unable to take the child at the necessary point.

Understanding Caregiving Constraints on Labor Market Choices

Detailing the amount of thought that goes into parenting and other caregiving activities is important for four reasons. First, the very familiarity of these activities makes it easy for us to think we understand what is involved without, in fact, having conceptual clarity about the nature of the work.

Second, the lack of clarity perpetuates a belief that the tasks can be transferred to the market, thereby eliminating the inequities between men and women in caregiving work, and freeing women to compete equally in the employment sector. While some services can conceivably be purchased, management is not accounted for in such a scheme, and it represents a significant proportion of the work. The managerial process behind the simple purchase of shoes for one child, for example, involves the gathering of information (on the child's feet, the shoes, the community resources, the family budget), the assessment of the information, negotiation with the child about the selection, the decision, and the evaluation of the decision made.

Third, this unaddressed absorptive issue is a major factor in the type of work that many women seek outside the home. Women with infants and small children, for example, may look for paid employment with flexible scheduling, minimal transportation concerns, generous sick leave and vacation benefits, and no after-hours demands. Failing to find employment opportunities that satisfy even half their needs, many women choose part-time work or take jobs not commensurate with their skills.

Women are overwhelmingly concentrated in a narrow range of jobs. The reasons for this are complex, including the demands of capitalism, division of labor by gender, sex discrimination, and also the choices women themselves make. This is not to argue that women choose to be in poorly paid positions, but merely to observe that choices about market work are constrained not by routine household drudgery, but by complex, often satisfying, and highly energy-absorbing caregiving work at home. It has been noted that when women choose careers, they frequently work in caregiving professions. The failure to choose business or engineering may reflect not a lack of assertiveness or a discomfort with mathematical concepts, but the choice of work in the market sector that has congruence with work in the domestic sector. This may help maximize available working time by reducing the stress of constantly changing mental gears, even though contrasting market work could provide a balance for the strains of caregiving. As long as domestic care work is primarily a female responsibility, many women, unless they have exceptional talents or interests, may continue to choose a market work life that complements the work they already do (Bonnar, 1986).

But the final reason is the most significant. Because homemaker activity has been labeled "housework," it has not been considered important for market sector work to be modified to meet the requirements of domestic sector work. Until very recently, governmental and corporate policy development has been geared toward enhancing paid employment, not personal caregiving such as parenting. Thus, caregiving of all sorts, and parenting in particular, has been squeezed for many people to the edges of available time and energy.

The Dual Work Roles of Women

Even with large variations in economic structure, political planning, national wealth, and the presence or absence of laws about sex discrimination, women who work for wages in every country carry dual occupational roles. Every international study of women's labor, without exception, has found that women who work for wages necessarily have a dual work life in which wage work is added to their domestic labor (Kamerman and Kahn, 1978; Leghorn and Parker, 1981; Scott, 1974). Responsibility for domestic labor is theirs regardless of what other type of work they do. In Sweden, China, and Cuba, the official policy that males must share the housework has been extremely hard to enforce. Although the percentage of women working for wages has jumped in the United States from 27.9 percent in 1955 to 51 percent in 1980, women remain overwhelmingly compressed into the lowest-paid positions in society. These jobs are characterized by low hourly wages, few benefits such as sick leave, no career ladders, frequent layoffs or seasonal work, and little or no investment in job training.

This compression of women into a narrow range of the lowest-paid jobs is as true in self-designated socialist countries as it is in the United States. For example, in Sweden it has long been official policy that "equality implies that both men and women shall have the same right and opportunity for a fully realized life. A job and financial independence are the basis for creating this equality" (Swedish Institute, 1983, p. 1). The Swedish government has, moreover, reported to the United Nations, "The goal of our long-range program of women's rights must be that every individual, regardless of sex, shall have the same responsibility for child upbringing and housework" (cited in Liljestrom, 1978, p. 33). But, Rita Liljestrom observes, "it is primarily women who have had to bear the conflict between parenthood and reproduction as well as between parenthood and production . . . the conflicts have been settled in favor of men at the expense of women" (1978, p. 21). Published wage rates for women in Sweden vary, but observers agree that there is a substantial discrepancy in income between men and women, with women's wages between 50 and 65 percent of men's. There is agreement that the problem stems from a segregated labor market in which women are concentrated in a narrow range of approximately 25 occupations, while males are found in more than 300. Predominantly female jobs are paid at lower wage rates than jobs that are predominantly male.

In Hungary, where everyone is guaranteed a job, Zsuzsa Ferge reports that wages for men are about 30 percent higher than those for women (1979, p. 184). There too, women remain in a much narrower range of occupations that generally pay lower wages. Hilda Scott, author of *Does Socialism Liberate Women?* states, "In all socialist countries, women still do most of the low-skill, poorly paid work, and the majority of women do work of this kind" (1974, p. 212).

Across all sectors of the labor market, nurturing jobs, occupied mainly by women, pay substantially less than jobs held by men that may require less skill or training. In commenting on the ranking of jobs by the U.S. government, Suzanne Stocking made the following observations:

> Foster Mothers, Child Care attendants, and Nursery School and Kindergarten teachers supposedly require no more training or responsibility than Restroom or Parking Lot Attendants. What is even more appalling is that every one of these parenting jobs ranks well below Dog Trainer. The job of a Nurse who works in every major department of her hospital and assists with surgery and birth is ranked as slightly less demanding than that of a Hotel Clerk. (Cited in Leghorn and Parker, 1981, p. 177)

The closer one comes to direct care, the less one earns. In the United States, high school teachers earn twice what preschool teachers do, and doctors earn more than four times as much as nurses, who in turn are paid better than patient-aides.

Consequences for Policy

Alternatives: Market Versus Domestic Sector Care

One factor contributing to the low wages of nurturing jobs in the market is that caregiving work and its attendant services in the home have traditionally been unwaged. Almost all policy has been oriented toward enabling women's paid employment, rather than enabling the caregiving they already do. Policy has also been devoid of efforts to enable men to do caregiving. It is a grave mistake to attribute the social product solely to those who work in market production and ignore and devalue the work of reproduction and human care without which society cannot continue. Under these circumstances the caregiver is encouraged, pushed, or coerced (Aid to Families with Dependent Children is a case in point) into valued market labor and unwittingly becomes the bearer of two workloads rather than one. Nowhere is this more evident than in child care. The failure to provide adequate time for parenting in general, and especially during critical times in a child's life such as early infancy, illness, or periods of developmental crisis, has produced hurried, worried parents raising hurried, worried children.

Both market and planned industrial economies have focused on increasing material wealth, often at the expense of human nurture. Increases in the standard of living have made life better for many people, but it is important to question the benefit of increases in material wealth that reduce the capacity of people to care for one another. It has been suggested that the nature of industrialization is such that it leads to the

> dependence of all social life, and indeed of all the interrelatedness of human kind, upon the market place. . . . thus the population no longer relies upon social organization in the form of family, friends, neighbors, [or] community. . . . In time not only the material and service needs but even the emotional patterns of life are channeled through the market. (Braverman, 1974, p. 276)

Are we locked into this prediction? I have suggested that although the market can produce shoes, it has a hard time producing nurture because the reproduction and care of people is not equivalent to the production of goods. Nurture involves constancy and personal care. Not only is personal caregiving work necessary, it is absolutely fundamental to life that people find valuable. If people are to thrive, not all caregiving can be transferred to group settings such as day care and nursing homes. Many women carry double workloads not because they have been overly socialized to notice "ring around the collar" but because they refuse to give up the personal caregiving activities they value in life.

Modifying the Time Variable

What alternatives for preserving personal care do industrial wage economies have? Economists argue that work decisions are influenced by trade-offs between time and money. I think we must consider policies aimed at both. The first option is to rearrange the time demand of employment. The requirements of parenting are incompatible with 8-hour-a-day, 5-day-a-week, 50-week-a-year work life. There are many times during the course of childhood when a child may need concentrated, individualized care from a parent. The most significant of these is, of course, immediately after birth, when bonding for parents and the infant is particularly critical. An older child may break a bone, suffer an illness, or have other mishaps that require intensive care from the primary caregivers. A system of guaranteed parental leave that permits extended care after birth and occasional leave for childhood emergencies is clearly the first step that must be taken to free time for parenting. Many industrial nations already provide for parental leave, and some have been doing so for years (Zigler and Frank, 1988). Meaningful parental leave policy requires paid leave. Unpaid leave may be better than none, but it is clearly not an option that most families could afford to take.

Another time option is to expand flextime arrangements that permit employees to vary their starting and stopping times to meet their particular caregiving needs. Such flexibility is critical for parents whose children may start school at 8:00 A.M. one year and 9:00 A.M. the next year. In addition, it provides time for parents to help children make necessary separation adjustments, to attend a school play, or to provide transportation for after-school activities.

Sweden and Israel, among other countries, have proposals for shortening the workday (Kamerman and Kahn, 1978). A six-hour day is being seriously discussed in Sweden and is already available to certain groups of employed parents. Reducing the length of the paid workday for everyone would not only open up full-time employment to many caregivers who are now employed part time but would enable many overworked men to become active caregivers as well. Shortening the work *week* has been suggested by many people concerned with high unemployment rates, but it would do little to aid caregivers with daily responsibilities. A shorter day, on the other hand, has the same potential for increasing employment while enabling many more people to do both market and domestic work.

Modifying the Wage Variable

The second option is to consider models for waging domestic sector work directly. Two such models have already been proposed. In the late 1960s David Gil proposed "Parent's Wages" in order to bring an alternative policy into the public debate on poverty. Essentially the model suggests paying wages to parents in relation to the time they devote to child care work or gainful employment respectively. Parents would be responsible for registering claims through Social Security. The entire program would be financed out of the general revenues of the federal government and integrated with the general tax systems (Gil, 1973, chap. 4; 1979, chap. 8).

In 1972 Mariarosa Dalla Costa and Selma James laid the groundwork for another model, Wages for Housework, which has grown into an international campaign. Essentially, they argue that people should be paid equally for the housework they do, whether married or single, employed or not, with or without children. Wages would come through government, financed by corporate taxes (Dalla Costa and James, 1975).

Both models clearly focus on the vast amount of unwaged labor that undergirds our productive system, but each is slightly off the mark. Gil's proposal limits the wage to parents, while Wages for Housework wages almost everyone and fails to target those whose market labor is most affected by domestic work—caregivers. Perhaps a more useful model is to wage caregivers. Caregivers include all those people who provide supervision and physical care to human beings whose ability to provide self-care is significantly limited. Because caregiving is complex and multifaceted work, flat payments should not be made. Caregiving for an infant is more demanding than caring for a 10-year-old, and caring for a severely disabled adult is more demanding than supervising an adolescent. Thus, a model could start with a flat rate, adding increments according to the intensity of care, the amount of time required, the number of people being cared for, and whether or not the caregiver is the household's only earner. The wage would be highest while one cares for very young children and would decrease as the children matured.

This model is raised here only to illustrate another policy alternative. We are talking about waging caregivers for roughly 90 million children, ill and disabled adults, and frail elders at a cost that is similar to the defense budget (Bonnar, 1985). The similarity in the figures for waging caregivers and paying for defense raises some troubling questions about the basis for the poverty of large numbers of women.

Objections to Waging Caregivers

Proposals for waging domestic sector work have raised intense opposition, which is to be expected. They are, after all, radical proposals that involve shifts in views about work, the separation of market and domestic spheres, and the traditional relation of dependency between the sexes, as well as major transfers of wealth. Some of the sources of this opposition are, however, surprising. In Sweden, the Communist party, socialists, and feminists actively worked against a proposal for homemaker wages in 1978. Of major concern to feminists were the reinforcement of women's traditional roles and the isolation—psychological, social, and political—that women experience doing individual labor in separate homes. However, keeping caregiving unwaged does nothing to decrease the isolation and, in fact, increases it. There is reason to believe that waging workers in the domestic sector would increase their mobility, their identification as a class of workers, their interest in unionization, and their political position (see James, 1975). Another way to address isolation would be to locate the wage in a larger package that envisions a new Social Security program for caregivers, much as the current Social Security program was developed for wage-earning men. Such a package should include increased funds for day care, a network of family resource centers, and training programs for parenting and other caregiving skills.

Paradoxically, the Wages for Housework Campaign argues that paying women for housework will allow women to refuse that work and thereby decrease the rigidity of conventional roles. Members point out that paying for the work allows it to be seen as work rather than love, moral imperative, or biological destiny. Women are then more free to choose between it and other labor. Moreover, while the dangers of locking women into sex-typed work must be considered, the other side of the issue—locking men into market roles—is rarely addressed. A wage in the domestic sector has the potential to enable men to assume more of this work, for they, too, could see it as work rather than a biological destiny. The idea that domestic work is trivial, unrewarding, and either unworthy of or too worthy for a wage fosters the one-sided sexual revolution the world is currently witnessing. Enabling men to do more caregiving has received very little attention from policymakers, yet it is becoming increasingly clear that we must find ways to engage men if we are to get beyond sex-stereotyped roles.

Money cannot buy love, some object. The lack of money cannot produce love either, whereas the lack of resources can rob people of their ability to care. The waging of caring work is not "buying love" but buying the circumstances of life that make love possible. As long as money is the currency that buys food, we cannot continue a system where half the world works for love and the other half works for money.

The Future

Some of the proposals outlined here may seem more realistic than others, but all focus on childrearing and other forms of caregiving as basic societal work. Massive amounts of this unpaid labor undergird industrial economies. The United Nations Decade for Women pushed to have women's unpaid labor counted as part of gross national products (Metz, 1989). If such work were counted, the U.S. GNP would immediately rise hundreds of billions of dollars.

Responsibility for domestic labor has traditionally fallen to women. Understanding this work as caregiving focuses on the essential contributions to society that women have always made. It clarifies that policies that propose Social Security credits for homemakers, children's allowances, shorter work hours, and parental leave are not simply to help women but are ways of ensuring that this vital human work will not only continue but will thrive. People need more than material well-being to survive; they need personal human nurture. Industrialized nations are organized to maximize material production as if it were society's most critical work. The task that lies in front of us is to change this seemingly universal assumption. It is an enormous undertaking, but we must begin by designing policy that both draws men into childrearing work and ensures that the caregiving that women already contribute can flourish in our daily lives.

REFERENCES

André, Rae (1981). *Homemakers: The Forgotten Workers*. Chicago: University of Chicago Press.

Bonnar, Deanne (1985). "Women, Work and Poverty." In David Gil and Eva Gil, eds., *The Future of Work*. Cambridge, Mass.: Schenkman.

—— (1986). "Toward the Feminization of Policy: Exit from an Ancient Trap by the Redefinition of Work." In Rochelle Lefkowitz and Ann Withorn, eds., *For Crying Out Loud: Women and Poverty in the United States*. New York: Pilgrim Press.

Braverman, Harry (1974). *Labor and Monopoly Capital*. New York: Monthly Review Press.

Burr, Rosemary (1981). "Love's Labour Lost . . ." *Financial Times*, November 11.

Della Costa, Mariarosa, and Selma James (1975). *The Power of Women and the Subversion of the Community* (3d ed.). Bristol, England: Falling Wall Press.

Edmond, Wendy, and Suzie Fleming, eds. (1975). *All Work and No Pay*. Bristol, England: Falling Wall Press.

Edmunds, Lynne (1978). "Should Wives Be Paid for Doing Housework?" *Woman's Journal*. March.

Engels, Friedrich (1972). *The Origin of the Family, Private Property and the State*. New York: International Publishers.

Ferge, Zsuzsa (1979). *A Society in the Making: Hungarian Social and Societal Policy 1945–75*. White Plains, N.Y.: M. E. Sharpe.

Gil, David (1973). *Unravelling Social Policy*. Cambridge, Mass.: Schenkman.

—— (1979). *Beyond the Jungle*. Cambridge, Mass.: Schenkman.

Gilman, Charlotte (1966). *Women and Economics*. New York: Harper & Row.

Kamerman, Sheila B., and Alfred J. Kahn, eds. (1978). *Family Policy: Government and Families in Fourteen Countries*. New York: Columbia University Press.

Keohane, Nannerl, Michelle Rosaldo, and Barbara Gelpi, eds. (1982). *Feminist Theory: A Critique of Ideology*. Chicago: University of Chicago Press.

Leghorn, Lisa, and Katherine Parker (1981). *Women's Worth: Sexual Economics and the World of Women*. Boston: Routledge & Kegan Paul.

Liljestrom, Rita (1978). "Sweden." In Sheila B. Kamerman and Alfred J. Kahn, eds., *Family Policy: Government and Families in Fourteen Countries*. New York: Columbia University Press.

Metz, Roberta (1989). "Women's Work Is Worth Something in Global Terms." *Boston Globe*. March 11.

Oakley, Ann (1974). *The Sociology of Housework*. New York: Pantheon Books.

Scott, Hilda (1974). *Does Socialism Liberate Women?* Boston: Beacon Press.

Swedish Institute (1982). "Equality Between Men and Women in Sweden." Stockholm: Swedish Institute.

Vanek, Joann (1980). "Time Spent in Housework." In Alice Amsden, ed., *The Economics of Women and Work*. New York: St. Martin's Press.

Zigler, Edward F., and Meryl Frank, eds. (1988). *The Parental Leave Crisis: Toward a National Policy*. New Haven: Yale University Press.

PART V

Employers' Experiences

11 Employers' Parental Leave Policies: Does the Labor Market Provide Parental Leave?

Eileen Trzcinski

The Need for Parental Leave

Parents require leave during the period before and after the birth or adoption of a child for two distinct reasons. The first is a result of disabilities from pregnancy and childbirth. By definition, female but not male employees require this protection. The second component of parental leave involves the care of newborn children. Parental leave gives parents the freedom to take time away from the labor market without relinquishing job security.

Psychological Needs of Parents and Infants

In recent years, the study of psychological development in infancy has expanded rapidly. This research shows that the need for parental leave stems from both the infant's and the parent's psychological needs. Previously researchers had focused on the parent–infant relationship as unidirectional in terms of the parents' effect on the child; they now are finding that the interaction works both ways: parent and infant influence each other's behavior. This interaction is a process through which parent and child come to know and to adapt to each other. (See Hopper and Zigler, 1989; Chapter 18 by Marsha Weinraub and Elizabeth Jaeger; and Chapter 19 by Lynne Sanford Koester for summaries of infant care research.) The length of time needed to develop this attachment, together with the mutual needs of parents and infants, makes parental leave an essential component of any family economic policy. Alternatives that are often suggested, such as flexible hours or high-quality child care, could alleviate some of the stresses working parents now experience, but they are not interchangeable with parental leave.

The lack of infant care leave has particularly serious repercussions for parents of adopted children. In some cases parents must assure the adoption agency that one of them can be at home with the newly adopted child for at least 6 months. Adoptive parents and the children themselves often face major transitions. Today many adopted children are entering a family of a different race, are handicapped, or have experienced abuse or abandonment. These factors can make the development of secure attachment to new parents more difficult (Hopper and Zigler, 1989).

The Economic Need for Parental Leave

Parental leave can affect the distribution of income between parents and nonparents, and hence the distribution of income to children. Without parental leave, caregivers have no choice but to leave the labor market if they desire to spend several weeks or months with their newborn child or if they are unable to work temporarily because of pregnancy and childbirth-related disabilities. Mandated parental leave allows caregivers to do both—to withdraw temporarily while remaining attached to their current job. Mandated leaves will thus increase job tenure for traditional caregivers. Research consistently shows that wages increase with job tenure (e.g., Corcoran and Duncan, 1979). Job-guaranteed leaves also provide protection against unemployment when the caregiver is ready to return to work.

Universally mandated parental leave can open up the range of occupations compatible with both childrearing and market work and thereby shift the choices of women, the traditional caregivers in our society, away from female-dominated occupations. If all occupations provide leave, women can select occupations that they might have previously rejected because these occupations provided neither leave nor easy labor market exit and reentry. Mandated leave would then improve women's employment position in four related ways: by reducing unemployment that can occur when the caregiver reenters the labor market, by increasing job tenure, by breaking down a structural barrier to women's entry into the higher-paid male-dominated occupations, and by reducing supply to female-dominated occupations, thus raising wages there.

These improvements in the labor market position of women will alleviate some of the economic pressures facing families. With mandated leave, children can receive short-term benefits, from a reduction in unemployment after leave and job search costs for their parents, and long-term benefits from a higher stream of family income and a reduced probability of falling into poverty in the future. (See

Chapter 3 by Roberta Spalter-Roth and Heidi Hartmann for estimates of the effects of the lack of leave on income for individuals
and families.)

A Market-Based Allocation of Wages and Fringe Benefits

The parental leave debate centers on the need for government-
mandated leave. Parental leave requires active participation by
employers. Government and private individuals can provide other
components of a family economic policy, such as child care, child
support enforcement, welfare programs, child allowances, and child
care tax credits, but only employers can provide leave with the necessary guarantee of job security.

Even the most vocal opponents of mandated leave, such as the
U.S. Chamber of Commerce, acknowledge that newborn children
benefit by having time to bond with their parents, but they question
whether government should actively encourage any specific behavior
on the part of parents. Opponents of mandated leave fear that leave
will create burdensome costs for employers. They also claim that the
market itself already provides employees with the optimal level of
parental leave.

Supporters of mandated leave are skeptical that the market will
provide parental leave to all who desire it. They are aware that parental leave will increase costs to employers, but they weigh these
costs against the costs of not having leave (see, for example, Chapter
3 by Spalter-Roth and Hartmann) and the long-term psychological
and economic benefits to children, parents, and society as a whole
(see, for example, Bush Center in Child Development and Social
Policy, 1988).

Theory of a Market-Based Allocation

Opponents of mandated leave contend that the labor market will
efficiently provide parents with adequate access to parental leave.
They base their argument on a specific theoretical model of how
markets allocate wages and fringe benefits. Some economists argue
that under certain specified conditions, markets allocate wages and
fringe benefits efficiently for both employers and employees. In a
free market economy that is untainted by institutional factors such as
custom and discrimination, the mix of wages and fringes should reflect the relative prices of wages and fringes interacting with the
preferences of employees. Since parental leave adds a cost to the
wage bill, firms that offer it will reduce other components of that

bill: wages may go down, health insurance coverage may be reduced, vacations may be shortened. According to this model, as long as employees value the parental leave more than another benefit that must be given up, employers will adjust the wage–fringe mix to reflect their employees' preferences.

As more women have entered the workplace, the mix of wages and fringes should theoretically reflect their needs and preferences. If working parents want parental leave, the model predicts that they need only search among the many different employers to find the one who offers the best mix of wages and fringes. In theory, employers will respond to these needs. In order to attract and retain good employees, employers must offer what employees want. Just as employers respond to employees' desire to have paid vacations, paid sick leave, health insurance benefits, and the wide range of fringe benefits now available, employers will theoretically respond to the desires of employees who want parental leave. But in order to provide this leave, employers must cut back on wages or other fringe benefits—a trade-off that these employees willingly accept, since they value parental leave more than other fringe benefits or the higher wages that would prevail in the absence of parental leave.

Some firms may find parental leave more expensive to provide than other firms. Where leaves significantly disrupt production, firms will cut back more on wages and other fringe benefits than firms that can provide leaves with greater ease. Rational employees will gravitate to firms that find leave less costly to provide because they will theoretically face less of a trade-off in wages.

Potential Problems with a Market-Based Allocation

Economists need to make a number of underlying assumptions for the above argument to hold: the labor market must be free of discrimination, employees must have perfect information about where the jobs are, they must be free to move wherever the jobs are located, and the economy must be at full employment. Violations of these assumptions result in market imperfections, which undermine the ability of the forces of supply and demand to yield efficient outcomes.

Even if these assumptions are satisfied, the efficient outcome implies a very specific result: that is, potential mothers and fathers must earn a lower wage than other individuals in society if they want to take parental leave. Under the conditions laid out in this theory, the labor market, the major institution for the distribution of income, requires parents to lower their income to obtain infant care leave. Parents must also end up in a different range of jobs from nonparents if the costs of providing leave differ across jobs.

The business community argues adamantly against mandated parental leave, claiming that parental leave will interfere with economic efficiency and hence with economic growth and productivity. These arguments deny any link between the welfare of children today and the welfare of society tomorrow. If employers benefit in the long run when children are well cared for, then employers must share the costs. Otherwise society faces a free rider problem: individual parents bear all the costs, while business in the future enjoys the benefit of well-adjusted, productive employees.

Other opponents of mandated leave object to its distributional consequences, labeling parental leave "yuppie welfare" and suggesting that the middle and upper-middle class will benefit from mandated leave but that poor families will not. Paid leave provides an obvious solution to this concern. Even an unpaid leave can, however, benefit low-income families. Without a job-guaranteed leave, low-income mothers who become disabled as a result of pregnancy and childbirth will be forced out of their jobs. Unpaid leave provides protection against unemployment.

Under the market solution, parents can be forced to choose between satisfying their children's developmental needs and their material needs. If one views children as consumption or investment goods yielding pleasure to their parents alone but providing nothing of use to society, then the market can be said to yield optimal economic efficiency. But if society recognizes the full implications of the often-used phrase "children are our future," then it will be apparent that the market may instead be producing an inefficiently low level of parental leave and a suboptimal level of human capital investment in its newest members. To what extent is the labor market currently providing parental leave?

The Incidence of Parental Leave

Under the Pregnancy Discrimination Act of 1978, an amendment to Title VII of the 1964 Civil Rights Act, employers must treat disabilities that result from pregnancy or childbirth on terms as favorable as other disabilities. If a firm provides sick leave or temporary disability leave, it must allow employees to use this leave for pregnancy- or childbirth-related disabilities. The reverse, however, is not true. In *California Federal Savings and Loan Association* v. *Guerra*, (1987), the Supreme Court ruled that a state statute can require firms to provide disability leave and special conditions of job reinstatement that apply to pregnancy- and childbirth-related disabilities but not to other disabilities. The PDA and the *Cal Fed* ruling shape our determination of how the market has responded to the growing participation of working women of childbearing age. We must distinguish between parental leave policies that result from compliance with the PDA and those that result from separate parental leave policies. If firms restrict parental leave to the period of disability, without providing leave for infant care, then we cannot directly attribute this leave to market forces of supply and demand.

Leave for Pregnancy- and Childbirth-Related Disabilities

As a consequence of the PDA, we can obtain a partial picture of the minimum level of leave available to employees during pregnancy and following childbirth by looking at sick leave and disability coverage. Coverage under these policies represents the lower bound of what is available, since employers are legally allowed to provide maternity leave over and above disability leave offered for other purposes.

For medium and large firms, the Bureau of Labor Statistics (BLS) Employee Benefit Survey (U.S. Department of Labor, 1986) provides the most reliable information at the national level. Table 11.1 presents the percentages of different categories of employees who are covered by paid sick leave and sickness and accident insurance. More than 93 percent of all employees in medium and large firms have some form of short-term disability coverage. This survey does not include information on whether firms guarantee employees the same job or a comparable one after a leave.

The National Federation of Independent Business (NFIB) surveyed its membership in 1985 on a range of employee benefits, including paid sick leave and dependent care leave. According to a study by Dunkelberg and Scott (1984), the membership of NFIB is representative of small businesses in the United States. The NFIB survey finds a far lower rate of paid sick leave coverage than does the BLS survey of medium and large firms, a finding that is consistent with other studies of the incidence of fringe benefits by firm size (e.g., Alpert and Ozawa, 1986). Of the firms in the survey, 52 percent provide no paid sick leave coverage; only 34 percent provide coverage for all full-time employees. As firms grow in size, they increase coverage, but they still tend to limit coverage to some but not all full-time employees: 54 percent of the firms with 1 to 4 employees offer no paid leave; this percentage drops to 32 percent for small firms with 50 or more employees.

TABLE 11.1

Short-Term Disability Coverage in Medium and Large Firms, 1985

(Percentage of Full-Time Employees Participating in Plan)

Type of Plan	All Employees	Professional and Administrative Employees	Technical and Clerical Employees	Production Employees
Short-term disability coverage	93	96	97	90
Sickness and accident insurance only	26	3	5	49
Paid sick leave only	42	66	60	21
Combined sickness and accident insurance/ paid sick leave	25	27	33	21

Source: U.S. Department of Labor, Bureau of Labor Statistics, (1986). "Employee Benefits in Medium and Large Firms, 1985," Bulletin no. 2262. Table 14, p. 14. Washington, D.C.: Government Printing Office.

This means that many women lack coverage, since women are more likely to work in small firms than in large ones, and the proportion of women working in small firms is greater than the proportion of men. Data from the 1983 Current Population Survey indicate that 59.3 percent of female wage and salary workers are employed by firms with fewer than 500 employees, compared with 56.8 percent of male wage and salaried workers. Almost half of all female employees (45.1 percent) work in establishments with fewer than 100 employees, compared with 43.7 percent of all male employees (*The State of Small Business*, 1986).

Leave to Care for Infants

Surveys of maternity leave policies have been conducted by Catalyst (1986), Kamerman, Kahn, and Kingston (the Columbia University Survey, 1983), the Bureau of National Affairs (1983), NFIB (1985), the U.S. Chamber of Commerce (1987), the Minnesota House of Representatives Research Department (1987), the National Council of Jewish Women (Bond, 1987), and the Bush Center (1988). Yet, because of restrictions concerning sample selection and size and low response rate, these surveys provide only a partial view of the availability of infant care leave.

Most of these surveys fail to distinguish between leave provisions for pregnancy- and childbirth-related disabilities and leave for infant care. For example, the Chamber of Commerce survey asked respondents about the provision of "parental leave" without defining that term. Some participants in the BNA survey indicated that they handled maternity leave requests under sick leave policy. Other firms in the same survey specifically stated that employees could not use sick leave for maternity absences. Since these studies do not differentiate between maternity leave for disabilities and infant care leave, we cannot reach a definitive conclusion concerning whether the market has responded to the needs of parents.

The percentage of large firms offering leave appears high. Catalyst (1986) found that 76 percent of the largest firms in the United States offered maternity leave coverage with a guarantee of the same or a comparable job on return from leave. Kamerman, Kahn, and Kingston (1983) found that 72 percent of the firms in their survey offered some form of maternity leave that guaranteed the same or a comparable job.

These results seem to imply that firms have responded to the increased presence of women in the labor market. Provision of maternity leave *without* the job guarantee corresponds closely to overall coverage for sickness and disability as reported in the BLS survey: 95 percent for Catalyst, and 88 percent for Kamerman, Kahn, and Kingston. These similarities suggest that the large firms may simply be complying with the PDA. Further support for this hypothesis comes from the Minnesota and Connecticut surveys (Minnesota House of Representatives Research Department, 1987; Bush Center, 1988), which do distinguish between infant care leave and leave for disabilities resulting from pregnancy and childbirth.

The Minnesota and Connecticut surveys, though restrictive in geographic scope, are both methodologically sound and comprehensive in terms of firm size. Here the parental leave landscape is far more sparse than that portrayed in surveys limited to large firms. Only 34 percent of the firms in the Minnesota survey offer nondiscretionary parental leaves, a percentage that includes leaves for sickness and disability. Another 12 percent sometimes provide leave, subject to employer discretion. Of the 34 percent that provide nondiscretionary leave, 72 percent specifically limited their leave policy to disabilities. Overall the survey found that less than 10 percent of Minnesota firms allow new parents time off to care for newborn children.

Tables 11.2 and 11.3 present the results of the Connecticut survey. Table 11.2 presents the extent to which firms offer parental leave policies that are separate from their other leave policies for sickness and disability. "*No Parental Leave*" indicates that the firm provides no leave to cover pregnancy- and childbirth-related disabil-

TABLE 11.2
Percentage of Connecticut Firms Providing Separate Job-Guaranteed Parental Leave by Firm Size

Number of Employees	Separate Parental Leave Policies		
	Disability Leave Only	Disability Leave and Infant Care Leave	No Parental Leave
10–49 (N = 307)	5.2	3.6	91.2
50–99 (N = 96)	12.5	7.3	80.2
100–499 (N = 122)	14.8	13.1	72.1
500 or more (N = 101)	13.8	13.9	72.3

Source: Bush Center in Child Development and Social Policy (1988). *Issues of Parental Leave: Its Practice, Availability, and Future Feasibility in the State of Connecticut.* Report to the Connecticut Task Force to Study Work and Family Roles. Chart 1.A. New Haven: Bush Center, Yale University.

TABLE 11.3
Percentage of Connecticut Firms Providing Job-Guaranteed Disability and Parental Leaves by Firm Size

Number of Employees	Disability Leave [a]	Parental Leave [b]	No Leave
10–49 (N = 310)	47.7	3.6	48.7
50–99 (N = 96)	63.5	7.3	29.2
100–499 (N = 126)	68.3	12.7	19.1
500 or more (N = 101)	65.4	13.9	20.8

Notes:

[a]The presence of disability leave indicates that leave is available for pregnancy- and childbirth-related disabilities. Any firm that provides sick leave, sickness and accident insurance, vacation leave that can be used for disabilities, unpaid leave for disabilities, and/or a separate maternity leave for pregnancy- and childbirth-related disabilities is included.

[b]Parental leave includes both maternity leaves as described in note a above and infant care leave.

Source: Bush Center in Child Development and Social Policy (1988). *Issues of Parental Leave: Its Practice, Availability, and Future Feasibility in the State of Connecticut.* Report to the Connecticut Task Force to Study Work and Family Roles. Chart 1.B. New Haven: Bush Center, Yale University.

ities over and above its other leave policies. Most firms, no matter how many workers they employ, offer no separate parental leaves for either disabilities or infant care. Even among the largest firms, a group that contains a substantial number of firms with more than a thousand employees, only 13.9 percent offer job-protected infant care leave. The percentages offering such leave are proportional to firm size; the figure declines to 13.1 percent for firms with 100 to 499 employees, to 7.3 percent for firms with 50 to 99 employees, to 3.6 percent for the smallest firms.

Table 11.3 shows that most maternity leave coverage stems from firms' standard policies regarding leave for sickness and disability. When general leave policies are combined with separate maternity leave policies, the percentage of firms offering no job-protected leaves ranges from 48.7 percent for the smallest firms to approximately 20 percent for firms with 100 or more employees. Where a firm has job-protected disability leave, protection exists for pregnancy- and childbirth-related disabilities.

The NFIB survey indicates that the low incidence of parental leave for infant care in Connecticut and Minnesota applies to the nation as a whole. Ninety-five percent of the firms surveyed provided no dependent care leave; only 3 percent provided dependent care leave for all their full-time employees.

Since these studies count firms and not employees, we cannot calculate the exact percentage of employees without leave for pregnancy- and childbirth-related disabilities and without leave to care for newborn children. But these percentages strongly suggest that a substantial majority of employees get no leave to care for infants. Those that do have leave are protected only while they are physically unable to work. In small firms even this protection is unavailable.

The lack of infant care leave suggests that the market has not responded in any real way to the large numbers of working women who are now of childbearing age. Although a substantial number of women in large firms do have coverage for pregnancy- and childbirth-related disabilities, this coverage flows from the broader protection that employees have achieved through paid sick leave and temporary disability insurance (TDI). The PDA, which requires that this leave be made available for pregnancy- and childbirth-related disabilities, seems a more likely source of the maternity leave that does exist than market forces of supply and demand. Any parental leave legislation will thus radically alter the provision of parental leaves. These laws will not just instruct firms to continue to offer what they now provide, institutionalizing existing practices, but will

drastically reshape the level of employer involvement in helping society provide care for its new members.

Determinants of Parental Leave Coverage

We have examined the incidence of leaves within firms; now let us
look at the incidence of leave from the employees' perspective.[1] Data
for this analysis come from the 1984 Panel Study of Income Dynamics (PSID).[2] What factors affect whether a female employee has
access to maternity leave and whether this leave is paid or unpaid:
percentage of women in an occupation or industry, age, union status? The proposed and enacted mandated leave statutes often have
coverage restrictions based on such employee characteristics as
length of service or full- or part-time status. Some treat government
employment differently from employment in the private sector.
Months of tenure at current job and part-time or government employment are included in the analysis, enabling us to ascertain the
effects of these provisions. Other public policy concerns are addressed through characteristics such as family income (excluding the
women's own labor income), years of education, wage rate, salaried
employment, marital status, and race. By examining whether these
characteristics affect maternity leave, we can determine whether lack
of mandated leave has a disparate impact, thereby exacerbating the
income inequality and stress encountered by different groups. Other
factors included in the analysis are county unemployment rate,
whether the employee works in a small-business-dominated industry,
and whether her state has mandated maternity leave or TDI.

Tests of Hypotheses Generated by Market Theory

The market-based theory of wage–fringe allocations has specific
implications for the effect of an industry's or occupation's sex ratio
on the incidence of maternity leave. First, according to this theory,
female-dominated occupations and industries should have a higher
incidence of maternity leave than male-dominated ones; second,
women might be expected to select these occupations and industries
because of the lower trade-offs in wages required to obtain leave.
Both hypotheses are refuted by the findings: the more female-dominated the industry, the less likely it is that a woman will have access
to maternity leave, whereas the percentage of women in an occupation has no effect on whether a woman has access to leave.[3]

These findings reinforce the implications of our review of mater-
nity/parental leave surveys. Since separate maternity leave policies

are rare, women obtain coverage for maternity-related disabilities through existing disability leave policies. Male-dominated occupations and industries tend to offer higher wages and more generous fringe benefits than female-dominated ones. Women in these occupations and industries are thus more likely to have access to disability leave than their counterparts in female-dominated industries.

One corollary of the market-based theory is that markets are more efficient than other institutions, such as unions, in determining the wage–fringe mix. The results in this analysis show no support for this contention. Women who belong to unions are more likely to have unpaid and paid leave than other women. Because we cannot separate general disability leave from maternity-specific disability or infant care leave with the available data, we cannot deduce whether unions are responding specifically to the needs of pregnant women and parents. Unionized workers are more likely to have sick or disability leave than other workers (see Freeman, 1981, and Freeman and Medoff, 1984, for a discussion of the effect of unionization on fringe benefits). The greater likelihood of maternity leave may reflect the joint effect of unionization on fringe benefits and the PDA.

In the Connecticut survey (Trzcinski, 1989), I found support for both of these hypotheses. The survey looked at the effect of unionization on the incidence of (1) general disability leave, (2) separate maternity-related disability leave, and (3) infant care leave. Unionization was associated with a substantial increase in the incidence of general disability leave coverage and infant care leave, but had only a marginal effect on separate maternity-related disability leave.

Women who are under 45 years of age are more likely to report that their jobs offer maternity leave than other women. This finding is consistent with the theoretical predictions of a market-based allocation of wages and fringes, which predicts that employees who want and need maternity leave are more likely to seek out jobs where it is offered.

Effects of Eligibility Requirements in Legislation

In order to benefit from parental leave legislation, individuals typically must be full-time employees and have worked for a year. Eligibility, however, differs from state to state where leave has been legislated; in Oregon, for example, the eligibility period was established at 3 months. By contrast, the proposed national parental leave requires that an employee have worked for 12 months and also have worked 900 hours or more during that time. In state legislation, no part-time employees have been considered eligible (see Bush Center, 1988, and Appendix B of this volume for a state-by-state review of these provisions).

Analysis of the PSID shows that these restrictions will continue to eliminate from coverage many employees who currently have no access to leave. Part-time employment lowers the likelihood that an employee has access to leave more than any other factor that was examined. Women with children tend to be overrepresented among part-time employees. Hence, these results indicate that many working mothers must withdraw permanently from the labor market if they are unable to work because of temporary disabilities resulting from a second or a later pregnancy.

How long an employee has worked at her current place of employment strongly influences access to paid or unpaid maternity leave: the longer an employee has worked at her current job, the more likely she is to have access to leave. The effect is stronger for paid leave: an increase in tenure from one year to five years increases the likelihood that she will have unpaid leave rather than no leave by more than 10 percent, whereas it increases the likelihood that she will have paid leave rather than no leave by 20 percent.

Some statutes differentiate between public and private employees. In this analysis, a woman who works in government employment is less likely to have either paid or unpaid leave than a woman in the private sector. Overall, these findings indicate that common legislative restrictions on coverage exclude the women who are already least likely to have protection through union contracts or employer policies.

Issues Surrounding Income, Class, and Race

Women with higher wages have greater access to paid leaves than other women. Those who work in salaried jobs also have greater access to paid leave than hourly employees. Since salaried jobs are typically marked by higher wages than hourly employment, these two effects combine to give high-income women far more access to leave than low-income women. Years of education have no direct effect on whether a woman has access to unpaid or paid leave, suggesting that any effects of education occur indirectly by providing women with better access to salaried jobs and jobs with higher wages.

For most factors in this analysis, effects are consistent across the alternatives: a factor that increases the likelihood that an employee has unpaid leave also increases the likelihood that she has paid leave, or it has no effect. Family income is an exception: those with lower incomes have greater access to unpaid leave than those with higher incomes, but less access to paid leave. Marriage sorting patterns and links between family income and labor force participation by married women provide possible explanations for this unusual effect. High-wage career women tend to be married to high-wage men. As noted above, high-income women in salaried jobs have greater access to paid leave than other women. Studies of wives' labor force participation have consistently found that increases in family income lower the likelihood that a married woman works in the labor market. Wives with high-earning husbands may anticipate withdrawing from the labor market for extended periods after the birth or adoption of a child; hence, they may have no use for unpaid leave that protects their jobs for a short period.

Marital status and race are the other factors investigated. Women who are married are more likely to report that their jobs offer maternity leave than are single, separated, or divorced women. This lower incidence of leave for unmarried women may contribute to the economic pressures facing single mothers, who are more likely than married women to be forced out of the labor market if they become disabled as a result of pregnancy- and childbirth-related disabilities. Black women are more likely to have access to paid leave than are white women or women of other races.

Other Factors

Firm size, as we have seen, has a major effect on whether a firm provides leave. Unfortunately, the PSID provides no information on firm size, so that a proxy for small business was used. The U.S. Small Business Administration designates an industry as small-business-dominated when over 65 percent of the firms in the industry are small businesses. The proxy used in this analysis was based on SBA's classification scheme at the three-digit SIC level. Despite the importance of firm size as a predictor of fringe benefit coverage, this proxy was insignificant, suggesting that it is too crude a measure to capture the effect of size.

In 1984, California, Connecticut, Massachusetts, and Montana had mandated maternity leave statutes, while California, New York, New Jersey, Rhode Island, and Hawaii had mandated temporary disability insurance (TDI). Women in these states are more likely than other women to have leave, indicating that employers in these states do at least partially comply with the provisions of the state statutes.

The final factor, county unemployment rate, does not affect the probability of leave.

Mandated leave will benefit only those who are currently without leave. These results indicate that women will gain the greatest protection from mandated unpaid leave if they are employed on a part-time basis, are not in unionized jobs, have short tenure at their jobs, and are unmarried. If the mandated leave is paid rather than unpaid, women in female-dominated industries and women with low wages will also benefit. Mandated paid leave would also affect women in low-income families, giving them greater access to paid leave. As noted above, these results show that legislative restrictions on coverage, such as requirements concerning job tenure and hours worked per week, exclude the women who are least likely to have protection. The findings lend little support to the prediction that the market will provide parental leave to those who need it.

State and federal legislatures are now actively formulating a series of new parental leave statutes. The evidence suggests that this legislation will significantly change the availability of leave. Job-guaranteed parental leave serves a unique function for families that other components of a family economic policy cannot adequately meet. Parental leave allows parents to stay attached to the labor market at the same time that they are providing care for and developing attachment to newborn biological or adopted children.

APPENDIX
Major Findings from Parental Leave Surveys

LEAVE POLICIES OF CONNECTICUT BUSINESSES

Universe: 1990 firms with 10 or more employees representing a cross section in terms of size, industry, and location. Response rate was proportional to firm size: among firms with 500 or more employees, the response rate was 90 percent; among firms with 100–499 employees, 73.7 percent; among firms with 50–99 employees, 49.8 percent; and among firms with fewer than 50 employees, 28.8 percent.

Findings:

- Less than 10 percent of Connecticut firms provide infant care leave; among firms with fewer than 100 employees, less than 5 percent provide leave for infant care.
- In a representative category of workers (clerical), 53.8 percent of all workers lack access to 6 weeks of maternity leave. The percentage of employees with no access to even 6 weeks of leave increases as size of firm decreases.

Publications: Bush Center in Child Development and Social Policy, 1988; Trzcinski, 1989.

MINNESOTA HOUSE SURVEY

Universe: 411 companies with 10 or more employees, a cross section in terms of size, industry, and location. Responses came from 254 companies.

Findings:

- 34 percent provided maternity/disability leave through a formal policy. An additional 12 percent provided discretionary leave.
- 22 percent provided leaves that were paid fully or partially, 75 percent provided either no pay or no leave, and another 3 percent paid the employee "to the extent of accrued sick leave."
- 40 percent provided a guaranteed return to the same or a comparable job.
- 28 percent provided continued health benefits during leave.

Publication: Minnesota House of Representatives Research Department, 1987.

PRELIMINARY REPORT ON MOTHERS IN THE WORKPLACE BY THE NATIONAL COUNCIL OF JEWISH WOMEN, CENTER FOR THE CHILD

Universe: Small, mid-sized, and larger businesses, and public sector organizations. A major limitation of this study is lack of random sampling.

Sample: 2,243 respondents from 100 communities across the nation, employing approximately 4,470,000 workers. 3,892 questionnaires were answered. Questionnaires were specific to type of business and classifications of workers.

Findings:

- 72 percent of those who worked for large employers received 8 weeks or more of medical leave (sick leave or disability) for pregnancy/childbirth.
- 51 percent of those who worked for small employers received the same.
- 37 percent of workers nationwide received some parental leave after maternity leave, regardless of employer size.

APPENDIX (*Continued*)

Publication: Bond, 1987.

CATALYST REPORT ON A NATIONAL STUDY OF PARENTAL LEAVES

Universe: 1,500 largest U.S. companies by level of annual sales (in its analysis of leave policies in relation to annual sales, Catalyst defines higher sales as $2 billion or more, medium sales as $501 million to $2 billion, and lower sales as $500 million or less).

Sample: Sample size was 1,500; responses came from 394 companies. One-third of the responding companies were located in the Northeast.

Findings:

- 95 percent provided short-term disability/maternity leave, but only 76 percent guaranteed a return to the same or comparable job.
- 51.8 percent offered an unpaid leave in addition to disability leave.
- 7.0 percent provided an unpaid leave of 20 weeks or longer.

Publication: Catalyst, 1986.

U.S. CHAMBER OF COMMERCE EMPLOYEE BENEFITS AND
PARENTAL LEAVE SURVEY

Universe: Participants in the Chamber's Employee Benefits Survey (including the Survey Research Section's business samples), names from *Fortune*'s lists, Polk's World Bank directory, and the directory of the American Compensation Association, and firms that asked to be included.

Sample: Sample size was 7,807; responses came from 700 companies.

Findings:

- 19 percent provided a formal parental leave plan.
- 31 percent provided parental leave that drew on sick and annual leave policies.
- 27 percent had no formal plan but provided leaves on a case-by-case basis.
- 23 percent offered no parental leave plan.

Publication: U.S. Chamber of Commerce, 1987.

NATIONAL FEDERATION OF INDEPENDENT BUSINESS (NFIB) REPORT ON
SMALL BUSINESS EMPLOYEE BENEFITS

Universe: Membership file of the NFIB, primarily small businesses, excluding firms with no full-time employees.

Sample: Sample size was 7,750; responses came from 1,439 companies.

Findings:

- 48 percent provided paid sick leave, but only 34 percent provided it to all employees.
- 20 percent provided disability leave, but only 12 percent provided it to all employees.

APPENDIX (*Continued*)

- 18 percent provided neither sick leave, vacation leave, nor health insurance.
- 5 percent provided dependent care to some full-time employees; only 3 percent provided dependent care leave to all full-time employees.

The findings of this survey are applicable to maternity leave, which is often made up of sick leave, disability leave, and vacation time.

Publication: National Federation of Independent Business, 1985.

COLUMBIA UNIVERSITY SURVEY OF MATERNITY BENEFITS AND LEAVES

Universe: Firms included in the Dun and Bradstreet *Million Dollar Directory* (approximately 90,000 companies).

Sample: The sample size was 1,000; responses came from 250 companies.

Findings:

- 88 percent provided maternity/disability leave.
- 72 percent guaranteed a return to the same or a comparable job.

No distinction was made between maternity/disability leave and parental leave.

Publication: Kamerman, Kahn, and Kingston, 1983.

BUREAU OF NATIONAL AFFAIRS REPORT ON POLICIES ON LEAVE FROM WORK

Universe: Members of BNA's Personnel Policies Forum, most of which had fewer than 1,000 employees. Private and public sector were represented.

Sample: Size not given; responses came from 253 firms.

Findings:

- 87–89 percent provided disability/maternity leave for white-collar employees.
- 82–95 percent provided disability/maternity leave for blue-collar employees.
- 75 percent in both groups guaranteed return to the same or a comparable job.

Leave surveyed was for pregnancy/childbirth; parental leave was not a category.

Publication: Bureau of National Affairs, 1983.

NOTES

Acknowledgments. Funding for this paper was provided in part by a 1987 small grant from the Institute for Research on Poverty, University of Wisconsin. The views and conclusions contained herein are those of the author and not necessarily those of the sponsor.

1. A multinomial logit regression was used to determine the probability that a female employee has employer-provided leave. These results are provided in the Appendix.

2. Besides the specifications discussed here, other specifications of the model were also run, including a version that corrected for selection bias regarding labor force participation. The magnitude and direction of the effects of the explanatory variables were robust across the different specifications of the models.

3. When the percentage of women in an occupation was included separately in a specification that did not include the percentage of women in an industry, this factor was also inversely proportional to the probability of having access to leave.

REFERENCES

Alpert, William, and Martha Ozawa (1986). "Fringe Benefits in Non-manufacturing Industries: How They Vary." *American Journal of Economics and Sociology* 45:189–200.

Bond, James T. (1987). Summary Statement Submitted to the U.S. House of Representatives Subcommittee on Labor–Management Relations and on Labor Standards of the Committee on Education and Labor, reported in *The Family and Medical Leave Act of 1987.* Hearings held in Washington, D.C., February 25 and March 5, 1987. Serial no. 100–200. Washington, D.C.: Government Printing Office.

Bureau of National Affairs (1983). *Policies on Leave from Work.* Personnel Policies Forum Survey no. 136. Washington, D.C.: BNA.

Bush Center in Child Development and Social Policy (1988). *Issues of Parental Leave: Its Practice, Availability, and Future Feasibility in the State of Connecticut.* Report to the Connecticut Task Force to Study Work and Family Roles. New Haven: Bush Center, Yale University.

Catalyst (1986). "Report on a National Study of Parental Leaves." New York: Catalyst.

Corcoran, Mary and Greg Duncan (1979). "Work History, Labor Force Attachment, and Earnings Differences Between the Races and Sexes." *Journal of Human Resources* 14:3–20.

Dunkelberg, William and J. A. Scott (1984). *Report on the Representativeness of the National Federation of Independent Business Sample of Small Firms in the United States.* Washington, D.C.: Small Business Administration.

Freeman, Richard (1981). "The Effect of Unionism on Fringe Benefits." *Industrial and Labor Relations Review* 34:489–510.

Freeman, Richard, and James Medoff (1984). *What Do Unions Do?* New York: Basic Books.

Hopper, Pauline, and Edward F. Zigler (1989). "The Medical and Social Science Basis for a National Infant Care Leave Policy." *American Journal of Orthopsychiatry* 58:324–28.

Kamerman, Sheila B., Alfred J. Kahn, and Paul W. Kingston (1983). *Maternity Policies and Working Women*. New York: Columbia University Press.

Minnesota House of Representatives Research Department (1987). *Maternity Leave Policies: A Research Report*. St. Paul.

National Federation of Independent Business (1985). *Small Business Employee Benefits*. Washington, D.C.: NFIB Research and Education Foundation.

The State of Small Business: A Report of the President (1986). Washington, D.C.: Government Printing Office.

Trzcinski, Eileen (1989). "Leave Policies in Connecticut Business: Findings from a New Survey on Parental Leave." Paper presented at the National Research Council Workshop on Employer Policies and Working Families, March 20–21, Washington, D.C.

U.S. Chamber of Commerce (1987). *Employee Benefits 1986*. Washington, D.C.: U.S. Chamber of Commerce.

U.S. Department of Labor, Bureau of Labor Statistics (1986). "Employee Benefits in Medium and Large Firms, 1985." Bulletin no. 2262. Washington, D.C.: Government Printing Office.

12 | How Does the Employer Benefit from Child Care?

Jules M. Marquart

More than ever before, American employees are torn between the competing demands of employment and family. This pressure has intensified as a result of demographic and social changes in the labor force, and particularly the increases in the number of employed women with pre-school-aged children and in the number of single-parent and two-wage-earner households. In the absence of a coherent federal policy in regard to family and work issues, the provision of such policies and programs has fallen to the discretion of individual employers. In recent years employers have made a limited, but increasing, commitment to child care assistance in particular.

According to the Conference Board, a nonprofit business research organization based in New York, the number of corporations providing some form of child care assistance to their employees increased from 110 in 1978 to 415 in 1982 and approximately 3,500 by 1989 (Axel, 1985; Friedman, 1989). If you consider that there are roughly 6 million companies in the United States, however, this means that only one employer in 2,000 is providing any kind of child care assistance.

Child care support is provided in a variety of ways, including resource and referral services, on-site and near-site centers, financial assistance through a vendor/voucher system or a flexible benefits plan, after-school care, sick child care, and support for family day care. A company may provide a child care benefit directly through a program it runs itself or as a member of a consortium, or indirectly through referral or financial or in-kind support to increase child care services in the community.

Of these methods, a child care center represents the greatest long-term investment by the employer. Such a center is often found where there is a specialized or highly trained labor force, a shortage of certain types of employees (such as nurses), or irregular shifts not covered by private child care facilities. It is not surprising, then, that more on-site child care centers are found in health care than in any other industry.

Employers give a variety of reasons for providing child care assistance: recruitment and retention of desired employees, improvement in morale and productivity, reduction in absenteeism, enhancement of the company's image, and response to employees' needs. Because of the substantial investment involved, it is important to know whether a program is achieving any of these goals. Furthermore, it is important for an employer to know from research on and evaluations of such programs what it is reasonable to expect from its own program.

To that end, this chapter will provide a synthesis of previous research on employer-supported child care programs. In addition, it will focus on the findings of a study of the effects of a multi-component child care program on employee attitudes and behavior. Because this study also took into account other organizational policies and programs, it provides information on a broader range of factors to consider in assessing the effects of employer-sponsored child care. Finally, recommendations will be offered for the development of such programs, along with implications for future research and evaluation.

What Do We Know About the Benefits of Child Care?

The focus of this chapter is on those effects of employer-supported child care programs that are of concern to the employer: that is, effects on employees' attitudes and behaviors as they influence their performance and value to the company, and not the effects of programs upon the child or the parent–child relationship. The published studies included in this review are ones that assess, either directly or indirectly, the causal relationship between the child care program and its effects on employees or the employer (Table 12.1). The five quasi-experimental studies typically have a research design that compares users and nonusers of the company child care program in terms of work-related attitudes and behaviors, and may include comparisons on these measures before and after the program began. The two cost–benefit studies translate program effects into cost savings to the employer. In the three surveys of employers, company representatives (usually human resource managers) were asked for their perceptions of how the child care program affected or might affect employees' attitudes and behaviors. Such studies cover the full range of child care assistance, from on-site centers to

TABLE 12.1
Studies of the Effects of Employer-Supported Child Care Programs

Study	Sample (Worksite)	Reported Effects
Quasi-Experimental Studies		
Marquart, 1988a	Users of on-site center, resource–referral, and family day care service; nonusers with preschoolers and non-users with school-aged children (hospital)	*Intention to continue employment at hospital *Recruitment *Recommendation of hospital as an employer *Satisfaction with child care arrangement Absenteeism Turnover Job satisfaction Organizational commitment
Dawson et al., 1984	Users of on-site and off-site centers or resource–referral services (29 companies, 311 respondents)	*Recommendation of employer *Acceptance of employment *Intention to continue employment *Availability to work overtime *Perceived positive effect on job performance Acceptance of a promotion Turnover Absenteeism
Youngblood and Chambers-Cook, 1984	Users of on-site center (textile company) and employees of similar company in same area	*Job satisfaction *Organizational commitment *Positive perception of organizational climate *Fewer turnover intentions Perception of company as better to work for Perception of job as satisfying Absenteeism Turnover
Milkovich and Gomez, 1976	30 users of on-site center, 30 non-users with pre-schoolers, 30 women with no children or school-aged children (computer company)	*Absenteeism *Turnover Job performance
Krug, Palmour, and Ballassai, 1972	Users of on-site center for OEO employees and other OEO parents of preschool-ers (gov't agency: Office of Economic Opportunity)	Absenteeism Tardiness Decision to seek/accept employment

TABLE 12.1 (*Continued*)

Cost–Benefit Studies[a]

Ransom and Burud, 1989	Users and nonusers of on-site center (bank)	Reduced turnover (for annual saving of $63,000–$157,000)
		Reduced absenteeism and maternity leave time (for annual saving of $35,000)
		Recruitment
		Morale
		Work performance
Tate (in Mann, 1984)	Users of on-site center (textile company)	Decreased turnover (for payroll reduction of 15 employees, lower recruitment and training costs)
		Estimated savings: $6 for every $1 spent

Surveys of Employers[b]

Burud, Aschbacher, and McCroskey, 1984 (National Employer-Supported Child Care Project)	178 companies providing child care assistance	Morale (90%)
		Recruitment (85%)
		Public relations (85%)
		Reduced turnover (65%)
		Lower absenteeism (53%)
		Productivity (49%)
	691 employees with children in employer-supported programs	Continuing employment with company (69%)
		More positive attitude toward company (63%)
		Recommendation of employer to others (>50%)
		Decision to take current job (38%)
Magid, 1982	204 companies with child care programs	Recruitment
		Improved morale
		Lower absenteeism
		Less turnover
		Return of employees on leave
Perry, 1982	59 employers (predominantly hospitals with on-site centers)	Ability to attract employees (88%)
		Lower absenteeism (72%)
		Improved attitude toward employer (65%)

Notes:
*Indicates a statistically significant effect at $p = .05$ or beyond in favor of program users.
[a]No statistical tests were reported.
[b]Percentages refer to proportion of employers reporting positive effects.

resource and referral services. Although they measure somewhat different outcomes, there are enough commonalities across them to permit summary judgments about the effects of employer-sponsored child care programs.

Among the quasi-experimental studies, statistically significant effects were more likely to be found on additional variables than on such behavioral variables as absenteeism and turnover. The strongest effects found were on recruitment, intention to continue employment at the company, and recommendation of the employer (Dawson et al., 1984; Marquart, 1988a, Youngblood and Chambers-Cook, 1984). Significant program effects were found on several variables that were unique to single studies: availability to work overtime (Dawson et al., 1984), and positive perceptions of organizational climate and of the company as an employer (Youngblood and Chambers-Cook, 1984).

Conflicting results were found for other variables, so that it is difficult to make a judgment about them. Job satisfaction and organizational commitment were found to be significant effects in one study (Youngblood and Chambers-Cook, 1984), but weak effects in another (Marquart, 1988a). In the Dawson et al. (1984) study, employees perceived a positive effect on their job performance, whereas the Milkovich and Gomez (1976) study, which actually measured job performance, found no such effect. In the Dawson et al. (1984) study, comparsions were made among three types of child care services: on-site centers, off-site centers, and information and referral. The study found significant attitudinal effects for the users of the on-site and off-site center programs, but not for the users of the information and referral services. This is a pattern of results that one might expect: more substantial effects from the more substantial programs. The Milkovich and Gomez (1976) study found significantly lower absenteeism and turnover among program users. Two other studies (Marquart, 1988a; Youngblood and Chambers-Cook, 1984) found a reduction in absenteeism among the users of the company-sponsored program, but no *statistically* significant differences between groups.

In the cost–benefit analyses, Ransom and Burud (1989) found that reduced absenteeism and turnover, and shortened maternity leaves, saved the employer an estimated $98,000 to $192,000 in one year. Deanna Tate (Mann, 1984) reported that decreased turnover enabled the company to reduce its payroll by 15 employees, resulting in lower recruitment and training costs and an estimated savings of $6 for every $1 spent on the child care program.

In the surveys of employers, the strongest effects of employer-sponsored child care programs generally were perceived to be on recruitment and morale, followed by absenteeism and turnover.

In the Burud, Aschbacher, and McCroskey (1984) study, which surveyed both employers and employees, it is interesting to compare the employers' perceptions and the effects reported by employees. Overall there is a fairly good correspondence between the two, although more employers than employees perceived effects on the outcomes. One notable discrepancy in perceptions concerns the effect on recruitment. It is difficult to say whether the employers' generally favorable and high expectations represent their true beliefs about the value of child care programs or a political wish to justify a program in which their company has invested. Moreover, most of these studies did not differentiate program effects according to the type of child care assistance provided or collect data on the actual child care arrangement.

A Study of a Multi-Component Child Care Program

A multi-component child care program has been provided by a large medical complex in the Midwest that includes a hospital and several other health care facilities.[1] Because of the diverse workforce of the complex, its child care benefit comprises two different services. The first is an on-site child care center accepting 110 children from 6 weeks through kindergarten age.

The second component is a resource and referral (R & R) service to a network of family day care homes in the community. The program staff visit and screen the family day care providers to guarantee that they meet their standards before placing them on the referral list. Those providers are allowed to use the toy and book resource library at the center and are invited to ongoing in-service training workshops. The benefits to the family day care providers of being on a referral list are obvious. The benefits to the organization of the dual services are important: the 110-child center would never meet the needs of all employees and, in fact, had a waiting list by the end of the first year. In addition, the family day care network provides alternative services for parents who prefer family care for whatever reason, or prefer care closer to home rather than at the workplace.

The R & R/family day care program was phased in gradually following parents' requests and the filling up of the on-site center, so that at the time of this study there were proportionately fewer users of this component than the on-site center. Currently, however, the R & R program has more users than the center.

Design of the Study

In the evaluation, the two groups of users of the employer-sponsored program (on-site facility or R & R/family day care) were compared with two other groups of employees who were not using the employer program: nonusers with pre-school-aged children who had made other child care arrangements and nonusers with school-aged children, because they also experience child-care-related problems (e.g., care during a child's illness or school holidays and vacations). In all the analyses, two kinds of comparisons were made: (1) between the combined groups of users and nonusers and (2) among the four separate groups. In addition to the data on employees' work attitudes and behaviors, considerable information was collected on their actual child care arrangements and attitudes about them. Data on the attitudinal variables were collected through a questionnaire mailed a little over a year after the program began, and information on absenteeism and turnover was collected from personnel records.

Sample

The overall sample comprises mainly technical and professional employees whose average age is 34. Nearly three-fourths of the respondents are female, and 85 percent are currently married. Of the married employees, slightly more than 80 percent are from two-income families. Fully half of all respondents have at least a college degree, and another 40 percent have some college; two-thirds have a family income of $30,000 or more. Among the full-time employees, one-quarter are salaried and 45 percent are hourly workers; 30 percent are employed part time. These summary characteristics reflect the composition of the workforce in the childbearing years at this hospital in this community; however, the predominance of female employees and the relatively high percentage of part-time employees are characteristic of hospitals in general.[2] There were no significant differences among groups on the other major demographic variables.

Findings

Work-Related Attitudes. The users of the employer-supported program were significantly more likely than the nonusers to report that the availability of the program affected (1) their recruitment to the organization, (2) their intention to continue employment, and (3) their recommendation of the company to prospective employees. In the four-group comparisons, the users of the on-site center ranked highest on those three attitudes, followed by the users of the R & R/ family day care component, and then by both groups of nonusers. This pattern is confirmatory, because one would expect greater effects from more substantial services. There were no significant differences in either the two- or four-group comparisons on job satisfaction, organizational commitment, or stress in balancing work and family demands.

Gender Comparisons. Women reported that their recruitment to the organization was affected by the availability of the child care program significantly more often than men did. Female employees also reported significantly more stress in balancing work and family than men. Women employees typically carry the major responsibilities for child care and other family demands in addition to their jobs, and are more likely to feel conflict between their work and family lives.

Absenteeism. The absenteeism rates of the groups were compared for the year prior to the initiation of the child care benefit and for the two subsequent years.[3] The program users had the highest absenteeism in the year before the child care program began, but experienced a decrease in absenteeism each subsequent year, while the nonusers' absenteeism remained about the same across all three years. The pattern of decrease was slightly different for the two user groups: the center users' absenteeism decreased by about one day the first year of the program and almost an additional half-day the second year, while the R & R/family day care program users' absenteeism remained the same the first year and then showed a decrease of almost three days the second year. This pattern is consistent with what one might expect: The effect on R & R users was delayed because that component developed slowly during the first year until the on-site facility reached capacity.

Turnover. The turnover rates for program users, nonusers with pre-school-aged children, and nonusers with school-aged children were 8 percent, 7 percent, and 5 percent, respectively. These differences were not statistically significant. Interestingly, these rates were considerably lower than the total organizational turnover rate of 12 percent for the same year, which itself is well below average for health care organizations. Furthermore, when the reasons for leaving were checked, the reasons most often given across all groups were acceptance of another job or moving from the area. We might conclude that although the use of an employer-sponsored child care program positively influences one's intention to remain in employment, other reasons for leaving the organization may become more compelling later on.

Actual Child Care Arrangement. Information was also collected on the actual child care arrangement used by employees—that is, how many hours preschoolers were in care in their own home, in someone else's home, or in center-based care; hours of self-care were added for school-aged children. The typical arrangement combined several types of child care, with the majority of weekly hours in one type but some hours spent in at least one other place. Since the most common arrangement was a combination, it is important to keep in mind that we were not evaluating the effects of one arrangement exclusively, but rather of the predominant type of care.

Few of the nonusers with pre-school-aged children used center-based child care: one group of them had all or most of the care performed in their own home, and the other group had most of it performed in someone else's home. Given that we were actually comparing very different types of care—a center-based program, care in one's own home, and care in someone else's home—it is all the more remarkable that the differences we found were in favor of the users of the employer-provided program.

Satisfaction and Problems with Child Care. Employees were also asked about their attitudes toward different aspects of their child care arrangement. Both groups of users of the employer's program were significantly more satisfied with their care arrangement than were nonusers.

The survey also asked about work-related problems caused by their child care arrangement[4] and problems with their regular care arrangement when a child was sick. On both those variables, the users of the on-site center and the nonusers with school-aged children cited significantly more problems than the other groups. Why might this be? Center-based care is a less flexible care arrangement than family day care, and parents of school-aged children often face greater scheduling difficulties because school calendars, hours, and demands do not correspond to work schedules.

On another question about stress related to child care, the nonusers with school-aged children were significantly lower than the other three groups—all with pre-school-aged children. It seems reasonable that employees with younger children feel more stress about child care.

Perceived Influence of Organization's Policies and Supervisor's Practices. Employees were also asked how helpful the organization's personnel policies and their supervisor's personnel practices were in dealing with their child care problems. The program users perceived the organization's policies *and* the supervisor's practices as significantly more helpful than did the nonusers. But, more interestingly, *all* four groups rated the supervisor's practices as *more* influential than the organization's policies in helping them deal with child care needs. This finding points out the direct and important influence of the supervisor on an employee's ability to handle work–family conflicts. A supervisor's sensitivity and flexibility on these issues can make all the difference in an employee's day-to-day work life, yet this area has been overlooked in many organizations.

Recommendations for Program Development

Child care centers at the workplace have the potential to be higher-quality programs than most because the presence of the parents nearby offers a built-in quality-control system. On-site centers must implement an open-door policy whereby parents are free to drop in for visits at lunchtime and other times during the day. Employees can discuss with other parent users the center's program, compare their children's teachers, and recommend changes in policies and operating procedures if they are not satisfactory. In order to take full advantage of this potential for high quality, several factors must be considered.

Design Program to Meet Employees' Needs

A company needs to develop the type of child care assistance that will meet both its corporate goals and employees' needs. The personnel or human resource department is usually given the responsibility of defining the company's needs and objectives, for example, in regard to recruitment and retention of desired employees. In addition, it is important to employees' needs and preferences, as well as child care available in the community. The employee needs assessment can be a formal survey or can be conducted through focus groups or informal meetings. It should obtain information on a variety of issues, including employees' current child care arrangements; their satisfaction as well as problems with those arrangements; needs and preferences for types of service, location, and hours of operation; how much employees are willing and able to pay for what services; and anticipated future needs (because the company is planning a long-term benefit).

Similarly, it is important to gather information on the supply, availability, and costs of child care services in the community. Often a local day care/child development council or the local licensing agency will have such information; the organization might even have a person who specializes in employer-sponsored programs. It can advise companies on options available, give information on what other companies are doing, and sometimes provide technical assistance on setting up services. Regarding the supply of child care, it is safe to say that almost any community today has a shortage of care for infants and children under two years, sick child care services, and before- and after-school care.

It is also important to consider the full range of employee needs in providing child care assistance. The medical complex described earlier recognized that an on-site center could not, by itself, respond to the range of employees' needs and preferences. The R & R service for family day care providers actually ended up serving more employees at a smaller cost. Multi-component programs have been found to serve a wider range of employee needs and may well prove more cost-effective to the company considering the greater benefits that can be expected.

In addition, it is useful to involve a diverse and representative employee group in the planning, design, and implementation of the child care benefit. Such a group can serve as a liaison with other employees, gather information about their needs and perceptions, and communicate progress; after a program is implemented, the employee group can serve as an advisory board and monitor the program's operations.

Provide for Sick Child Care

A major cause of employee absence, second only to the employee's own illness, is the illness of a child. Although individual employees are reluctant to acknowledge this cause of absence for fear of penalty in the typical corporate environment, human resource departments and front-line supervisors are well aware of its common occurrence. Policies and programs need to be designed for two levels of illness: one for children who can attend an appropriate group setting, and the other for children who need to be confined to their homes.

One way to handle the first level of illness is to provide a separate sick room in a center-based program. In some communities separate facilities for sick children are now available, although they are still rare. One might expect hospitals, given the nature of their business, to show more creativity in providing sick child care services.

The second level involves a more complex approach. Some companies have a sick child care benefit that provides a partial or full subsidy for a home health care service whereby an agency sends a professional into the home to care for the child (see Chapter 13 by Mitzi Dunn). Companies have found this to be more cost-effective than losing an employee's services or training a substitute for the duration of the child's illness.

Moreover, organizations need to assess their policies regarding the use of leave for family-related absences so that the policies reflect more realistically what employees are doing. This means having a policy that applies equitably to both exempt and nonexempt employees and permits employees to use their own sick leave for sick child care or, better yet, allocates a small number of family leave days for the range of family-related illnesses and appointments that regularly occur. It is better for the company to establish a formal and equitable policy than for employees to have to rely on supervisor leniency in interpreting unrealistic absence rules.

Assist Employees with School-aged Children

A few employers have incorporated before- and after-school programs into on-site centers and, there are other policies that can help employees with school-aged children. Working parents with children in school need a level of flexibility in the workplace that allows for such normal occurrences as the after-school "check-in" call and the need to leave work for a child's medical appointment or a school conference, as well as other special and unexpected events. Sensitivity to such issues may appear to complicate the administration of an organization but, in fact, would more realistically respond to the needs of working parents and permit a greater correspondence between formal policies and actual employee behaviors.

Provide Training for Supervisors on Work and Family Issues

The importance of the supervisor's role in helping working parents cope with their multiple responsibilities is emerging in research (Galinsky, 1988a). Many organizations provide in-service training for supervisors in a variety of organizational policies and procedures. Since work–family issues are important to a majority of employees today, this topic needs to be incorporated into regular supervisory training.

For supervisors to be most effective in supporting employees' needs as family members, they must work in a corporate environment that is conducive to such support. In turn, a company that seeks to provide a pro-family corporate climate must train and utilize its supervisors as the front-line implementers of responsive policies and programs.

Implications for Evaluation and Research

Define Program Carefully

Employer-sponsored child care encompasses a wide range of services, yet most of the research to date provides little information on actual programs and generally has treated child care as though it were one entity. Even though defining a program sounds straightforward, it is not always easy (McClintock, 1987). For example, in the study described, the R & R/family day care component was a resource and referral service on the part of the organization, while the actual child care service came from family day care providers. Complex child care arrangements, and particularly combinations of arrangements, may be the norm rather than the exception (Emlen and Koren, 1984; Galinsky, 1988b). Rather than merely following the classification of an employee's care arrangement, it is important to collect detailed information on the number of hours the child spends in each type of care.

Investigate Relationship between Type of Child Care and Size of Effect

It does not seem reasonable to expect that a less substantial form of child care assistance, such as a resource and referral service, will have as much impact on the expected outcomes as a more substantial service, such as an on-site center. We need to examine the size and pattern of effects from different types of child care programs as we would with any other kind of intervention program.

This paper has focused on program effects of concern to the employer and less so on effects of concern to the parents, while the child development literature has focused on the effects on the child or the parent–child relationship. Research models are needed that simultaneously take into account all three groups—the employer, the parents, and the children—and that hypothesize and test patterns of effects across those groups.

Examine Relationship between Child Care and Other Organizational Programs

Companies provide an array of human resource policies and programs to recruit and retain employees and to increase their morale and productivity. Although it may be desirable from a social science perspective to try to separate out the effects of different programs, it was found in an earlier study that it is usually not feasible to do so (Marquart, 1985a). Companies typically regard employee benefits and other human resource programs as a "package" that is provided to employees. In addition, evaluation of specific programs (other than training) is not commonly done in companies unless a specially targeted program is implemented, such as one to reduce absenteeism.

In a study related to the program evaluation described above, a conceptualization activity was conducted with a group of administrators of hospitals providing a child care program to obtain their perceptions of the relationships among organizational efforts (see Marquart, 1988a, 1988b). The group first defined the effects or outcomes they expected from the child care program. The group members then identified those outcomes which they expected to be most and least affected by the program. From these ratings we calculated an expected pattern of effects for the group. The administrators also rated the ability of the child care program, compared with other organizational activities, to influence those outcomes. For example, if the administrators expected recruitment and absenteeism to be strong effects, they were asked to list what other actions their companies were currently taking to influence recruitment and absenteeism, and then to rank the influence of the child care program compared with those other activities. We found that the administrators rated the child care program as much more influential when they considered it in isolation than when they considered it in relation to other organizational efforts.

Such a procedure can be useful in assessing the benefits of the child care program to the employer, while also taking into account other company policies and programs.

Perform Some Type of Cost Analysis

Both costs and benefits are important to consider in planning and evaluating child care programs. Although it may not be feasible to conduct a strict cost–benefit analysis, other procedures are possible. In "break-even" analysis (Boudreau, 1984), managers estimate the magnitude of effects necessary to "break even" with program costs. This form of utility analysis requires less precise information than other cost analysis methods, but is often sufficient as a decision tool. It also offers flexibility in incorporating qualitative information; for example, the value of recruiting several highly valued employees could be considered. In addition, it enables a value to be attached to important although less tangible benefits, such as the company's image in the community.

Conclusion

The employees using the employer-sponsored child care program were found to be more satisfied with their child care arrangement and their employer than their co-workers in the organization. The other positive effects of the program found in this study—on recruitment, intention to continue employment with the hospital, recommendation of the organization as a good place to work, and decreased absenteeism—support the growing body of evidence of the impact of company-supported child care programs on employees' attitudes and behaviors.

Employer-supported child care programs represent important initiatives in helping to meet the child care needs of working parents. Although the need still far exceeds the supply, such programs have grown in number, diversity, and sophistication during the past decade. With greater attention to program design and evaluation, employer-sponsored programs may realize their potential of offering the highest-quality and most affordable child care available to working parents.

NOTES

Acknowledgments. I am grateful for the thoughtful and constructive comments of Irving Lazar, Charles McClintock, Sylvia Schmidt, and three anonymous reviewers.

1. Details on this study are provided in Marquart, 1988a.

2. The database on hospital employees from which our samples were drawn showed that the population was 94 percent white, so that it was not possible to conduct subgroup analyses by ethnicity.

The user groups were made up of the entire group of on-site center users (N = 108) and R & R/family day care users (N = 23) at the time of data collection. The original research plan was to randomly select the sample for each comparison group. However, the population of nonusers with pre-school-aged children was found to be small enough (N = 261) that sampling was neither desirable nor necessary. A random sample of 210 employees with school-aged children (at least one child between the ages of 6 and 13) was selected. Because of employment changes during the one-year gap between the 1983 database and the questionnaire mailing in December 1984, a small loss of potential respondents occurred in each comparison group. For further information, see Marquart, 1988a.

3. Absenteeism was operationalized as the annual total of sick hours used, based on the types of leave employees reported using to care for a sick child and the data available in the personnel records. However, there are numerous difficulties in the measurement and analysis of absenteeism data (Hammer and Landau, 1981), particularly when the goal is to obtain a valid and reliable measure of absences related to child care (Marquart, 1985b).

4. A composite measure included problems in getting to work, being late or missing work, being able to stay late, and needing to leave work for child-related matters.

REFERENCES

Axel, Helen (1985). *Corporations and Families: Changing Practices and Perspectives*. Conference Board Report no. 868. New York: Conference Board.

Boudreau, John (1984). *Decision Theory Contributions to HRM Research and Practice*. Ithaca, N.Y.: Industrial and Labor Relations Press.

Burud, Sandra L., P. R. Aschbacher, and Jacquelyn McCroskey (1984). *Employer-Supported Child Care: Investing in Human Resources*. Dover, Mass.: Auburn House.

Dawson, Ann G., C. S. Mikel, C. S. Lorenz, and J. King (1984). *An Experimental Study of the Effects of Employer-Sponsored Child Care Services on Selected Employee Behaviors*. Grant no. 90-CJ-51701. Washington, D.C.: DHSS, Office of Human Development Services.

Emlen, Arthur, C., and P. E. Koren (1984). *Hard to Find and Difficult to Manage: The Effects of Child Care on the Workplace*. Portland, Oreg.: Regional Research Institute for Human Services, Portland State University.

Friedman, Dana E. (1989). "Estimates from the Conference Board and Other National Monitors of Employer-Supported Child Care." Memorandum. New York: Conference Board.

Galinsky, Ellen (1988a). "The Impact of Supervisors' Attitudes and Company Culture on Work/Family Adjustment." Paper presented at the annual convention of the American Psychological Association, Atlanta, August.

———(1988b). *Child Care and Productivity*. New York: Bank Street College of Education.

Hammer, Tove H., and J. Landau (1981). "Methodological Issues in the Use of Absence Data." *Journal of Applied Psychology* 66:574–81.

Krug, D. N., V. E. Palmour, and M. C. Ballassai (1972). *Evaluation of the Office of Economic Opportunity Child Development Center*. Rockville, Md.: Westat, Inc.

McClintock, Charles (1987). "Conceptual and Action Heuristics: Tools for the Evaluator." In L. Bickman, ed., *Using Program Theory in Evaluation: New Directions for Program Evaluation*, no. 33. San Francisco: Jossey-Bass.

Magid, Renée Y. (1982). "Parents and Employers: New Partners in Child Care." *Management Review* 71:38–44.

Mann, Judy (1984). "Public Policy Report: Child Care." *Young Children*, November, p. 73.

Marquart, Jules M. (1985a). "Balancing Work and Family Demands: Eight Corporate Views." Manuscript. Cornell University Department of Human Service Studies, Ithaca, N.Y.

―――― (1985b). "Evaluating Human Resource Programs: The Elusive Bottom Line." Paper presented at the 1985 joint meeting of the Canadian Evaluation Society, Evaluation Network, and Evaluation Research Society, Toronto, October.

―――― (1988a). "A Pattern Matching Approach to Link Program Theory and Evaluation Data: The Case of Employer-Sponsored Child Care." Ph.D. dissertation, Cornell University, Ithaca, N.Y.

―――― (1988b). "Measurement and Outcome Pattern Matches: Examples from an Employer-Sponsored Child Care Program Evaluation." Paper presented at the annual meeting of the American Evaluation Association, New Orleans.

Milkovich, George T., and L. R. Gomez (1976). "Day Care and Selected Work Behaviors." *Academy of Management Journal* 19 (1):111–15.

Perry, Kathryn S. (1982). *Employers and Child Care: Establishing Services Through the Workplace.* Washington, D.C.: U.S. Department of Labor, Women's Bureau.

Ransom, Cynthia, and Sandra Burud (1989). "Productivity Impact Study of an On-Site Child Care Center." *Unpublished manuscript.* Pasadena, Calif.: Burud and Associates.

Youngblood, Stewart A., and Kimberly Chambers-Cook (1984). "Child Care Assistance Can Improve Employee Attitudes and Behavior." *Personnel Administrator*, February, pp. 45–46, 93–95.

13 | Employers' Child Care Policies: Sick Child Care

Mitzi Dunn

Time Insurance Company decided in 1987 to offer a sick child care program as a subsidized corporate benefit to all of its employees. Time Insurance has about 1,900 home office employees, with an average age of 32. About 75 percent of those employees are female, and a significant number of them are mothers, married and single. Over the past several years, day care has been a recurring issue. The Corporate Services Department conducts an attitude survey every two years, with focus groups in between for feedback, and the president meets each month with employees who are celebrating a work anniversary and encourages them to express their concerns. The issue of quality child care is frequently mentioned. As a result, we have done substantial research on the subject.

Time Insurance Company participates in a task force of downtown Milwaukee employers that is considering some type of consortium day care arrangement. Research by a Time Insurance affiliate in St. Paul, Minnesota, suggests, however, that this is an expensive way to provide what is still considered to be a somewhat selective benefit. The St. Paul survey of employee interest produced some surprising results. Only 3 percent indicated that they would be willing to bring their children to work. Thus, expected revenue would not be sufficient to cover the cost of the study, much less warrant actual construction of a day care center on site.

As part of our research, we also began to look at a somewhat different dimension of the child care issue that has been, at least until recently, overlooked. This is the area of sick child care. The following statistics are taken variously from *Working Mother*, the *Wall Street Journal*, and *Pension World*. When a child is seriously ill, 70 out of 100 times Mom stays home. One-fourth of women report that their husband relieves them one-half of the time, as long as the child is not too sick. Grandmothers appear to be the best bet for reliable sick child care on short notice, but they are available in only one in six cases, and seem to prefer short duty to longer-term care. Two-thirds of women workers must still use vacation or sick days, and one-fourth of them must take the time off without pay. In 1986 only 6 percent of employers offered sick family days up front as an option, and 6 percent were reported as blatantly giving employees a hard time about time off for family reasons. Survey results indicated that small companies were more accommodating than larger ones. Despite the greater disruption that absenteeism can cause in a small company, these companies tended to be a bit more empathic with their employees in such situations. Clerical and sales personnel appeared to fare the worst. And even when the employer was understanding, the loss in productivity due to absenteeism, tardiness, and workplace stress and tension was considerable.

After considering all these statistics, in light of the demographics of our workforce and the fact that many of our employees regularly work overtime, we felt that there was both reason and opportunity to try to address the special needs of employees with sick children—that is, employees who are unable to use their normal day care arrangements because their child is too sick or too contagious to leave the home. If working parents cannot find acceptable substitute care, often at short notice, one of the parents must stay home. It is that simple. For the employee it is not necessarily a question of finance, but rather of outright necessity. It becomes a problem for the company as well when it loses the experienced services of the employee and frequently has to pay the high costs of a temporary replacement as well.

In our initial attempt to find some alternative to which parents could turn for sick child care, we looked at what was available in the community and what other Milwaukee employers were doing. In 1987, that was not much. Most employers were doing nothing about sick child care. In terms of providers of this service, one local hospital had six beds available to the public on a first come, first served basis. Employees were required to register during work time, in advance, before the child became ill. They would still have to take the very sick child out of the home and hope that, when they got there, one of those six beds would be available. Even though the cost was very affordable (approximately $2.50 an hour), we felt that this was not the best solution for the cross section of our workforce who might need this service.

Then we looked at Sick Child Plan (SCP), which I had personally used on an unsubsidized basis and found to be a very satisfactory service. SCP is a division of Medical Placement Services, Inc. (MPS), which is in turn owned by Columbia Hospital in Milwaukee. MPS has been a provider of home care and institutional nurses in the Milwaukee metropolitan area since 1972.

To join SCP, employees must still register in advance, before a child becomes ill. However, they can call SCP and arrange for an at-home interview at their convenience. The supervising nurse (an R.N.) comes to the home and notes the exact location to aid potential caregivers in arriving on time. This is important, since SCP serves several counties in the greater Milwaukee area.

The R.N. completes a file of background information for SCP's records, including each child's daily schedule, diet, food preferences, allergies, and favorite activities and the employee's work phone number and work schedule. The employee is given a folder of information about SCP, including a checklist to fill out if a child becomes ill. The checklist is designed to make available to the caregiver pertinent information for the day. The R.N. also discusses billing arrangements at the registration interview. SCP prefers that the user charge through Visa or MasterCard, but it will arrange for direct billing if necessary.

The cost of the registration interview (in 1990) is $30.00. Time Insurance pays half of the cost but expects the employee to pay the other half. In 1990 the fee for care provided is $8.75 an hour. Time also subsidizes half of this cost, and is billed directly for its portion.

SCP can be reached 24 hours a day. If the employee calls the night before, a caregiver will arrive at the home prior to the time that the employee needs to leave for work, in order to discuss any special needs of the child. If the call is made in the morning, a caregiver can be there in 90 minutes at the latest. The supervising R.N. is available for consultation with the caregiver throughout the day.

When we first considered SCP, we had some concerns about its hiring practices and criteria, the kind of experience it looked for, its selection process. We wanted to know what training was given, since its brochure indicates that these are specially trained caregivers. We wanted to know what some SCP users had to say. Our president also had some concerns about the legal aspects of such a program if it was subsidized by Time Insurance, such as SCP's bonding policies and our potential liability if there was a question of negligence. And, of course, we wanted to know what our utilization would be, how much we should subsidize, and how much it would cost.

We had several meetings with the president of MPS and the supervising R.N. from SCP to address these subjects. We discussed their hiring practices in detail. SCP caregivers must have experience either in childhood education or in direct child care. SCP views its employees as professionals in this area, so it must charge enough to offer a good wage and benefits. It tries to find candidates like the woman who came to my home, who was working on her master's degree and attended school three days a week. She was available for SCP on a regular basis the other two days. SCP also considers people starting later-life careers. SCP screening includes required references and continuing psychological assessment during the interview and training periods. It has rejected some applicants on the basis of their psychological assessment.

SCP candidates must complete their training in a satisfactory manner. While not registered nurses, caregivers are medically trained personnel. They have completed classes in nutrition and child behavior and development, and they must have successfully completed a heart savers course and CPR training. They are also trained in first aid, home and fire safety, and age-appropriate play activities. SCP was as concerned as we were that its staff maintain the excellent reputation that MPS had developed over its years of service to the Milwaukee community.

We also talked with some SCP users. First, we reviewed the evaluation forms parents are asked to complete whenever care is provided. We then contacted some of the parents directly, and received very positive feedback.

With regard to the legal aspects, our in-house counsel reviewed SCP's insurance and bond policies. They had a one million dollar, per individual, per incident bond with St. Paul Insurance, with no claims to date. Our counsel wrote a contract that included an indemnification agreement with SCP to hold us harmless from any action arising as a result of its employees' negligence. We also put in writing that SCP must maintain its current bonding with St. Paul Insurance.

With regard to potential cost, we reviewed SCP's statistics on sick child care usage. SCP was able to give us detailed information on how many children get which sicknesses and when, whether they get sick more when they are going to school or in the summer, and so on. We then had one of our actuaries estimate how many people at Time might use the service. The final estimate, based on our decision to subsidize half the cost (i.e., $3.50 an hour in 1988) was a cost to us of $4,500 per 100 users.

We decided to offer the program. Although $7.00 an hour (the rate in 1988) was expensive for anyone, including exempt (salaried) employees, we felt that the $3.50 an hour payable by the employees was at least marginally affordable and was closer to what parents were paying their regular caregivers. It is also important to keep in mind that this is an extraordinary type of service. The employee would not use it on a daily basis, but only for a short period, when he or she absolutely had to go to work and no alternative care was available.

We decided to subsidize the program for up to 52 hours per year, which is not as arbitrary as it sounds. Time Insurance has an attendance bonus program, which credits employees with one hour per week for sick days. Any unused hours are paid for with a separate check to the employee at year end. We tied the SCP benefit to the same plan, though we may increase the number of subsidized hours in the future, depending on our experience. We prorate the 52 hours according to when an employee registers with SCP. Someone who signs up before the beginning of the year is eligible for the full 52 hours. Someone who signs up on July 1 would get 26 hours. Again, our purpose was to ensure that employees do not wait for a child to become ill before signing up.

We introduced SCP via brown bag lunches as part of our ongoing wellness promotion. SCP provided very articulate and informed speakers to explain their program to our employees at no cost. We also promote the program during new employee orientations.

We have a written agreement with the employee to provide some safeguards. For example, we require that employees list the names of their dependents so that we are not subsidizing the neighbor's day care children. We indicate that the purpose of the program is to enable them to come to work. Some of our employees work second or third shift, and many work on weekends. We are willing to extend this service to those times if employees need the service to enable them to work.

We considered potential situations when a child is not really sick, or when the regular care provider is sick. Because the caregivers are not R.N.s, SCP was hesitant to have them venture a medical opinion as to whether or not a child is really sick. Therefore, we decided in the first year not to make any attempt to audit for sickness or to determine why employees were using SCP. If it appeared that the program was being abused, we would reconsider this issue. So far, we do not think that it has been.

We offered SCP on a trial basis in 1988 so that we could assess the actual costs, employee satisfaction, and what problems might evolve. So far, it has been received very favorably, and we have not had any complaints or problems.

We were surprised, though, that for the first year only 25 employees signed up, which is fewer than we had expected. However, a few of them have already exhausted all 52 hours, and almost all have used SCP at least once. Registrants represent all levels of the company, and over a third were men.

An unexpected bonus to us was the positive value of this program in recruiting. In 1987 we introduced a flexible spending account plan (Flex) that allows employees to pay for eligible out-of-pocket child care expenses with before-tax dollars. We also offer a before-tax health expense account to reimburse expenses such as well baby care that are not covered under our group insurance plan. We found that even if new employees did not enroll immediately, they seemed to feel that the availability of Flex and SCP signaled something about our company and its concern for the needs of our employees.

One year into this program, we feel that it is truly an innovative idea whose time has come. We are pleased to offer this benefit, and we are the first in Milwaukee to do so, although several other employers are now considering it. We feel that it has enhanced the perception of Time Insurance as a caring employer, improved employee relations and productivity, and promoted good community public relations as well, for a minimal cost.

Our first-year costs were substantially less than budgeted. So, for a modest investment, and minimal paperwork, and administrative time, we have a benefit that returns much value for the dollars spent.

14 | Family Leave Policymaking in a Mid-sized Professional Firm: A Case Study

Linda M. Clifford

The History

Our law firm was founded as a two-lawyer partnership in 1946. Since then, it has grown to 26 lawyers—15 partners, 9 associates, and 2 lawyers of counsel—and a 23-member staff of paralegals, secretaries, messengers, bookkeepers, and administrators.

The firm is structured as a partnership. The attorneys who are partners own and manage the business after buying a portion of the firm's assets, and each partner shares in the firm's profits or losses. Attorneys who are associates and the staff do not own the business or share in the profits but are paid a salary or wages. Associates are trained and supervised by partners for a period of time during which the partners evaluate their eligibility and qualifications to become a partner. At the end of that time, an associate can expect to receive an invitation to join the partnership—or not. If invited to join, the associate changes status from employee to employer, from worker to owner, and the lawyer takes on a new relationship with his or her partners. This period of evaluation—the partnership track— recently has lasted from four to six years at our firm.

Lawyers and staff historically had followed separate patterns of family leave-taking. For example, members of the staff were generally permitted to take a 4-month unpaid maternity leave plus paid accumulated sick leave and vacation. Most staff members took the full unpaid leave and the full paid leave, less enough sick days to make it through a few years of caring for ear infections and the flu. The typical result was a 6-month leave.

By comparison, until 1980 only two lawyers, one a partner and one an associate, had given birth. Both returned to work full time within weeks, if not days, of their deliveries. As role models, they inspired awe, but their successors did not necessarily share the same willingness to get back to their desks at the cost of giving up time with their newborns.

In 1982 the firm hired an associate who was interested in working for several years part time until her children reached school age. It was understood, however, that she would not be considered for partnership until she was working full time and that the length of her partnership track would be extended in proportion to her part-time employment. She went full time in 1985 and became a partner in 1988. Her experience demonstrated the firm's willingmess to consider part-time work by associates, but also its unstated beliefs that part-time lawyers could not be partners and that part-time work should not be accorded full weight toward the partnership track.

Between 1982 and 1984, two other associate lawyers gave birth. Each arranged for a full-time, 6-month maternity leave. One ultimately left the firm for unrelated reasons and moved to another city. The other, who had earlier agreed to return to work full time after 6 months and was close to completing her partnership track, decided that she would prefer to work only part time for an indefinite period.

Instead of returning to full-time work, the associate offered to work part time as an associate and then part time as a partner upon completion of her partnership track and the expected invitation to join the partnership. The firm, committed to a philosophy of no part-time partners, offered her a choice of joining the firm as a full-time partner or working part time as an associate with the understanding that, upon her return to full-time work, she would be considered for partnership. She declined both choices and left the firm.

In 1987 another associate became pregnant. She had already been invited to join the partnership but was due to commence partnership the same week she was to deliver her child. Preferring to return to work part time, she arranged to delay her partnership in recognition of the firm's policy of having no part-time partners. She returned to work part time after a 6-month leave, went full time 3 months later, and then became a partner.

The Need for A Policy

The same lawyer became pregnant again soon after she returned from maternity leave and became a partner. Confusion about her status solidified the need for a more comprehensive, flexible policy, not only to handle her next leave but to establish a leave policy for all of the firm's lawyers.

The firm at the time had 12 partners, 2 of them women. There were 12 associates, 5 of them women. Concern was building based on the misperception that the partnership hierarchy was institutionally hostile to women lawyers' family leave needs. Moreover, dealing with family leave issues case by case tended to personify the decision making. A pregnancy that coincided with a decision on partnership, for example, could lead to the undesirable possibility of mixing the partners' views on part-time partners with their views on the associate's readiness for partnership. The lack of a policy made it difficult for associates or partners to plan their careers or their families.

The absence of a clear policy also affected recruiting. Lawyers on the hiring committees for both associates and law clerks were regularly faced with questions about maternity or family leave. The absence of a clear policy and outside misperceptions of the firm's handling of prior maternity leave situations created a real handicap in hiring talented young women out of law school.

The firm was acutely aware that family leave for its lawyers was a more sensitive issue than family leave for its secretarial and clerical staff. The partners perceived that the absence of a professional had more of an impact on the firm's short-term and long-term viability than the absence of a secretarial or clerical employee. The same perception applied when comparing the impact of family leave taken by owner–partners with the impact of family leave taken by employee–associates.

The perception probably has some basis in reality, specifically in the functional differences between the firm's owners and employees. As owners of the firm, partners are ultimately responsible for the quality of legal services provided to clients, for client development, for the general management of the firm, and for the long-term financial viability of the firm.

By comparison, as employees, associates and staff members have none of these ultimate responsibilities. They have a responsibility to provide quality legal services for clients, to be sure, but their work generally is under the supervision and direction of the partners, and it is the partners who answer to the clients for the results. Certainly, associates are encouraged to attract new clients, but they primarily focus on their own training and development as lawyers.

In good times and in bad times, associates and staff members are paid their salaries. In bad times, however, partnership income may decline and the partners may not realize much in the way of profits after paying employee salaries and wages and other office overhead.

The ultimate responsibility to generate business, to retain business, and to keep the business viable lies with the partners.

Painful conflicts grew out of these distinctions for some of the firm's women lawyers. And those conflicts underscored the need for the firm to strike a balance between professional and personal responsibilities, especially at the partner level.

The Policymaking Process

The firm's managing partner appreciated the need to develop consistent policies to handle issues that the firm had historically dealt with ad hoc. In early 1988 he appointed a family leave committee composed of two male partners and a junior woman partner who was designated the chair. He also asked that an associate assist the committee in performing legal research about the necessity for and restrictions on maternity or family leave policy.

The senior of the male partners in the past had been skeptical of the concept of part-time partners; the other male partner appeared more open to the concept. The female partner had worked part time as an associate but semed to have completed her family and was not likely to recommend policy based on her immediate personal self-interest or needs. The associate member of the committee was male, unmarried, and had expressed no views on the matter. He, too, did not seem to have an immediate personal family leave agenda.

The managing partner directed the committee to formulate a family leave policy and recommend whether it should cover both attorneys and staff, whether it should cover maternity as well as parenting or family leave, and whether family leave should include care of family members experiencing a serious illness.

The chair assigned the associate to research the legal requirements of maternity leave and family leave and to follow current efforts in the Congress and the state legislature to enact family leave policies. The chair herself surveyed the maternity and family leave policies adopted formally or informally by other law firms and agencies in the state.

Legal Research and Survey of Other Firms

The legal research indicated that, as an employer, the firm must treat an employee disability caused by or associated with pregnancy in the same manner as it treated other temporary medical disabilities. While not required to offer nondisability parenting leave, if the firm offered parenting leave at all, it had to offer it to both men and women. These provisions applied generally to employers and employees, but did not appear to cover how partners must treat other partners.

The survey indicated that governmental or nonprofit agencies employing lawyers had more liberal family leave policies than private law firms. It also confirmed that most law firms composed of partners and associates treated partners and associates differently. The most common response, though, was that the surveyed firms had never needed to address the issue of family leave for partners. Evidently, most firms hoped they would never have to.

Eleven examples of leave polices came out of the survey. Each is summarized below, following a generic identification:

Proposed federal law:
> Employers of 50 or more must provide 10 weeks unpaid, job-protected leave to males and females for birth, adoption, or serious illness of child or dependent parent.

State law:
> Employers of 50 or more must provide 6 weeks unpaid leave to males and females for family leave.

State administrative rule covering state employees:
> Six months unpaid parenting leave with option to renew or extend another 6 months. May be used in combination with paid sick leave with medical excuse, not to exceed 6 months. Unpaid paternity leave up to 6 months.

State legal services office:
> Six weeks leave using paid sick or vacation leave plus unpaid leave for mothers and fathers with 4 weeks notice.

State Judicare office:
> Six months unpaid leave taken not more than once in a 12-month period.

State legal aid office:
> Maternity leave for medical reasons up to one year. Childrearing leave for 4.5 months.

Medium-sized firm in medium-sized city:
> *Associates*: Paid maternity medical leave. Additional unpaid child care leave from 3 to 9 weeks depending on length of employment. May be extended at partners' discretion. Firm continues paying life, health, disability, and malpractice insurance. Limited to two leaves.
> *Partners*: Handled case by case. Several partners are on leave; some have been on leave and have returned half time.

Medium-sized firm in medium-sized city:
> *Associates*: Two months paid maternity disability–related leave with optional 30 days unpaid leave. Part-time leave has not been addressed.
> *Partners*: Continue to share the firm's profits during medical disability. Post-disability leave not yet addressed.

Medium-sized firm in medium-sized city:
> *Associates*: Paid medical disability (if a doctor certifies its necessity) plus personal leave for childrearing at discretion of partners.
> *Partners*: Not yet addressed.

Large statewide firm:
> *Associates*: Two months paid leave plus 4 months unpaid leave. Option for part-time work on return.
> *Partners*: Not yet addressed.

Large statewide firm:
> *Associates*: Three months paid leave plus 3 months unpaid leave. Four weeks parenting leave for fathers and mothers within 13 weeks of birth. Several fathers have used parenting leave already, though usually not the full 4 weeks. Part-time work available for those with firm two years or more. Must work at least half time, for no longer than one year, but half-time schedule can be renewed at discretion of administration.
> *Partners*: Handled case by case. One partner has worked part time (a 75% schedule) with an adjustment in compensation.

Initial Consideration and Discussion

To facilitate discussion at its first meeting, the chair distributed to the committee members the results of the legal research and the survey with an explanatory memorandum and a recommendation for a proposed family leave policy. The committee then met to discuss the goals of the committee and the scope of its mission.

Initially, the questions included (1) whether the staff, associates, and partners all should be subject to the same policy; (2) whether the policy should include leave to care for sick family members; and (3) what effect parenting or family leave should have on an associate's partnership track. Discussion later was expanded to the question of full-time and part-time leave for partners.

Several months later, the committee recommended and the partnership adopted family leave policies covering staff members, associates, and partners. There were two policies, one for employees (including associates) and one for partners. Along the way, the firm encountered several sensitive issues, some of which were only halfway resolved.

Sensitive Issues and Their Resolutions

The Associates' Partnership Track

One issue in almost all law firms is whether extended leaves should have any effect on an associate's partnership track. Most firms hire associates with the expectation that they either will leave or be asked to leave the firm or will join the firm as a partner or shareholder after several years on the partnership track. The length of the partnership track varies from firm to firm. There is never a guarantee of partnership at the end of the track.

The track in our firm now lasts six years. It is used not just to "season" the associate, but also to provide an extended opportunity for all of the partners to work with the associate long enough to train him or her, if necessary, and to evaluate the associate's professional development and potential as a partner.

The survey showed that women in some firms are insisting that childbirth and family leave have no effect on their partnership track. They hope to be able to graduate into partnership with their incoming "class." Our firm rejected the notion that an extended absence should have *no* effect on the associate's development and experience.

The partners felt that a long leave or a series of several shorter leaves during the partnership track could affect the partnership's ability to train or evaluate the associate. Clearly, having fewer years on the job will reduce the associate's exposure to assignments, cases, clients, and other members of the firm. Two or three family leaves within the six-year track could translate into one or two years absence from active participation in firm matters, effectively reducing the track to four or five years for the leavetaker. In firms where the partnership track is shorter than six years, this could have an even greater impact on the time the associate actually practices with the firm.

Balancing these concerns against the practical application of a parenting leave policy, the firm adopted a "one free kid" rule. Family leave of 4 months in the aggregate—which could be combined with sick leave and vacation for nearly 6 months leave—would not affect the associate's partnership track. The partners were convinced that our current partnership track was long enough to absorb one family leave period without jeopardizing the purpose and goals of the track. The policy adopted preserves the partners' right to shorten or lengthen the track for any reason, however.

The new policy tells associates for the first time how family planning will affect their careers. The policy is consistent with the way the firm treated its former part-time associates. It also retains flexibility and confirms the firm's inherent authority to shorten the partnership track for the exceptional associate (for example, the experienced associate or the lateral hire) or to lengthen it for those who need extra evaluation or training.

Expansion of Maternity Leave to Parenting and Family Leave

There was little controversy about the desirability of expanding the employee's leave policy to include parenting leave and leave to care for sick family members. Both were consistent with trends in leave policy at the state and federal levels. Several firm members already had faced the need to care for terminally ill parents, and a former member of the firm had cared for a spouse during a terminal illness. The availability of unpaid leave in such circumstances seemed an appropriately humane and compassionate response.

Application to Males and Females

It was unclear at first whether the firm would make parenting or family leaves available to both men and women. The legal research confirmed, however, that the firm had no choice. If unpaid parenting or family leave was available at all, it had to be available to all, at least when it came to employees.

One other firm had reported in response to the survey that a young father had taken family leave to care for a newborn. No male attorney or staff member at our firm had ever asked for extended leave to care for a child or sick family member, although, if a policy had been in place, perhaps there would have been an interest in it. We did not survey firm members to determine whether they would have taken such leave if it had been available.

It became clear when the new policy was announced, however, that male associates interested in starting families were as interested as female associates in the availability of family leave. In fact, most of the questions raised when the policy was introduced came from the male associates. Most have spouses who work outside the home and who enjoy maternity or family leave benefits. The family could potentially combine leaves to make possible a full year of in-home parental child care.

Part-Time Partners

Part-time work for associates and staff never generated much controversy. It was relatively simple to reduce compensation in proportion to the reduction in hours from the normal work week. The firm had employed associates on a part-time basis in the past and merely confirmed that practice by adopting a written policy clarifying its implications.

Part-time practice for partners, however, was a different matter, and it generated the most controversy. Part-time partners include partners on a full-time leave for a designated period and those working part time for a period. Both situations were problematic.

One objection focused on the problem of fairly compensating full-time partners when some partners took full-time leaves or worked only part time. Our partners, as in many other firms, receive a share of the profits of the firm on a monthly basis in accordance with annually set percentages. Profits fluctuate, however, and are not directly related to any one partner's current working hours. Instead, they reflect efforts by many partners over previous months and years to develop and serve the firm's clients. The absence of income generated by one partner, even a partner who reduces her own compensation, means a corresponding reduction in the income of all of the other partners, who would oridnarily share in that income after paying for fixed expenses.

Unfair compensation could result, moreover, if the partner on part-time status reduced her percentage distribution during years of modest profits but not during years of high profits generated by efforts made by full-time partners during her full-time or part-time absence, or vice versa. Working out a fair method of compensation during an extended period of family leave is, to say the least, complicated.

Another objection to part-time partners stemmed from concern for the strength of a partnership in which some "owners" are only partially committed to its advancement. The survival of small and medium-sized law firms in a competitive legal marketplace depends upon each partner's ability to attract, serve, and retain clients. A partner's job is to guarantee his or her clients personal and prompt legal services, including evening and weekend services for the client in crisis. The firm's ability to retain clients depends on the partner in charge of a matter being easily accessible to the client.

A part-time schedule arguably works against the accessibility needed to meet client needs or objectives. It is one thing for associates to work part time, since the partner in charge remains available to the client or can assign another associate to work on the matter, but part-time partners, it was feared, could endanger the firm's client base.

Related to that objection was a concern that client development itself requires a partner's active involvement in trade associations, public speaking, and participation in clubs and civic functions—activities that occur in addition to normal work hours at the office. It was unclear how part-time partners could deliver the time that these activities demand.

Some partners, concerned for the prospective part-time partner's best interest, also believed that the part-time partner would acquire "second-class" status as a decision-maker and participant in the firm. Permitting partners to practice part time, the partners feared, could hurt both the partnership and the partner. In addition, some partners felt strongly that the first year of partnership is critical and that an incoming partner should not undertake that status on a part-time basis but should delay the onset of partnership until he or she could work full time.

Advocates for overturning the policy against part-time partners argued that a new, flexible policy could be structured to emphasize the firm's philosophy that partners must make a wholehearted commitment to the firm. Such a policy could permit disapproval of requests for lengthy periods of part-time work and continue to treat requests for part-time practice on an ad hoc basis.

A flexible policy, moreover, could take into consideration the firm's current workload, the partner's area of practice, the ability and willingness of the other partners in the same practice area to continue providing high-quality service to the firm's clients in that area, the partner's track record, the partner's particular family needs, the partner's financial investment in the firm, the number of other partners working or wanting to work part time, and other factors that would balance a partner's temporary reduction in time commitment with a total psychological commitment. Every partner agreed that a wholehearted commitment to the firm was essential to its long-term well-being. However, advocates for part-time work argued, 1 year of part-time work out of a potential 40-year history with the firm is a small deviation that the firm should be willing to accept in the interest of a greater social good—the care and well-being of our families—and in the interest of job satisfaction.

Ultimately, the partners accepted the concept of a limited period of family leave for partners, on either a full-time or a part-time basis. Acceptance of the concept does not guarantee family leave for every partner, however. Family leave for partners remains in the discretion of the partnership on a case-by-case basis, with adjustment in compensation—for now, undefined— and a delay in partnership for associates working part time during the "transition" year.

Maternity Disability Policy for Partners

The law requires employers to treat their employees' medical disability equally. An employer cannot withhold paid medical leave for childbirth if it grants paid medical leave for other medical disabilities, for example. Partnerships, however, generally are not bound by laws affecting employer–employee relationships. In other words, partnerships can discriminate among partners' disabilities and permit medical leave for some medical disabilities and not others, even if the decision discriminates against females denied medical leave for childbirth-related medical disabilities.

The partners in our firm do not have sick leave in the sense of accumulating sick days over time and accounting for sick days taken. Although some partners have disability insurance, the partnership has never adopted a medical leave policy covering the partner who becomes disabled or ill for an extended period. Rather, there is a perception that such partners would probably be "carried" through major illnesses for at least some period of time without a reduction in compensation. The partnership, however, has never established a policy or formula to determine how long that would be.

It seemed a step in the right direction, notwithstanding the ambiguous nature of partner sick leave, to encourage the partnership to treat the medical complications of childbirth the same as other medical disabilities. The partners, after consideration, agreed to follow the spirit of employment law and treat maternity- or childbirth-disabled partners as they would treat other medically disabled partners. If a partner needed to recover from a caesarean delivery or a broken tailbone before returning to work, for example, she would be treated and compensated like a partner recovering from hernia surgery.

Because the partners have no established medical disability leave policy for themselves, however, the practical effect of this policy is still unclear. The committee considered tackling the broader issue of partner medical disability leave, but the scope of that issue went so far beyond the scope of family leave that the committee decided to defer that to another day. It was enough to send the signal that women partners would not be hurt by maternity and childbirth disabilities to any greater or lesser extent than male partners with other medical disabilities. They could now expect to be "carried" during a period of medical disability for a reasonable time.

The Policies

The firm implemented its decisions with two sets of written policies, one affecting employees (including the associates) and one affecting the partners. The policies are reproduced below, with introductory comments.

New Policies Affecting Employees

Vacation Leave. The firm's former vacation leave policy permitted staff members to accrue paid vacation leave at two weeks per year, and associates at three weeks. This remained unchanged but was supplemented to include the following language on use of vacation in conjunction with family leave:

> *Vacation leave. . . .* Vacation leave may be used in conjunction with maternity disability leave or family leave.

Sick Leave. The firm's former sick leave policy permitted employees to accrue up to 60 days of sick leave at one day per month. Upon voluntary termination, the employee received compensation for 25 percent of the accrued sick leave. This remained unchanged but was supplemented to include the following language offering unpaid family leave for medical reasons:

> *Sick leave. . . .* Employees, upon request and in the discretion of the partnership, may take unpaid family leave for the employee's own medical disability upon exhaustion of accrued sick leave.

Maternity Disability Leave, Family Leave, Part-Time Employment, and Partnership Track. The firm's former written policy on maternity leave authorized the use of paid sick and vacation leave for maternity and childbirth purposes. This remained unchanged, but the new written policy clarified definitions by using the term "maternity disability leave" to distinguish paid disability leave from unpaid parenting leave.

The firm also reduced to writing for the first time its ad hoc policy on part-time work by staff members and associates and the effect of part-time employment on the partnership track.

> *Maternity Disability Leave.* Employees may take paid leave for pregnancy and childbirth-related medical disability using the employee's accrued sick leave or accrued vacation. The firm will continue all existing insurance coverage during the maternity leave. Employees also may be eligible for long-term disability leave for pregnancy and childbirth complications in accordance with the terms of the firm's long-term disability income plan.

Family Leave. Family leave constitutes unpaid leave to care for a new-born child, a newly-adopted pre–school age child, or a seriously ill parent, a child, or a spouse or similarly significant person. Employees, male and female, may take unpaid family leave for up to four months. This leave is independent of and in addition to maternity disability leave.

Family leave for child care purposes must be taken within six months of the birth or adoption. The employee shall give at least eight weeks notice to the partnership before taking family leave for child care purposes. The firm will continue all existing insurance coverage during the family leave. Family leave may be extended upon request in the discretion of the partnership. An employee may take no more than one family leave during any 12-month period.

Part-time Employment for Family Leave. Employees, male and female, may request part-time employment to accommodate family obligations qualifying for family leave under [the previous paragraph]. The partnership will consider such requests on a case-by-case basis with appropriate adjustments to compensation and benefits, if applicable. In no case may an employee be employed less than half time.

Associate Partnership Track. Use of accrued sick leave or vacation time to cover a maternity disability leave will not affect an associate's partnership track.

Use of up to four months of family leave in the aggregate during employment as an associate will not preclude consideration for partnership at the conclusion of the associate's normal partnership track. However, the partnership always reserves the right to extend or shorten an associate's partnership track to reflect extended absences from full-time employment and other relevant considerations.

New Policies Affecting Partners

The firm had never had a written leave policy covering partners. The resulting written policy still leaves much to the partnership's discretion, however, and does not provide an entitlement.

Maternity Disability Leave. A partner may continue to receive a draw at her established share of participation during any leave taken in connection with pregnancy or childbirth medical disability to the same extent as partners receive draws for other medical disabilities. The partnership may require a written report from the treating physician to support a request for a partner's compensated maternity sick leave.

Family Leave. Family leave constitutes unpaid full-time or part-time leave to care for a newborn child, a newly-adopted pre–school age child, or a seriously ill parent, spouse, or child. This leave is independent of and in addition to maternity disability leave. Partners, male and female, upon request and in the discretion of the partnership on a case-by-case basis, may take family leave for up to six months. Family leave may be extended upon request and in the discretion of the partnership.

Absence from the firm on a full-time or part-time basis may affect the partner's draw and capital contribution. The extent of its effect will be determined by the partnership on a case-by-case basis.

Summary

The family leave policy project in our firm was a success. Guided by policies in place elsewhere, the partnership expanded leave so that both male and female employees could use family leave to care for newborn or ill family members. It clarified the effect of family leave on an associate's partnership track and opened the door for partners to take family leave full time or part time.

The woman partner whose back-to-back pregnancies inspired us to address these issues was the first to request leave under the new policies. The firm accepted her proposal that she be granted a paid medical disability leave of 2 months and an unpaid full-time family leave of 3 months, followed by part-time family leave for one year. Her compensation while working part time will be converted to a 12-month basis and reduced by 50 percent. The agreement recognizes that when the partners set partnership percentages at the beginning of next year, they may consider her part-time status in determining her percentage share of profits.

None of the family leave policies at our firm is a true entitlement. While the firm's history demonstrates that the partners have been generous with leave in the past, both employees and partners must still request and obtain approval for family leaves. And while the partners have reversed the philosophical prohibition against part-time partners, they still require that incoming partners work full time their first year and will delay partnership for those requesting family leave during the transition year from associate to partner.

Yet the part-time partners policy reflects a good faith attempt to balance the responsibilities professionals have to their business partners against the responsibilities professionals have to their families. The balancing effort itself did much to alleviate concerns about the working environment the firm offered its women lawyers. Implementation of the firm's family leave policy can now be accomplished within a framework built upon a full discussion of the critical competing values and goals.

PART VI

Parental Leave and Its Effects on Women's and Men's Health

15 | The Wisconsin Parental Leave Study: Maternity Leave and the Health of Women and Their Families

Janet Shibley Hyde and Roseanne Clark

Parental leave is a policy issue on which social scientists ought to be able to provide research and expertise. For example, expert testimony for Representative Patricia Schroeder's Parental and Medical Leave bill was provided by the Bush Center in Child Development and Social Policy, which is headed by the eminent psychologist Edward Zigler. However, when one examines social science research on this issue, most of it focuses on infants and their well-being. When the issue is parental leave, we believe that mothers' and fathers' perspectives and well-being should be addressed as well. Our research uses a family systems approach, focusing on the mother, the father, the infant, and their relationships. This chapter examines the results of our research on mothers and infants; Chapter 16 by Marilyn Essex and Marjorie Klein presents the data on fathers.

The Longitudinal Design

We have been conducting a study of 55 women and their families. The women were recruited from lists of registrants for childbirth education classes in Milwaukee and from a clinic for low-income women. The women were interviewed initially during the ninth month of pregnancy (Time 1); both the women and their husbands/partners were then interviewed one month after the birth (Time 2); we later collected follow-up data (Time 3) on the women and their husbands/partners 12 months after the birth. In addition, mother–infant interactions were videotaped when the babies were 4 months old, and again when they were 16 months old.

The Sample

Because we recruited through childbirth education classes, our sample is somewhat better-educated and more affluent than the general American population. Almost half (47 percent) of the women were college graduates or had advanced degrees. Before the birth, 44 percent of the families had incomes of $40,000 per year or more; on the other hand, 10 percent had family incomes between $10,000 and $14,000. The mean age of the women was 28 years; ages ranged from 19 to 36 years. Almost all (95 percent) of the women were married, and for 78 percent this was the first child.

Measures

We define health as comprising three components (World Health Organization, 1948): physical, mental, and social. By "social health" we mean the woman's relationships, including the marital relationship, the mother–infant relationship, and the quality of her social supports. Our focus is on the effect of maternity leave on women's health and on the family system. To this end, we measured the following variables:

Physical health, including the woman's current symptoms and complications of pregnancy and/or delivery

Mental health, including depression (measured by the Center for Epidemiological Studies Depression Scale, or CES-D: Radloff, 1977) and anxiety (Spielberger's State Anxiety Inventory: Spielberger, 1983)

Social health, including the quality of the marital relationship as perceived by the woman and her husband/partner (Dyadic Adjustment Scale: Spanier, 1976; items developed by Pearlin: for example, Pearlin and Johnson, 1977), the quality of the mother–infant relationship (Parent–Child Early Relational Assessment: Clark et al., 1985), and the quantity and quality of social supports available to and used by women to meet their instrumental and emotional needs

Maternity leave variables, including the employer's policy and the woman's decision (that is, whether to work full or part time or be a homemaker, and the number of weeks of leave if she returns to work)

Psychosocial variables that mediate the process, including the woman's personality (need for affiliation, need for achievement, autonomy, and anxiety from the Jackson Personality Inventory: Jackson, 1976; self-esteem: Rosenberg, 1965), her attitudes on parental leave policy, work/career commitment, and the needs of an infant (Greenberger et al., 1988), and her husband/partner's corresponding attitudes

Situational factors that mediate the process, including child care arrangements, the infant's temperament and health, and the husband/partner's parental leave options and decision, willingness to share tasks, mental health, and work stress

Background characteristics, including income, occupation, ethnicity, age, and education

Based on our theoretical model, we are investigating the relation between maternity leave variables (length of leave, company policy) and women's physical, mental, and social health, recognizing that many variables mediate this relation, including such factors as the infant's temperament, the woman's attitudes, family income, and the father's attitudes and adjustment. Put simply, are women better off taking shorter leaves or longer leaves, in terms of their physical health? in terms of their mental health? in terms of their relationship with their baby and with their husband/partner? Are they better off returning to work part time or full time? And what other factors play into this equation?

Attitudes: What Do Women Want?

Although there have been several surveys of corporations' policies on parental leave, we know of no survey that has asked working women and their husbands/partners, who are the relevant consumers, what kind of leave they desire.

In response to the statement "Women should have a right to job-guaranteed maternity leaves (that is, the right to the same or comparable job upon return from a leave during late pregnancy and/or after the birth of a child)," 98 percent of the women said they agreed (90 percent agreed strongly, 8 percent somewhat) when interviewed a month after the baby's birth.

On the issue of job-guaranteed parental leave for fathers, nearly half the women (49 percent) agreed strongly and another 29 percent agreed somewhat. That is, these women are very supportive of leaves for men.

On the issue of income replacement during leave, there was also a strong positive consensus. In response to the statement "Women should have a right to some pay (either full pay or reduced pay) during their maternity leave," over half the women (55 percent) agreed strongly, and another 23 percent agreed somewhat. On the issue of continuation of benefits, the consensus was nearly perfect, with 92 percent of the women agreeing that benefits such as health insurance should continue during maternity leave.

We also asked women for their opinions about the proper source of maternity leave policy. The majority (69 percent) believed that job-guaranteed maternity leave should be provided by federal or state laws (54 percent favored federal laws, 11 percent favored state laws). The remainder favored voluntary policies by employers.

In regard to the length of leave, 69 percent of these women believed that women should have a right to a job-guaranteed leave that lasts between 3 and 6 months (18 percent favor 2 months leave or less; 31 percent favor 3 months; 38 percent favor 4 to 6 months; and 9 percent favor more than 6 months).

Two things strike us about these results. First, women want considerably more leave than current state legislation and pending federal legislation requires. The state of Wisconsin, for example, mandates only 6 weeks of job-guaranteed parental leave. As of this writing, the U.S. Senate version of the Family and Medical Leave Act has been so weakened by compromises that it calls for only 10 weeks of parental leave (and businesses with fewer than 20 employees are exempted, so that only 12 percent of U.S. firms and 47 percent of U.S. employees would be covered). In Sweden (see Chapter 22 by Linda Haas), all women and men are guaranteed a leave of 12 months, 9 months at 90 percent pay and another 3 months at reduced pay. In those countries with government-mandated longer leaves, parents believe that those leaves are their right. We believe that adequate leaves are the right of American parents, too.

It is important to take seriously mothers' opinions about the appropriate length of parental leave. It may well be that women have an intuitive sense of the right time for them to return to work, in terms of their own needs, their baby's needs, and the needs of their husbands/partners. Research in psychology has described "intuitive parenting," an intuitive sense of the way to care for an infant (Papoušek and Papoušek, 1987). We should not dismiss lightly parents' sense of what will be best for them and their family.

Women's Mental and Social Health

In investigating maternity leave and its consequences for women's mental and social health, we are especially interested in differences according to the woman's current or planned work status at Time 2, a month after the birth. At the time of that interview, 7 percent of the women were back at work full time, and 28 percent planned to be working full time by the time the baby was 12 months old; 13 percent were back at work part time, and 41 percent planned to be part-time workers by the baby's first birthday; 26 percent were currently full-time homemakers, and all of them planned to remain homemakers; and an additional 5 percent had other plans, such as becoming students.

Depression is a major mental health variable in this study because depression is known to be elevated in late pregnancy and in the postpartum period (see, for example, O'Hara, 1986) and because it is associated with a wide variety of life stresses (Pearlin et al., 1981). We use the CES-D, a self-report instrument, to measure depression (Radloff, 1977). For this project, we excluded three items that reflect a normal part of late pregnancy and the early post-partum period ("I did not feel like eating; my appetite was poor," "I felt that everything I did was an effort," "My sleep was restless"). The analyses reported here reflect that modified scoring.

Group differences in depression scores at Time 2 are interesting, with women who were working part time or planned to work part time reporting the fewest depressive symptoms ($M = 7.3$), and women who were working or planned to work full time and homemakers reporting the most ($M = 9.2$ and $M = 9.0$, respectively). Those differences are not statistically significant, probably because of the small number of subjects when they are divided into these employment subgroups. However, the pattern showing that part-time workers fare best appears repeatedly in our analyses, suggesting a genuine advantage.

We are investigating women's social health in a number of areas, including the marital relationship. Although there are no significant group differences in ratings of marital intimacy (e.g., "My partner is someone I can really talk with about things that are important to me") or affirmation (e.g., "My partner appreciates me just as I am"), the results indicate that homemakers and women who work or plan to work part time report the most equity in their marriages, and those who work or plan to work full time report the least. The design is not experimental, of course, and we must be careful about inferences. But it is ironic that those who will work full time and need the most equity in their marriage actually perceive that they have the least. Again, we see that women who work or plan to work part time fare well.

We used the statistical technique of regression analysis to investigate what factors were most associated with mothers' depression at Time 2, one month after the baby's birth. Consistently, the father's depression and the mother's rating of the affirmation she feels in her marriage had the strongest relationship to her depression. The mother's work status interacted with these factors. Consistently, having a husband/partner who is depressed and low ratings on marital equity and affirmation is *least* likely to increase depression for women who work or plan to work full time; it is most likely to increase depression for those who work or plan to work part time. On the other hand, having a husband/partner who is not at all depressed and rating marital equity and affirmation very high is associated with reduced depression for women who work or plan to work part time, while these factors are least associated with reduced depression for women who work or plan to work full time.

We will summarize only briefly numerous analyses that we conducted examining the relationship between the length of maternity leave (for those who are employed) and the mental health and social health measures. Most of those analyses showed no significant relationships, much to our surprise. (There were a few exceptions: for example, there is a positive, significant correlation between the number of weeks of leave a woman has and perceived equity in the marriage. This means that those who return to work later feel that their marriages are more equitable.) There may be several explanations for the null findings. One possibility is that our sample is simply too small to detect the relations that exist. Another may be that we had too little variation in the length-of-leave variable in our sample. Virtually all of the women were returning to work 2 to 3 months after the baby's birth.

Two important conclusions emerge from the findings reported in this section. First, the distinction between part-time and full-time work status is important in this research because of its relation to mental health and because of the potential that work has for buffering against stresses that women may encounter in the family. Second, parental leave research must include fathers, not only because it is conceptually sound and politically correct, but because fathers undoubtedly exert a strong influence. This may sound obvious, but few other scholars have examined the role of fathers in parental leave (an exception is the work of Pleck, 1988, and Chapter 16 by Essex and Klein).

The Mother–Infant Relationship

Some mothers experience anxiety about leaving their infant or being apart from him or her. Ellen Hock and her colleagues (DeMeis, Hock, and McBride, 1986) have developed the Maternal Separation Anxiety scale to measure these feelings, and we administered this scale to our respondents. The results indicate that at the time of the first interview, full-time homemakers express the most anxiety (although the effect is not quite significant). One month after the birth, however, there are no group differences in maternal separation anxiety. It is relevant to note here that our sample consisted mostly of first-time mothers (78 percent), no doubt because we recruited many subjects through childbirth education classes. The results might look considerably different if we had more multiparous women in the sample.

Those who have been following the great infant day care debate know that the evidence on whether a mother's employment in the first year is harmful to the infant has rested almost solely on one measure: Ainsworth's Strange Situation procedure (see, for example, Ainsworth and Wittig, 1969), which assesses the infant's attachment to the mother. In this paradigm, the mother and infant are in a strange situation (usually the psychologist's laboratory). This procedure is conducted in a stressful social situation that includes eight episodes, two of which involve brief separations from the mother and the introduction of a stranger to the infant in this unfamiliar environment. The focus is on the baby's behavior when the mother returns. Does the infant approach her and react happily (secure attachment) or do other things, such as avoid her (insecure attachment)?

This measure has some limitations. Among others, it assesses only a small slice of the mother–infant relationship—the infant's behavior at the time of a reunion. Certainly an important public policy debate such as the one over day care should not be based on a single concept and method of measurement. Therefore, we have sought to use a measure that captures more of the complex quality of the mother–infant relationship by assessing the affect and behavior of the mother and the infant, as well as the mother–infant interaction.

A member of our research group, Roseanne Clark, has been instrumental in developing an important new measure, the Parent–Child Early Relational Assessment, or simply the Early Relational Assessment (ERA!), which assesses the quality of the mother–infant relationship on six factors: maternal affective involvement and responsiveness; maternal negative affect; infant regulation, attentional, and social skills; infant disregulation, irritability, and negative behavior; dyadic (i.e., mother–infant) mutuality and reciprocity; and dyadic tension (Clark et al., 1984, 1985). This measure assesses the affective and behavioral quality of the mother–child relationship, the contribution each makes to it, and the quality of dyadic functioning. The dyad is videotaped in three situations: feeding, a structured task (changing diapers and playing with a rattle), and a free-play situation (playing with chosen toys).

The videotape is replayed for the mother and, during the replay, a semistructured interview is conducted in order to assess her phenomenological experience of her child, of herself in the parenting role, and of their interaction. The mother, for example, is asked whether this interaction was typical or unusual; she is also asked about her perception of her infant's temperament and behavior and about her own sense of competence and effectiveness in this relationship. We believe that this measurement technique is an excellent example of feminist methodology. The mother becomes a true interactive *participant* in the research, rather than being a passive *subject*.

Through the use of three different situations, each tapping different areas of competence and conflict, and the use of both objective and subjective assessments, we are better able to understand both the mother's and the child's experience of the relationship and the quality of interpersonal functioning. As a means of collecting data to inform public policy debates, we believe that this methodology goes beyond the Strange Situation paradigm in assessing the quality of the mother–infant relationship—for two reasons. First, it provides a richer and more complex assessment by looking at the mother–infant relationship rather than just the infant's behavior. Second, the method can be used at various ages over the first five years (in contrast to the Strange Situation, which typically is used only around 12 months of age), so that the effects of the mother's work status, or the effects of child care, can be assessed over longer periods in the child's life.

Trained coders, who are blind to the work status of the mother, objectively rate the interactions recorded on the videotapes.

When the babies were 4 months old, we videotaped 20 of the 55 mother–infant pairs; at that time, 26 percent of the mothers were working full time, 42 percent were working part time, and 32 percent were full-time homemakers.

Results of preliminary analyses with this small sample indicate that there were no significant differences in the quality of mother–infant interactions depending on whether the mother was employed or was a full-time homemaker. However, the means were higher (more positive) in all areas of mother–child interaction for the mothers who were working part time. Thus, these preliminary results do not support the belief that a mother's return to work is damaging to the mother–infant relationship, at least when she is able to do so part time.

We videotaped the mothers and infants when the latter were 16 months old, but the data are not yet analyzed. This should be a rich source of information on the long-term effects of the mother's employment during the first year of the baby's life.

The 4-month videotaping also yielded rich qualitative data from the women. At that time, the mothers reported that they were still learning to read their infants' cues and beginning to feel more competent as parents. The working mothers' concerns focused on the infant's not sleeping through the night and their own feelings of fatigue. At that age, babies' patterns of sleeping and feeding are in flux, requiring adaptation from the mother and father (see Chapter 19 by Lynn Sanford Koester). The mothers said that they hoped that changing from breastfeeding to bottlefeeding as they went back to work would not be too difficult. They were concerned about whether babysitters would be able to read the baby's cues well. At odds were the pulls they reported at 4 months, feeling that they must become more structured and get work done quickly, and at the same time that their infants required them to be more flexible and patient.

Summary and Conclusions

Part-Time Work Options

Our data provide some evidence that women who work or plan to work part time in the first year after the baby's birth seem to fare the best. This suggests that public policy should guarantee women an option to choose part-time work during an infant's first year, and perhaps longer.

Timing of Return to Work

Our research failed to uncover effects related to the timing of the return to work. It would be premature, however, to conclude that the length of leave is unimportant. The main reason for caution is that our sample was small. In addition, almost all the women who returned to work in the first year after the birth did so when the baby was around 2 to 3 months of age. Thus, we were not able to examine how women fared if they returned at 6 months or 12 months. These findings also need to be understood in conjunction with the findings on women's beliefs about the ideal length of leave, which they saw as 3 to 6 months. Certainly the length of leave is an important variable that requires further investigation. In addition, as the notion of parental leaves becomes more recognized and socially acceptable (for example, through federal or state legislation or union contracts), women may feel comfortable acknowledging that they would prefer longer leaves.

This research has raised many interesting and important questions and opens up new avenues for research. We are tentative about many of these conclusions because our sample was small (55). Surely we need larger studies of these issues. We are currently planning an expanded study of 600 women, funded by a grant from NIMH. Most important, women's health—physical, mental, and social—should not be ignored in the parental leave debate.

REFERENCES

Ainsworth, Mary D. S., and B. A. Wittig (1969). "Attachment and Exploratory Behavior of One-Year-Olds in a Strange Situation." In B. M. Foss, ed., *Determinants of Infant Behavior*, vol. 4. London: Methuen.

Bretherton, Inge (1985). "Attachment Theory: Retrospect and Prospect." In *Growing Points of Attachment Theory and Research*. Monographs of the Society for Research in Child Development, vol. 50. 1–2, serial no. 209.

Clark, Roseanne, J. S. Musick, F. M. Stott, and K. B. Klehr (1985). *The Parent–Child Early Relational Assessment*. Madison: University of Wisconsin, Department of Psychiatry.

Clark, Roseanne, J. S. Musick, F. M. Stott, K. Klehr, and B. Cohler (1984). "Mother–Child Dyads at Risk: Assessment of Maternal and Child Affect and Behavior." *Infant Behavior and Development* 7, special ICIS issue.

DeMeis, D. K., Ellen Hock, and S. L. McBride (1986). "The Balance of Employment and Motherhood: Longitudinal Study of Mothers' Feelings about Separation from Their First-Born Infant." *Developmental Psychology* 22: 627–32.

Greenberger, Ellen, W. A. Goldberg, T. J. Crawford, and J. Granger (1988). "Beliefs About the Consequences of Maternal Employment for Children." *Psychology of Women Quarterly* 12: 35–59.

Jackson, D. N. (1976). *Jackson Personality Inventory*. Goshen, N.Y.: Research Psychologists Press.

O'Hara, Michael W. (1986). "Social Support, Life Events, and Depression During Pregnancy and the Puerperium." *Archives of General Psychiatry* 43: 569–73.

Papoušek, Hanuš, and Mechthild Papoušek (1987). "Intuitive Parenting: A Dialectic Counterpart to the Infant's Precocity in Integrative Capacities." In J. D. Osofsky, *Handbook of Infant Development* (2d ed.). New York: John Wiley.

Pearlin, Leonard I., and J. S. Johnson (1977). "Marital Status, Life-Strains, and Depression." *American Sociological Review* 42: 704–15.

Pearlin, Leonard I., M. A. Lieberman, E. G. Menaghan, and J. T. Mullan

(1981). "The Stress Process." *Journal of Health and Social Behavior* 22: 337–56.

Pleck, Joseph H. (1983). "Husbands' Paid Work and Family Roles: Current Research Issues." In H. Lopata and J. H. Pleck, eds., *Research in the Interweave of Social Roles*, vol. 3: *Families and Jobs*. Greenwich, Conn.: JAI Press.

———(1988). "Fathers and Infant Care Leave." In Edward F. Zigler and Meryl Frank, eds., *The Parental Leave Crisis: Toward a National Policy*. New Haven: Yale University Press.

Radloff, Lenore (1977). "The CES-D Scale: A Self-Report Depression Scale for Research in the General Population." *Applied Psychological Measurement* 1: 385–401.

Rosenberg, Morris (1965). *Society and the Adolescent Self-Image*. Princeton: Princeton University Press.

Spanier, Graham B. (1976). "Measuring Dyadic Adjustment: New Scales for Assessing the Quality of Marriage and Similar Dyads." *Journal of Marriage and the Family* 38: 15–30.

Spielberger, Charles D. (1983). *Manual for the State–Trait Anxiety Inventory*. Form Y. Palo Alto, Calif.: Consulting Psychologists Press.

Zigler, Edward F., and Meryl Frank, eds. (1988). *The Parental Leave Crisis: Toward a National Policy*. New Haven: Yale University Press.

16 | The Wisconsin Parental Leave Study: The Roles of Fathers

Marilyn J. Essex and Marjorie H. Klein

Men's family roles will be influenced greatly by the resolution of the current parental leave debates. If policy reforms maintain the traditional view of parental leave as necessary only for women to recover from the medical disabilities of childbirth, employed fathers will be effectively barred from participation in child care. Similarly, paternity leaves will be unavailable if maternity leave is mandated as a "special protection" for working mothers. On the other hand, if policy reforms are aimed at avoiding sex discrimination and directed more broadly to include family leave (leave to take care of newborns and adopted infants, as well as sick children and other family members) in addition to medical disability leave, fathers stand to gain considerably more parental leave options.

Unfortunately, these debates are being carried out without the benefit of comprehensive research on the effects of parental leave on the family. Although there are some studies on the effects on infants, relatively little is known about women's desires or needs, or the effects of maternity leave on them, and except for the work of Joseph Pleck (1986), almost nothing is known about the issues and policy implications of fatherhood, employment, and child care. In a recent overview of current research, Pleck (1988) summarized the evidence on the availability, use, and effects of paternity leave in the United States and Sweden. Although there are numerous studies of Sweden (e.g., Hwang, 1987; Lamb and Levine, 1983), data on the United States consist of a few surveys that show a very low number of organizations giving paid paternity leaves of any duration, the more common approach of giving unpaid personal leaves or leaves of absence, and generally low rates of use (Bureau of National Affairs, 1986; Catalyst, 1986; Kamerman, Kahn, and Kingston, 1983). To date, however, no studies exist on the attitudes of men toward parental leave, their reasons for using (or not using) their paternity leave options, or the effects of paternity leave on men and their families, especially over time.

This chapter is a first step toward providing this information. It reports on our study of the effects of parental leave options and decisions on the family system, focusing specifically on paternity leave and the family roles of fathers (see Chapter 15 by Janet Shibley Hyde and Roseanne Clark for data on the mothers and infants).

Sample and Measures

The sample consisted of 55 women, their husbands/partners, and their infants recruited from lists of registrants for childbirth education classes and from a clinic for low-income families at a major hospital in Milwaukee. Initially, only the women were interviewed during the ninth month of pregnancy (Time 1). Subsequently, 1 month after the birth (Time 2), 45 of the fathers agreed to be interviewed. They and their wives/partners were interviewed a final time 12 months after the birth (Time 3). This chapter is based on the 39 couples for whom complete data were available at Time 2 and Time 3.

The fathers were somewhat better-educated and more affluent than the general American population. Half (52 percent) were college graduates or had advanced degrees, and all had graduated from high school. Before the birth, 44 percent of the families had incomes of $40,000 per year or more, although 10 percent had family incomes under $14,000 and a third had family incomes under $30,000. The mean age of the fathers was 29 years; ages ranged from 21 to 40.

The key variables in this study are defined and described in Chapter 15. Paternity leave variables include the men's attitudes toward maternity and paternity leave, their employers' policies, and the fathers' actual use of leave. The fathers' family role variables include the degree to which they shared in child care and household tasks, and the amount of disagreement between the fathers and mothers concerning these tasks. These variables, in turn, have important effects on the family system, assessed here by the fathers' and mothers' perceptions of the quality of their marital relationships, using items developed by Leonard Pearlin (for example, in Pearlin and Johnson, 1977).

Parental Leave Attitudes: What Do Men Want?

Men's attitudes toward parental leave, for themselves and for their wives, are important underlying factors in their actual experience of paternity leave as well as their family roles and marital relationships over time. One month postpartum (Time 2), we asked the fathers their views on the appropriate length, pay, and benefits of maternity leave and whether men should also have the right to paternity leaves. In response to the statement "Women should have a right to job-guaranteed maternity leaves," 73 percent of the men agreed strongly and 22 percent agreed somewhat, for a total of 95 percent in agreement. However, they were significantly less likely to agree with the statement "Men should have a right to job-guaranteed (paternity) leaves": 24 percent agreed strongly, 36 percent agreed somewhat, and 22 percent disagreed (t[38] = 6.77; p = .00). When asked about the maternity leave issues of income replacement, continuation of benefits, and the length of leave, 24 percent of the men agreed strongly that women should have a right to some pay, either full or reduced, during their maternity leave, while 33 percent disagreed. Almost all (96 percent) agreed that benefits such as health insurance should continue during maternity leave. And 69 percent of the men believed that job-guaranteed maternity leaves should last 3 months or less.

Although the fathers were generally supportive of women's right to maternity leave benefits, they felt significantly less strongly than the mothers about all of these issues except for the continuation of benefits. Almost all (90 percent) of the women agreed strongly that they should have a right to job-guaranteed maternity leaves (t[38] = 2.05; p < .05); over half (55 percent) agreed strongly that they should have a right to some pay (t[38] = 2.69; p = .01); and they were significantly more likely than fathers to believe that maternity leaves should last 3 months or longer (t[38] = 2.37; p < .03). Furthermore, the fathers felt significantly less strongly than the mothers about their own rights to paternity leaves. Almost half (48 percent) of the women agreed strongly, and only 8 percent disagreed, with the idea that men should have a right to job-guaranteed paternity leaves (t[38] = 2.82; p < .01).

If we agree with Hyde and Clark (see Chapter 15) that what women want is quite modest compared with what is available to women in many other countries, it is distressing to realize that the fathers feel less strongly about women's right to maternity leaves, and even less strongly than that about their own right to paternity leaves. However, it is also clear that men want considerably more leave than is typically available to them or than current and proposed legislation provides. These results support Pleck's (1988) suggestion that the number of fathers who want paternity leave rights is more than the small minority represented in known legal and media cases.

Paternity Leave Options and Use

It would make sense if men's attitudes toward paternity and maternity leave had a significant effect on their actual use of leave. However, our findings show that the men's attitudes had no significant effect on whether they took a leave or on the length of leave taken. Pleck (1988) suggests that men's actual use of leaves may be based more on the availability of leaves and the specific benefits given (such as paid leave as opposed to unpaid).

What paternity leave options were available? Only 21 percent (N = 8) of the men's employers allowed a job-guaranteed paternity leave following the birth of a baby, and only 2 of those (or 5 percent of the total) guaranteed pay for some or all of that time. Of those fathers who were allowed a leave, half (N = 4) were unsure of the length allowed, probably because the leaves were unpaid and thus of little interest. On the other hand, the half who knew the maximum time allowed were either guaranteed fully paid leaves (N = 2; leaves of 1 week and 4 weeks) or had special circumstances that increased the likelihood that they would know the leave policy even though the leave was unpaid (one was self-employed, guaranteed 1 week; one was guaranteed 6 months, an unusually long parental leave).

Given the scarcity of paternity leaves, what did the fathers do after the births of their babies? Three-quarters (75 percent) took some time off immediately after the birth, 15 percent rearranged their work schedules, and 10 percent did neither. Of those who took some time off, 57 percent took 2 to 3 days of leave, and 36 percent took off 1 week. Only two fathers took longer leaves (2 weeks and 3 weeks).

These results might be seen as evidence that fathers do not take, and therefore may not want, paternity leaves of much more than a week. In fact, when asked a month after the birth whether they would prefer to be working full time, working part time, or on paternity leave at that time, over three-quarters of the fathers said they preferred to be working full time. However, a substantial minority said they would prefer to be working only part time (10 percent) or on paternity leave (13 percent). And we do not know how many who preferred to be working full time would have liked to rearrange their schedules in order to spend more time with their babies. We do know, however, that almost half (47 percent) of the fathers said that finances were at least somewhat important in their decisions about paternity leave; 78 percent said that practical considerations were at least somewhat important. Furthermore, although there are virtually no national data available on the actual use of paternity leaves in the United States, the leaves taken by the fathers in our study correspond to the leave policies reported by U.S. organizations (Bureau of National Affairs, 1986; Catalyst, 1986; Kamerman, Kahn, and Kingston, 1983). This suggests that fathers may, indeed, take leaves to the extent that they are available and do not cause financial hardship.

A closer look at individual cases provides additional evidence that fathers typically took leaves that corresponded to the options they had available. The father who took 2 weeks off was given that amount of fully paid paternity leave. And the father who took 3 weeks had that amount of fully paid vacation available, though taking the leave meant that he had no more vacation available for the next year. Many fathers who took paid vacation or personal leave for a week or less also rearranged their work schedules for a further time, and they often planned to take vacation later in the year or to continue to rearrange their work schedules indefinitely. Only 18 percent (N = 5) of the fathers who took leave were unpaid during that time, presumably because they had no other paid options. In fact, one father stated that he took personal leave because he had no vacation left. Furthermore, except for one self-employed father, those who rearranged their work schedules were not allowed paternity leave. Finally, at least some of the 10 percent (N = 4) of the fathers who neither took time off nor rearranged their schedules spent considerable amounts of time with their babies (one was self-employed at home; another babysat while the mother worked a night shift); we cannot tell from the data what the others did. However, the fact that one of these fathers said he would like to have been on paternity leave suggests that circumstances prevented him from doing so. And the fact that all of these fathers said that finances and practical considerations were important or very important in their paternity leave decisions suggests that fathers felt that they could only take or dream about short leaves. The provision of paid leaves (and longer leaves) might change the picture dramatically.

Pleck (1988) suggests that the situation may be complex, with fa-

thers' use of paternity leaves also affected by their desire to participate in child care and the family, among other things. Unfortunately, our data do not include assessments of these desires, and so
we cannot address this question adequately. A month after the birth
(Time 2), however, we did ask the fathers whether they would prefer to spend more or less time than they usually did, or the same
time, on four specific child care tasks. There were no significant differences between the fathers who took longer or shorter (or no) paternity leaves in their preferences regarding time spent feeding, diapering, or playing with their babies. Almost all the fathers said they
would prefer to spend the same amount of time or more feeding the
baby (few of the fathers were able to share in this task, since most of
the mothers were breastfeeding) and playing with the baby (the most
desirable child care task); changing diapers, on the other hand, was
the least desirable task. There were significant differences, however,
on the fathers' preferences regarding time spent quieting their
babies, with fathers who had taken longer leaves significantly more
likely than fathers who had taken shorter or no leaves to prefer to
spend the same or more time on this task ($r = .34$; $p = .04$). Although this is scant evidence, it does suggest the possibility that
fathers who want to participate more in child care take longer paternity leaves. Conversely, because these are cross-sectional and correlational data, they might suggest that fathers who take longer leaves
immediately after the births of their babies continue to want to participate more in child care after they return to work. The effect of
paternity leaves on fathers' participation in the family and the long-
term effect on the marital relationship are crucial areas of study.

Fathers' Contributions to Child Care and Household Tasks

At Time 2, a month after the babies' births, the fathers reported that
they spent an average of 2.80 hours per day quieting (1.10 hours) and
feeding (0.98 hour) their babies and changing diapers (0.72 hour);
they spent an average of 1.90 hours per day playing with their
babies. We suspect that the fathers' estimates are a bit inflated. The
self-report measures we used cannot be verified, and more sophisticated studies that have asked fathers to keep actual time diaries of
their activities show them spending about one-quarter of an hour
per day caring for their children (Pleck, 1983). However, those
studies were not conducted shortly after the babies' births, a time
when fathers are most likely to spend time at home with their wives
and babies. When we looked at the time the fathers in our survey
spent on child care a year after their babies' births, we found that it

had decreased significantly: the fathers reported that they then spent an average of 1.40 hours per day on the tasks of quieting (0.60 hours; ([38] = 3.69, p = .001) and feeding (0.52 hours; ([38] = 2.89, p = .006) their babies, and changing diapers (0.31 hours; ([38] = 2.95, p = .005). The time they spent playing with their babies, however, did not change significantly in that year (1.60 hours; ([38] = .78; p = .44). These subjective estimates of time still may be a bit inflated compared with the more objective measures used in some other studies. But the estimates also include the time fathers spent in primary caretaking while their wives worked, making the estimates higher than they would be otherwise.

When we asked the women who was doing the housework during the first month after the births of their babies (Time 2), 59 percent said they did all (5 percent) or most of it (54 percent); 36 percent said it was divided equally between them and their husbands; and 5 percent said their husbands did most of it. None of the women said her husband did all of the housework. There were no significant differences a year later (Time 3). Thus, although the fathers spent significantly more time on child care during the first month after the births, they did not spend additional time on housework beyond their typical arrangements.

The fathers' attitudes toward maternity leave had significant effects on the degree to which they shared in child care during the first month after their babies' births (Time 2). Their attitudes toward their own paternity leaves and their actual use of leaves, however, had no effects. Fathers who were more supportive of women's right to paid maternity leaves spent significantly more time playing with their babies (r = .33; p = .04) and changing diapers (r = .34; p = .04) than did fathers who were less supportive of maternity leaves. Since changing diapers was the least preferred child care task, it is a good indicator of the extent to which the fathers were committed to sharing child care. Thus, the fact that the fathers who were more supportive of maternity leave (at Time 2) continued over the next year to spend significantly more time changing diapers (at Time 3) is especially noteworthy (r = .32; p < .05). Fathers' attitudes toward parental leave (both maternity and paternity) and their actual use of leaves, however, had no effect on their contributions to household tasks either immediately after their babies' births or a year later.

The constraints of the situation might also be expected to have important effects on fathers' contributions to child care and household tasks. At Time 2, we found that the fathers whose wives had already returned to work (either full or part time) contributed significantly more time to child care than the fathers whose wives remained at home ($M = 4.65$ hours and $M = 2.39$ hours, respectively; [37] = 2.29; p < .03). This finding contradicts other research on men's contributions to work in the home, which typically shows that men with working wives contribute no more than men married to full-time homemakers (e.g., Pleck, 1983). However, child care is only a part of the total work in the home. When we considered the degree to which fathers whose wives were working shared in household tasks at Time 2 compared with fathers whose wives remained at home, we found no differences. Furthermore, most of the research on fathers' contributions to the household has been done in families with older children, not newborns. When we considered the amount of time fathers spent on child care at Time 3, when their children were a year old, the differences between those with working wives and those whose wives remained at home disappeared ($M = 1.50$ hours and $M = 1.19$ hours, respectively; [37] = 0.82; p = .42).

Together, these results paint a picture of rather traditional sex-role differentiation, with mothers still primarily responsible for the home and family. Although the fathers helped to some extent with child care for a short period after their babies' births, especially if they were supportive of maternity leaves and/or their wives returned to work early, their contributions generally decreased significantly over the next year. Only the fathers who most strongly supported paid maternity leaves continued to do significantly more diapering than did the fathers who were less supportive of maternity leave. Furthermore, a month after the births many fathers wished they could spend even less time on child care: 39 percent wished to spend less time quieting their babies, and 41 percent wished to spend less time changing diapers. These feelings persisted throughout the year (no significant differences at Time 3). In fact, at both Time 2 and Time 3 the majority of fathers wanted to spend more time only on the most preferred tasks of feeding and playing. Finally, the fathers provided no extra help with household tasks either shortly after births or over the next year.

It is possible, of course, that mothers also wished to spend less time quieting and diapering, and that this is a common parental reaction to less pleasant child care tasks. Unfortunately, we do not have the data to answer this question. One indication, however, of whether the fathers' contributions to child care and household tasks were acceptable to their partners was the frequency with which couples disagreed on who should do these tasks. When we asked the

fathers at Time 2 how much disagreement there was between themselves and their partners, 56 percent said they occasionally or frequently disagreed about household tasks, and 31 percent said they
occasionally disagreed about child care tasks (none frequently disagreed). There were no significant differences at Time 3. Thus, although we do not know whether the disagreement was over the
amount of time spent on these tasks or other aspects of task sharing
(e.g., when the tasks were done), there was clearly more dissension
between fathers and mothers over household tasks, into which the
fathers had put no extra effort, than over child care tasks, into
which the fathers had put effort for at least a short time after the
birth.

The Father–Mother Relationship

Father's attitudes toward paternity and maternity leave, their actual
use of leave, and their contributions to child care and household
tasks had important effects on the family system over time. Here, we
focus on the effects on the father–mother relationship, looking specifically at the couples' perceptions of the affirmation, intimacy, and
equity in their relationships. Affirmation was assessed by asking the
fathers and mothers how strongly they agreed or disagreed with the
following statements: "My (partner) seems to bring out the best in
me"; "My (partner) appreciates me just as I am"; "My marriage (relationship) doesn't give me enough opportunity to become the sort
of person I'd like to be" (reverse coded). Marital intimacy was assessed with the following statements: "My (partner) is someone I can
really talk with about things that are important to me"; "My (partner) is affectionate toward me"; "My (partner) is a good sexual partner." Equity was assessed with the following statements: "My (partner) insists on having her/his own way"; "My (partner) usually
expects more from me than she/he is willing to give"; "Generally, I
give in more to my (partner's) wishes than she/he gives in to mine"
(all reverse coded).

One month after their babies' births, the fathers agreed very
strongly that their relationships were affirming, intimate, and equitable. Over half (56 percent) said they agreed very strongly with the
statements of affirmation, and only 5 percent disagreed. Similarly,
59 percent agreed very strongly with the statements of intimacy, and
only 8 percent disagreed. They felt a little less strongly about the
degree of equity in their relationships, however, with 39 percent
agreeing very strongly that their relationship was equitable, and only

10 percent saying it was not. The mothers felt similarly about the intimacy and equity in their relationships, though they felt significantly less strongly than their partners about the degree of affirmation ([38] = 2.03; p = .05).

Over the course of the first year after the babies' births, significant differences developed between fathers' and mothers' feelings about their relationships. Between Time 2 and Time 3, there were no significant changes in the way the fathers felt about the quality of their relationships. By the end of that first year, however, their partners felt significantly less affirmation, intimacy, and especially equity than they had shortly after the births. Thus, by the time the babies were a year old, the mothers felt significantly less affirmation and equity than the fathers felt. And although there were no significant differences between the fathers' and the mothers' feelings of intimacy at either Time 2 or Time 3, the mothers' feelings of intimacy dropped from being higher than the fathers' to being lower.

It is possible that the greater stability in the fathers' feelings about their relationships reflects traditional sex roles and the corresponding fact that the changes resulting from parenthood are less salient to fathers than to mothers. And, in fact, our results show that the fathers' parental leave attitudes, use of leave, and contributions to child care and household tasks had fewer effects on their own feelings about their relationships than on their partners' feelings.

The fathers' attitudes toward paternity and maternity leaves as well as their actual use of leave had little effect on their feelings of marital affirmation, intimacy, and equity at either Time 2 or Time 3. However, although the amount of time they spent on child care had no significant effect on their feelings about their relationships shortly after the birth, that amount had important effects on those feelings during the next year. By the end of the first year, the fathers who spent more time playing with their babies felt significantly more intimacy than did the fathers who spent less time (r = .38; p = .02). But the fathers who spent lots of time feeding their babies felt significantly less marital equity than did the fathers who spent less time (r = 47; p < .01). The amount of time the fathers spent on household tasks had no effect on their feelings about their relationships at either Time 2 or Time 3. They did, however, feel significantly less affirmation and intimacy at Time 3 if they and their partners disagreed very often on who should do the household tasks (r = .39, r = .43, respectively, p < .01 for both coefficients).

These parental leave and family role variables had a much stronger effect on the mothers' feelings about their relationships. The mothers whose partners were more supportive of their own rights to paternity leaves felt significantly more marital affirmation, intimacy, and equity shortly after their babies' birth ($r = .44$, $r = .46$, $r = .42$, respectively; $p < .01$ for all coefficients), as well as over the next year ($r = .52$, $r = .59$, $r = .34$, respectively; $p < .05$ for all coefficients). Similarly, when the fathers took longer paternity leaves, their partners felt significantly more intimacy and equity over time ($r = .32$, $r = .33$, respectively; $p < .05$ for both coefficients at Time 2; and $r = .34$, $r = .43$, respectively; $p < .04$ for both coefficients at Time 3). And the amount of time the fathers spent on child care and household tasks had a significant effect on their partners' feelings about their relationships, but only at Time 3. Thus, by the time their babies were a year old, the mothers whose husbands spent more time playing with their babies and shared more equally in household tasks felt significantly more affirmation ($r = .37$, $r = .34$, respectively, $p = .03$ for both coefficients), intimacy ($r = .37$, $r = .32$, respectively, $p < .05$ for both coefficients), and equity ($r = .37$, $r = .41$, respectively; $p < .03$ for both coefficients) in their relationships.

Earlier, we saw that the fathers whose partners returned to work within the first month after the baby's birth spent significantly more time on child care during that month than did the fathers whose partners remained at home. However, by the time their babies were a year old, the fathers whose partners were employed were no more likely than those whose partners remained at home to spend time on child care. We might expect that this would affect the employed mothers' sense of equity. And, indeed, the employed mothers felt no less equity at Time 2, when their partners were putting in extra effort on child care, but they felt significantly less marital equity at Time 3, when they were receiving no more help with child care than were the mothers who remained at home.

Overall, these results suggest that relationships are often better and quite special for a short period of time right after a baby's birth. While fathers' feelings about their relationships are quite positive and stable, their partners' feelings are strongly affected by the fathers' commitment to sharing family responsibilities. Thus, because fathers are more likely to spend time sharing in child care shortly after baby's birth, mothers are more likely to feel that their relationships are affirming, intimate, and equitable. And fathers who are supportive of parental leaves and/or whose partners return to work early are especially committed to sharing child care, so that their partners feel even better about the relationship. Furthermore, although fathers' actual use of paternity leave has little to do with the amount of time they spend on family tasks, taking a longer leave is indicative of their family commitment, with additional positive effects on their partners' feelings.

Over the course of the first year after the birth, however, the honeymoon disappears. The fathers spend significantly less time and energy sharing in the responsibilities of child care. And if the fathers spend much time feeding their babies, their sense of equity decreases significantly. Furthermore, although the degree to which fathers share in household tasks has little effect on either partner's feelings about the relationship shortly after the baby's birth, mothers feel significantly less affirmation, intimacy, and equity when their partners do not share much in household tasks by the end of the first year. Fortunately, however, fathers continue to play with their babies, and this increases both their and their partners' positive feelings about the relationship. On the whole, then, fathers (but not mothers) maintain their earlier rather positive feelings about the relationship. And the mothers who are employed outside the home are particularly likely to feel that their relationships are increasingly inequitable. The fact that their partners cut back on child care and do no extra housework means that the mothers must balance increasing responsibility for the family tasks with the demands of outside employment.

Conclusion

Our research emphasizes the importance of fathers in parental leave, child care, and the well-being of families over time. Although it may seem puzzling that fathers are not more supportive (although for the most part they are supportive) of policies guaranteeing job rights for both mothers and fathers of new babies, the results may indicate that gender roles have not changed much in regard to child care. The primary responsibility is still seen to be the mothers', so that fathers do not take—or may not even want—paternity leaves that extend beyond a week or two. Even the fathers who rearrange their schedules do so only for an additional few weeks. This means, of course, that fathers' time commitments to child care and the family decrease significantly after the first month or two. Our research has shown that this damages the couple's relationship over time. Viewing child care as the mothers' responsibility ignores women's commitments to their own work or career and the need to change family roles in order to achieve equality between partners in terms of total work (job plus family) hours. And it ignores women's important function as wage earners, which makes income replacement essential during leave.

On the other hand, it may be that fathers' lack of interest in longer paternity leaves is more a result of economic factors and employers' formal and informal policies. If leaves are unpaid, fathers may take very short leaves or no leave simply because they cannot afford to take more. Or fathers may feel subtle pressure or disapproval from their employers if they want to take a leave, especially a longer one. Yet our research makes it clear that when fathers are supportive of parental leaves, and when they take longer leaves and participate more in child care and family tasks *beyond* the period right after the baby's birth, their partners especially feel more affirmation, intimacy, and equity in the relationship. This is undoubtedly important to the health and well-being of the larger family system, including the infant, over time. The provision of paid and longer paternity and maternity leaves, as well as family leave, may change the picture dramatically, making it possible for parents to arrange their child care and other family responsibilities in ways that fit their specific needs and desires.

REFERENCES

Bureau of National Affairs (1986). *Work and Family: A Changing Dynamic.* Washington, D.C.: BNA.

Catalyst (1986). *Report on a National Study of Parental Leaves.* New York: Catalyst.

Hwang, C. P. (1987). "The Changing Role of Swedish Fathers." In M. E. Lamb, ed., *The Father's Role: Cross Cultural Perspectives.* Hillsdale, N.J.: Erlbaum.

Kamerman, Sheila B., Alfred J. Kahn, and Paul W. Kingston (1983). *Maternity Policies and Working Women.* New York: Columbia University Press.

Lamb, Michael E., and J. A. Levine (1983). "The Swedish Parental Insurance Policy: An Experiment in Social Engineering." In M. E. Lamb and Abraham Sagi, eds., *Fatherhood and Family Policy.* Hillsdale, N.J.: Erlbaum.

Pearlin, Leonard I., and J. S. Johnson (1977). "Marital Status, Life-Strains, and Depression." *American Sociological Review* 42: 704–15.

Pleck, Joseph H. (1983). "Husbands' Paid Work and Family Roles: Current Research Issues." In H. Lopata and J. H. Pleck, eds., *Research in the Interweave of Social Roles*, vol. 3: *Families and Jobs.* Greenwich, Conn.: JAI Press.

—— (1986). "Employment and Fatherhood: Issues and Innovative Policies." In M. E. Lamb, ed., *The Father's Role: Applied Perspectives.* New York: John Wiley.

—— (1988). "Fathers and Infant Care Leave." In Edward F. Zigler and Meryl Frank, eds., *The Parental Leave Crisis: Toward a National Policy.* New Haven: Yale University Press.

17 Factors Influencing Recovery from Childbirth

Lorraine Tulman and Jacqueline Fawcett

A basic question in any discussion of parental leave and child care is how long a leave is necessary or desirable. This question cannot be answered without consideration of maternal recovery from childbirth, how recovery is defined and measured, and the nature of the factors affecting recovery.

The Pregnancy Discrimination Act of 1978 specifies that childbirth is to be regarded as a temporary disability and therefore treated like other disabilities with regard to insurance and related matters. This law did not, however, identify a specific period of disability for childbirth. Medical tradition has set the time of recovery from childbirth at 6 weeks, based on the healing of the reproductive organs rather than on a broader, more health-oriented definition of recovery that encompasses the resumption of usual activities and the assumption of the new responsibilities entailed by the birth. Inasmuch as discussions of parental leave have not taken this broader definition into account, our current work has been directed toward determining just how long recovery from childbirth requires. More specifically, our work focuses on two questions. How long does it take a woman to resume her usual activities and assume care of the newborn? What factors are related to recovery?

We have begun to answer these questions by visiting 100 women in their own homes at 3 weeks, 6 weeks, 3 months, and 6 months after delivery. This study reports the responses of the 50 women for whom we currently have complete data. Our recommendations for length of parental leave are based on the 50 women's responses to questionnaires and an interview guide. One questionnaire measured the extent to which usual self-care, household, social and community, and occupational activities had been resumed and infant care responsibilities assumed at the time of the home visit (Fawcett, Tulman, and Myers, 1988). Another questionnaire measured psychological and social adjustment following delivery (Lederman, Weingar-

294

ten, and Lederman, 1981). A third questionnaire measured the woman's perception of her infant's temperament (Bates, Freeland, and Lounsbury, 1979). Demographic and obstetrical data were collected by means of a semistructured interview schedule.

The women resided in metropolitan and suburban areas of southern New Jersey and eastern Pennsylvania. They ranged in age from 22 to 38 years and were mostly well educated and middle-class. Almost half of the women were college graduates, and almost two-thirds reported annual household incomes of over $40,000. The vast majority were white. Ten percent of the women classified themselves as homemakers, and 50 percent were in professional or managerial occupations. All the women delivered healthy, full-term babies. None of the women had any major prenatal complications or chronic medical problems; 72 percent had vaginal deliveries. For 68 percent, the baby was their first child; for 26 percent, their second; and for the remaining 6 percent, their third.

Recovery from Childbirth

Obstetrical textbooks indicate that the physical recovery of reproductive organs after childbirth takes about 6 weeks and imply that the woman is fully recovered from childbirth at that time. This period corresponds to the interval required for the uterus to return to its approximate pre-pregnant size (Pritchard, MacDonald, and Gant, 1985). However, research findings have suggested that recovery from childbirth involves more than the healing of the reporductive organs. Marcia Gruis (1977) found that 36 (90 percent) of the 40 vaginally delivered women she studied at 4 weeks after delivery were still concerned about their ability to coordinate the demands of housework, family, and infant care. The majority reported concerns about fatigue, tension, changes in their figures, and lack of time for personal activities. Similar findings were reported by Harrison and Hicks (1983) and Fawcett and York (1986). Furthermore, Virginia Larsen (1966) found that the 130 women she studied 3 months after delivery reported physical discomforts, fatigue, depression, nervousness, difficulty in adjusting to the needs of the baby and other children, difficulty with housework and routines, and worry about the ability to cope with the family's needs.

We ourselves found (Tulman and Fawcett, 1988) that only 51 percent of the 70 women in a retrospective survey reported that they had regained their usual level of energy by the end of the traditional 6-week period after delivery. By 6 months after delivery, 87 percent of the women reported that they had regained their usual level of energy. The women frequently commented that although they resumed certain activities shortly after delivery, they did not regain their energy until quite a while later. These findings suggest that recovery is not complete 6 weeks after delivery, but it *is* complete for a large percentage of women at 6 months.

Finally, clinical observations and research findings suggest that cesarean birth reguires a longer period of recovery than vaginal birth. Cesarean-delivered women have reported delayed assumption of infant care responsibilities and have stated that for the first 2 months after delivery, much of their energy went into coping with recovery from the surgery in addition to caring for a new infant around the clock. Many of these women seemed not to have fully recovered 2 months after delivery, and some seemed to have limited ability to perform usual activities beyond that time (Lipson, 1981; Lipson and Tilden, 1980; Tilden and Lipson, 1981; Tulman, 1986; Tulman and Fawcett, 1988).

Our current study findings revealed that recovery from childbirth progressed steadily during the first 6 months after delivery, as measured by the resumption of usual self-care, household, social and community, and occupational activities, as well as assumption of infant care responsibilities. Further data analysis indicates that infant care was fully assumed more rapidly than either household or social and community activities were resumed, and that household activities were fully resumed more rapidly than social and community activities. However, at the traditional 6-week point, just 32 percent of the women had fully resumed usual household activities, and only 30 percent had fully resumed usual social and community activities. Moreover, 22 percent had not fully assumed infant care 6 weeks after delivery. In addition, 6 months after delivery, 14 percent still had not fully resumed usual household activities, and 26 percent had not fully resumed usual social and community activities. Contrary to our expectations, we found no differences in the resumption of household, social and community activities, and self-care activities between cesarean- and vaginally delivered women at any of the time periods.

We also found that when women over 30 were compared with those under 30 at 6 weeks after delivery, the younger women had a higher level of recovery in all areas that we measured. This difference had disappeared by 3 months after the birth.

In our present sample, physical energy was strongly correlated with recovery at 3 and 6 weeks after delivery. Interestingly, this correlation was not present at 3 months and 6 months after delivery. At 3 weeks, only 27 percent of the women reported having regained their usual levels of energy; at 6 weeks, only 57 percent; at 3 months, 71 percent; and by 6 months, 90 percent. Thus, by the end of the traditional 6-week recuperative period, 43 percent of the women had still not reached their usual energy levels. These results are consistent with our previous work (Tulman and Fawcett, 1988). Women again frequently mentioned that they had fully resumed many activities, even though they were still fatigued, because they had no choice.

Interpersonal factors—and social support in particular—are thought to have an impact on women's adjustment and recovery after childbirth (Crnic et al., 1984; Cutrona, 1984; Kahn, 1980; Norbeck and Tilden, 1983; Turner and Noh, 1983). We found that support from friends and family members was positively related to the women's assumption of infant care responsibilities at 6 weeks and 3 months after delivery. In addition, the quality of the marital relationship is thought to influence the transition to parenthood. Findings on the effect of the marital relationship on maternal role performance have been mixed, however, and may reflect differences in samples and changes over time (Dyer, 1963; Hobbs, 1965; Hobbs and Cole, 1976; LeMasters, 1957; Russell, 1974). We found that the quality of the woman's relationship with her husband was positively related to her assumption of infant care responsibilities at 3 and 6 weeks and resumption of household activities at 6 weeks, as well as to all areas of recovery 3 months after delivery.

We also found that factors related to assuming the role of mother were associated with recovery. More specifically, satisfaction with motherhood and infant care was positively related to all areas of recovery 3 weeks and 6 months after delivery, but not at the intervening times. However, women's confidence in their ability to cope with the tasks of motherhood was positively related to the level of resumption of social and community activities at 3 months.

The infant's temperament also may affect recovery from childbirth. A difficult infant—one who is fussy, unpredictable in schedule, unadaptable to changes in surroundings, and unresponsive to the mother's attention and efforts at play—can undoubtedly make life, and hence recovery, more difficult for the new mother. We found that infant temperament, as measured by his or her unpredictability, fussiness, unadaptability, and dullness, was related to a woman's recovery, with a higher degree of difficulty being associated with a lower level of maternal performance of usual activities. Infant unpredictability was associated with all areas of recovery at 3 weeks, 6 weeks, and 6 months, and with resumption of social and community activities at 3 months. Fussiness was associated with resumption of social and community activities at 6 weeks and 3 months and with all areas of recovery at 6 months. Unadaptability was associated with resumption of occupational activities at 3 months, and dullness was associated with resumption of social and community activities at 6 weeks and occupational activities at 3 months.

Another infant characteristic, nighttime sleeping patterns, can be hypothesized to affect a woman's recovery from childbirth. Surely an infant who awakens several times during the night, and perhaps stays awake for long stretches, can tax recovery. In our sample, 5 percent of the infants were sleeping through the night by 3 weeks after delivery; 40 percent, by 6 weeks; 82 percent, by 3 months; and 86 percent, by 6 months. Many women reported that their infants had begun sleeping through the night but then reverted to awakening during the night. Most infants awoke briefly for a feeding and then went back to sleep. Quite surprisingly and despite what common sense would indicate, whether or not the infant slept through the night did not affect either the resumption of usual activities or the level of energy as reported by the women in our sample. These counter-intuitive results clearly merit replication.

Recovery and Work

Most of the women (88 percent) in our sample were employed during their pregnancies, almost all until the week of delivery. Of the employed women, 73 percent were employed full time and 27 percent part time. Of the women who were employed during pregnancy, 80 percent were planning to return to work after delivery. Of these women, only 67 percent were granted parental leave from their jobs, 15 percent were not granted leave, 15 percent were self-employed, and 3 percent had resigned from their jobs during or at the end of the pregnancy.

The average length of parental leave for those who had it was 12.1 weeks, with a range of 6 to 52 weeks. Almost half (45 percent) of the leavetakers had salary support from their employer during the leave, through use of accrued sick leave and vacation time and/or through actual paid parental leave. (It must be kept in mind that those who used accrued sick leave and vacation time had none left in their "banks" for time off during the first year back at work, either for their own illness or that of their infant or other family members.)

An additional 24 percent of the women who had leave were paid a percentage of their salaries through New Jersey's disability compensation program. New Jersey's Temporary Disability Benefits Law provides most employees in that state with partial wage compensation for up to 26 weeks for medical disability, including disability resulting from childbirth (N.J.S.A. 43:21–25 to 21–50). Not all of the women in our study who were employed in New Jersey received state disability, however, since towns may elect not to cover their municipal workers under the state program. Women in our sample who worked in Pennsylvania did not receive disability, because that state does not provide temporary disability insurance.

Of the women who were planning to return to their former jobs after delivery, 77 percent stated that they would get the same position back; another 12 percent stated that they would get a comparable position. How "comparable" the new position would be was not known in advance by most of the women. In several cases, the position eventually involved less desirable hours.

Most (71 percent) of the women who planned to return to work reported that they had the option of easing their return by either part-time hours or flextime. This seeming flexibility on the part of the employers may be a function of the very low (3 percent) unemployment rate that the region was experiencing at the time we collected our data. Most businesses were short of well-trained, experienced personnel and were making extensive efforts to accommodate the needs of the workers they had.

Of the 35 women who reported that they planned to return to work within 6 months after delivery, 10 (28 percent) had done so by 6 weeks, 26 (74 percent) by 3 months, and 31 (89 percent) by 6 months after delivery—16 on a part-time basis and 15 full time. Whether a woman had returned to work was not related to her level of recovery from childbirth at the time of return. Most women indicated that they returned when they did either because their leave was over or because their family needed the money to maintain its current standard of living.

There were no overall differences in recovery between the group of women who returned to work full time and the group who returned part time. However, a greater percentage of women who worked part time reported full resumption of household and social and community activities at both 3 and 6 months after delivery and full assumption of infant care responsibilities at 3 months after delivery.

The number of children a woman had was found to be related to level of performance of occupational activities at 3 and 6 months after delivery. More specifically, women who had two or more children had a higher level of performance in occupational activities than women who had just had their first child. It may be that prior experience with returning to work after delivery is an advantage.

At 3 weeks after delivery, women who had cesarean deliveries were less likely to report that they were planning to return to work than women who had vaginal deliveries. However, there were no differences between the cesarean- and vaginally- delivered women in the timing of their actual return to work. Women who had delivered vaginally did, however, report a higher level of performance in occupational activities at 6 months after delivery.

Conclusions

Our preliminary findings indicate that unlike physiological recovery from childbirth, which is usually complete by 6 weeks after delivery, recovery as measured by performance of usual activities is not complete until at least 6 months after delivery for many women. As we have noted, the vast majority of women have not recovered by the traditional 6-week period, and some have not recovered even by the end of 6 months. Factors that may assist or impede recovery in various spheres of life include type of delivery, number of children, satisfaction with motherhood and infant care, confidence in ability to cope with the tasks of motherhood, quality of the relationship with the husband, support from friends and family members, maternal age, and level of physical energy, as well as infant temperament.

Our findings extend the available knowledge of factors associated with recovery from childbirth. The results of our study may help women to have more realistic expectations of themselves and sensitize others, especially employers, to the complexity of recovery from childbirth.

Although complete recovery may take up to 6 months, 31 of the 50 women in our study (62 percent) had returned to work by that time. Most of the women who returned to work stated that they had done so when they had either because their leave time was over or because of financial need. We did not find a relationship between the time that women returned to work and their level of recovery, suggesting that some women return to work before they are fully recovered from childbirth. The physical and psychological costs of doing so require systematic study. Our data also showed that those women who return to work part time rather than full time tend to have better recovery. Therefore, any policy on parental leave should include the option of returning to work on a part-time basis.

The large percentage (62 percent) of women in our study who returned to work within 6 months of delivery contrasts with the latest available U.S. Department of Labor (1988) figure (50.8 percent of mothers with children less than one year of age in the workforce). It is, of course, difficult to determine whether our figure is an aberration based on our particular sample or whether it is indicative of the rapid shift occurring nationwide as a result of which women return sooner and in greater percentages to the workforce after childbirth, a trend that has been accelerating over the past 15 years (Hayghe, 1986; Kamerman, Kahn, and Kingston, 1983). We believe the latter may be the case. With this large a percentage of women returning to the workforce after childbirth, the issue of parental leave becomes even more pressing because it affects not a small fringe minority of our citizenry but the vast majority of women *and* men as they move through their childbearing years.

Proposals being discussed at the federal and state levels vary in the length of parental leave involved. Ultimately, the length of leave will be based on political compromise as well as research data. Our data clearly support the recommendation that the minimum leave should last 6 months and perhaps longer in certain cases. It should be a paid leave, and the option of returning to work on a part-time basis should be included. We would be remiss, however, if we did not temper our recommendations with the provisos that some women are ready to return to work prior to 6 months after delivery and that, in the absence of fully paid leave, some women *must* return quite soon after childbirth for financial reasons. Thus, parental leave policies must not establish a standard that would *prohibit* a woman from resuming her place in the workforce before the end of the allotted leave time. Legislation on parental leave must be framed with a view toward providing assistance to women and their families during childbearing without creating workplace discrimination and impediments to career advancement.

REFERENCES

Bates, John E., Claire A. Freeland, and Mary L. Lounsbury (1979). "Measurement of Infant Difficultness." *Child Development* 50: 794–803.
Crnic, Keith A., Mark T. Greenberg, Nancy M. Robinson, and Arlene S.

Ragozin (1984). "Maternal Stress and Social Support: Effects on the Mother–Infant Relationship from Birth to Eighteen Months." *American Journal of Orthopsychiatry* 54: 224–35.

Cutrona, Carolyn E. (1984). "Social Support and Stress in the Transition to Parenthood." *Journal of Abnormal Psychology* 93: 378–90.

Dyer, Everett D. (1963). "Parenthood as Crisis: A Re-Study." *Marriage and Family Living* 25: 196–201.

Fawcett, Jacqueline, Lorraine Tulman, and Sheila Myers (1988). "Development of the Inventory of Functional Status after Childbirth." *Journal of Nurse–Midwifery* 33: 252–60.

Fawcett, Jacqueline, and Ruth York (1986). "Spouses' Physical and Psychological Symptoms During Pregnancy and the Postpartum." *Nursing Research* 35: 144–48.

Gruis, Marcia (1977). "Beyond Maternity: Postpartum Concerns of Mothers." *American Journal of Maternal-Child Nursing* 2: 182–88.

Harrison, Margaret J., and Sue A. Hicks (1983). "Postpartum Concerns of Mothers and Their Sources of Help." *Canadian Journal of Public Health* 74: 325–28.

Hayghe, Howard (1986). "Rise in Mothers' Labor Force Activity Includes Those with Infants." *Monthly Labor Review* 109 (2): 43–45.

Hobbs, Daniel F. (1965). "Parenthood as Crisis: A Third Study." *Journal of Marriage and the Family* 27: 367–78.

Hobbs, Daniel F., and Sue P. Cole (1976). "Transition to Parenthood: A Decade of Replications." *Journal of Marriage and the Family* 38: 723–31.

Kahn, Steven (1980). "Social Support in the Transition to Parenthood." *Journal of Community Psychology* 8: 332–42.

Kamerman, Sheila B., Alfred J. Kahn, and Paul W. Kingston (1983). *Maternity Policies and Working Women.* New York: Columbia University Press.

Larsen, Virginia L. (1966). "Stresses of the Childbearing Year." *American Journal of Public Health* 56: 32–36.

Lederman, Regina P., Carol G. Weingarten, and Edward Lederman (1981). "Postpartum Self-Evaluation Questionnaire: Measure of Maternal Adaptation." In Regina P. Lederman, Beverly S. Raff, and Patricia Carool, eds., *Parinatal Parental Behavior: Nursing Research and Implications.* Birth Defects: Original Article Series, vol. 17, no. 6. New York: Alan R. Liss.

LeMasters, Ersel E. (1957). "Parenthood as Crisis." *Marriage and Family Living* 19: 352–55.

Lipson, Juliene G. (1981). "Cesarean Support Groups: Mutual Help and Education." *Women and Health* 6 (3/4): 27–39.

Lipson, Juliene G., and Virginia P. Tilden (1980). "Psychological Integration of the Cesarean Birth Experience." *American Journal of Orthopsychiatry* 50: 598–609.

Norbeck, Jane S., and Virginia P. Tilden (1983). "Life Stress, Social Support, and Emotional Disequilibrium in Complications of Pregnancy: A

Prospective, Multivariate Study." *Journal of Health and Social Behavior* 24: 30–46.

Pritchard, Jack A., Paul C. MacDonald, and Norman F. Gant (1985). *Williams' Obstetrics* (17th ed.). Norwalk, Conn.: Appleton–Century–Crofts.

Russell, Candyc S. (1974). "Transition to Parenthood: Problems and Gratifications." *Journal of Marriage and the Family* 36: 294–302.

Tilden, Virginia P., and Juliene G. Lipson (1981). "Cesarean Childbirth: Variables Affecting Psychological Impact." *Western Journal of Nursing Research* 3: 127–41.

Tulman, Lorraine (1986). "Initial Handling of Newborn Infants by Cesarean– and Vaginally Delivered Mothers." *Nursing Research* 35: 296–300.

Tulman, Lorraine, and Jacqueline Fawcett (1988). "Return of Functional Ability After Childbirth." *Nursing Research* 37: 77–81.

Turner, R. Jay, and Samuel Noh (1983). "Class and Psychological Vulnerability Among Women: The Significance of Social Support and Personal Control." *Journal of Health and Social Behavior* 24: 2–15.

U.S. Department of Labor (1988). *Labor Force Participation Unchanged Among Mothers with Young Children.* USDL Publication no. 88–431. Washington, D.C.: Department of Labor.

PART VII

Infants and Infant Care

18 | Timing the Return to the Workplace: Effects on the Mother–Infant Relationship

Marsha Weinraub and Elizabeth Jaeger

When should mothers return to the workplace? In this chapter we review different recommendations and present data from a preliminary study designed to investigate the effects of the timing of the maternal return to the workplace on the developing mother–child relationship. Our findings have implications for individual families and for social policy decisions.

A Review of the Recommendations

Strong arguments exist for the importance of mothers' staying home with their newborn infants for at least the first 4 to 6 months of the infant's life. Lynne Sanford Koester presents these arguments in Chapter 19 in this volume. A mother needs time to regain her endurance, tolerance, patience, and enthusiasm so that she can respond sensitively to the developmental and idiosyncratic needs of her child. Moreover, the mother and child need sufficient time together to learn about each other and develop a mutually responsive "rhythm." T. Berry Brazelton (1985) has specifically advocated that mothers spend the first 4 months at home and then return to employment during the fifth month. Similarly, Edward Zigler and Susan Muenchow (1983) have argued for a 6-month child care leave following childbirth. In another paper, Thomas J. Gamble and Edward Zigler (1986) argue that parental leave should be provided "during the first months of life."

Some of these recommendations imply that 4 to 6 months is the *minimal* amount of time for a mother to be at home with her child; it is even better if a mother can delay her return to employment longer. On the basis of their data, Barglow, Vaughn, and Molitor

307

987), and Belsky and Rovine (1988), argue that returning to employment for more than 20 hours per week at any time during the infant's first year places both the infant's social and emotional development and the mother–infant relationship at risk. From a theoretical point of view, John Bowlby (1973) argues that mothers and infants should continue in an exclusive one-to-one relationship until the child is approximately three years of age.

However, from a developmental perspective, arguments can be made that return to employment within the first 6 to 8 months after childbirth is *more desirable* for the health and security of the mother–child relationship than a return later in the first year or at any time during the second year of the child's life (Ainsworth, 1973; Hoffman, 1984). Although an early return is sometimes difficult for the mother, who must separate from her new baby, it is quite easy for the very young infant, who can readily form a new and additional attachment to the nonparental caregiver. Later return to the workplace may be easier for the mother, who is often ready and sometimes eager to leave the home, but more difficult for the infant, who by 8 months is already focused on the mother as attachment object. Infants whose mothers have returned to the workplace before they are 8 months of age will have developed a system of interacting with their mothers within the context of daily and predictable separations; continued daily separations for these children will not be unusual and may not engender unusual distress. In contrast, a mother's return to the workplace after 8 months may violate the infant's expectations concerning her behavior, and the infant may be distressed and angry about it. In addition, after the onset of clearly defined stranger wariness and with the beginnings of separation distress—somewhere around 8 months—infants may have more difficulty forming new relationships with nonparental caregivers, and may become extremely distressed when left with new and unfamiliar caregivers.

Several classic studies (Schaffer and Callender, 1959; Schaffer and Emerson, 1964; Yarrow, 1964) in the field of developmental psychology have suggested that, at least for long-term separations, a separation that takes place before 6 months has no lasting effect on the infant. After 6 months, there may be effects that continue as long as 10 years. Thus, contrary to popular belief, return to employment during the second part of the first year, or at any time during the second year of life, might be *more* disruptive to the mother–infant relationship than a return before or after this period.

The Evidence So Far

Though no studies have directly addressed the timing of the maternal return to the workplace, there is some evidence that later return to employment is *more* disruptive of the attachment relationship than early return. Studies that have included only mothers who returned to employment in the first 3 months after childbirth have not found adverse effects on the quality of mother–child interaction generally (Hock, 1980; Pedersen et al., 1983; Stith and Davis, 1984) or on the security of mother–infant attachment specifically (Chase-Lansdale, 1981; Chase-Lansdale and Owen, 1987; Hock, 1980). On the other hand, researchers examining children whose mothers returned to employment later within the first year have sometimes found negative results of maternal employment (Barglow, Vaughn, and Molitor, 1987; Belsky and Rovine, 1988; Schwartz, 1983; Vaughn, Gove, and Egeland, 1980).

Several studies are particularly suggestive that a later onset of maternal employment might have more negative effects. In one of these studies, Rita Benn (1986) found that boys of *early*-returning mothers may be more securely attached than boys of *late*-returning mothers. Carollee Howes and Judith Rubenstein (1985) report that toddlers who had entered group care *earlier* in the first year had more pleasurable relationships with alternative caregivers than children who entered it later in the first year. Howes and her colleagues (1988) found that at 18 months, children who were classified as securely attached to nonparental caregivers had entered child care at earlier ages than children who were not considered securely attached. Only Wendy Goldberg and Ann Easterbrooks (1988) provide conflicting evidence. In their study, children whose mothers resumed employment before 6 months were less likely at 12 months to be securely attached to either mother or father than children whose mothers returned later. It should be noted, however, that Goldberg and Easterbrooks did not find timing effects when only attachment to the *mother* was considered. Several other researchers have looked at their data to see whether the effects of employment differed as a function of the timing of the maternal return to employment (Barglow, Vaughn, and Molitor, 1987; Belsky and Rovine, 1988), but they have been limited by the small number of children in their sample whose mothers returned to employment during the second half of the first year.

The Present Study

The study we report here was designed specifically to test for differences in child development and in characteristics of the mother–child relationship as a function of different durations of parental leave following childbirth. We were interested in several questions. Will children whose mothers returned to employment after attachment behaviors have fully emerged (that is, after 8 months) have more or less secure attachments at 18 months than children whose mothers returned to employment earlier? How will the attachment patterns of children of late-employed mothers compare with the attachments of children whose mothers have not yet returned to employment? Since attachment is related to cognitive development (Bell and Ainsworth, 1972; Bretherton et al., 1979; Easterbrooks and Lamb, 1979; Main, 1973), we also examined differences in infants' developmental levels. Finally, we explored the effects of mediating variables, such as frequency of stressful life events, social supports, marital satisfaction, role satisfaction, and nonmaternal child care arrangements on optimal child outcome in families with employed mothers.

Participants

We report data from 65 mother–infant pairs. The infants were all between 17 and 19 months of age. Twenty-nine of our families had "early-employed" mothers, who returned to employment before their children were 8 months of age; 10 had "late-employed" mothers, who returned to employment when their children were between 8 and 16 months. This group is quite small, despite our determined effort to recruit these mothers. We assume this is because few mothers have leave benefits beyond 5 months after the birth (Catalyst, 1985). Twenty-six of our mothers were nonemployed.[1]

All the mothers were married, and their husbands were employed. Mothers who were employed worked away from their infants at least 25 hours per week. Early-employed mothers were employed outside the home a mean of 38.5 hours per week ($SD = 6.9$); late-employed mothers, 37.2 hours per week ($SD = 8.2$). Mothers and infants were Caucasian and middle-class. Employed mothers had more years of education than nonemployed mothers; early-employed mothers earned more than late-employed mothers, and family income was higher in early-employed mothers' families than in nonemployed mothers' families. Of the children in the early-employed group, 69 percent were firstborns, as were 100 percent of the children in the late-employed group and 46 percent of the children in the nonemployed group. Data from an additional eight mothers who had unusual family histories or who had been separated from their infant for more than one week were excluded from the sample, as was one nonemployed mother whose child was in day care for 25 hours per week and two families in which the father was unemployed. Arrangements for substitute child care were varied.

Procedures

Mother–infant pairs were seen twice—once in the lab and once more, a week later, for two hours at home. Mothers were given a series of questionnaires and the Attachment Q-set (Waters and Deane, 1985) to complete between the lab and home visits. Measures of attachment, dependency, and developmental level on the Bayley Scales of Infant Development (Bayley, 1969) were obtained. Observations were coded from videotape by well-trained, reliable coders. All data were collected and coded by individuals unaware of the mother's employment status. We also observed and coded mothers and children interacting naturally in a number of situations in the laboratory and at home, but the results of these observations will not be included in this report.

Measures

Psychologists have been concerned about the possibly disruptive effects of employment on the quality of mother–infant "attachment." Does the mother provide for the child a "secure base" from which to explore the world? The most reliable technique for assessing whether or not a child is "securely attached" is known as the "Strange Situation" (Ainsworth et al., 1978), a semistructured laboratory procedure consisting of eight three-minute episodes involving the infant, the mother, and an unfamiliar person. The infant is observed playing alone in the unfamiliar room and responding to an unfamiliar woman in the presence of the mother, responding to maternal departure when left with the stranger and then when left alone, and responding to the reunion with the mother after each of these separations. With each episode, the situation becomes increasingly stressful to the child, and children demonstrate certain characteristic patterns of behavior. On the basis of their behavior, infants are classified into three major types. Type B infants are considered securely attached to their mothers: they actively seek proximity to or contact with their mothers during the reunion episodes, and if they are distressed, they are easily comforted by maternal contact. Type

A infants are considered insecure–avoidant because they ignore or reject their mothers upon reunion; and Type C infants are considered insecure–resistant because they show anger or resistance even while seeking proximity during reunion. Despite the simplicity of this measure, these categorizations have been shown to be reasonably predictive of socioemotional development as long as nine years later, with more favorable patterns of development observed in children who were categorized as securely attached.

To perform correlational analyses, Strange Situation scores were transformed into continuous "felt security" scores following the procedures employed by Owen and Cox (1988).[2] Felt security scores ranged from 1 (least secure) to 4 (most secure).

Because there is some controversy surrounding the Strange Situation attachment measure, we also included another set of measures, less well researched, known as the Q-set (Waters and Deane, 1985). This measure requires mothers to sort 75 descriptions of infant behavior into nine categories, from "most characteristic of my child" to "not at all characteristic of my child." From these sortings, we were able to obtain a second measure of attachment and a measure of dependency based on the mother's report of the child's behavior in both familiar and unfamiliar settings.

Results

We did not find any differences among the three groups in scores on our developmental test or in the Q-set scores for maternal reports of attachment and dependency. However, using the more standardized and better-validated measure of attachment—the attachment classifications obtained from the Strange Situation—we did find significant differences between early-employed and late-employed mothers. These data are presented in Table 18.1.

When mothers returned to employment in the first 7 months following childbirth, 45 percent of their infants were classified as insecure–avoidant, 48 percent as securely attached, and 7 percent as insecure–resistant. Particularly interesting—and unexpected—are the results for the children of late-employed mothers. All of the children whose mothers waited 8 months before returning to employment were securely attached. The difference in the attachment category distributions between the early- and late-employed groups is significant ($\chi^2 = 8.55$, df = 2, p < .02). There were no differences, however, between attachment security ratings for the children of late-employed mothers and the children of nonemployed mothers ($\chi^2 = 1.72$, df = 2, NS).

TABLE 18.1
Mother–Child Attachment Class as a Function of Child's Age at
Mother's Return to Employment

	Early-Employed (<8 months)		Late-Employed (>8 months)		Nonemployed	
	Percentage	*Number*	*Percentage*	*Number*	*Percentage*	*Number*
A	45	13	0	0	8	2
B	48	14	100	10	81	21
C	7	2	0	0	12	3
Total		29		10		26

Note:
A = avoidant   B = secure   C = resistant

We also examined the correlations (using Pearson Product Moment Correlations Coefficients) between the child's age when the mother returned to employment and the various child outcome measures. For all the children of employed mothers, the length of time the mother waited before returning to the workplace was not significantly related to outcome as measured by Q-set scores of attachment and dependency or developmental level. There was, however, a trend observed for the relationship between the child's age when the mother returned to employment and the child's felt security score (derived from the child's Strange Situation attachment categorization). The older the child when the mother returned to the workplace, the more likely the child was to be securely attached ($r = .30$, $n = 39$, $p < .06$). Within each of the employment groups, however, there were no relationships between the child's age at onset of maternal employment and attachment security.

Finally, there were no relationships between the type of substitute care used and the child outcome measures. Infants in center day care, infants in family day care, and infants at home with a relative or babysitter were not observed to be different on any of our outcome measures.

Discussion

We have reported two important results. First, mothers who returned to the workplace for 25 hours per week or more before the infant was 8 months of age had children who appeared less likely to be securely attached (according to the Strange Situation measure of attachment security) than the children of mothers who returned to the workplace for 25 hours per week or more after the infant was 8 months of age. Second, infants whose mothers were employed but who returned to the workplace when the infant was between 8 and 16 months of age were all securely attached, and the distribution of their attachment categories was not different from that of infants of nonemployed mothers. How old the child was when the mother returned to the workplace tended to predict how securely attached the child was to the mother.

While the data seem clear, the interpretation of these data is not. First, we think the data suggest that maternal employment during infancy—in and of itself—is not detrimental to children or to the mother–child relationship. What does seem important is something about the *timing* of the mothers' return to employment. Mothers who waited until their children were 8 months of age before returning to the workplace had children who were *all* securely attached, while mothers who returned earlier had children who were nearly evenly split between secure and insecure attachments.

It is important to remember that no differences among the three groups were observed using the measures of attachment or dependency obtained from the mother's Q-set descriptions of the child's behavior. The only differences observed were based on the Strange Situation measure of attachment. But researchers (Clarke-Stewart, 1988; Hoffman, 1984; Weinraub, Jaeger, and Hoffman, 1988) have raised questions about the construct validity of this measure when used with children of employed mothers, arguing that being left in a strange situation may be differentially stressful for children of employed mothers and for children of nonemployed mothers. Thus, these findings have to be interpreted with caution. Future research will have to confirm the validity of using the Strange Situation to compare children of employed and nonemployed mothers.

However attractive it might be to use these data to support arguments in favor of parental leave, it would also be inappropriate to attribute the differences observed in the Strange Situation attachment classifications solely to the timing of the mother's return to employment. First, if timing is an important variable, then we might expect to find relationships between the age of the child when the mother returned to employment and child outcome *within* each of the employed mother groups. However, we found no evidence of within-group relationships. Returning to work when the infant was 1 month old was not likely to produce more or less secure attachment than returning when he or she was 4 or 6 months old. The failure to find within-group correlations might suggest that there is a qualitative shift around 8 months of age in the nature of the child's attachment to the caregiver, and might even raise the possibility of the existence of a critical period in the development of attachment. However, it is also possible that our failure to find relationships between age and attachment is due to the small number of subjects. Thus, a fair test of these within-group analyses is precluded. Until research with much larger samples can examine the specific age parameters that might be operative, practitioners will have to refrain from recommending specific ages at which mothers should return to employment.

Second, and much more important to remember here, is that none of these mothers was randomly assigned to an employment group. It is not at all unlikely that the variables that account for why a mother was in the early-employed group and no the late-employed group were the variables that influence attachment, and not the timing per se. (See Hoffman, 1989, for more detailed discussions of the problem of the self-selection of mothers into employment groups.) Ellen Hock's longitudinal data are relevant here. She interviewed mothers shortly after childbirth and found that mothers who returned to employment in the next few months showed more commitment to their careers and less anxiety concerning separation from their infants than mothers who did not return or who returned later (DeMeis, Hock, and McBride, 1986; Hock, Morgan, and Hock, 1985). In our study, there were several ways in which early-employed mothers were different from late-employed mothers. Early-employed mothers earned more money on the job, and they tended to be older (32 years versus 29). In addition, all of the late-employed women were first-time mothers.

Unfortunately, we do not have longitudinal data or any information on some of the more interesting psychological characteristics on which these mothers might differ and which might account for or contribute to the differences in child attachment security ratings between the groups. It is possible, in line with Hock's findings, that these mothers differ from each other in their attitudes toward child-rearing and motherhood. All mothers are not alike, and not every mother is imbued equally with the qualities that make for secure mother–infant relationships. Mothers who derive less satisfaction from interacting with very young infants may return to employment earlier than other mothers. If these mothers were to stay at home with their infants, both infants and mothers might be the worse for it. On the other hand, mothers who especially enjoy young infants might be more likely to be found among the late-employed. These are mothers who want to be employed but who postpone their return to the workplace, sacrificing the employment experience and additional income. They might be especially sensitive and patient in interacting with young babies, characteristics that contribute to the formation of secure parent–child bonds whenever the mothers return to employment.

We have some data to support this possibility from our questionnaires. Several of our late-employed mothers went back to the job *later* than they had initially planned. When asked about this change in their plans, two mothers reported problems separating from their young infants. One said, "I couldn't leave the baby after 4 months," and the other said, "Four months seemed too soon to go back." Interestingly, two mothers in the early-employment group returned *earlier* than they had planned, citing financial or job-related concerns. Said one mother, "There was pressure from my boss plus financial need and enticement." Belsky and Rovine's (1988) finding that employed mothers of insecurely attached infants scored lower on interpersonal sensitivity and empathy and higher on career motivation than employed mothers of securely attached children lends further support to this interpretation.

Directions for Future Research

It is dangerously premature to attribute the differences in attachment we found between the children of early- and late-employed mothers to the timing of the return to employment. The data in fact raise a number of questions about our study and other studies of this kind. First, in what ways do the mothers who are employed—early or late—differ from each other and from nonemployed mothers? Second, can it be that there are fundamental differences between mothers that determine both their employment choice and their relationship with their child? Would children of mothers in the early-employed groups really be more securely attached if their mothers had simply waited longer before returning to the workplace? Third, are there parametric relationships between variables relating to the maternal separation—such as length of absence and how often it occurs—that predict child outcome? Could there be such a thing as too many hours away from the infant? Mothers employed on the usual full-time schedule—40 hours—may have sufficient time remaining in the week to develop a healthy relationship with their infants, but there is some evidence that more than 40 hours of employment a week is associated with greater maternal anxiety and strain (Owen and Cox, 1988).

Finally, are there some transitions from being at home with the baby to being employed full time that are healthier for the mother–infant relationship than others? Mothers who have returned to the workplace gradually over a period of several weeks sometimes report that they feel this approach is better for their recovering health and gives their infant a smoother transition to being with the substitute caregiver. The data on part-time employment suggest that this alternative might be best for both mothers and children (Hoffman, 1989). Because of the constraints of our study, mothers who returned gradually to the workplace or who were employed fewer than 25 hours per week were not included in our sample. Future studies may want to examine parent and child adjustment when mothers return more gradually.

Longitudinal data might help to answer some of these questions. Researchers and funding agencies, most notably the National Institute of Child Health and Development, are becoming increasingly aware of the need for longitudinal data from large groups of children studied from a point before the family even begins alternative care arrangements. Another strategy that might help illuminate the processes by which maternal employment affects parent and child outcome is one we at the Infant Behavior Laboratory and other researchers around the country (see, for example, Belsky and Rovine, 1988) have been working on for some time—within-group analyses. Of the infants of employed mothers, for example, approximately half appear securely attached, half not. What factors predict which of these children will appear securely attached? This is the information that would be most useful: theoretically, by illuminating the development of attachment; practically, since mothers will continue to be employed, by clarifying which factors are more likely to contribute to favorable child outcomes; and politically, by highlighting those changes in the lives of employed families that would really make a difference.

What we have found in these within-group analyses is that, for employed mothers, the mother's satisfaction with her employment role is very much related to the child's attachment status. This holds whether attachment is measured with the Strange Situation felt security score ($r = .38$, $p < .04$) or with the Q-set score ($r = .39$, $p < .04$). Moreover, the best predictor of the employed mother's role satisfaction appears to be her evaluation of the quality of the care her child is receiving in her absence ($r = .62$, $p < .0005$). Improving access to satisfactory child care might go a long way toward increasing mothers' role satisfaction and, subsequently, the probability of secure attachment in their children.

Conclusions

We must be very wary of making policy decisions based on data obtained from self-selected groups of employed and nonemployed mothers. Mothers are not randomly assigned to employment situations, and so differences in their children's development cannot be attributed solely to the mothers' employment situation. Rather than simply examining differences between children of employed and nonemployed mothers, a more illuminating strategy might involve looking at the factors that predict optimal outcome *within* each group.

Mothers are not all alike. Under optimal conditions mothers may select the employment situation that is best for themselves and their children; under less than optimal conditions, mothers may select the best of the available options. For some mothers, an early return to employment may be best. Such mothers may know, consciously or not, that they would not be happy with full-time mothering and that their infant might not profit from being with them on a full-time basis. For these mothers, access to adequate substitute child care may be the primary concern. For other mothers, an early return to employment may be very difficult; the mother may need time to recover her strength and stamina, or she may feel distressed about separating from her new infant. For still other mothers, especially mothers of infants with unusual medical or educational needs or infants with very difficult temperaments, return to employment within one or two years of childbirth may not be possible. These families may not be able to obtain care adequate to the child's special needs, and for them, especially, family leave programs may be necessary.

Since not all mothers, children, and families are alike, social policy is needed not to guarantee equal family care leaves to all families, but to give families the opportunity to choose those provisions that best meet their needs.

NOTES

Acknowledgments. Work on this paper was supported by a grant from the National Institute of Child Health and Human Development (RO1HD25455).

The research reported here was partially supported by grants from the Temple University Biomedical Research Support Fund. We are extremely grateful to Lois Hoffman for inspiring this study, for assisting in the design, and for critically reviewing the manuscript. We are also grateful for assistance in all aspects of this research from Susan Ansul, Rose DiBiase, Maureen O'Brien, Loretta Newell, Beverly Coulson, Shirley Landis, Robert Gress, and Kim Perez. This study could not have been done without the cooperation and support of the families who participated in the project. Requests for reprints should be sent to Marsha Weinraub, Department of Psychology, Temple University, Philadelphia, PA 19122.

1. Sociologists, demographers, and social scientists who are used to working with large data sets are often surprised and disturbed by reports of data from such small samples. Samples under 100 are difficult for them to accept; samples of fewer than 15 make them shudder. And yet it is important to remember that the use of inferential statistics balances sample size against effect size. For large samples, an effect that accounts for only 1 percent of the variance can be significant—that is, is considered not due to chance. But in a small sample, a large effect is necessary to be considered statistically significant. Small as our sample is, the effects we report are large and reliable using nonparametric or parametric statistics. Of course, when a person is claiming "no effects," large samples are more useful than small ones, but if an effect is found, it is as reliable if found with a small sample as with a large one.

2. Felt security scores were obtained by recoding the Strange Situation subcategories (A1, A2, B1, B2, B3, B4, C1, and C2). B3 children were considered the most securely attached and given scores of "4"; B1 and B2 children were considered next most securely attached and given scores of "3"; B4 children were rescored as "2"; and A and C children were rescored as "1."

REFERENCES

Ainsworth, Mary D. Salter (1973). "The Development of Infant–Mother Attachment." In Bethye M. Caldwell and Henry N. Riccuiti, eds., *Review of Child Development Research*. Chicago: University of Chicago Press.

Ainsworth, M. D. S., Mary Blehar, Eve Waters, and Sally Wall (1978). *Patterns of Attachment*. Hillsdale, N.J.: Erlbaum.

Barglow, Peter, Brian E. Vaughn, and Nancy Molitor (1987). "Effects of Maternal Absence Due to Employment on the Quality of Infant–Mother Attachment in a Low-Risk Sample." *Child Development* 58: 945–54.

Bayley, Nancy (1969). *Manual for the Bayley Scales of Infant Development*. New York: Psychological Corp.

Bell, Silvia, and M. D. S. Ainsworth (1972). "Infant Crying and Maternal Responsiveness." *Child Development* 43: 1171–90.

Belsky, Jay, and Michail Rovine (1988). "Non-maternal Care in the First Year of Life and the Security of Infant–Parent Attachment." *Child Development* 59: 157–67.

Benn, Rita K. (1986). "Factors Promoting Secure Attachment Relationships Between Employed Mothers and Their Sons." *Child Development* 57: 1224–31.

Bowlby, John (1973). *Attachment and Loss*, vol. 2: *Separation*. New York: Basic Books.

Brazelton, T. Berry (1985). *Working and Caring*. New York: Basic Books.

Bretherton, Inge, Elizabeth Bates, Laura Benigni, Luigia Camioni, and Virginia Voltera (1979). "Relationships Between Cognition, Communication, and Quality of Attachment." In E. Bates, ed., *The Emergence of Symbols: Cognition and Communication in Infancy*. New York: Academic Press.

Catalyst (1985). *Preliminary Report on a Nationwide Survey of Maternity/Parental Leaves*. Position Paper, RR no. 17. New York: Catalyst.

Chase-Lansdale, P. Lindsay (1981). "Effects of Maternal Employment on Mother–Infant and Father–Infant Attachment." Ph.D. dissertation, University of Michigan.

Chase-Lansdale, P. Lindsay, and Margaret T. Owen (1987). "Maternal Employment in a Family Context: Effects on Infant–Mother and Infant–Father Attachments." *Child Development* 58: 1505–12.

Clarke-Stewart, K. Alison (1988). "'The Effects of Infant Day Care Reconsidered' Reconsidered: Risks for Parents, Children and Researchers." *Early Childhood Research Quarterly* 3: 293–318.

DeMeis, Debora K., Ellen Hock, and Susan L. McBride (1986). "The Balance of Employment and Motherhood: Longitudinal Study of Mothers' Feelings About Separation from Their Firstborn Infants." *Development Psychology* 22: 627–32.

Easterbrooks, M. Ann, and Michael Lamb (1979). "The Relationship Between Quality of Infant–Mother Attachment and Infant Competence in Initial Encounters with Peers." *Child Development* 50: 380–87.

Gamble, Thomas J., and Edward F. Zigler (1986). "Effects of Infant Day Care: Another Look at the Evidence." *American Journal of Orthopsychiatry* 56(1): 26–41.

Goldberg, Wendy, and Ann Easterbrooks (1984). "The Role of Marital Quality in Toddler Development." *Developmental Psychology* 20: 504–14.

—— (1988). "Maternal Employment when Children are Toddlers and Kindergartners." In Adele E. Gottfried and Allen W. Gottfried, eds., *Maternal Employment and Children's Development: Longitudinal Research*. New York: Plenum.

Hock, Ellen (1980). "Working and Nonworking Mothers and Their Infants: A Comparative Study of Maternal Caregiving Characteristics and Infant Social Behavior." *Merrill–Palmer Quarterly* 26: 79–101.

Hock, Ellen, K. C. Morgan, and M. Hock (1985). "Employment Decisions Made by Mothers of Infants." *Psychology of Women Quarterly* 9: 383–402.

Hoffman, Lois W. (1984). "Maternal Employment and the Young Child." In
M. Perlmutter, ed., *Parent–Child Interaction and Parent–Child Relations in
Child Development.* Minnesota Symposia on Child Psychology, vol. 17.
Hillsdale, N.J.: Erlbaum.
—— (1989) "Effects of Maternal Employment in the Two-Parent Family:
A Review of Recent Research." *American Psychologist* 44(2): 283–92.
Howes, Carollee, Carol Rodning, Darlene C. Galluzzo, and Lisabeth Myers
(1988). "Attachment and Child Care: Relationships with Mother and
Caregiver." *Early Childhood Research Quarterly* 3: 403–16.
Howes, Carollee, and Judith Rubenstein (1985). "Age of Entry and Quality
of Child Attachment." *Child Care Quarterly* 14: 140–51.
Main, Mary (1973). "Exploration, Play, and Cognitive Factors as Related to
Mother–Child Attachment." Ph.D. dissertation, Johns Hopkins University.
Owen, Margaret T., and Martha J. Cox (1988). "Maternal Employment and
the Transition to Parenthood." In A. E. Gottfried and A. W. Gottfried,
eds., *Maternal Employment and Children's Development: Longitudinal Research.* New York: Plenum.
Pedersen, F. A., R. L. Cain, M. J. Zaslow, and B. J. Anderson (1983). "Variation in Infant Experience Associated with Alternative Family Role Organization." In L. Laesa and I. Sigel, eds., *Families as Learning Environments for Children.* New York: Plenum.
Schaffer, H. R., and W. M. Callender (1959). "Psychological Effects of Hos-
pitalization in Infancy." *Pediatrics* 24: 528–39.
Schaffer, H. R., and P. E. Emerson (1964). "The Development of Social
Attachment in Infancy." Monographs of the Society for Research in
Child Development, vol. 23. Serial no. 94. Chicago: University of Chi-
cago Press.
Schwartz, Pamela (1983). "Length of Day Care Attendance and Attachment
Behavior in Eighteen-Month-Old Infants." *Child Development* 54: 1073–
78.
Stith, Sandra, and Albert J. Davis (1984). "Employed Mothers and Family
Day Care Substitute Caregivers: A Comparative Analysis of Infant
Care." *Child Development* 55: 1340–48.
Vaughn, Brian E., Frederick L. Gove, and Byran Egeland (1980). "The Re-
lationship Between Out-of-Home Care and the Quality of Infant–
Mother Attachment in an Economically Disadvantaged Population."
Child Development 51: 144–48.
Waters, Everett, and Kathleen Deane (1985). "Defining and Assessing Indi-
vidual Differences in Attachment Relationships: Q-Methodology and
the Organization of Behavior and Early Childhood." In I. Bretherton
and E. Waters, eds., *Growing Points in Attachment Theory and Research.*
Mongraphs of the Society for Research in Child Development, vol. 50.
Serial no. 209. Chicago: University of Chicago Press.
Weinraub, Marsha, Elizabeth Jaeger, and Lois W. Hoffman (1988). "Predict-
ing Infant Outcomes in Families of Employed and Nonemployed
Mothers." *Early Childhood Research Quarterly* 3: 361–78.

Yarrow, L. J. (1964). "Separation from Parents During Early Childhood." In
    M. L. Hoffman and L. W. Hoffman, eds., *Review of Child Development
    Research*, vol. 1. New York: Russell Sage Foundation.
Zigler, Edward F. and Susan Muenchow (1983). "Infant Day Care and In-
    fant Care Leaves: A Policy Vacuum." *American Psychologist* 38: 91–94.

19 | Supporting Optimal Parenting Behaviors During Infancy

Lynne Sanford Koester

Changes in an infant's physiological, cognitive, and social needs over the first year of life continually affect the functioning and needs of his or her entire family. To ensure the optimal development of the next generation, future policy decisions should be based on current knowledge regarding the conditions required by both parents and their babies.

In recent years a great deal of research on early parent–infant interactions has focused on the mutual influence of both partners, and we have become particularly aware of the infant's competence as a responsive social being (Brazelton, Koslowski, and Main, 1974; Fogel, 1984; Tronick, Als, and Adamson, 1979). As a result, we now view each member of this early dyad as both contributor and recipient in a dynamic flow of communication, with each partner influencing and being influenced by the behavior of the other. It is widely accepted that a healthy, normally developing infant is indeed an active social partner, much better at perceiving, communicating, learning, and remembering than was previously acknowledged. For example, Anthony DeCasper and William Fifer (1980) have demonstrated that a short time after birth, babies are capable of distinguishing their mother's voice from other female voices; in addition, healthy newborns can easily learn to perform an action that will make the mother's voice (on tape) reappear.

After several decades of research on infant development, most developmental psychologists now agree that it does not take long for a healthy newborn to make others fully aware of his or her skills as a socially interactive being. There is, of course, a period of time, approximately the first quarter-year after birth, during which infants expend a great deal of energy simply stabilizing the functions of their central nervous systems as well as refining the social and mental capacities with which they were born.

Surprisingly, many recent researchers have all but overlooked the contribution of the other half of this reciprocal relationship—the parents. There has been little emphasis on the important observation that *parents* who are adapting well to the birth of an infant, and who are adequately supported in that role, engage in many subtle and nonconscious behaviors that are indeed very well matched to the cognitive and socioemotional needs of their offspring (Papoušek and Papoušek, 1981).

The Role of the Parent in the Parent–Infant System

Infants require protection, support, stimulation, and reinforcement from the social world in order to develop their capabilities. Until recently, researchers have paid relatively little attention to ways in which parents, caregivers, and the social environment in general support and enhance newborns' inherent qualities.

In fact, the parent–infant dyad is an excellent example of what might be called a teaching partnership, but with one striking feature that makes it unique: it consists of two members with widely discrepant levels of maturity. On the one hand, we have the newborn, who has virtually no prior experience in communicating with another person and is unable to understand or use a spoken language. How then, one might ask, does the "naive" parent establish an effective means of interacting with one so inexperienced? Surely it is safe to assume that the less competent of the two—the infant—requires the support of a partner who will use sensitive and appropriate methods to bridge this gap (Koester, Papoušek, and Papoušek, 1987). Kenneth Kaye describes the empathetic caregiving necessary to help the young organism "become human":

> This kind of behavior is not specifically maternal or paternal. We see it in any adult, even in children, whenever they interact with another person lacking their own level of competence in a particular situation. It is a basic birthright of the human species, and a remarkable one from the point of view of behavioral evolution. It is remarkable because its adaptive value, the reason this set of behavior patterns evolved, is directly related neither to the individual's survival nor to reproduction. Instead, its raison d'etre is education, bringing up the young. (Kaye, 1982, p. 68)

Hanuš and Mechthild Papoušek have extensively studied this issue in looking at parental sensitivity and responsiveness to infant cues (for a recent review of their work, see Papoušek and Papoušek,

1987). Their concept of "intuitive parenting" refers to the many subtle and nonconscious behavior patterns that parents frequently use
in interactions with their infants; the Papoušeks contend that these
"intuitive" behaviors turn out on closer examination to be extremely
well suited to the baby's perceptual, cognitive, and developmental
needs. For example, their studies have shown that parents typically
interact with the baby face-to-face and at a very short distance,
closely matching the newborn's limited range of focus; they vary and
exaggerate their normal pitch, as in "baby talk," which helps the infant perceive and pay attention to this communication and to recognize that it is meant for him or her; and they use frequent repetition, simplification, and reinforcement to support the infant's
limited abilities.

In fact, the strategies used by parents in nonstressful interactions
with their infants are very similar to what we already know to be
optimal and necessary for successful infant learning:

- The infant must be awake, alert, and attentive to the interacting partner.
- Stimulation must be structured (for example, simplified) to match the
infant's level of understanding.
- Tasks must be repeated frequently and paced carefully so that the infant
is not overwhelmed.
- The infant must be rewarded and reinforced for efforts so that he or
she will be motivated to continue and will gain pleasure from small
accomplishments.
- Caregivers must be sensitive to signals that indicate limitations, fatigue,
and tolerance levels.

Many developmental psychologists involved in infancy research
are impressed by the reciprocal nature of parent–infant behaviors
and by the matching that can so often be observed in these early
interactions. Clearly, the infant's adaptation to his or her social and
physical environment can be greatly facilitated by responsive and
nurturant caregivers. It is important to emphasize, however, that the
parent's or caregiver's goal should not be to *accelerate* the infant's
normal rate of learning and adaptation, or to create a "super-baby,"
but simply to ensure the environmental and social support necessary
to maximize the infant's opportunities for further healthy developmental progress.

Unfortunately, there are far too many instances of disturbing
*mis*matches between parent and child, of conflicting needs, and of
parents who are too tired, too stressed, or too much in need of nurturance themselves to provide this kind of support for the child's
development. Thus, the behaviors associated with "intuitive parent-

ing" are not necessarily automatic, guaranteed, or immune to external influences. Rather, they may be inherent but vulnerable to disruption if relaxed time is not available in which to learn the infant's idiosyncratic signals and responses. Indeed, parent–infant interaction can often be a strikingly beautiful dance, with finely tuned nuances; and as in any dance, both members of the dyad need time and practice to learn not only the steps, but also the pacing and turn-taking that are required. This may be particularly true of adult–infant dyads, since one partner is still communicating entirely on a nonverbal basis.

Infant Development and Influences on the Parent–Infant System

Predictable changes in the infant's development within the first few months of life inevitably influence the relationship with his or her caregivers (see Table 19.1). It is normally not until about 3 months of age that the infant's patterns of eating, sleeping, and elimination become regular enough to allow the parents to plan their own schedules around that of the child; it is also not unusual, especially if the child has colic or was born prematurely, for this process to take considerably longer. A major developmental task during the infant's first few months is to establish stable, predictable cycles of sleeping, waking, and eating (Dittrichová, 1969; Dreyfus-Brisac, 1974; Korner, 1979). Again, this is not a one-way street: not only is the caregiver affected by the infant's early biological rhythms, but he or she may also play a role in shaping their development (Koester, 1987). In terms of face-to-face interaction, babies alternate between states of attention and nonattention, and most parents are sensitive to these signals (Brazelton, Kowslowski, and Main, 1974); that sensitivity contributes to a gradual increase in attentiveness.

Similarly, parents of a newborn require a certain amount of time (depending on their own age, physical stamina, number of other children, and workloads in general) to adapt to the demands of caretaking during these early months. Not only must the mother regain her physical strength and normal activity level after childbirth, but all members of the family may be affected by the strain of interrupted sleep and the need to provide care for a relatively helpless being who makes his or her wishes known primarily by crying. Parents who must return to work before this transition has been satisfactorily maneuvered may find themselves lacking the endurance,

TABLE 19.1
Tasks and Changes over the First Year of Life

	Infant	Parent
Prenatal	Experiencing maternal rhythms and sounds (physiological functions, voice, sleep/wake/activity cycles)	Creating image of idealized infant; being aware of fetal rhythms and activity cycles
Birth	Adapting to life outside the womb Recognizing mother's voice Showing preference for human stimuli	Adjusting to infant's caregiving needs, tempo, and temperament Helping baby control reflexes
0–3 Months	Alternating cycles of attention/nonattention Gradually increasing ability to regulate arousal; stabilizing physiological functions Giving preliminary social signals ("I'm ready to play." "I've had enough." "Don't overload me.") Using eye-to-eye gaze; visually exploring faces Initiating social smiling	Gradually prolonging interactions with baby Assisting child in modulating attention, excitability, distress "Reading" baby's signals; recognizing when child is alert or tired Learning which behaviors will bring about social response by infant
3–6 Months	Visually recognizing significant caregivers Being most responsive to parents Becoming aware of strangers Cooing, vocalizing to express pleasure Developing reach/grasp coordination (leads to games)	Being reinforced by infant in role as significant caregivers Anticipating and interpreting baby's signals Still "guessing" about infant's intentions, but attributing much meaning to baby's actions and sounds Engaging in mutual play (now possible)
6–9 Months	Taking more initiative in social exchanges Becoming more object-oriented Developing greater mobility Showing increased interest in exploring the environment Grasping *and* releasing (throwing and dropping games) Anticipating "surprises" in games, others' intentions Showing some anxiety around strangers	Responding more to infant's lead in playful interactions Using toys to mediate attention, entertain, and teach Monitoring infant's safety and exploratory ventures Supporting child's growing memory by more use of explanations

TABLE 19.1 (continued)

	Infant	Parent
9–12 Months	Being more discriminating about partners Actively seeking out "special" people Becoming anxious about separations, or suddenly seeming more dependent	Becoming distressed if infant is upset by separation Experiencing a period of temporary disorganization (especially if working outside the home) if baby is "clingy"
1 Year	Babbling, imitating sounds, leading to first meaningful words Communicating desires in more diverse and effective ways Using familiar caregivers as a secure base for exploring the environment Preparing for independent mobility (standing, walking) Becoming a more equal partner in social interactions	Interpreting words and giving feedback to help shape language Experiencing a greater need to set limits, define expectations Supporting child's motivation to explore, discover Reaching a milestone for both parent and child: preverbal infant becomes toddler, understanding and using language

Note: This is an approximate timetable of some important developmental changes in infants and the ways in which these changes are typically responded to and supported by parents. Time of onset or completion of any given task may vary greatly with individual children, although the influence on the parents is likely to be similar.

tolerance, patience, and enthusiasm to fully enjoy and respond to their infant's developmental needs.

During the early months, the infant stabilizes his or her levels of internal physiological activity and balances these efforts with increasing attention to the outside world. Parents assist in this process through the timing, repetition, and rhythms of stimulation they provide—for example, the soothing rhythms of rocking or carrying, and the more playful rhythms of tapping, tickling, and bouncing games are effective means of calming or alerting the young child. These patterns play an important role in early mutual regulation, although few parents are aware of their potential benefits or use them consciously (Koester, Papoušek, and Papoušek, 1989; Tronick, 1981).

The effective caregiver must be guided by an implicit understanding of the infant's limitations; otherwise, much of the successful communication that one sees in such dyads would not occur. For the caregiver, the challenge is to be constantly ready to alter the tempo,

strategy, or intensity of his or her behavior in response to the fluctu-
ating needs of the infant (Stern et al., 1977). This is no small task,
even though it is largely nonconscious, and it is not as easily or
smoothly accomplished if parents themselves are already overex-
tended or torn by the demands of work and family.

While regulating his or her biological rhythms over the first few
months, the infant may reach several important social milestones.
Having learned the caregivers' identities, unique features, and communication styles, the infant usually engages in truly social smiling
by around 3 months. The impact of this event on the parents is
tremendous. Concurrent with the infant's increasing vocalizations
(cooing and eventually babbling), smiling serves as an important
reinforcement for the caregivers' routine and playful behaviors,
thereby creating a new excitement and enthusiasm within the relationship. Clearly this milestone has many positive implications for
the parent–child relationship, as is apparent when one watches how
hard parents work to elicit these early smiles—and how delighted
they are when the infant rewards their efforts!

Similarly, by 6 weeks of age, most infants will have begun to explore visually the inner details of a partner's face, thus seeming to
look another person in the eye (Fogel, 1984). Many parents report
that the onset of this developmental stage makes the infant seem
"human" for the first time, and the emotional attachment between
infant and parent that is thought to be so crucial to further healthy
development is enhanced by such seemingly small modifications in
the infant's own responsiveness. But as the infant learns to make
things happen, to influence and gradually to master the environment, it continues to need an emotionally invested audience to share
in these small pleasures and provide encouragement for further ex-
plorations (Papoušek, Papoušek, and Koester, 1987).

Obviously, parents have an intense emotional investment in their
infant and take great pleasure in witnessing the vast amount of development that the child undergoes in the first few years after birth.
At the same time, it is important that they be able to spend relaxed
time with their infant, beyond the routine caregiving tasks, in order
to focus on the child him- or herself and on the sometimes small,
incremental changes in cognitive, motor, and social skills that occur
during this stage. Child care workers also play an important role by
observing and taking note of each child's new accomplishments, and
by communicating them enthusiastically to the parents. This implies
that staff–child ratios must permit the caregivers to become attuned
to each child's signals, needs, and development.

Kaye (1982) refers to the first 3 months as a period of "shared rhythms and regulations," during which the infant's inborn rhythms (such as sucking and cycles of attention and nonattention) become the basis for an interactive dialogue between the two partners. "One could say the mother is entrained by the biological rhythms of the infant, but it is just as correct to say that the mother uses these rhythms to entrain the infant into patterns of a dialogue that characterize the adult world" (Kaye, 1982, p. 66). Beginning at around 2 months, parents and infants also enter a period of "shared intentions," in which parents infer increasingly sophisticated meaning, emotional content, and intention from the infant's limited cues. As Kaye explains, "Until recently we have missed the importance of the way parents take over these indices of intention and interpret them as if they were messages" (Kaye, 1982, p. 67).

It is not until about 8 months, however, that these shared intentions take on a truly bi-directional quality in which the *infant* is also capable of perceiving, remembering, and even anticipating the *adult's* intentions (such as Mother's or Father's departure). This milestone ushers in another new phase of parent–infant interactions, which Kaye (1982) aptly calls the period of "shared memory." Thus, the short-lived crisis that may be brought on by separations from the parents may be gradually alleviated as the child is helped to remember and anticipate that the parents also *return* each time.

Throughout each phase of the infant's development, parents typically expect more from the child than he or she is capable of producing at that time. In this way, parents subtly and patiently stretch the child forward into an increasingly balanced partnership, becoming the child's first teachers as well as nurturers and social partners.

Implications for Research

There is, of course, much controversy regarding the potential disruption of the attachment process in infants who experience out-of-home group care from a very early age (Belsky, 1986, 1987; Belsky and Steinberg, 1978; Chase-Lansdale and Owen, 1987; Hock, 1980; Phillips et al., 1987; Schwartz, 1983; Vaughn, Deane, and Waters, 1985). Most of these studies have examined this issue from the perspective of the infant's behaviors, specifically those that might signal undue anxiety or avoidance of parents or other adults. It is time now also to address parental behaviors and the ways in which they may contribute to or influence the child's social and emotional development. Many of the naturally occurring, nonconscious features of optimal parent–infant relationships have been described. Researchers should now be able to address the question of whether these patterns are adversely affected in situations in which parents must spend a great deal of time away from their infants in the early months, during what appears to be such an important period for becoming closely acquainted with the new family member. That is, do optimal parenting behaviors depend, for their full development, on being elicited by infants' signals? If so, how can we maximize the time available to parents for recognizing and responding appropriately to these infant cues? What amount of time together should be considered adequate to ensure the full nurturance and blossoming of these parenting behaviors?

Taking this one step further, we must also consider whether caregivers other than parents can be trained in optimal "parenting skills" or nurturing behaviors, and whether a certain amount of transition time might be advisable for a new caregiver—time during which infant and partner can become familiar with each other's communicative styles, signals, and rhythms of interaction. By approximately 6 months, the infant's involvement with objects and range of emotional and communicative expressions have increased the scope of his or her world beyond the early one-on-one interactions. One might hypothesize that a new caregiver entering the scene in the latter half of the first year could establish rapport with the infant more quickly and with less effort. On the other hand, as the child's awareness of the world and people in it increases, there is also greater potential for anxiety around strangers or distress when separated from familiar caregivers; thus, the transition to substitute (or nonparental) care might actually be more difficult if it is initiated at a time when the child is experiencing these tensions. It might be helpful for both parents and infants in this situation if the parents had the opportunity to return to work gradually, slowly increasing the number of work hours or days as the family adjusts to this change in scheduling, routines, and caregiving responsibilities.

In Chapter 18, Marsha Weinraub and Elizabeth Jaeger contribute data that may shed some light on this issue. Comparing the attachments of children whose mothers returned to out-of-home jobs during the child's first 8 months with those whose mothers returned to employment later, they found that only in the "late-employed" group were *all* of the children "securely attached." As Weinraub and Jaeger assert, the timing of a mother's return to employment may have important implications for the child as well. It would be erroneous (as they observe) to assume that timing is the only crucial variable. Motivation, the need to return to employment at a particular time, and individual differences in both parental and infant behaviors must be addressed before one can make firm policy recommendations. What is clear, however, is that parents need a variety of *options*—options that will enable them to choose the combination of employment and parenting arrangements that will be most compatible with their own needs and the best interests of the child.

Implications for Policy

On the basis of our current knowledge about changes in infant behavior over the first 3 to 4 postnatal months, it seems safe to assert that new parents need—at the minimum—the option of spending as much time as they desire with their infant during this quarter-year. To date, as Edward Zigler and Susan Muenchow have noted, "there is no recognition that a healthy parent may have a psychological need for some time off to be with a new baby, or that a baby, in turn, may need some time to establish a relationship with at least one parent" (1983, p. 92). By a logical extension, one should not forget that adoptive parents, like biological parents, also need sufficient time to become acquainted with a new child, regardless of age at adoption.

The complex relationships among parental employment, age of infant, and the infant's subsequent socioemotional development have been the topic of numerous research efforts. As should be evident from the present review, however, it is equally important to consider the implications (for all members of the family) of secure or insecure *parenting*. That is, parents need to feel competent; they need to have feedback from their infant that tells them that they are doing a good job responding to his or her signals and needs; and they need to grow in their own confidence and skills just as the infant is developing. While this may be true throughout the child's maturation into adulthood, it is especially significant during the preverbal infancy period, for reasons that have been mentioned earlier.

Individuals and families alike are particularly vulnerable when going through a transition to a new stage, as when an important new skill is being mastered; the plateaus before and after always seem easy in comparison to the disequilibrium brought on by these periods of change. Infancy is indeed a period of many rapid and significant changes, and thus one that has the potential to disrupt even those families that appeared to function most smoothly prior to the child's birth.

Public policies are needed that reflect and respond to the complexities of varying individual and family situations in our society. Clearly, employed parents with infants need the assurance that their jobs will not be jeopardized when they spend time at home after the birth or adoption of a child; legislation currently under consideration would at least provide such assurance for the first 4 months and would be an important step in this direction. But parents also need considerable flexibility regarding the timing of their return to work and the scheduling of daily home and workplace responsibilities, and they need child care arrangements that will let them feel comfortable leaving the child in the care of another adult.

Both employers *and* caregivers can play important roles in supporting these needs, thus in the long run enhancing the job satisfaction, performance, and commitment of the employee, as well as the optimal development of infants and their parents. On the employers' side, more on-site (or nearby) child care facilities are one of the best ways to ensure that parents can remain in closer proximity to their children during the day, allowing them to join their infants during meals or breaks and generally to observe their behavior and daily progress and adjustment in the out-of-home child care setting. Child care providers, on the other hand, must be responsive to and concerned about the needs of parents as well as children; this may take the form of flexibility regarding daily schedules, receptiveness to parents who want to spend time with the child in the center or family day care home, parenting support groups and sick child care on the premises, and in some cases serving as models of appropriate and effective caregiving techniques.

Finally, it is important to point out that the descriptions of infant and parent development I have offered are those of presumably "normal," healthy individuals in situations supportive of optimal early adaptation. While this may be the goal toward which we should be striving, it is obvious that for many families this description is far removed from the reality of their lives. In addition to the innumerable societal and economic causes of family disruption, the infant may bring with him or her characteristics that make the job of early parenting a particularly stressful one with fewer rewards than may be needed to keep the interaction system functioning smoothly. Many infants are born seriously premature, are too weak or ill or poorly nourished to be responsive social partners, or have temperaments that make normal caregiving efforts frustrating and ineffective. These infants run the additional risk of not providing their caregivers with enough positive feedback to reward and sustain the nurturing responses that the child needs in return. In such cases, the best solution may *not* be to have a parent remain at home all day with the child, but rather to offer support and relief by others who have also had experience with a difficult child. These parents need suggestions and help to cope with a stressful home situation; they certainly do not need the additional stress of a nonsupportive or inflexible work environment.

No single alternative or childrearing decision will be right for all families, or even for a single family over time; optimally, parents would have an array from which to choose—a "cafeteria plan," such as those currently offered for health insurance by many employers, with options that can support the individual needs and unique situations of each set of parents and children.

Optimal parenting may often appear to be simply a matter of "doing what comes naturally." However, it also requires the support of a society that values this early phase of development enough to offer parents the time and financial cushion necessary to nurture the emerging relationship.

NOTE

Acknowledgments. Many of the ideas in this chapter were developed during a postdoctoral appointment at the Max Planck Institute for Psychiatry in Munich, while on leave from the Department of Child Development and Family Relations at the University of North Carolina–Greensboro. The support of the Alexander von Humboldt Foundation and the Max Planck Society is gratefully acknowledged, as are the intellectual stimulation and opportunity for collaborative research provided by Hanuš and Mechthild Papoušek.

REFERENCES

Belsky, Jay (1986). "Infant Day Care: A Cause for Concern?" *Zero to Three* 6 (5): 1–7.
———— (1987). "Risks Remain." *Zero to Three* 7 (3): 22–24.
Belsky, Jay, and Lawrence Steinberg (1978). "The Effects of Day Care: A Critical Review." *Child Development* 49: 929–49.
Brazelton, T. Berry, Barbara Koslowski, and Mary Main (1974). "The Origins of Reciprocity: The Early Mother–Infant Interaction." In Michael

Lewis and Leonard Rosenblum, eds., *The Effect of the Infant on Its Caregiver*. New York: John Wiley.

Chase-Lansdale, P. Lindsay, and Margaret T. Owen (1987). "Maternal Employment in a Family Context: Effects on Infant–Mother and Infant–Father Attachments." *Child Development* 58: 1505–12.

DeCasper, Anthony J., and William P. Fifer (1980). "Of Human Bonding: Newborns Prefer Their Mothers' Voices." *Science* 208: 1174–76.

Dittrichová, Jaroslava (1969). "The Development of Sleep in Infancy." In R. J. Robinson, ed., *Brain and Early Behavior*. New York: Academic Press.

Dreyfus-Brisac, C. (1974). "Organization of Sleep in Prematures: Implications for Caretaking." In Michael Lewis and Leonard Rosenblum, eds., *The Effect of the Infant on Its Caregiver*. New York: John Wiley.

Fogel, Alan (1984). *Infancy: Infant, Family, and Society*. St. Paul: West.

Hock, Ellen (1980). "Working and Nonworking Mothers and Their Infants: A Comparative Study of Maternal Caregiving Characteristics and Infant Social Behavior." *Merrill–Palmer Quarterly* 26: 79–101.

Kaye, Kenneth (1982). *The Mental and Social Life of Babies: How Parents Create Persons*. Chicago: University of Chicago Press.

Koester, Lynne Sanford (1987). "Multimodal, Repetitive Stimulation in Parent–Infant Interactions: A Look at Micro-Rhythms." Paper presented at the biennial meetings of the Society for Research in Child Development, Baltimore, Md., April 23–26.

Koester, Lynne Sanford, Hanuš Papoušek, and Mechthild Papoušek (1987). "Psychobiological Models of Infant Development: Influences on the Concept of Intuitive Parenting." In Helga Rauh and Hans Christoph Steinhausen, eds., *Psychobiology and Early Development*. New York and Amsterdam: Elsevier Science Publishers.

——— (1989). "Patterns of Rhythmic Stimulation by Mothers with Three-Month-Olds: A Cross-Modal Comparison." *International Journal of Behavioral Development* 12(2): 143–54.

Korner, Anneliese F. (1979). "Conceptual Issues in Infancy Research." In Joy D. Osofsky, ed., *Handbook of Infant Development*. New York: John Wiley.

Papoušek, Hanuš, and Mechthild Papoušek (1981). "How Human Is the Human Newborn, and What Else Is to Be Done?" In Kathleen Bloom, ed., *Prospective Issues in Infancy Research*. Hillsdale, N.J.: Erlbaum.

——— (1987). "Intuitive Parenting: A Dialectic Counterpart to the Infant's Precocity in Integrative Capacities." In Joy D. Osofsky, ed., *Handbook of Infant Development* (2d ed.). New York: John Wiley.

Papoušek, Hanus, Mechthild Papoušek, and Lynne Sanford Koester (1987). "Sharing Emotionality and Sharing Knowledge: A Microanalytic Approach to Parent–Infant Communication." In Carroll E. Izard and Peter Read, eds., *Measuring Emotions in Infants and Children*. Cambridge: Cambridge University Press.

Phillips, Deborah, Kathleen McCartney, Sandra Scarr, and Carollee Howes

(1987). "Selective Review of Infant Day Care Research: A Cause for Concern!" *Zero to Three* 7 (3): 18–21.

Schwartz, Pamela (1983). "Length of Day-Care Attendance and Attachment Behavior in Eighteen-Month-Old Infants." *Child Development* 54: 1073–78.

Stern, Daniel N., Beatrice Beebe, Joseph Jaffe, Stephen Bennett (1977). "The Infant's Stimulus World During Social Interaction: A Study of Caregiver Behaviors with Particular Reference to Repetition and Timing." In H. Rudolph Schaffer, ed., *Studies in Mother-Infant Interaction*. London: Academic Press.

Tronick, Edward (1981). "Infant Communicative Intent: The Infant's Reference to Social Interaction." In Rachel E. Stark, ed., *Language Behavior in Infancy and Early Childhood*. New York and Amsterdam: Elsevier Science Publishers.

Tronick, Edward, Heidelise Als, and Lauren Adamson (1979). "Structure of Early Face-to-Face Communicative Interactions." In Margaret Bullowa, ed., *Before Speech: The Beginnings of Human Communication*. Cambridge: Cambridge University Press.

Vaughn, Brian E., Kathleen E. Deane, and Everett Waters (1985). "The Impact of Out-of-Home Care on Child–Mother Attachment Quality: Another Look at Some Enduring Questions." In Inge Bretherton and Everett Waters, eds., *Growing Points in Attachment Theory and Research*. Monographs of the Society for Research in Child Development, vol. 50. Serial no. 209. Chicago: University of Chicago Press.

Zigler, Edward F., and Susan Muenchow (1983). "Infant Day Care and Infant-Care Leaves: A Policy Vacuum." *American Psychologist* 38: 91–94.

20 The Child Care Preferences of Parents with Young Children: How Little Is Known

Freya L. Sonenstein

Since the end of World War II, mothers with pre-school-aged children have increasingly entered the labor force, but the past decade has brought a further dramatic change—the remarkable rise in the employment of mothers with infants. Whereas 31 percent of new mothers were in the labor force in 1976, the proportion passed the 50 percent mark in 1986 (O'Connell and Bloom, 1987). In 1988, 52 percent of mothers with children under the age of three were in the labor force (Zill, 1989).

Various explanations have been offered for this shift. Some have argued that the economic squeeze experienced by the baby boomers maturing in the 1970s pushed both parents into the labor market as these families struggled to maintain their standard of living (Levy and Michel, 1986). Others have stressed the pull of the labor market as women's expectations have expanded to include occupational roles. This change occurred gradually over the twentieth century, but was jolted by the feminist movement in the late 1960s and the 1970s. However, whether mothers of young children have been pushed or pulled into the labor force, demands for increased child care services and expanded parental leave options have resulted. What forms of care do parents with very young children prefer? And, specifically, what are the preferences of low-income, welfare mothers, who face especially constricted choices and who are often targeted for special assistance by public policy? The available evidence is limited.

Although most of the recent policy debates about child care have paid lip service to the importance of maximizing parental choice, in practice parental preferences have rarely been considered when child care policy was formulated. Indeed, what parents want has been considered so unimportant that 15 years have passed since the last national survey of parents as potential child care consumers (Unco, 1975). Meanwhile, the employment of mothers has grown and initiatives have been launched to expand publicly supported child care and to require employers to provide dependent care leave. Proponents of these initiatives argue that they represent parents' interests, and it is clear that public opinion does support some expansion of options. However, it is not clear what the exact mix of options should be, nor what the take-up rate for different options would be if parents were able to exercise more choice in making child care arrangements. More information about what parents would like is therefore crucial to the development of child care policies that are responsive to parents' needs.

The measurement of parental preferences regarding child care has proven to be an uncommonly difficult task. Two approaches are offered in the literature. The first assumes that child care operates like any other economic market in which consumers of the service purchase an arrangement that maximizes their preferences at a price that fits their monetary resources. If the child care market is performing well—that is, the supply of child care is responsive to changes in demand—then the actual child care arrangements that parents make reflect their preferences. Using this approach, one might argue that utilization patterns reveal what parents want and are therefore the correct measure of parents' preferences.[1]

A second approach assumes that child care choices are often made under conditions in which the supply of available and affordable options is very constricted. If these conditions prevail, the arrangements that parents use may not necessarily reflect their preferences. When asked, these parents will say that they would prefer alternative arrangements. The second approach, therefore, is to ask parents hypothetical questions about the forms of child care they would prefer if existing constraints were not operating. Parents' answers to these hypothetical questions are believed to reveal their real child care preferences. Although this approach corrects for the questionable assumption that actual choices generally reflect preferences, it is problematic from a different perspective. The hypothetical nature of the questions offers no assurance that parents will actually behave in accordance with their answers. If, in fact, some of the market constraints were removed, we do not know whether parents would actually implement the child care choices they predict they would make. For example, in the Gary and Seattle/Denver Income Experiments, free or low-cost licensed child care was offered to the participants in these welfare demonstration projects, but the number of parents using this service was much lower than expected (Kurz, Robins, and Spiegelman, 1975).

The research literature therefore offers two imperfect approaches to measuring parents' child care preferences. In this chapter we will examine the evidence from this literature about parents' preferences for child care for young children. Two types of choices will be examined: (1) the choice between parental care and nonparental care, and (2) the choice among nonparental arrangements. Actual child care utilization patterns will be examined as well as hypothetical answers to questions about desired child care characteristics. Whenever possible, the presentation of the evidence will be limited to findings related to families with children under the age of one.

Preferences for Parental Versus Nonparental Care

Utilization patterns for the winter of 1984–85 indicate that just under two-thirds of U.S. children under the age of one were primarily cared for by their parents. These children include those whose mothers were not employed (52 percent in 1985), those whose mothers cared for them while they were employed (4 percent in 1984–85), and those whose fathers were their primary caretakers while their mothers were employed (9 percent in 1984–85). The remaining children (35 percent) were primarily cared for by relatives, family day care providers, and centers while their parents were employed.[2] If behavior reveals preferences, then approximately two-thirds of U.S. parents could be said to prefer parental care as the primary mode of care for children under the age of one.

There is also some evidence from hypothetical data that parental care is considered the ideal form of care for young children by many U.S. parents, even when the other forms of care are actually used. For example, in a recent *USA Today* poll of 439 employed parents with children under the age of 13 (1988), 77 percent of fathers and 70 percent of mothers responded affirmatively to the following hypothetical question: "If money was not a factor, would you or your spouse stay home to care for your child?" Breakdowns of these responses by children's ages were not available.

Karen Mason and Karen Kuhlthau (1989) examined the child care ideals of mothers of pre-school-aged children in the greater Detroit metropolitan area, asking, "What kind of daytime care is ideal for children at different ages, that is, care that is best for the child's happiness" under different scenarios. One scenario was "when a family has no financial worries." For children under the age of one, parental care was chosen under this scenario by 97 percent of non-employed mothers and 64 percent of employed mothers. About 3 percent of the nonemployed mothers and 36 percent of the employed mothers chose nonparental care: child care centers and nursery schools (0.5 percent of nonemployed mothers, 1 percent of employed mothers); care by relatives (2 percent of nonemployed mothers, 31 percent of employed mothers); care by nonrelatives (1 percent of nonemployed mothers, 3 percent of employed mothers). These data show that if money were no object, the majority of mothers might be expected to prefer parental care for children under the age of one. Among employed mothers, care by relatives would probably be the next most frequently chosen option.

The Detroit study also shows that parental preferences shift as children grow older. When the same respondents were asked about the ideal kind of care for children between the ages of three and four when a family has no financial worries, 68 percent of the nonemployed respondents and 42 percent of the employed respondents still chose parental care. However, almost one-third of the nonemployed mothers and over half of the employed mothers now chose nonparental options: nursery schools and child care programs (26 percent of the nonemployed mothers, 34 percent of the employed mothers), or care by relatives (5 percent of the nonemployed mothers, 31 percent of employed mothers). Care by nonrelatives remained an infrequently chosen option (2 percent of nonemployed mothers, 4 percent of employed mothers). Thus, while large proportions of employed and nonemployed respondents preferred parental care for infants when a family has no financial worries, the proportions expressing this preference were significantly lower when the scenario asked about children between the ages of three and four.

The *USA Today* poll and the Detroit study asked parents to choose ideal arrangements when money was not a factor. Other researchers have examined data gained in response to different hypothetical questions that do not remove financial constraints but still try to assess what parents want. For example, Harriet Presser (1989) reports analyses of the May 1985 Current Population Survey, which asked employed mothers, "If you had a choice, would you prefer to: (1) work the same hours and earn the same money, (2) work fewer hours at the same rate of pay and earn less, or (3) work more hours at the same rate of pay and earn more money?" In response to this question, two-thirds of married mothers employed full time who had children under the age of six preferred their present arrangement (option 1), while 17 percent preferred fewer hours and 17 percent preferred more. Among unmarried mothers, 61 percent preferred their present arrangement, 35 percent desired more hours of work and higher earnings (option 3), and only 4 percent preferred fewer. Presser reports that the proportions were virtually the same for the employed mothers of children under the age of one. From these data she concludes that the majority of mothers of young children who are employed full time would not opt to take unpaid parental leave if it were offered.

As for mothers who are not employed, there is some evidence that a portion of them would seek employment if child care were available at a reasonable cost. In this case, the constraint removed in the hypothetical question is the lack of available and affordable child care. In 1982, when this question was posed in a special Census Bureau survey of mothers of children under the age of five, 26 percent of nonemployed mothers indicated that they would look for work if such child care were available. The proportion was similar among nonemployed mothers with children under the age of one (U.S. Bureau of the Census, 1983). Further analyses of these data by Martin O'Connell and David Bloom (1987) indicate that the proportions of nonemployed mothers answering yes to this question were higher among never-married women (50 percent), black women (52 percent), women who had never finished high school (36 percent), and women from low-income families (36 percent). This evidence suggests that if affordable child care were available, perhaps as many as one-quarter of the nonemployed mothers of young children might "prefer" to be employed. Among mothers in poverty, the proportion might be substantially higher.

It is clear that actual care arrangements of infants may not necessarily reflect parental preferences. Among mothers at home, there are those who say they would seek employment if affordable child care were available. Among employed mothers who use nonparental care, there are those who would prefer to be at home if there were no economic impact on the family from staying home, but who might opt for their current employment status if there were such an impact. Presumably there are also employed mothers who would currently prefer parental care to their present form of nonparental care but who might have different preferences if other alternatives were available. For example, an employed mother currently using a low-quality arrangement might prefer to provide her own child care if she could afford to forego earnings. However, if she were offered an affordable, high-quality arrangement (evaluated according to her own criteria), she might *not* choose parental care. The crux of this decision rests on how parents define high-quality care, care that fits their ideals. To answer this question we must turn to the research evidence about what parents want in their child care arrangements.

Preferences Among Child Care Arrangements

National data about the child care arrangements preferred by the parents of very young children are limited. Data do exist about the arrangements that parents use. Some of the use patterns may reflect choice, and some may reflect compromises reached at the time the parent searched for child care. In the winter of 1984–85, more than one-quarter of children under age one with employed mothers used parental care arrangements.[3] Of the remaining children in nonparental care arrangements, 38 percent were primarily cared for by their grandmothers or other relatives, 14 percent in the child's home and 24 percent in someone else's home. Another 43 percent were cared for by nonrelatives, usually outside the child's home; and 19 percent were in organized child care facilities. (U.S. Bureau of the Census, 1987).

The distribution of arrangements for children of three and four with employed mothers was different. Twenty-two percent of these children were cared for by their fathers or their mothers, a proportion just slightly lower than that for children under the age of one. However, among the remaining children in nonparental care, 27 percent were cared for by relatives, 29 percent were cared for by nonrelatives, and 44 percent were in organized child care facilities. Thus, as children grow older, the child care use patterns indicate that preferences for organized child care facilities may rise substantially, while preferences for care by relatives and nonrelatives drop.

Another potential indicator of parents' child care preferences is how satisfied they are with their present care arrangements. In general, very few parents report that they are "dissatisfied." For example, in the last national survey of child care consumers conducted in 1975, less than 10 percent of the parents voiced dissatisfaction with their present arrangements (Unco, 1975). This measure has been severely criticized, because it may be difficult for parents to admit that their children are in unsatisfactory child care. Alternatively, high levels of satisfaction may indicate that unsatisfactory arrangements are quickly terminated, so that their numbers are small in cross-sectional samples. In the same 1975 consumer survey, however, almost one-quarter of the parents said that they would like to change their present arrangement (Hofferth and Phillips, 1987).

More recent data are available from a 1988 Random-Digit Dialing telephone survey of 989 employed[4] mothers of children under six in three low-income cities: Camden and Newark, New Jersey, and South Chicago. These mothers were asked whether they would prefer some other child care arrangement for their child "if all arrangements were available free of charge." Mothers of fewer than one-third of the children in each site reported that they would prefer something else (27 percent in South Chicago, 31 percent in Newark, and 32 percent in Camden). The authors of this study report that the mothers of children under the age of one appeared more satisfied with their arrangements than the mothers of older children, at least in two of the sites, because the proportions preferring another arrangement were much lower (16 percent in South Chicago, 24 percent in Newark). Although mothers of older pre-school-aged children were likely to say that they wanted a change so that their children would learn more, the mothers of children under one were more likely to cite convenience of location or hours as the main reason for wanting a change. When a change was desired, care in a child care center or a preschool program was the preferred arrangement for pre-school-aged children of all ages, although the proportions were a little lower for children under the age of one. There were no differences across present child care arrangement types in the mothers' reported preferences for a change (Kisker et al., 1989).

These data indicate that as many as two-thirds of employed parents of pre-school-aged children may be satisfied with their present arrangements. When a change is desired, the overwhelming preference is for a formal program in a center or preschool, suggesting that these programs should be expanded so that they are available at affordable prices. We are, of course, extrapolating from data obtained in three localities. New national data will be available from the 1990 National Child Care Survey (Hofferth, 1990).

Child Care Preferences Among Welfare Mothers

More detailed information about child care preferences is available in a study of welfare mothers (Sonenstein and Wolf, 1988) developed to explore the forms of child care and child care subsidies that are related to successful transitions off welfare. This question has become increasingly important as the role of Aid to Families with Dependent Children has changed. The AFDC system was crafted in the 1930s to assist mothers to stay home; now its role is to assist mothers to become self-sufficient. The Family Support Act, which created welfare reform in 1988, requires the participation of mothers with children over two years of age (or over one year, at state option) in employment programs. For these mothers, the option of parental care has been foreclosed.

The study sample consisted of 554 AFDC mothers with children under the age of 10 randomly drawn from welfare rolls in Boston, Charlotte, and Denver in 1983. The sample was stratified to oversample mothers with earnings; in the subsequent analyses, sampling weights are applied to make the results generalizable to mothers on the caseloads in the three cities. The analyses in this chapter are limited to the 204 mothers in the sample with children under the age of three. The mothers were followed over a 14-month period through two interviews, one 8 months after the sample selection data and the second 6 months after the first interview. In the two interviews, retrospective information was gathered in a life events format about the respondent's employment, training, school participation, job search, and child care arrangements. In addition, case record data were abstracted for the 14-month period.

Over the 14 months, 63 percent of the mothers with children under the age of three reported that they had used a child care arrangement for their youngest child at least once while they were employed, looking for work, or going to school or a training program. Among those who used child care, more than two-thirds (68 percent) had most recently used relatives as the main source of care (43 percent in the home, 25 percent outside the home). In addition, 16 percent used care by nonrelatives and 16 percent used care in a child care center or nursery school (see Table 20.1). In this sample, the utilization patterns indicate a preponderance of care by relatives, not unlike the results of the Camden, Newark, and South Chicago study when adjustments are made for the fact that the latter study included arrangements for children up to seven years of age (Kisker et al., 1989). If preferences are revealed in actual utilization patterns, one might conclude that the mothers in our study preferred care by relatives.

However, at a separate point in the first interview with the mothers, we asked them to look at a card listing different kinds of child care arrangements and to indicate which would be their first choice for their youngest child, if they could choose any one at all.[5] Table 20.1 contrasts the mothers' first-choice child care arrangements with their actual ones. Only 36 percent of the mothers using

TABLE 20.1
Actual versus Preferred Child Care Arrangements of Welfare Mothers with
Youngest Child Under Three Years of Age (Weighted Percentages)

Type of Arrangement[c]	Actual Arrangement (N = 153)	Percent in Preferred Arrangement (N = 153)	Preferred Arrangement	
			Users[a] (N = 153)	Nonusers[b] (N = 51)
Relative in home	42.7	41.2	26.6	29.2
Relative out of home	25.2	28.9	24.7	28.9
Nonrelative	16.3	1.6	1.6	0
Center/preschool	15.8	70.8	47.1	41.9
Total	100	36.3	100	100

Notes:
[a]Mothers who used child care in the 14-month period
[b]Mothers who did not use child care in the 14-month period
[c]Main arrangement

child care in the study were using an arrangement that would be their first choice if they could choose any at all. There were distinct differences by child care type. Mothers using child care centers and preschool programs appear to have their first choice arrangement 71 percent of the time, whereas mothers using relatives in the home had their first choice 41 percent of the time. The proportions were even lower for mothers using relative care outside the child's home (29 percent) and for mothers using nonrelative care—care by babysitters and family day care home providers (2 percent).

The first-choice child care arrangement of mothers using care in the study was care by relatives either in or outside their own homes: 51 percent chose this option. Organized child care programs were almost as popular (47 percent). Very few of the mothers indicated a preference for care by a nonrelative. Mothers who had not used child care in the last 14 months expressed preferences similar to those of mothers who had used child care.

These data indicate a serious mismatch between the child care arrangements that welfare mothers prefer and the arrangements that they actually make. Sixty-four percent of the mothers were using arrangements for their children under three that were not their first choice. According to these reports, group care is preferred by almost half the mothers, although only 16 percent actually use it. Relative care was preferred by 51 percent of the mothers, yet the proportion using it was substantially higher (68 percent). These findings suggest that policies that expand the range of group care options for very young children would be consistent with the preferences of many welfare mothers.

Mothers in the sample were also asked to indicate the characteristics of care that would be important when they looked for care for their youngest children. A list of characteristics was read, and the respondent categorized each one as "very important," "important," or "not very important." Table 20.2 displays the proportions of mothers with children under three who thought the listed characteristics were "very important." The characteristics receiving the highest ratings from the most mothers were (1) reliability and dependability of the caregiver, (2) cleanliness and safety, (3) cost, and (4) sick child care. Mothers who had used child care in the past 14 months showed some interesting differences from mothers who had not. Child care users were significantly more likely to give higher importance to (1) the child's having a chance to learn new things, (2) care when the child is sick, (3) convenience to home or work, and (4) convenient hours. In contrast, nonusers gave higher importance to affordability, suggesting that cost may be a barrier for them.

So far we have examined what mothers *say* they would prefer in their child care arrangements for children under three. Since articu-

TABLE 20.2
Proportion of Welfare Mothers Rating Child Care Characteristics
"Very Important" (Weighted Percentages)

Characteristics	Nonuser (N = 51)	User (N = 153)	Total (N = 204)
Reliable and dependable	82.2	85.9	84.5
Experienced caregiver	77.8	65.7	70.4
Special training in child care	62.2	64.3	63.5
Warm and loving person	68.9	76.1	73.3
Discipline given	48.9	57.7	54.3
Chance to learn new things	64.4*	77.5*	72.4
Clean and safe	71.1*	85.9*	80.2
Cares for sick child	77.8*	90.1*	85.3
Convenient location	37.8*	54.9*	48.3
Convenient hours	18.1*	41.4*	59.5
Affordable	82.2	78.6	80.0
Child likes arrangement	60.0	59.2	59.5
Adult supervision	73.3	78.9	76.7

Note:
*Difference significant at .05 level.

lated preferences may not always predict actual behavior, we examined which care characteristics contributed the most to a mother's reported satisfaction with her most recent child care arrangement. An ordered logistic multiple regression specification (Walker and Duncan, 1967) was used to fit models of mothers' satisfaction with care arrangement for their youngest child. In these analyses satisfaction levels were coded "0" for "not very or not at all satisfied"; "1" for "somewhat satisfied"; "2" for "mostly satisfied"; and "3" for "completely satisfied." Half (51 percent) of the mothers reported that they were completely satisfied with their youngest child's care arrangement; 23 percent were mostly satisfied; 13 percent were somewhat satisfied; and 13 percent were not satisfied.

Initially a model was specified containing the types of care arrangement (relative care in home, relative care out of home, group care, and nonrelative care—the omitted category) and other variables anticipated to affect mothers' satisfaction with child care. These other variables included demographic descriptors of the mother (race, education level, number of children under nine years old, and city of residence), other descriptors of the child care arrangement (number of arrangements she had simultaneously, and number of hours in main child care arrangement), and descriptors of her main activity when she used this care arrangement (looking for work, going to school, and working—the omitted category). This model of the predictors of satisfaction had very little estimated explanatory power ($R = .000$), but four variables emerged as significant independent predictors of satisfaction. The number of children the mother had under the age of nine was negatively associated with satisfaction, as was the number of child care arrangements made for the youngest child and residence in Charlotte. Care in a center or preschool program was positively associated with satisfaction.

At the second step of the analyses, the mother's rating of her child's most recent arrangement on each of the characteristics of care listed in Table 20.2 was also entered into the model. These variables increased the estimated explanatory power of the model, and several emerged as significant independent predictors of satisfaction: the number of days the mother had to stay home from work in the past 8 months because child care was not available, an indicator of reliability, and a negative predictor, and convenience of hours and location, each of which predicted higher levels of satisfaction. When the mother rated adult supervision of her child as just right, satisfaction was higher; but when she rated her arrangement as having just enough discipline when her child misbehaved, her satisfaction was lower. While the number of arrangements made for the youngest child remained a significant predictor of satisfaction, care in a center or preschool was no longer a significant independent predictor in the second model. This shift suggests that a mother's ratings of specific care characteristics are more directly related to her satisfaction than whether care occurred in a particular type of arrangement. Residence in Boston replaced residence in Charlotte as a significant predictor of satisfaction, and the sign of coefficient changed, indicating a positive association with satisfaction.

These analyses point to the importance of specific characteristics for explaining reported satisfaction with child care arrangements. In particular, a number of factors related to convenience are associated with satisfaction. These include the number of arrangements a mother had to make, the number of days missed from work because the arrangement was not available, location, and hours. This finding for the mothers of very young children is corroborated in the recent study of child care in Camden, Newark, and South Chicago (Kisker et al., 1989). While care type (specifically center or preschool) was associated with higher satisfaction levels before the ratings of individual care characteristics were entered into the model, its salience disappeared after these ratings were added. This finding suggests that the characteristics of care are more directly related to mothers' satisfaction than whether care takes place in a center or a family day care home or is provided by relatives. Yet most survey research to date has failed to make distinctions beyond this simple typology.

The analyses are also revealing for the variables that were shown *not* to contribute independently to the mother's satisfaction with child care. Although adult–child ratio and the specialized training of caregivers are commonly used in the literature as indicators—admittedly rough ones—of the quality of child care arrangements, they added little to the explanatory power of the model of mothers' satisfaction.[6] Instead of focusing on these criteria, mothers in our sample appear more concerned about the location of the arrangement and avoiding the need to make multiple arrangements or to lose days from work.

This examination of the child care preferences of welfare mothers points up the mismatch between what mothers say they want in terms of child care for their young children, what they get, and what policy advocates think they should get. Only one-third of the mothers of children under three were using the arrangements that would be their first choice. Just over half the mothers indicated that care by relatives would be their first choice, while just under half selected formal, group-based programs. Very few parents opted for nonrelative care as a first choice, even though family day care homes are considered by many professionals as desirable arrangements for very young children. This finding suggests a certain dissonance between professional and parental child care agendas. Further evidence of dissonance can be seen in the mismatch between the characteristics of care that contribute most to parental satisfaction and the characteristics that are considered by some professionals to be indicative of the quality of care. While the ratio of adults to children and the training of the caretakers are often used as indicators of quality in licensing regulations, for example, these characteristics had no significant independent effect on levels of parental satisfaction in the multivariate model.

Summary and Conclusions

The study of welfare mothers indicates that parents' child care objectives do not necessarily mesh with public child care policy objectives. For the U.S. population of parents in general, there are no data available to assess the discrepancies between parents' preferences, their actual child care situations, and the remedies advocated in public policy discussions. The National Child Care Survey conducted in 1990 may remedy this situation (Hofferth, 1990). The absence of information in the past is perhaps one reason why policy has not been explicitly framed to address parents' concerns. Yet its absence may also be symptomatic of a lack of interest in these concerns.

A brief review of the limited available data suggests that descriptions of parents' current child care patterns are not sufficient to reveal their preferences. There are clearly some parents who use alternative child care arrangements when they would prefer to provide the care themselves, and there are parents who care for their own children but who would seek employment if alternative care were available. Among the users of various types of child care, there are parents who are not using arrangements that they consider ideal.

Data from studies of low-income and welfare populations suggest that these parents are the least likely to have their preferred arrangement. Low-income mothers who are not employed and are therefore providing parental care to their children are the most likely to say that they would seek employment if affordable child care were available (U.S. Bureau of the Census, 1983). Among welfare mothers who used child care while they worked, only one-third used the arrangement that would be their first choice.

There is some evidence that parental care is considered ideal for infants by the majority of parents, especially if money is no object. Financial constraints are, however, extremely difficult to remove. When parental care cannot be arranged, care by relatives, child care centers, and preschools are said to be preferred alternatives. It is troublesome that in several studies (Kisker et al., 1989; Sonenstein and Wolf, 1988; Unco, 1975), very few parents select family day care homes as a preferred arrangement. National data indicate that 23 percent of employed mothers with infants used family day care homes in 1984–85. Either there are a lot of parents using family day care regardless of their preferences, or there is something wrong with the way the preference questions have been posed in the past. This discrepancy points up the need for far more refined techniques for measuring parents' child care preferences.

The study of welfare mothers suggests that parents using child care may be more concerned about location, hours, and dependability than about aspects of quality that might be important to child care professionals. Agencies and policymakers may focus on quality to the detriment of the convenience factors. For example, one-third of the employed mothers in the welfare study worked in the evening, when child care centers and preschools are generally not available. If public resources directed to increasing child care quality are concentrated on programs that operate during regular business hours, the needs of many parents may not be met. The potential mismatch between what parents and professionals want also suggests the need for educational efforts to help parents choose arrangements that will enhance their children's safety and development.

Clearly both parents' preferences and the quality and safety of programs need to be addressed when child care policy is framed. This coordination of concerns cannot happen until more reliable information is available about what parents want and need. There is a corollary need for more information about the components of child care quality. Furthermore, research should also address the issue of whether parents' dissatisfaction and stress regarding their actual child care arrangements lead to developmental decrements for their children. Is it bad for children when their unemployed parents would prefer to be employed or when their employed parents would prefer to be at home? Is it bad for children when their employed parents experience stress related to child care arrangements that they do not consider ideal?

Much more research needs to be done before a knowledge base is available to inform the public policy debate about parental leave and child care options. This information is crucial for ensuring that child care programs and policies are indeed responsive to the needs of all parents and children. Particular attention should be paid to addressing the needs of low-income and welfare families, whose care options are perhaps the most limited of all. A full 30 percent of U.S. children under six lived in families that received welfare at least once during a 32-month period between 1983 and 1986 (U.S. Bureau of the Census, 1989). When parental leave and child care policies are framed, the preferences of parents in these families should not be ignored.

NOTES

Acknowledgments. Funding for this research was provided by the Rockefeller Foundation and the U.S. Department of Health and Human Services.

1. A number of recent reports and papers have emphasized the economic model of the child care market. See the series of working papers prepared for the Child Care Action Campaign (1988) and a report by Rachel Connelly (1988) for examples.

2. These statistics were developed using U.S. Bureau of the Census data on the employment participation rates of mothers of newborns, cited in O'Connell and Bloom (1987), and U.S. Bureau of the Census (1987) data on the primary child care arrangements of employed mothers.

3. Of children under the age of one with employed mothers, 18.2 percent were primarily cared for by their fathers, and 8.1 percent were cared for by their mothers while they worked (U.S. Bureau of the Census, 1987).

4. The employed mothers category also includes mothers who were in school or job training.

5. The choices were as follows: care by child's brother or sister, child's grandparent, other relative of the child; care by nonrelative of the child; mother watching child at work; mother working at home; child caring for him- or herself; child in school; child in nursery school/preschool/Head Start; and child in day care center. A second question asked if the care would be in the child's home or somewhere else.

6. These two variables were added to the first-step model, but the explanatory power of the model did not increase, and they were not significant. Thus, they were subsequently incorporated into the second model along with the ratings of other characteristics of care.

REFERENCES

Child Care Action Campaign (1988). "Child Care and the Bottom Line: An Ecocomic and Child Care Policy Paper." New York: Child Care Action Campaign.

Connelly, Rachel (1988). "Utilizing Market Child Care: An Economic Framework for Considering the Policy Issues." Paper presented at the National Academy of Science, New York, February.

Hofferth, Sandra L. (1990). "Enrollment in Preschool Programs." Paper presented at annual meeting of the American Educational Research Association, Boston, Massachusetts, April 16–20.

Hofferth, Sandra L., and Deborah Phillips (1987). "Child Care in the United States, 1970 to 1995." *Journal of Marriage and the Family* 49: 559–71.

Kisker, Ellen E., Rebecca Maynard, Ann Gordon, and Margaret Strain (1989). "The Child Care Challenge: What Parents Need and What Is Available in Three Metropolitan Areas." Princeton, N.J.: Mathematica Policy Research, Inc.

Kurz, Mordecai, Philip K. Robins, and Robert Spiegelman (1975). "A Study of the Demand for Child Care by Working Mothers." Research Memorandum 27. Stanford, Calif.: Center for the Study of Social Policy, Stanford Research Institute.

Levy, Frank S., and Richard C. Michel (1986). "An Economic Bust for the Baby Boom." *Challenge*, March–April, pp. 33–39.

Mason, Karen O., and Karen Kuhlthau (1989). "Determinants of Child Care Ideals Among the Mothers of Preschool Children." *Journal of Marriage and the Family* 51: 593–603.

O'Connell, Martin, and David Bloom (1987). *Juggling Jobs and Babies: America's Child Care Challenge.* Population Trends and Public Policy Pamphlet No. 12. Washington, D.C.: Population Reference Bureau.

Presser, Harriet B. (1989). "Can We Make Time for Children? The Economy, Work Schedules and Child Care." Presidential address, annual meeting of the Population Association of America, Baltimore, Md.

Sonenstein, Freya L., and Douglas A. Wolf (1988). "Caring for the Children of Welfare Mothers." Paper presented at the annual meeting of the Population Association of America, New Orleans, Louisiana.

Unco, Inc. (1975). *National Day Care Consumer Study: 1975.* 4 vols. Arlington, Va.: Unco.

U.S. Bureau of the Census (1983). "Child Care Arrangements of Working Mothers: June 1982." *Current Population Reports*, no. 129. Series P-23. Washington, D.C.: Government Printing Office.

—— (1987). "Who's Minding the Kids? Child Care Arrangements: Winter 1984–1985." *Current Population Reports*, no. 9. Series P-70. Washington, D.C.: Government Printing Office.

—— (1989). "Characteristics of Persons Receiving Benefits from Major Assistance Programs." *Current Population Reports*, no. 14. Series P-70. Washington, D.C.: Government Printing Office.

USA Today Child Care Poll (1988). Unpublished tabulations. November 10–12.

Walker, S. H., and D. B. Duncan (1967). "Estimation of the Probability of an Event as a Function of Several Independent Variables." *Biometrika* 54: 167–79.

Zill, Nicholas (1989). *Basic Facts About the Use of Child Care and Preschool Services by Families in the U.S.* Washington, D.C.: Child Trends, Inc.

21 | The Regulation Controversy in Family Day Care: The Perspective of Providers

Margaret K. Nelson

Family day care, defined as "non-residential child care provided in a private home other than the child's own" (Fosburg et al., 1981, p. 1), is the prevalent form of out-of-home care for very young children. It accounts for 23 percent of the care of children under the age of one, 26.8 percent of the care of children aged one and two, and 17.7 percent of the care of children aged two and three (U.S. Bureau of the Census, 1987, p. 5). If paid and unpaid care by relatives (including grandparents) is included, these figures rise to a total of 40.6 percent for children under the age of one, 41.9 percent for children aged one and two, and 31.0 percent for children aged three and four (U.S. Bureau of the Census, 1987, p. 5).

Family day care is also much maligned. Critics are quick to acknowledge that family day care providers can offer excellent substitute care; they also note that there are wide variations in quality and that consumers are not always able to assess the level of care (Greenman, 1984; Jackson and Jackson, 1979; Kahn and Kamerman, 1987; Morgan, 1984; Sale, 1984b).

To many, regulation is one obvious and necessary solution to the problem family day care presents. Although divided about the best regulatory system, some child care advocates argue that effective monitoring can ensure at least minimal levels of safety for children (Class and Orton, 1980; Kendall and Walker, 1984; Morgan, 1979, 1984; NAEYC, 1987; Tobin, 1985; Young and Zigler, 1986). They also point to a number of additional possible benefits such as increasing the stability and reliability of day care providers and ensuring access to training (Anderson, 1986). Regulation thus enters the debate about family day care from the perspective of the consumers who will be protected by increased control over, and eventually a reshaping of, child care. Even when proponents acknowledge that the "rights" of consumers and providers might conflict, the bias is toward a concern for the most vulnerable party in the relationship—children who cannot speak for themselves (Morgan, 1984).

Although opponents of regulation draw on a different arsenal, they also generally ignore the needs and concerns of providers. Some argue on ideological grounds that it is inappropriate for the government to intervene in private arrangements between parents and caregivers, particularly when the care of relatives is involved (Alexander and Markowitz, 1982; Inman, 1982; Morgan et al., 1986). Others argue, on more practical grounds, that regulation has a deleterious effect on the supply of family day care providers, is unwieldy and ineffective, drives many providers "underground," and depletes scarce resources better allocated to salaries and direct services (Kahn and Kamerman, 1987; Morgan, 1979; Rose-Ackerman, 1983; see also Young and Zigler, 1986). By default, at this point the opponents of regulation can claim victory: although almost every state now has some system of licensing or registration on the books, observers estimate that between 50 and 90 percent of all family day care remains unregulated in fact (Morgan et al., 1986).

These debates take place in the context of limited data about providers' attitudes toward regulation. Because unregulated providers are difficult to locate, most studies of family day care have focused on regulated providers. As a result, relatively little is known about differences between the two groups and whether regulation has the intended effects. Even studies that explore noncompliance have relied on interviews only with regulated providers who attempt to guess why others evade regulation (Anderson, 1986; for exceptions, see Enarson, 1990; Fosburg et al., 1981).

This chapter attempts to replace guesswork with data, exploring reasons for providers' resistance to regulation and suggesting that their attitudes toward, and decisions about, regulation are reflections of major dilemmas they encounter in their relationships with children, parents, and their own family members. Providers attempt to balance competing affective and contractual claims; they also attempt to maintain autonomy with respect to the conditions of their work. A comparison of registered and unregistered providers demonstrates that the differences between them have to do with the availability of resources and the needs or interests with which they address the same occupational concerns.

Methods

My data come from two complementary sources. In the summer of 1986 I mailed a questionnaire to each of the 463 registered day care providers in the state of Vermont; responses were received from 225 (a response rate of 49 percent). The following summer I distributed a similar questionnaire to 110 unregistered family day care providers located through snowball sampling techniques. (While I was distributing these questionnaires, an additional 10 registered providers completed the survey.) Only 2 of the providers surveyed were men. The questionnaires covered a range of issues, including the number of years in child care, reasons for opening a day care home, characteristics of children in care, working conditions, attitudes toward child care, problems, and background information.

Much of the analysis relies on another methodology. Over a two-year period, I conducted lengthy, semistructured interviews with 28 registered providers (21 of whom also completed questionnaires) and 39 unregistered providers (10 of whom also completed questionnaires). Interviews dealt with such issues as relations with children and parents, the impact of the work on the provider's family, attitudes toward government regulation, and sources of stress and satisfaction. The interviews were conducted in the provider's home and lasted at least one hour; many ran considerably longer.

Family day care as an occupation for women in Vermont does not draw from an underclass. In fact, family day care providers are quite representative of the population of Vermont women as a whole (and are therefore also similar to those who use their services). Median family income among the providers falls into the $20,000 to $25,000 category; in 1980 median family income in Vermont was $21,137 for households where the husband was present and the wife was employed (U.S. Bureau of the Census, 1980). Providers' previous occupations were distributed among the major occupational groups, much as Vermont's female labor force as a whole is (Nelson, 1988). Vermont's population is extremely homogeneous in terms of race; 99 percent of the population is white (U.S. Bureau of the Census, 1980). All of the women interviewed for this study were white.

In spite of its racial homogeneity, Vermont is an appropriate research site for two reasons. First, although most data about family day care focus on urban populations, it is, in fact, a more common form of child care in rural areas (Fosburg et al., 1981). Second, Vermont's two-tiered system of regulation, which offers both licensing (used primarily by day care centers) and voluntary registration (for family day care homes), represents a current trend in regulatory efforts (Adams, 1982; Collins 1983; Dames, 1983). This new regulatory pattern has contradictory aspects: on the one hand, because rules for registration are generally much less stringent than those applying to licensed facilities, it is perceived by some to be a form of deregulation (Adams, 1984; Cohen and Zigler, 1978; Kendall and Walker, 1984; Young and Zigler, 1986); on the other hand, because of this "loosening of standards," it attracts larger numbers of providers and thus brings more homes within the regulatory net (Adams, 1984; Kendall and Walker, 1984; Sale, 1984a).

In Vermont, registration is required of those who offer care to children from more than two families. A registered provider may care for no more than six children of preschool age on a full-time basis and no more than four school-aged children on a part-time basis. (The provider's own children are not included in these numbers.) At the time of this study, registration guidelines focused on such safety issues as smoke detectors, furnace inspection, and first aid kits; there were no training requirements. Registered providers, however, were informed of conferences, received a monthly newsletter, and some were visited by outreach workers. Only registered providers can have their names placed on lists made available to potential clients by Information and Referral Centers, offer care for children who are supported by the state, and participate in the federal food program. Women caring for any number of children from two or fewer families may remain unregistered. Those who care for children from more than two families and who fail to register constitute the illegal population of day care providers (State of Vermont, 1986). In Vermont, as elsewhere, a significant proportion of family day care remains outside the regulatory framework: a recent study estimated that approximately 75 percent of pre-school-aged children received unregulated care (both legal and illegal) from approximately 1,200 different providers (Davenport et al., 1985).

Understanding Evasion

A variety of explanations for evasion are tendered in the literature (Fosburg et al., 1981; Kahn and Kamerman, 1987; Kappner, 1984). Two frequent explanations—that providers are ignorant of the requirement to register and that providers want to avoid the costs of regulation—can be eliminated as possibilities among the group of women under investigation here. Only 3 percent of the unregistered providers said that they had never heard of registration or licensing; those who were interviewed expressed strong feelings about the issue. The issue of cost is more complex. Regulation simultaneously places a cap on the possible income that can be earned (by limiting the number of children cared for at any given time), entails paying taxes on earned income (because it brings the operation to the government's notice), and requires the direct outlay of money (in order to purchase such devices as smoke detectors and fire extinguishers). Even so, anticipated costs cannot account for resistance to registration among the women in this study. The unregistered providers generally cared for fewer children than did the registered providers (see below); many unregistered providers noted that they did report their incomes; and only 4 percent of the unregistered providers who responded to the questionnaire said that they could not afford the purchases or modifications registration entailed.

Other explanations for evasion, such as the assertion that providers regard licensing as a "complex government hassle and unnecessary intrusion" (Kahn and Kamerman, 1987, p. 233), are best understood not as abstract ideological stands but as positions that emerge from the context of their daily work as they negotiate their relationships with children, parents, and their own family members (for a similar argument about opposition to government regulation among home-based knitters, see Boris, 1987).

Relationships with Children

A major dilemma for family day care providers is how to define and defend one's caregiving style. Almost all providers see themselves as offering homelike care and being like a mother to the children who come to them on a daily basis: 79 percent of the unregistered questionnaire respondents felt that it was "very important" to provide a homelike atmosphere; 83 percent of these respondents agreed strongly with the statement, "A family day care provider should be like a mother to the children in her care." In discussing their feelings about the children, the women use familial analogies: "They are my part-time kids." "I'm like a second Mom." "I think of them as extended members of my family."

Unregistered providers view regulation as a multifaceted threat to this style of care. They associate regulation with the notion of reorienting care toward an emphasis on educational activities. The "home base" from which they offer care, however, inhibits this approach; preschool pedagogy is expensive. As one woman said, "I'm a *home* day care. I can only do so much with what I can afford. I can't buy luxurious things." Moreover, most family day care providers deal with more than one age group and have to handle a variety of tasks (for example, housework) as well as the care of children; most are unable to tie all parents to the same (or even similar) schedules. They cannot take on the additional burden of an educational program.

But providers are not just defending a style based on limitations. Most providers feel that their approach to caregiving is preferable to that which might be offered in a day care center or preschool. When asked about the differences between the care they give and that offered to children in institutional settings, they are articulate and insistent: day care centers do not encourage the "warmth, love, and intimacy" that can be found in a family day care home; preschools exert too much pressure on children and deny them the luxury of a "real childhood."

Family day care providers also feel that regulation will introduce more formal elements into their relationships with children. They defend the flexible nature of the care they now provide, and they point with pride to their willingness to make accommodations. They feel these accommodations would be impossible if they were to comply with the full range of regulatory provisions:

> If I were registered and an inspector happened to come in on a certain day when I had one of the children that had the light temperature or a green runny nose, I would be closed down because you're not supposed to have those children around other children. And that's why day care has gotten the bad name. Because they cannot be as accommodating with all the regulations as somebody who's not regulated can be. And it's too bad because the children suffer for it.

Regulation is also associated for providers with the requirement of training as preparation for work with children (over a quarter of the unregistered providers think—falsely—that registration necessitates ongoing training) and with professional evaluation of their care. Most providers, however, locate their skills in their own experiences. They talk about the knowledge they have acquired through years of babysitting, caring for younger siblings, and raising their own children. They contrast this basis for skill development with formal training:

> Well, if they're going to have training I don't think they're a very good babysitter. I wouldn't want to put my kids [with] someone that needs book training and stuff like that. No way. I would say if they don't have the ability without being trained, I wouldn't want them to babysit.

When faced with the possibility of official oversight, they wonder whether their experience equips them to undergo scrutiny. Among some, this doubt emerges as a rejection of a practice that locates quality control in an outsider rather than in the provider's assessment of her own capabilities. Although providers acknowledge that regulation might be appropriate for those who cannot be trusted to

impose appropriate limits, they differentiate themselves from
others:

> [Regulation] is a good idea because it helps to limit the number of kids
> a person is watching. But I wouldn't take more kids anyway.

> I just don't see what the big deal is. . . . I just figure if I don't take on
> any more [children] than I can handle, I'm fine.

Relationships with Parents

Relationships between providers and parents are enormously
complex, alternating between two sets of contradictory norms. On
the one hand, both parents and providers have reason to want to
follow the norms of a market exchange. That is, both parties have
some interest in assuming that the relationship is characterized by
clearly specified obligations, stated rules, and social distance. And, to
a certain extent, this style of interaction prevails. Providers and parents agree to hourly or weekly fees for the care of young children;
they may agree to other conditions as well (for example, the providers will supply snacks and not meals, a fee will be charged for
time scheduled if parents do not give prior notice of a child's absence, parents must bring diapers and a change of clothing). They
thus mimic the form of a contractual service. But the full range of
obligations between mothers and providers is rarely so simply defined. Both parents and providers also have reason to find unsatisfactory the impersonality of the market (with its suggestion of com-
modifying care) and to view the relationship as embedded in the
norms of a social exchange. That is, both parties have an interest in
assuming that the relationship is characterized by diffuse obligations,
negotiated decision making based on trust, and intimacy.

Regulation threatens this delicate balance because it focuses exclusively on the contractual elements of the relationship, emphasizes
the rights of parents over those of providers (State of Vermont,
1986), and introduces a third party into the negotiations. Unregistered providers are concerned that this shift will erode the good
will that now prevails in their relationships with parents. One provider who had been registered in the past but had recently dropped
her registration said that she now felt less worried about the possibility of a lawsuit: although no one had ever threatened her in this
manner, she said that as long as she was registered, she felt "it could
happen."

Providers are also concerned that when official certification is
substituted for parental trust, the latter is diminished as a reward. In

the absence of significant material benefits for this kind of child care, providers rely heavily on expressions of appreciation and approval:

> The moms are intelligent enough to choose whether or not I am a good babysitter and they feel that I am. So I never felt the need to register. I feel that it should be the moms' decisions. I'm friends with everybody I babysit for and they know me, and if they felt that I wasn't capable, they wouldn't bring their children to me. And everybody I babysit comes first with their children. And I would hope that everybody would do that and realize—you can tell what a person is like by visiting or through word of mouth.

As this comment suggests, the providers carefully distinguish between parental and official oversight. They are critical of parents who do not exercise sufficient judgment in the choice of a family day care home. But they are unwilling to locate quality control in an impersonal bureaucracy that uncritically grants a stamp of approval to providers.

Relationships with Family Members

The fact that this business is located within the home and that it has to be accommodated to family needs (although it often conflicts with those needs) is relevant to evasion as well. Most providers enter the occupation out of a dual motivation: they want to stay home and be responsible for their own families; they also want to earn money. Some family day care providers are under pressure to deny that they are working at all in order to assure a spouse that he remains the "breadwinner."

Like other home-based workers, almost all providers experience enormous tension in mediating between family and occupation (Allen and Wolkowitz, 1987; Christensen, 1985, 1987; Hoy and Kennedy, 1983). But family day care providers want to maintain the right to resolve conflicts in favor of their families. Arguments about the privacy of the domestic domain are used to defend these priorities:

> I didn't want to have to hang a paper towel rack in my bathroom because they're not allowed to use towels. I just don't want to rearrange my whole house. My house is clean and it's neat and it's childproof. I didn't want the regulations. I think [registration] is appropriate. Yet that's touchy because it is still your house . . . you're talking about, or your family, and you don't want to change your whole lifestyle.

Two themes thus predominate as providers discuss their opposition to regulation: providers seek to resolve competing affective and contractual claims; and they strive to protect their autonomy.

Ambivalence about whether they are working for love or money marks entry into the occupation and is sustained in each of their relationships. Unregistered providers suggest repeatedly that registration threatens this delicate tightrope walk. Unregistered providers speak contemptuously of registered providers, who are, they feel, simply "in it for the money." They imply that regulation will inevitably alter the basis of their relationships with children ("I wouldn't want regulation; I just feel like I'm a mommy taking over for the daytime"), parents ("I wasn't doing it as a business. I not only babysat their kids, I was a mother to them"), and their own families ("I just wanted to earn a little extra *for the family*"). In short, they are concerned about a redefinition of an activity that they have balanced with, and occasionally subsumed within, a social or domestic ideology.

Providers also struggle to sustain autonomy. Substantial limits to autonomy exist because providers offer a service to individuals in wage labor, deal with many clients (with whom they establish personal relationships), and have obligations to their own families (Nelson, 1988). Providers defend adamantly their few remaining options, such as the right to make decisions about food and discipline. They also learn from friends, or they simply guess, about the many ways in which registration can become a hassle:

> Other people that I know who are registered or licensed have had major problems. One had a problem with an inspector outside of their home questioning the parents, another one had problems with them just walking in in the middle of the day, and another one had them walking in at six-thirty in the morning.

> I would probably close down rather than become registered because of the red tape and all the picky little things. The punishment thing is fine with me, but there are all kinds of little things such as so much space. There's just so much that it wouldn't be worth the aggravation.

In short, regulation is perceived as an additional constraint in an already overconstrained setting.

Differences Between Registered and Unregistered Providers

In many ways registered and unregistered providers are remarkably similar. But there are differences between the two groups as well.

This analysis cannot distinguish among providers at different stages of involvement with regulation: some providers open their family day care homes under the auspices of the regulatory framework; others decide to become registered after a number of years in the occupation. Nor can it, in the absence of longitudinal data, say whether observed differences precede or follow from regulation. Therefore, rather than speaking definitively about cause and effect, I will place these differences in the context of the issues discussed above.

Relationships with Children

With respect to relationships with children, it is significant that the two groups of providers hold essentially similar attitudes. Approximately the same proportion of each group define themselves as being like a mother to the children in their care (71 percent of the registered providers and 83 percent of the unregistered providers). And there are no differences in the *ordering* of their caregiving priorities: providers in both groups stress "good nutrition" and a "homelike atmosphere" as most important; "training in social skills" and "consistent discipline" follow; "educational activities" and "a structured or planned day" trail way behind. There are, however, some differences in the absolute weight registered and unregistered providers place on issues relating to consistent discipline and training in social skills. These issues were scored from "1" (very important) to "5" (not important at all): among registered providers the mean scores for consistent discipline and training in social skills were 1.3 and 1.5 respectively; among unregistered providers these scores were 1.6 and 1.8 respectively. These childrearing practices are likely to be affected by the number of children in care: because registered providers generally deal with more children, they may have to place greater emphasis on maintaining control.

The registered providers do feel that the possibility of observation affects superficial issues (for example, neatness, cleanliness) and keeps them on edge; fundamentally, however, they feel that the content of care is unchanged by regulation:

> I feel like I have to be "so so" now and run it a little differently just in case I get checked up on or something. . . . But actually, I don't feel any differences. I could have a pigsty here and the kids would still be happy with me.

Moreover, registered providers, like unregistered providers, root their abilities in their own experiences. Although registered providers are more likely to say that they are interested in training, half of them have never attended a conference or workshop. Many of those who do go dismiss the content:

> As far as their advice and stuff . . . it sounds great when they are talking about it, but it can't be put into effect.

> [The conference I attended] was a waste of time. It didn't really deal with kids. It didn't help you with any situation.

Regulation is thus irrelevant to the content of child care. Nevertheless, on average, registered providers have a higher level of education than do unregistered providers: whereas only 41 percent of the unregistered providers have education beyond the high school level, 54 of the registered providers do. They are thus better equipped to *defend* their caregiving style in the face of official scrutiny.

Relationships with Parents

Relationships with parents are not always smooth sailing, and all providers bitterly resent the abuses they feel they suffer at the hands of parents. Because registered providers generally deal with more children than do unregistered providers, they experience some of these problems more often. The frequency with which these kinds of problems were experienced were scored from "1" (often) to "5" (never). Among registered providers, mean scores for frequency of "late payments from parents" and "parents coming late to pick up children" were 2.5 and 2.0 respectively; among unregistered providers the scores were 2.8 and 2.3 respectively. In this context, registration, with its emphasis on formal contractual agreements, might offer a welcome promise of relief. Furthermore, registered providers are more likely to have two problems that impinge on trust: they more often deal with children they find difficult to handle (mean score of 2.5 versus 2.8 for unregistered providers), and they more often deal with children they dislike (mean score of 3.5 versus 3.6 for unregistered providers). In cases where the social element of the relationship between parents and provider might be especially strained, the additional assurance that comes with registration enables the provider to take risks without worrying that an angry parent will turn her in to a state official.

Relationships with Family Members

Although finding the proper balance between family and occupation is difficult for all providers, three sets of differences between registered and unregistered providers enable the former to acknowledge a limited shift in their priorities. First, more of the registered providers are single women (14 percent versus 6 percent); the single women do not have to accommodate their work lives to the needs and interests of a spouse. Second, registered providers are less likely to be caring for their own pre-school-aged children (52 percent versus 77 percent); hence, fewer have to mediate between their own children's needs and those of the children who come to them on a daily basis. Finally, registered providers care for more children (an average of 7.7 different children each week versus an average of 4.6) for longer hours (an average of 48.7 hours versus an average of 42.9). And they earn not only more money as a whole (an average of $196 per week versus an average of $118 per week), but a higher proportion of the family's income (an average of 41 percent versus an average of 28 percent). They thus have more claim to the right to impose business concerns on their households.

These shifts do not signify that the registered providers have embraced governmental control: registered providers, like unregistered providers, express ambivalence about whether the government should be involved in the regulation of a home-based business:

> In the overall view of things, I don't know how I feel about whether [government regulation] is a good thing in the long run or not. The Big Brother kind of thing. The government getting more involved kind of thing. Who knows what that will be like 20 years from now.

> I haven't found anything that's unfair . . . but I have a problem with regulation in the first place—that you even have to be registered at all if you are taking care of more than two kids. . . . The state's always got their hands in everything.

But registered providers more openly acknowledge that their homes have, indeed, become work sites: "It's not just my home any more. It's my place of business."

The two themes identified as characteristic of resistance to registration thus appear transformed among those who comply. Many of the differences are relevant to the manner in which providers balance contractual and affective relationships. The data as a whole, however, do not indicate that registered providers should be seen as single-mindedly driven by a market perspective. They, like unregistered providers, speak contemptuously about women who are only in it for the money. Like unregistered providers, they become enormously attached to the children in their care:

> [One child] came to me when he was six months old and I had him up until he was two. He was like my own because I'd have him from seven

in the morning till six-thirty or seven at night from Monday through
Friday and some Saturdays. And it's like this kid's my own. This is the
kid I was second mamma to. . . . I even trained that kid—I potty-
trained him. [The mother] did the nighttime bit but I did the daytime.
The talking—everything. I watched this kid grow up.

They also develop lasting ties to the parents of those children:

To this day there is a bond there with the whole family. We've seen the
mother come a long way. . . . When she graduated from Alcoholics
Anonymous [my husband] bought her a watch, and I was so touched.
That's how you get involved in some of these things. You're not just
getting involved in the babysitting. . . . You take on the whole family
sometimes.

And registered providers, like unregistered providers, find themselves giving free care and extending their working hours to accommodate the needs of parents and children with whom they have
forged these strong emotional bonds. They do so even when making
these accommodations entails stretching their own rules or those
contained in the registration guidelines:

The latest leaves close to six. It's too long for me. But what happened
with one of them is . . . I had her before when her mother worked [in
town] and she was getting picked up at four, four-thirty. And then her
mother changed jobs and was working [farther away]. And because I
had already had her and there was so much going on anyway with the
family . . . I decided to keep her. She'd been through enough changes
and I didn't want her to go through another change.

I usually have just two infants. I hate to say no to anybody that I've
taken care of before. . . . This last week and this week I've three children I haven't watched in about a year. The girl is two, and I started
taking care of her when she was six months old . . . and her mother
now has multiple sclerosis. And I won't say no to her.

But registered day care providers have been in the occupation
longer (an average of 5.1 years compared with an average of 4.1
years for unregistered providers), and they learn to acknowledge the
reality of the market perspective: "After being in it for four years,
you have to look at it as a business." They become eager to obtain
the support services registration can provide:

My sister was telling me about the benefits like the food program was
available and the butter and cheese programs. And then when I figured when you live [in a rural area] you cannot get the price . . . and I
was really putting all my money into food and supplies . . . and I wasn't

making a dime. Now I am on the food plan and, boy, does it help me. [Now] I'm not doing it for nothing.

Someone came to help with a contract. That's hard to do on your own. I now have parents sign contracts.

Registration is also relevant to the issue of autonomy in two ways. First, unregulated providers are vulnerable to complaints filed with state officials and harassment by these same persons. Regulation confers the benefits of legality (Weitz and Sullivan, 1990). (In fact, 70 percent of the registered providers said that they became registered simply because "I wanted to be legal.") Providers who have decided (for whatever reason) to enlarge their clientele are often particularly concerned about getting this protection:

I became registered because I wanted to take more children. . . . I had always just had the two little kids, and once in a while I'd have the extra kid around and I always felt guilty, as if somebody was going to be popping in at any minute. I figured if I was going to take that many kids . . . I didn't want to fool around with not being registered.

Second, regulation confers a status that is relevant to the *claim* of autonomy. Registered and unregistered family day care providers do not differ significantly in most of their attitudes about their work. They do, however, differ in their attitudes toward being called "babysitters" (Greenman, 1984, p. 9). Whereas only 19 percent of the unregistered providers said that they minded this title, 55 percent of the registered providers said that it was a problem for them. A provider who registered as a result of a complaint against her suggested that this shift sat uneasily on her shoulders: "I call myself a day care provider. But I guess I am really just a babysitter." In contrast, a voluntarily registered provider said, "I say I run a day care. I don't babysit. I run a day care. We used to be babysitters and now we are a day care provider or whatever. [That change] is really important to me."

Summary and Discussion

Evasion of regulation is rooted in providers' perceptions of its implications and, in particular, its threat to transform their ongoing relationships and to challenge the ideology and freedom with which they conduct their business. These protected patterns are linked to the broader context in which family day care exists: although there is an enormous demand for this kind of care, there have been few material or ideological changes that would support or legitimize this activity. Family day care providers carve out a self-definition in the context of persistent notions about women's proper place, broad social uneasiness about the commodification of care, and a devaluation of caregiving in all contexts. The evidence from registered providers suggests that regulation can give them access to significant resources, offer limited protection, and serve as a basis for claiming a higher status. But these possibilities are not yet sufficient to overcome the hesitation, or dispel the anxieties, of many providers.

The lesson for those interested in advancing the goal of regulation is that perceived threats must be neutralized. Certainly incentives are needed: registration must continue to offer such benefits as the federal food program, conferences, support from outreach personnel, and newsletters. The fact that some providers have come to see regulation as a resource is evidence that these incentives have an impact. But regulation must also offer these benefits in a manner that confirms and supports the provider's orientation toward homelike care for young children. For example, resources such as lending libraries of books and toys that come to the provider's home might be more welcome than an invitation to leave home to attend a conference or workshop (Sparkes, 1978). It must also recognize her rights *as well as* those of employing parents. However, both the underlying rationale of regulation (the protection of children) and the current bias in regulation (which minimizes provider concerns) reduce the likelihood that registration will become widespread.

Inevitably the question arises of whether more regulation is an appropriate goal. The evidence presented here cannot evaluate whether registered or unregistered providers offer better care to young children: not only is quality notoriously difficult to assess, but any assessments may reflect biases (Enarson, 1990; Greenman, 1984; Stallings and Wilcox, 1978). Because "a key aspect of quality is a congruence with the beliefs and values of the families served" (Greenman, 1984, p. 15), both social class and ethnicity are likely to have an impact on parental and official evaluations of the adequacy of care. Nevertheless, some assessment of the shifts associated with regulation is in order; a comparison with another group of caregivers who have recently moved into the regulatory orbit offers a useful guide.

In a careful study of Arizona lay midwives five years after a licensing system had been introduced, Weitz and Sullivan (1990) noted that the midwives had moved toward a more medicalized model of childbirth. Although the midwives had initially offered their services in order to provide a distinct alternative to the hospital method of childbirth, in the years following licensure they became increasingly aware of the potential for medical problems to arise and more accepting of intervention. They also edged away from a commitment to holistic care and introduced more hierarchical elements into their relationships with clients.

Registration among family day care providers appears to be associated with similar subtle shifts. Registered providers are more self-conscious about such issues as discipline and training in social skills; they acknowledge more fully the market component of their relationships with parents; they recognize the possibility of resolving some conflicts in favor of work; and they eagerly accept a status that differentiates them from unregistered "babysitters." Cause and effect in this process, however, are enormously difficult to untangle. Some of these differences can be attributed to having more children in care and may therefore be a cause of registration: providers who, for whatever reason, decide to enlarge their child care group come to see registration as both a useful resource and a necessary protection. But a willingness to deal with more children can also be an effect of registration: registration abets this process by providing access to clients and the means to ensure reimbursement for such expenses as food. Thus, providers who think that they want no more than a few children may find that once registered they can handle more, particularly if they "allow" themselves to learn techniques for group management suggested by outreach workers or workshop leaders. Some of these changes might have an even more complex origin. As more women enter the labor force (Hayghe, 1986), the demand for this service grows; what was once a set of casual arrangements achieves the public recognition and acknowledgment that the name "family day care" suggests. All providers can now advertise their services by calling on the new nomenclature. As they enlarge the pool from which they draw clients beyond the confines of kinship and friendship, opportunities for conflict (over childrearing style, for example) increase. And as they see more children, they may also encounter pathologies outside the realm of everyday experience and thus may come to need the assistance of professionals.

At the same time, too much can be made of these differences. This study did not find that regulation resulted in *fundamental* shifts in orientation toward either the content of family day care or the experiential basis for caregiving skills. This lack of change may be due to the particular manner in which regulation impinges on providers. For them, regulation does not yet mean extensive, direct contact with professionals; nor does it require formal training. More important, regulation alone does not alter the context of family day care: parents still seek care outside institutions for very young children; they still have limited resources with which to pay for this care. Thus, while registration might facilitate the movement toward a more regularized and impersonal business orientation, it alone is insufficient to shift providers' priorities or enable them to resolve in an entirely new manner the conflicting claims, interests, and concerns that mark this occupation.

NOTE

Acknowledgments. Data collection was supported by the Middlebury College Professional Development Fund and Vermont Experimental Program to Stimulate Competitive Research. I thank Burke Rochford and two anonymous reviewers for their helpful comments.

REFERENCES

Adams, Diane (1982). *National Survey of Family Day Care Regulations, Statistical Summary.* ERIC Document Reproduction Service no. 220–207.

——— (1984). "Family Day Care Registration: Is It Deregulation or More Feasible Public Policy?" *Young Children* 39 (May):74–77.

Alexander, Cheryl, and Ricka Markowitz (1982). "Attitudes of Mothers of Preschoolers Toward Government Regulation of Day Care." *Public Health Reports* 97:572–78.

Allen, Sheila, and Carol Wolkowitz (1987). *Homeworking: Myths and Realities.* Basinstoke, England: Macmillan.

Anderson, Elaine A. (1986). "Federal Day Care Provisions: A Legislative Response." *Child Care Quarterly* 15 (1):6–14.

Boris, Eileen (1987). "Homework and Women's Rights: The Case of the Vermont Knitters, 1980–1985." *Signs* 13:98–120.

Christensen, Kathleen E. (1985). "Women and Home-Based Work." *Social Policy,* Winter, pp. 54–57.

——— (1987). *Women and Home-Based Work: The Unspoken Contract.* New York: Henry Holt and Company.

Class, Norris, and Richard Orton (1980). "Day Care Regulation: The Limits of Licensing." *Young Children* 35 (June):12–17.

Cohen, Donald J., and Edward F. Zigler (1978). "Federal Day Care Standards: Rationale and Recommendations." *Young Children* 33 (March): 24–32.

Collins, R. C. (1983). "Child Care and the States: The Comparative Licensing Study." *Young Children* 38 (5):3–11.

Dames, Kateri (1983). "Registration for Child Care Homes." *Day Care and Early Education*, Fall, pp.21–23.

Davenport, Amy, et al. (1985). *The Economics of Child Care.* Montpelier, Vt.: Governor's Commission on the Status of Women, Childcare Task Force.

Enarson, Elaine (1990). "Experts and Caregivers: Perspectives on Underground Care." In Emily K. Abel and Margaret K. Nelson, eds., *Circles of Care.* Albany: State University of New York Press.

Fosburg, Steven, et al. (1981). *Family Day Care in the United States: Summary of Findings, National Day Care Home Study, Final Report.* Washington, D.C.: U.S. Department of Health and Human Services.

Greenman, James (1984). "Perspectives on Quality Day Care." In James Greenman and Robert Fuqua, eds., *Making Day Care Better.* New York: Teachers College Press.

Hayghe, Howard (1986). "Rise in Mothers' Labor Force Activity Includes Those with Infants." *Monthly Labor Review* 109 (2):43–45.

Hoy, Jane, and Mary Kennedy (1983). "Women's Paid Labor in the Home: The British Experience." *Research in the Sociology of Work: Peripheral Workers*, Vol. 2: Greenwich, Conn.: JAI Press.

Inman, Virginia (1982). "Stunted Growth." *Wall Street Journal*, October 26.

Jackson, Brian, and Sonia Jackson (1979). *Childminder: A Study in Action Research.* London: Routledge & Kegan Paul.

Kahn, Alfred J., and Sheila B. Kamerman (1987). *Child Care: Facing the Hard Choices.* Dover, Mass.: Auburn House.

Kappner, Augusta (1984). "Factors Affecting Provider Movement Along a Continuum of Visibility." Ph.D. dissertation, Columbia University School of Social Work.

Kendall, Earline D., and Lewis H. Walker (1984). "Day Care Licensing: The Eroding Regulations." *Child Care Quarterly* 13:278–90.

Morgan, Gwen (1979). "Regulation: One Approach to Quality Childcare." *Young Children* 34(June):22–27.

——— (1984). "Change Through Regulation." In James Greenman and Robert Fuqua, eds., *Making Day Care Better.* New York: Teachers College Press.

Morgan, Gwen, Carol S. Stevenson, Richard Fiene, and Keith O. Stephens (1986). "Gaps and Excesses in the Regulation of Child Day-Care: A Report of a Panel." *Reviews of Infectious Disease* 8:634–43.

National Association for the Education of Young Children (NAEYC) (1987). "NAEYC Position Statement on Licensing and Other Forms of Regulation of Young Children." *Young Children* 42 (May):64–68.

Nelson, Margaret K. (1988). "Providing Family Day Care: An Analysis of Home-Based Work." *Social Problems* 35 (1):79–84.

Rose-Ackerman, Susan (1983). "Unintended Consequences: Regulating the Quality of Subsidized Day Care." *Journal of Policy Analysis and Management* 3:314–30.

Sale, June Solnit (1984a). "Family Day Care: The Registration Controversy."
    Day Care and Early Education 8 (1):10–14.
—— (1984b). "Family Day Care Homes." In James Greenman and Robert
    Fuqua, eds., *Making Day Care Better*. New York: Teachers College Press.
Sparkes, Kathleen (1978). "The Magic Bus Provides Magic Moments to
    Family Day Care Homes." *Day Care and Early Education* 5 (Spring):55–
    56.
Stallings, Jane, and Mary Wilcox (1978). "Quality Day Care: Can It Be Mea-
    sured?" In Philip Robins and Samuel Weiner, eds., *Child Care and Public
    Policy*. Lexington, Mass.: D. C. Heath.
State of Vermont (1986). *Journal for Family Day Care Home Registration*. Wa-
    terbury, Vt.: Division of Licensing and Registration, Social and Reha-
    bilitation Services.
Tobin, Catherine J. (1985). "Overhauling State Licensing Requirements:
    Making Quality Child Care a Reality." *Journal of Legislation* 12:213–24.
U.S. Bureau of the Census (1980). *1980 Census of Population*, vol.1: *Charac-
    teristics of the Population: Part 47—Vermont*. Washington, D.C.: Govern-
    ment Printing Office.
—— (1987). "Who's Minding the Kids? Child Care Arrangements: Winter
    1984–1985." *Current Population Reports*, no. 9. Series P-70. Washington,
    D.C.: Government Printing Office.
Weitz, Rose, and Deborah A. Sullivan (1990). "Licensed Lay Midwifery and
    the Medical Model of Childbirth." In Emily K. Abel and Margaret K.
    Nelson, eds., *Circles of Care*. Albany: State University of New York Press.
Young, Kate, and Edward F. Zigler (1986). "Infant and Toddler Care: Reg-
    ulations and Policy Implications." *American Journal of Orthopsychiatry*
    56(1):43–55.

PART VIII

Historical and Cross-Cultural Perspectives

22 | Equal Parenthood and Social Policy: Lessons from a Study of Parental Leave in Sweden

Linda Haas

In every known society, women have had primary responsibility for the physical care and emotional well-being of infants, while men's responsibility for babies has been mainly economic (Katz and Konner, 1981). Even the dramatic increase in the labor force participation rate of mothers of small children, which is common in most industrial societies, has not substantially changed the sexual division of labor where child care is concerned. Studies show that fathers in dual-earner families are no more likely to share the responsibility for child care equally than are fathers in traditional families where the mothers are not employed (Pleck, 1985).

The pattern of mothers being responsible for child care is sometimes blamed on fathers' lack of access to parental leave—time off from work to care for the new baby. Most industrial societies, in contrast to the United States, grant mothers a generous amount of paid maternity leave with job security (Kamerman and Kahn, 1980; Sidel, 1986). An increasing number of societies also allow fathers to take paid parental leave, including Finland, Norway, Sweden, West Germany, and Yugoslavia (Morgan, 1984; Pleck, 1988, Sharman, 1987). The first country to institute paid parental leave for both mothers and fathers was Sweden, in 1974 (Sidel, 1986). The Swedish parental leave program remains the most generous and flexible in the world.

With return to his original job assured, a Swedish father—married or unmarried—has 15 months of paid leave to share with his partner, so that one parent can stay at home to care for a newborn or adopted child. For the first 12 months, the pay is generally at the level of 90 percent of salary; the last 3 months are paid at a level equivalent to about 10 dollars a day. A father is legally entitled to half of the leave; if he chooses not to take it, he must inform the social insurance office in writing. Social insurance offices handle the dispensation of benefits, which are financed mainly by employers' payroll taxes.

The Swedish parental leave system is a radical attempt to break the centuries-old tradition of women's primary responsibility for baby care. It is perhaps a model for the type of legislation many would like to see enacted in the United States. It is therefore useful to study the development and evaluate the success of this unique social program. What circumstances prompted Sweden to develop a parental leave program, and how do these compare with circumstances in the United States? How likely is it that the United States will develop a similar policy? A year-long study of the Swedish parental leave program, conducted during 1985–86, provides statistics regarding fathers' actual participation in parental leave. Examining the barriers that appear to keep Swedish fathers from taking the leave will allow us to recommend the types of parental leave programs that would most likely be attractive to American men, to pinpoint the social forces that operate to prevent men and women from sharing the parenting role equally, and to suggest additional types of social programs that might need to be instituted to encourage fathers to share parental leave.

There are considerable dangers involved in holding Sweden up as a model for American family policy. Each society represents a peculiar configuration of historical, economic, political, and social forces; programs that exist in one society cannot be readily adapted to another social setting. Still, a study of Swedish society can help us gain new insight into the social forces likely to be associated with greater interest in child care on the part of fathers, as well as the difficulties involved in trying to change gender expectations through social policy.

Methods

The main body of data comes from a 1986 mail survey of 319 sets of Gothenburg parents who had children during 1984. Permission was obtained from the social insurance headquarters in Gothenburg to survey couples who were registered at two local offices as having taken parental leave. The offices were chosen to represent, respectively, a generally middle-class area of the city and an area where predominantly factory workers lived. Couples were included in the study if they met the following criteria: they had a child in 1984; they had lived together before the baby was born and were still living together in the Gothenburg area in early spring 1986; they had both been employed outside the home before the child was born; and they were both eligible to receive parental leave. (Eligibility at that time depended on having been employed 270 days before the leave was to begin. Until rule changes in 1987, both the mother and the father had to be eligible for the father to take leave.) Couples were excluded from the study if a multiple birth or an adoption was involved, since these situations lead to special parental leave arrangements. Two questionnaires were sent out to all 721 couples who qualified according to these criteria. Forty-four percent completed and returned questionnaires, yielding information on 319 sets of parents. Under normal mail survey procedures, several reminders would have been sent out to increase the response rate, but a new law regarding the confidentiality of public records had made government bureaucrats nervous, and officials at the central insurance office prohibited repeated contacts with the sample.

An attempt was made to assess what biases might emerge from such a low response rate by drawing comparisons between characteristics of respondents and known characteristics of parents in the Gothenburg area (available from census bureau records). Demographically, it appeared that the respondents were quite similar to Gothenburg parents in general—for example, in terms of percentage foreign-born, percentage married, family size, and, most important, average amount of parental leave taken by fathers. A social class bias appeared to remain, however. Because a middle-class area was deliberately chosen as one of two areas for the study, a larger proportion of the sample were in professional occupations than was true for the population of parents as a whole.

To understand the history and development of parental leave policy, as well as potential determinants of fathers' taking parental leave, I read numerous reports and books by Swedish academics, feminists, and government bureaucrats. It was also possible to follow coverage of the issue in the mass media by being in residence for one year. In addition, I had the opportunity to discuss the study and preliminary findings with governmental officials and academics.

Reasons for the Development of Parental Leave in Sweden

The Swedish government developed a parental leave program in response to three concerns: worry about a low birth rate, a need to encourage women's employment, and a desire to liberate men from gender stereotypes. Particular demographic, economic, political, and ideological circumstances gave rise to these concerns; in turn, the unique nature of political and economic institutions in Sweden led to the development of the parental leave program as a way to address them.

The Population Crisis

Sweden's policy of advocating shared parenthood has its roots in a concern for the survival of the Swedish population, a concern that first arose in the 1930s. The worldwide depression aggravated an already low birth rate; if the birth rate dropped below replacement levels, a smaller workforce would have to support a growing number of older citizens. The nature and importance of the declining birth rate were brought to the attention of the public by sociologists Alva and Gunnar Myrdal in Kris i befolkningsfrågan (The Population Crisis) published in 1934. The Myrdals recommended that the government, as part of a general plan of social security, subsidize the well-being of the family so that couples would find childbearing more economically feasible. The Myrdals' proposals went further, however; they proposed that the government take steps to help women combine employment outside the home with motherhood. In such drastic economic times, many people begrudged women jobs that could be held by unemployed men. But the Myrdals argued that women would have more children if government programs helped them combine motherhood with employment, that children would be better off with mothers who had a chance to fulfill their ambitions in outside employment, and that two incomes in a family would provide the economic security and comfort that are prerequisites for the willingness to bear and raise children. To the critics who might reply that there were not enough jobs, the Myrdals answered that public works projects, sound economic planning, and a growing national economy would create enough jobs for all adults to work if they chose.

The victory of the Social Democratic party in Parliament in 1932 had set the stage for the needed reforms. The Myrdals' recommendations were eventually implemented because they coincided with the Social Democratic party's commitment to social equality and enhanced material welfare. Measures enacted to improve the economic situation of the family included public works jobs, child allowances, and public housing. Other policies were instituted to improve the quality of Swedish family life: antipollution measures, rehabilitation of housing to eliminate slums, a national health insurance program, and limited public ownership of industries providing the basic necessities of life (Forsberg, 1984). Working mothers' employment opportunities were protected through a law forbidding employers to dismiss women for getting married or being pregnant, and a law granting mothers 3 months of unpaid maternity leave (Näsman, 1986).

Welfare state policies led to dramatic improvements in Swedes' economic standard of living, job security, and health (Hadenius, 1985). But family size stayed small; at its lowest point, in 1983, the average Swedish woman had 1.63 children (Ericsson and Jacobsson, 1985). Furthermore, the percentage of wives and mothers who were employed stayed low for another 30 years after their employment rights were assured (Scott, 1982).

While early policies to promote childbearing were essentially failures, it was significant for later developments that the Social Democratic government of Sweden, which has now been in power for most of the last half-century, has always had an official concern for the birth rate and a policy of promoting maternal employment. Concern for the birth rate and children's welfare, as well as an acceptance of working mothers, first manifested in the 1930s, continued to be a driving force behind Swedish welfare and family policy and contributed eventually to the enactment of legislation for parental leave for both mothers and fathers.

Need for Women's Labor Power

Women's right to employment was thus established in Sweden in the 1930s. It was not, however, until the 1960s that a revolution in women's labor force participation rates occurred. During the 1960s the Swedish economy greatly expanded; there was a shortage of male workers to fill positions created by expanding industry and the growing private and public service sectors. (Foreign workers were imported, but the difficulties of assimilation led the government to choose not to rely too heavily on them for labor power.) Swedish economists stated that it was no longer economically "efficient" for female talent to be wasted—one claimed that the Swedish gross national product could be increased by 25 percent by allowing women to fill positions they were best suited for. The shortage of male workers and a desire to increase economic productivity prompted the Swedish government to start new programs to encourage more women—particularly mothers—to take jobs.

Several programs were instituted to increase women's qualifications for employment. Public vocational training programs were expanded to include more housewives; in 1960, only 14 percent of the people retrained were women, but by 1975 the figure was over 50 percent (Gustafsson and Lantz, 1985). The government also increased the number of study grants for higher education, which led to a great increase in the recruitment of females to colleges and universities (Wistrand, 1981).

Women's access to nontraditional jobs was also enhanced by government policies and programs. All protective legislation limiting women's participation in certain jobs was abolished during the 1960s, generally by extending protections to all workers (Baude, 1979). To combat sex segregation of jobs, the government sponsored pilot programs to retrain women for nontraditional occupations, instituted financial subsidies for employers who hired women for nontraditional jobs, placed special counselors in schools to encourage girls to consider nontraditional occupations, and mandated that schoolchildren visit job sites in the fields that were not traditional for their sex (Baude, 1979). A new national school curriculum in 1962 recommended "that girls with a leaning toward technical and scientific subjects be encouraged" (Sandlund, 1971).

The government also promoted equal pay for equal work. Equal pay legislation for government employees was enacted as early as 1947. The Social Democratic party heartily supported trade union efforts to eliminate wage differentials between male and female workers from wage contracts in the 1960s. The Social Democrats also supported the union-initiated "wage solidarity policy," which was not explicitly motivated by a concern for women's wages but in the end resulted in women (as the lowest-paid workers) receiving equal pay for comparable work. In 1963, female industrial workers made 72 percent of what male workers did; by 1982, they made 90 percent (Gustafsson and Lantz, 1985).

One institutional restriction on women's employment was a tax policy whereby mates were forced to pool incomes for tax purposes. In Sweden's highly progressive income tax system, this had the effect of increasing the tax burden in families with two earners. In 1966, therefore, the tax laws were changed so that income taxes could be levied on individuals instead of families. By 1971, the individual tax system was made obligatory (Gustafsson and Lantz, 1985).

To encourage more mothers to work, the government decided in the 1960s to assume more responsibility for the provision of day care centers. The national government pays 45 percent of day care costs; municipal governments also pay 45 percent, allowing parents to pay 10 percent of actual costs. These subsidies, as well as a commitment to expand the number of places, have led to a dramatic increase in the number of children using center- or family-based child care. In

1968, for example, 20,000 Swedish children were in center-based child care; by 1974, 60,000 were; and by 1985, 188,900 were (Sandberg, 1975; Swedish Institute, 1987). Now 45 percent of all preschool-aged children are in day care centers or family day care; the government is committed to meet the demand for child care fully by 1991 (Swedish Institute, 1987).

Last but not least, maternity leave was extended to 6 months of fully paid leave in 1963. Maternity leave policy was designed to encourage women to join the labor force; women had to be employed before childbirth to qualify for benefits. Maternity leave also shortened the work interruption at childbirth because a woman would keep her old job and did not lose time looking for another (Gustafsson and Lantz, 1985).

Swedish women are now almost as much a part of the labor force as men. In 1985, 82 percent of Swedish women between the ages of 20 and 64 were employed, compared with 90 percent of men; 83 percent of all mothers with pre-school-aged children were employed (Statistiska Centralbyrån, 1986). The need for female labor power diminished somewhat as the Swedish economy weakened in the late 1970s. Nevertheless, the concern for women's employment opportunities remained a permanent part of social policy. Two incomes are seen as vital for a family's economic security, and women's economic independence is seen as a prerequisite for sexual equality (Statens Offentliga Utredningar, 1982). In this context, programs like parental leave are justified as ensuring women continued access to employment.

Desire for Men's Liberation

During the early 1960s government leaders subscribed to the philosophy that women should have two roles: housewife–mother and wage-earner, a model first proposed by the Myrdals in the 1930s. Policies were therefore designed to help women meet the requirements of both roles. This all changed in the mid-1960s as a result of an intensive public debate about gender roles. This debate was begun by a feminist journalist, Eva Moberg, in an essay widely circulated in Swedish intellectual circles and later reprinted in popular magazines. She argued that women would never achieve equal employment opportunities as long as it was assumed that women should adopt a double role of worker and housewife–mother. She saw no reason why women should be held primarily responsible for child care and housework:

> Actually there is no biological connection whatsoever between the
> function of giving birth to and nursing a child and the function of
> washing its clothes, preparing its food, and trying to bring it up to be
> a good and harmonious person. . . . The concept of double roles can
> have an unhappy effect in the long run. It perpetuates the idea that
> woman has an inherent main task, the care and upbringing of children,
> homemaking, and keeping the family together. . . . Both men and
> women have one main role, that of being human beings. (Moberg,
> 1962; my translation)

Moberg made specific recommendations about changing men's
roles. She felt that men were too pressured to advance, compete,
and raise the family's living standard. Swedes should lower their expectations regarding economic and social success and raise expectations regarding men's participation in domestic work and bringing
up children.

By the mid-1960s, the growth of public support for this more
radical view of men's and women's roles led the Social Democratic
government to adopt it as official policy. The head of the Social
Democratic party and prime minister of Sweden, Tage Erlander,
said in 1964: "Equality between the sexes . . . means that men are
allowed increased possibilities to be close to children and to increase
their influence over the new generation's upbringing" (Arbetsgruppen om Mansrollen, 1985; my translation). In 1968, a government
report to the United Nations stated: "The division of functions as
between the sexes must be changed in such a way that both the man
and the woman in a family are afforded the same practical opportunities of participating in both active parenthood and gainful employment" (Sandlund, 1971, p. 214).

Swedish social scientists have historically played an influential
role in the development of Swedish social policy (witness the role of
Myrdals played in 1930); their writings echoed the sentiments of
Moberg and the United Nations report. In 1962, Edmund
Dahlström, a Swedish sociologist, edited *Women's Life and Work*. In it,
he stated:

> Equality cannot be realized as long as the majority of women are
> content to bear by themselves the main responsibility for the care of
> the home and children. . . . The concept of "the two roles of women"
> is . . . untenable. Both men and women have *one* main role, that of a
> human being. For both sexes, this role would include childcare. (1971,
> p. 179)

An extension of maternity benefits to men was seen early on as a
way to symbolize the commitment to the "human being model." In

1967 the Swedish Parliament appointed a family policy commission to investigate how the social insurance system could be changed to increase opportunities for both women's employment and sexual equality. This committee presented reports in 1968 and 1969 recommending that maternity leave be converted into a parental leave system so that fathers could have access to benefits (Familjepolitiska Kommittén, 1969). A 1969 report prepared by Alva Myrdal for the Social Democratic party convention also advocated that parental leave be shared between mothers and fathers, as did reports prepared by the two largest trade union confederations (Landsorganisationen, 1976; Qvist, Acker, and Lorwin, 1984).

In 1974, the Parliament voted to replace the maternity leave policy with a parental insurance system, which allowed fathers as well as mothers to take time off with pay after the birth of a child. In addition, fathers were granted another 10 days off with pay at the time of childbirth, and parents were allowed 10 paid days off per year to take care of sick children.

Parental leave clearly had the support of the trade unions, the Social Democratic party, and influential Swedish social scientists. The policy fitted in well with the concern for the low birth rate, an interest in preserving women's employment opportunities, and a new concern for men's liberation. There are, however, some additional reasons why parental leave was legislated so easily, reasons that relate to the political, economic, and social climate of Sweden.

One important reason may have been that by 1974, the year parental leave was legislated, women made up 21 percent of the Parliament—at that time the highest female representation in any democracy or socialist state (Hedvall, 1975). Swedish women thus had an unusual amount of political clout, reflecting both the history of the feminist movement in Sweden and the type of political system Sweden has. Most Swedish feminists chose to work within the women's auxiliaries of the major political parties, rather than in autonomous women's groups. In 1970, for example, 198,000 Swedish women belonged to the women's auxiliaries of the four main political parties, while only 11,000 belonged to the autonomous feminist organization, the Fredrika Bremer Society (Lyle and Qvist, 1974). Sweden's political system is based on proportional representation; the party picks the slate, and the popular vote determines the actual proportion each party has of parliamentary seats. As women worked their way up their party hierarchies, they were elected to Parliament.

Another reason for the easy passage of parental leave legislation is related to the changing structure of the labor market. As women gained more employment opportunities, fewer women were content with being private domestic workers. When domestic workers were in plentiful supply, middle-class women relied upon them to help them manage the double role of worker and housewife–mother. Thus, middle-class women (who dominated the debate about changing gender roles) became more interested in changing men's responsibility for housework and child care than they might have been if they had still been able to purchase help (Sandqvist, 1987b).

Sweden's religious climate may also have played a role in the passage of a law designed to reduce the traditional sexual division of labor. While Swedes generally pay tithes to the state-supported Lutheran church, and feel it is important to have their children christened, religious sentiments are generally weak. A strong fundamentalist religious movement advocating adherence to traditional gender roles is thus absent from Sweden.

Finally, competition for voters may have been a factor. Although they have not been in power for most of the last half-century, the bourgeois parties have come close to the Social Democrats in the popular vote; indeed, because of the Social Democrats' refusal to ban nuclear power, the bourgeois parties won control of the Parliament for six years from 1976 to 1982. Consequently, all political parties have advocated equality between the sexes as part of their campaign promises. The nonsocialist coalition even extended parental leave as well as other benefits for working parents during their short reign.

The concern for men's liberation did not end with the passage of the 1974 parental leave legislation. In 1979, family law was changed to say explicitly that spouses should share breadwinning, housework, and child care (Statens Offentliga Utredningar, 1982). In 1983, joint custody of children after the parents' divorce became automatic; this change was seen as furthering the development of equality between men and women (Forsberg, 1984). In 1983, the government appointed a "working group" to study men's roles; this group conducted seminars and research studies and published several books advocating men's liberation (Arbetsgruppen om Mansrollen, 1985; Jalmert, 1983, 1984); its work was also widely publicized in the mass media.

A concern for men's rights fueled further changes in parental leave legislation. Paid parental leave was eventually extended to 12 months, and with these extensions fathers gained the legal right to half of the leave. Unpaid leave to parents until their children were 18 months old was mandated in 1979, as was a policy that stated that parents of children under the age of seven could reduce (without compensation) their work hours to six a day (Kamerman, 1988). In the most recent change (1987), the father's eligibility for the leave is no longer dependent on the mother's eligibility (Försäkringskassan, 1987).

While interest in changing men's roles is still high, there is considerable social scientific evidence that Swedish men are far from "whole human beings" when it comes to participation in housework, child care, and, as will be discussed shortly, parental leave benefits. A 1983 study of 5,000 men revealed the widespread existence of the "in-principle man"—men who thought that men *in principle* ought to devote themselves to housework and take care of children but who found that for them personally this was difficult to do (Trost, 1983). Other studies of the Swedish domestic division of labor have also found complete equality to be lacking, although there is evidence that Swedish men are more involved in domestic work than American men (Haas, 1981, 1982; Konsumentverket, 1982; Sandqvist, 1987b; Statens Offentliga Utredningar, 1982; Statistiska Centralbyrån, 1980). Even at the national level, where equality rhetoric is widespread, a conservative party leader was recently ousted partly because of criticism by party regulars that he left too many meetings early to care for his pre-school-aged children.

Parental Leave Policy: Implications for the United States

The circumstances that led Sweden to adopt a radical program of parental leave have now been presented. On the basis of these findings, can we predict that the United States will develop and adopt a similar policy?

Until recently, the three concerns that led Sweden to adopt parental leave—a low birth rate, recognition of the need for female labor power, and an interest in men's liberation—have been absent in the United States. Historically, the U.S. birth rate has been above replacement level; indeed, the post–World War II baby boom led to a concern about *over*population. The U.S. government and businesses, except for a short period during World War II, have not acknowledged the important role American women play in the labor force. Indeed, the government has in effect discouraged women from working—for example, through its lack of support for day care and its poor enforcement of equal employment opportunity legislation. Lastly, the feminist movement in the United States has focused more on changes in women's role than on changes in men's role. Support for greater participation by fathers in child care, in particular, has been retarded by prominent pediatricians and psychologists who maintain the uniqueness of the mother–child bond.

But all this may be changing. Rather suddenly, we are seeing a concern for the birth rate, recognition of the importance of female labor power, and interest in men's liberation. The 1980 census revealed that the U.S. birth rate had dropped to 1.9 children per woman, which is less than the rate needed for population replacement. Women's labor force participation has been shown to have a negative impact on childbearing, which suggests that women find it difficult to combine the two roles (Kagan, Klugman, and Zigler, 1983). The sudden awareness that women's labor force participation may not be conducive to childbearing is reflected in an outburst of legislative proposals for government-subsidized child care as well as the proposal to allow employees time off without pay to care for family members.

The lack of recognition of the economic importance of women's employment, as well as the resistance to the fact that mothers are in the labor force to stay, seems also to be at an end. Economists are now pointing out to government officials and business leaders that two-thirds of the new entrants into the labor force by the year 2000 will be women. As companies increasingly compete for these new entrants, government and businesses will have to adopt policies to recruit women for the labor force and support them once they are in it. The importance of women's labor power is also underscored in publicity about the national shortage of certain groups of workers (notably nurses). Employers are also becoming aware that worries about child care will affect women's and men's productivity (Kamerman and Kahn, 1987).

Probably least developed is a concern for men's liberation, but we are seeing an increased interest, at least in women's magazines and on talk shows, in the "new male," and, in particular, "the new father." There are national men's liberation organizations and newsletters and a burgeoning list of books on men's roles, and some feminists are advocating greater concern for changing men's, as well as women's, roles. We might expect that some people will press for social policies that do not discriminate against men when it comes to opportunities to be with children. We see, already, a greater concern for men's access to custody of children after divorce, and the national proposal to provide unpaid family leave includes men as well as women. (Indeed, this inclusion of men in the proposed Family and Medical Leave Act may be due to a concern that such a law would be regarded as unconstitutional if it provided benefits only to women, as other laws and policies granting women special maternity benefits have been deemed; see Clay and Feinstein, 1987.)

While the precipitating conditions for parental leave in the United States may exist, unique features of American society operate to prevent such a policy from being developed, at least in the form that exists in Sweden. Sociologist Alvin Schorr (1979) has outlined three major American traditions that prevent the government from adopting an explicit family policy. These traditions would seem to work against the adoption of parental leave in particular.

The first such tradition is "individualism." There is a lack of concern for the common good, and the concept that children are society's resource to be supported by all is absent (Bronfenbrenner, 1986). This tradition makes unpalatable to many any proposal whereby society would pay for parental leave through employers' payroll taxes. People are also unwilling to accept the possibility of an increased workload when a colleague is off work to care for children. (In Sweden, temporary workers are hard to find; commonly, when an employee is on parental leave, co-workers take up the slack.) Another aspect of individualism is the high regard in which small business is held in the United States. Studies show that the majority of Americans aspire to own their own business someday, and this, combined with the image of America as a land of opportunity, gives small businesses and their organizations considerable political influence. Small businesses are the most strenuous opponents of even unpaid parental leave in the United States (Press, 1987). Market competitiveness is seen as jeopardized by the need to do without or replace an employee absent on parental leave.

The second tradition that operates against the development of parental leave in the United States is "suspicion of government," particularly in matters "private, sentimental, or sexual" (Schorr, 1979, p. 465). This tradition has retarded the development of child abuse legislation, battered women's shelters, and a national child care policy. Not surprisingly, child care is regarded as a problem of individual families, not to be solved or meddled in by government. Furthermore, the Swedish model of parental leave would call for federal involvement in employer–employee relationships. There is considerable resistance in the United States to such federal involvement (Malo and Murray, 1986). To "sell" parental leave, government officials would need to make the case that economic productivity is enhanced by programs that support employees in meeting their family responsibilities (Clay and Feinstein, 1987). Certainly, such a case can be made in Sweden, which enjoys marked prosperity.

Finally, the nature of our political process works against parental leave policy. That process, Schorr maintains, "does not lend itself to broad agreement on principles to which subsequent policies are subordinated" (1979, p. 465). Swedes agree on principles such as children's welfare and equality between the sexes; Americans do not. Such agreement is possible in a society that is fairly homogeneous in terms of social class and ethnicity (although one out of eight Swedes is foreign-born); it is more difficult in a society like ours with more dramatic social divisions. But our political system also encourages piecemeal reforms; legislation arises out of deals and compromises at the national level rather than out of a genuine concern for solving social problems. The Swedish legislative style, in contrast, is not only oriented toward social problems but more "organized" (Quarfort, McCrea, and Kolenda, 1988). The Parliament first recommended consideration of a change in maternity leave policy in 1967; a commission then studied the proposal and revised it, according to criticisms from industrial shop floors, neighborhood study circles, local union meetings, and women's organizations. The process took seven years; only then was parental leave adopted by the Parliament. The Swedish process, more than the American, leads "to compromise and acceptance of a measure that may have seemed at the outset too radical and innovative" (Childs, 1980, p. 5).

In short, it seems unlikely that the United States will adopt a parental leave program similar to that of Sweden in the near future. Awareness of the difficulties involved, brought to light by a study of the Swedish case, however, may help those who look forward to such a policy.

Fathers' Participation in Parental Leave

Will fathers take advantage of a program that allows them to stay home to take care of their newborn baby with nearly full pay? The Swedish program, now long established, allows us to answer that question.

Only 3 percent of fathers took parental leave the first year, 1974. By 1976 (when the leave had been extended to 7 months), 5 percent of fathers took leave (Riksförsäkringsverket, 1979). These small percentages are not surprising. The program was new, and the fathers who took part were engaged in a dramatic social experiment. The statistics may also be a little misleading. Many fathers were not eligible for the program at that time, since their eligibility depended on the mother's having been employed before the baby was born. Statistics concerning women's labor force participation during this era suggest that at least 20 percent of fathers were ineligible for leave (Statistiska Centralbyrån, 1986, p. 2). Perhaps the most important obstacle was the strong pressure put on Swedish women to breast-feed for the first 6 months; interestingly, the campaign to get all Swedish mothers to nurse began about the time parental leave was extended to fathers (Sandqvist, 1987a).

In 1978, parental leave was extended: 8 months fully paid, 1 month paid at the minimum level. Statistics became available for dual-earner households, where all fathers were eligible to take leave. As parental leave was extended, more fathers participated. By 1980, 23 percent of eligible fathers took leave in the child's first 12 months of life; if the time span considered was extended to 18 months, 27 percent of eligible fathers had taken parental leave (Riksför-säkringsverket, 1985, p. 4).

In 1980, parental leave was extended to 12 months: 9 months with nearly full pay, and 3 months with a minimum stipend. In 1981, the percentage of fathers who took advantage of the leave remained about the same as in 1980—22 percent during the child's first year, 27 percent during the child's first year and a half (Riksför-säkringsverket, 1985, p. 4). This lack of progress may have been due to the new changes in the law. Mothers are more likely than fathers to take the portion of the leave with a low stipend because they tend to earn less money than fathers. Extending the minimally paid period from 1 to 3 months may have increased women's proportion of the leave taken, or at least masked any gains in fathers' participation in the higher-compensated portion of the leave. If we look only at couples who take 7 or 8 months of the leave (when parents can get nearly full pay), we find as many as 44 percent of all fathers taking parental leave (Riksförsäkringsverket, 1985, p. 4).

Although Swedes are allowed to take their parental leave in part or full days, it is most common to take it in full days. Only 10 percent of all days taken by mothers, and 25 percent of days taken by fathers, are taken in less than whole days. Parents are thus given the opportunity to work part time and be home part time, but the vast majority do not take advantage of this.

Mothers usually take the parental leave during the child's first 5 or 6 months of life. If a father takes leave at all, he will take it when the child is 5 or 6 months old. This means that the mother will return to work temporarily; when the father's average month and a half stint is over, she returns home to use the rest of the parental leave. Sandqvist (1987b) has suggested that a pattern of shared leavetaking is an option only when the mother's employer is willing to tolerate her leaving and returning to the job twice in a short span of time.

The survey I conducted in Gothenburg in 1986 included only dual-earner couples (Haas, forthcoming). I found exactly the same percentage of such fathers taking parental leave (27 percent) as the last available survey of the national social insurance board (its figures covered children born in 1982). These results suggest that fathers' participation in parental leave has leveled off. My study was based only on a regional sample, but it included a larger proportion of middle-class men than does the nation as a whole. As a consequence, we might assume that I should have discovered a rate of parental leave usage higher than the national average. The Swedish government seems also to be aware that fathers' participation in parental leave is not increasing; rule changes instituted in 1987 that made more fathers eligible for the leave (those with partners who were not employed before childbirth) seemed designed to encourage greater usage.

Moreover, although a sizable proportion of Swedish fathers take parental leave, the average number of days taken remains small in comparison to the number of days taken by mothers. For children born in 1982, the national social insurance board found that fathers took, on average, 15 percent of the days taken by the couple (fathers who took leave did so for an average of 45 days, in contrast to mothers' average of 262). Fathers were reported to have taken 43 days in 1978 (Riksförsäkringsverket, 1985). In my study, fathers took somewhat more leave (53 days) and mothers somewhat less (225) than was reported nationally for two years earlier; this added up to fathers in my study taking 19 percent of all leave days taken. These differences may reflect an upward trend in use of parental leave *for those fathers who are inclined to take it*, or they may be due to a sampling bias. Since I could look at days taken by both partners in the Gothenburg study, it was possible to calculate what percentage of fathers took an equal part of the leave—defined as at least 40 percent of all leave days taken. Only 4 percent of all the fathers in the study had taken an equal portion of the parental leave. Only 14 percent of all fathers *who took leave* had.

Swedish fathers' participation in parental leave is lower than their participation in other social programs designed to increase their involvement in child care. In 1983, 85 percent of Swedish fathers took advantage of the 10 paid days off at childbirth, for an average of 8.5 days (Riksförsäkringsverket, 1984, p. 12). In 1983, fathers took 35 percent of all paid days off to take care of sick children, for an average of 7 days per year (Sandqvist, 1987b). Why is there such a discrepancy between fathers' participation in these programs and fathers' participation in parental leave? Karin Sandqvist (1987b) has suggested that participation in parental leave is more radical in that it involves complete role reversal—the mother goes back to work while the father stays home. In contrast, the other programs have a smaller role reversal component. When taking "daddy days" (the 10 days off after childbirth), the father is home along with the mother. When assuming responsibility for a sick child, the father does it only a day or so at a time, and usually takes turns with the mother.

The participation rate of fathers in the Swedish parental leave program suggests that a program that would be attractive to American men would likely need to have two features: it should be available to fathers beyond the months mothers typically spend in breastfeeding, and it should be fully paid. An increase in fathers' participation in parental leave was noticed in Sweden as soon as the leave was lengthened beyond 6 months. However, increasing the amount of poorly compensated time off seems to have *reduced* Swedish men's overall participation. A year-long fully paid system would seem optimal, so that a father could stay home for 6 months following the mother's 6-month stay (assuming that she would be breastfeeding around the clock at this stage). Of course, to be truly optimal, such a policy needs to be complemented by an adequate supply of quality day care for one-year-olds, as well as the opportunity for both parents to reduce their workday to 6 hours until the child reaches school age, to prevent children from spending 9 to 10 hours a day in an institutional setting. These latter policies are in place in Sweden but are virtually undiscussed in the United States.

The study of Swedish fathers' participation also suggests that it will take a long time and considerable effort to involve American men in a parental leave program. The Swedish program has been in place for 14 years, yet equal participation of fathers and mothers is clearly far off.

Barriers to Fathers' Participation

Why don't more Swedish fathers take parental leave? Potential barriers to fathers' involvement in child care fall into four categories— biology, social psychology, lack of social support, and economics. (This typology is a blending of those offered by Hwang, 1985, and Lamb, 1986).

Biological Obstacles

In the recent past, Swedes (as well as Americans) assumed that men were less biologically suited for childrearing than women. The physical acts of giving birth and breastfeeding were assumed to forge a tie between mother and child that made the mother better able to meet babies' needs for physical care and emotional security. There is, however, no scientific evidence that, among humans, females are innately better qualified than males to care for infants; studies show that fathers can respond as appropriately as mothers to infants' signals for assistance and, when given the opportunity, spend about the same amount of time as mothers talking, teaching, soothing, and showing affection (Belsky, 1979; Field, 1978; Lamb, 1981; Lamb et al., 1985; Parke and Tinsley, 1981). Studies also show that babies are capable of establishing intimate relationships with more than one primary caretaker, are interested in contact with both parents, and are likely to attach themselves strongly to both parents once attachment behaviors begin at about 6 months of age (Clarke-Stewart, 1978; Hwang, 1985; Jalmert, 1980; Lamb, 1981; Nettelbladt, 1984).

One real biological difference between the sexes is women's unique ability to breastfeed. Especially in Sweden, where 90 percent of mothers nurse for at least 5 months, the fact that fathers cannot breastfeed could be an important obstacle to their participation in parental leave. Indeed, we find that fathers seldom take parental leave before the child's fifth month of life (Riksförsäkringsverket, 1985, p. 4) and that when parental leave is lengthened past the period of breastfeeding, fathers' rates of participation go up. Some Swedish studies have found that parents believe breastfeeding is a barrier to fathers' participating in child care (Hamrin et al., 1983; Hwang, 1985; Statens Offentliga Utredningar, 1978). In the Gothenburg survey, however, no significant association was found between the number of months mothers breastfed (an average of 5) and fathers' likelihood of taking parental leave (Table 22.1). It appears, then, that if parental leave is long enough, this biological difference between the sexes will not prevent fathers from participating in parental leave.

Social–Psychological Obstacles

A second, more important set of potential barriers is social–psychological in origin, related to fathers' motivations, skills, and attitudes toward gender roles. How a man was raised, how much education he has, and the extent to which he has been exposed to new

TABLE 22.1
Factors Associated with a Father's Taking Parental Leave

Independent Variables	Took Leave (1 = no / 2 = yes) (N = 319)		Proportion of Leave Taken (N = 85)	
	r	β	r	β
Social–Psychological Variables				
Belief: men should be breadwinners	− .25*	.14*	− .31*	.30*
Belief: success is men's main goal	− .08		− .19*	
Belief: men can be close to children	− .03		− .14	
Belief: men can do child care	− .07		− .10	
Number of acquaintances who took leave	.12*	.22*	.05	
Attention to parental leave debate	− .15*		− .23*	
Years of education	.16*		.20*	
Own father's participation in child care	− .08		− .19*	
Amount of prior child care experience	.05		.13	
Social Support Variables				
Support from friends	.27*		.23*	
Support from mother	.19*		.08	
Support from father	.22*		.13	
Support from partner	.18*		.17	
Partner:				
Desire to stay home	.07		− .24*	
Own mother's employment status	.14*	.13*	.29*	.31*
Own father's participation in child care	.08		.27*	.29*
Attention to parental leave debate	.11*		.10	
Belief: men should be breadwinners	− .16*		− .18	
Belief: success is men's main goal	− .18*		− .03	
Belief: men can be close to children	.00		.12	
Belief: men can do child care	.06		.19*	
Economic Variables				
Employer support	.13*		.16	
Supervisor support	.24*		.13	
Male co-workers' support	.23*		.21*	
Female co-workers' support	.15*		.26*	
Work regarded as an obstacle	− .21*		− .27*	
White-collar job	.07		.01	
Job satisfaction before childbirth	.06		.11	
Work in public sector	.21*		.13	
Own income before childbirth	− .07		− .23*	
Partner:				
Income before childbirth	.12*		.11	
Income relative to partner's	.16*		.15	
White-collar job	.21*	.16*	.02	
Education level	.22*		.14	
Employer support	.05		.07	
Supervisor support	.04		.04	
Variance explained (R^2)		.22		.25

*Difference significant at .05 level. The reported standardized regression coefficients are those that remain significant when all independent variables are included in multiple regression analyses.

models of fathering could potentially affect his participation in parental leave.

Fathers may feel that domestic work, including child care, is less valued in society than is paid employment; they may not see what benefits for the baby and for their own personality development can be gained by staying home on parental leave. Fathers may feel that they are less capable of taking care of a baby—perhaps because of a lack of positive role models and experience. And a man who feels that men are responsible for providing the family income, that success should be men's main goal in life, and that women are more suited to and capable of parenting would seem less likely to want to take parental leave.

It is notoriously difficult to examine the extent to which such factors influence behavior. People are often unconscious of the role motivations and attitudes play in their behavior. In asking why the father did not take leave, or did not take more leave, this study, like others, found that people tend *not* to mention men's lack of interest or motivation, but instead blame institutional barriers, such as finances or workplace support (Hamrin et al., 1983; Statens Offentliga Utredningar, 1978, 1982).

In this study, I was able to gather information on attitudes toward the male role, exposure to new models of fathering, and upbringing. Orientation to the breadwinner role was found to be an important influence on fathers' tendency to take parental leave. About three-quarters of fathers believed to some degree that men should be more responsible for breadwinning than women, and those with more traditional attitudes were less likely to take parental leave (Table 22.1).

Lack of exposure to new models of fathering was also found to be an important obstacle to participation in parental leave. The majority of men in the study (73 percent) knew at least one other man who had taken parental leave, but the number known was low, an average of four. The fewer such men a father knew, the less likely he was to take parental leave. Similarly, relatively few Swedish fathers (15 percent) said they had paid a lot of attention to the media coverage of parental leave; those who had paid less attention were less likely to take it. Less educated men were less likely than others to take parental leave; education was found to be significantly associated with gender role attitudes.

The ultimate goal of Swedish family policy is a society where men and women share equally the responsibilities of child care. A milestone would be men's sharing parental leave equitably with their partners. In this study, I looked at factors associated with fathers sharing a higher than average *proportion* of the leave. This was calculated by dividing the number of days of leave the father took by the total number of days both the mother and the father took; only fathers who took leave were considered. Feeling that men should be the breadwinners, inattention to publicity about parental leave, and having less education remained as important correlates of fathers' proportion of parental leave taken (Table 22.1). In addition, it was found that fathers were less likely to take a bigger proportion of the leave if they believed that success was men's goal in life, a view that two-thirds of Swedish fathers subscribed to in some degree. An unexpected finding concerned the relationship between a man's upbringing and the relative amount of parental leave he took: men whose own fathers had participated little in child care were found to be *more* likely to share parental leave than other men.

This study failed to find support for some often presumed social–psychological reasons men do not participate in child care. Only 18 percent of the men in the study had a lot of prior experience doing child care before they became parents, yet amount of prior experience was not found to relate either to taking parental leave or to taking a bigger proportion. Only a small minority of the fathers in the study believed that a father could not be as close emotionally to his child as a mother (11 percent); only a few (15 percent) thought women were more capable than men at child care. These attitudes played no role in fathers' tendency to take parental leave.

Lack of Social Support

A third potential barrier to fathers' participation in child care is lack of social support. Fathers might hesitate to take parental leave because they think those close to them will think they are weird. Men who receive support from others have been found to participate more in child care than men who lack such support (Hamrin et al., 1983; Lein, 1979; Pleck, 1986). One can look at support from friends and parents, and most important, at the support expressed by the child's mother.

The majority of fathers in the study did not receive positive support for taking parental leave from their friends and parents. Only 44 percent said their friends were positive; the same proportion said their mothers were. Only one-third (32 percent) said their fathers were positive. Results showed that the less support men received from friends, mother, and father, the less likely they were to take parental leave (Table 22.1). Support from friends was also found to affect men's proportion of leave taken.

The vast majority (73 percent) of fathers reported that their partners were positive toward their taking parental leave; however, when his partner's attitude was not positive, a father was less likely to take parental leave. Another way to look at the extent of mothers' support for fathers' leave-taking is to look at mothers' interest in monopolizing the leave. Each father was asked specifically if the mother's desire to take more of the leave was an obstacle to his taking a bigger portion. Forty percent of fathers admitted that this was the case, and such reports were significantly correlated with fathers' taking a smaller proportion of the parental leave.

Some features of mothers' upbringing and attitudes appeared to be a factor in their willingness to share parental leave. Women whose own mothers had not been employed were less likely to share parental leave with their spouses than were women whose mothers had been employed. Women whose own fathers had not participated in their upbringing were less likely than others to have partners who took a bigger proportion of parental leave. In addition, the less attentive a woman had been to the publicity about parental leave (only one-fourth had been very attentive), the less likely her partner was to take it. Holding traditional attitudes about men's role was also found to be an important barrier to women's sharing parental leave, as has been found in other studies (Hamrin et al., 1983; Schönnesson, 1986). Women's attitudes toward these issues tended to be less traditional than men's. Still, 60 percent of women agreed to some degree that the man should be the primary breadwinner and that success should be men's main goal in life. Only 10 percent, however, felt that men were not capable of doing child care as well as women. The more traditional her attitudes toward the breadwinner role and success as men's main goal, the less likely a woman was to have a partner who took parental leave. In addition, the more skeptical a woman was about men's ability to do child care, the less equitably was parental leave shared by the couple.

Economic Obstacles

A last, and much lauded, set of potential barriers to men's involvement in child care is institutional in character, related to both the man's and the woman's workplaces, jobs, and economic situation.

Men's jobs are widely regarded as the most important obstacles to men's participation in child care (Lamb, Russell, and Sagi, 1983; Pleck, 1986). Previous studies of parental leave in Sweden have also suggested that lack of workplace support is a major factor in fathers' failure to use parental leave benefits. Workplaces in the public sector are widely regarded as friendlier toward men taking parental leave, partly because they feel an obligation to follow governmental directives encouraging men to be more active fathers, and partly because they tend to be less male-dominated, employing more women workers in higher positions than the private sector (Hamrin et al., 1983; Hwang, Eldén, and Fransson, 1984; Trost, 1983).

In general, men in the study reported a lack of support for leave-taking from those at their workplace. Only 15 percent described their employers as positive, and only 18 percent reported their supervisors as positive. Co-workers, especially female ones, were more supportive, but still the majority were not positive. Over one-fourth (27 percent) of male co-workers were regarded as positive, while almost half (46 percent) of female co-workers were. The attitudes of employers, supervisors, and male and female co-workers were all found to be strongly associated with fathers' likelihood of taking leave. The attitudes of supervisors and male co-workers seemed the most crucial. If male and female co-workers were positive, fathers were also likely to take a bigger proportion of leave.

Some jobs are structured in a way that makes it difficult for people to take extended time away from work. Several researchers have suggested that inflexible jobs would make it difficult for men to participate in parental leave (Calleman et al., 1984; Pleck, 1986; Statens Offentliga Utredningar, 1978, 1982). Over half the men in the study (55 percent) reported that work conditions were an important obstacle to their taking (or taking more) parental leave. Moreover, if a man perceived his job as an obstacle in this way, he was less likely to take leave and less likely to take an equal portion of leave.

Additional features of fathers' jobs were examined for potential impact on their decision to take parental leave. Having a white-collar job proved not to be a factor influencing parental leave usage among men, nor did the level of satisfaction with one's job. If he worked in the public sector, he was more likely to take parental leave; however, public sector employers were *not* found to be more supportive of leave-taking than private sector ones.

Additional economic barriers might prevent fathers from participating in parental leave. A 1981 study found that many parents said that they could not share parental leave more equitably for economic reasons (Statens Offentliga Utredningar, 1982). Although they are compensated while taking leave, parents typically get only 90 percent of their former pay, and then only up to a certain income level (which today would be around $20,000). The last months of parental leave are only minimally paid. Both features discourage couples from having the higher-paid worker—usually the father—stay home. Government employees usually have higher compensation levels—typically 100 percent of their former pay. It is therefore not surprising that fathers working in the public sector were found to be more likely to take parental leave. Father's income levels were also found to be negatively related to their likelihood of taking a greater proportion of leave. Correspondingly, women's income levels positively influenced fathers' likelihood of taking leave. The higher the woman's income before her baby's birth (both absolutely and relative to her mate's), the more likely her partner was to take parental leave.

The nature of the woman's job seemed likely to be an important factor in her willingness to share parental leave. Previous studies of parental leave suggested that women will monopolize the leave if they have a job they are unhappy with or if they have a low-status job, both likely effects of women's poor job opportunities (Hamrin et al., 1983; Hwang, Eldén, and Fransson, 1984; Schönnesson, 1986; Statens Offentliga Utredningar, 1978; 1982). Women's job satisfaction proved not to influence their partners' likelihood of taking leave; two-thirds of the women were very satisfied with the jobs they held before their children were born. Job status, however, did have an influence, with women in blue-collar jobs being more likely to monopolize parental leave. Women's educational level, strongly associated with job type, was also found to correlate significantly with fathers' taking parental leave, with more educated women having partners who took leave.

It seemed possible that mothers might be more likely to share parental leave in situations where their own workplaces were hostile toward their taking parental leave. Mothers' employers were more positive than fathers' employers had been toward their taking parental leave, with 41 percent of employers and 48 percent of supervisors being perceived as positive. Reactions from employers and supervisors, however, had no impact on mothers' likelihood of sharing parental leave with their partners.

Many of the factors found to be associated with fathers' leave-taking and the proportion of leave fathers took were highly intercorrelated, so stepwise multiple regression analyses were conducted to sort out which factors had the strongest independent effects on fathers' participation. What was most interesting about this exercise was the fact that economic factors disappeared completely as having strong independent relationships with fathers' participation in parental leave. As potential barriers to fathers' taking leave, what remained was the man's attitude toward the breadwinner role, the number of men he knew who had taken parental leave, lack of support from friends, and factors associated with the mother's willingness—whether or not she had a white-collar job, and whether or not her own mother had been employed. (See Table 22.1 for the standardized beta coefficients.) For proportion of leave taken, the variables found to be most important were the man's attitude toward the breadwinner role, his partner's mother's employment status, and his partner's father's level of participation in child care.

These findings suggest the possibility that workplace attitudes and economic barriers are less real obstacles to participation than they are rationalizations. Gender role attitudes, lack of exposure to new models of fathering, and lack of social support seem more important than economics as barriers to fathers' greater participation in child care.

Multiple regression results also suggested that it would be important to look more closely at the impact mothers have on fathers' participation in child care. Women's interest in monopolizing child care may be difficult to change if it is as deeply rooted in childhood socialization practices as indicated here.

The first set of variables explained 22 percent of the variance in fathers' leave-taking; the second set explained 25 percent of the variance in the proportion of leave fathers took. While these amounts are respectable, it suggests that we still need to look for additional factors associated with fathers' participation in parental leave if we are to have a fuller understanding of the barriers involved.

Use of Parental Leave: Implications for the United States

A study of the Swedish parental leave program can be helpful in increasing our understanding of what social forces operate to keep fathers from participating fully in a program designed to involve them in infant care. One set of barriers is social–psychological, related particularly to fathers' traditional attitudes about breadwinning and mothers' desire to monopolize child care because of the way they themselves were raised. Such barriers are difficult to dismantle quickly, and we might expect that it will take generations to do so.

We have also seen the importance of role models and social support. This is an area where intervention might be more possible. Support groups for men contemplating and taking parental leave could be established. In Sweden, such groups could easily be organized through the prenatal education classes and well-baby clinics that also provide parental education. In the United States, where prenatal and infant care is more decentralized, it might be more difficult to locate and put in touch fathers interested in parental leave, although it might still be done through hospitals, medical practices, or health maintenance organizations.

Another potentially thorny barrier is the workplace. A recent study found that two-thirds of U.S. companies do not see the need for parental leave for fathers (Catalyst, 1986). The law in Sweden makes it clear that an employer must release employees to take parental leave and guarantee them the same job or an equivalent one on their return. Still, I found that the majority of Swedish employers, supervisors, and workers were not positive toward fathers' taking parental leave, and that the perception of a lack of support had an impact on fathers' doing so. If workplace support is lacking in Sweden, we can imagine how difficult—but how necessary—it will be to convince American employers of the importance of parental leave, both for their economic productivity and for guaranteeing the well-being of the next generation of workers.

While the obstacles are considerable, lessons from Sweden also suggest that it is possible to increase fathers' participation in parental leave, albeit slowly. More Swedish men will probably take parental leave in the future because of the impact of the current group of pioneering fathers. Although few fathers have taken leave, those who have serve as important models for those contemplating staying home. Knowing someone who had taken parental leave was a powerful determinant of men's taking leave, and being exposed to publicity about leave helped as well. A snowball effect may gradually lead to a large group of fathers who have tried parental leave because they know others who have done it. We might expect such a snowball to accumulate in our own society once parental leave is instituted.

The other social forces that might lead more Swedish men to take parental leave in the future relate to the work attitudes and employment situations of women. Study results showed that having a working mother was a crucial factor in women's tendency to share parental leave with their mates. Women felt better about going back to work if their own mothers had been in the labor market, and this opened the way for the father to participate in baby care. As time goes on, increasing numbers of women will have had working mothers, in both the United States and Sweden, so we could expect that, over time, increasing numbers of fathers would be given the opportunity to stay home to care for children. The study also showed that as women gain greater access to higher-status jobs, they are more interested in seeing men take on a greater share of the responsibility for child care. As they make more money, the financial losses of having the father stay home diminish. The improving economic opportunities of women, present in both countries although in differing degrees, can be seen as increasing fathers' opportunity and likelihood of participating in parental leave.

Summary

A study of the Swedish experience suggests that it would be difficult to win support in the United States for a parental leave program whereby fathers are encouraged to stay home to care for their new babies, but that social trends in the form of decreasing birth rates, a need for women's employment, and a desire to liberate men from traditional gender stereotypes may be hastening the day when such a program can be put into place. The study also suggests that even when men are given opportunities to take paid parental leave, many will not take advantage of them. While some structural obstacles to fathers' taking parental leave may exist (in the form of intolerant employers and restrictions on income compensation), adherence to traditional gender attitudes and lack of social support seem to be even more important reasons why mothers take most of the parental leave in Sweden. Clearly, not just men, but women too, are still most comfortable with a situation in which women are primarily responsible for child care. If equal use of parental leave is still so far off in Sweden, a society ideologically committed to the concept of equal parenthood for the past 25 years, we can expect that it will take a long time and considerable effort to involve American men in a future parental leave program.

NOTE

Acknowledgments. This research study was sponsored by grants from the American–Scandinavian Foundation and Indiana University. I would like to thank Philip Hwang, Karin Sandqvist, Lena Nilsson Schönnesson, and Ain Haas for their support and encouragement in regard to this project.

REFERENCES

Arbetsgruppen om Mansrollen [Work group on the male role] (1985). *Mannen i förändring* [The changing man]. Stockholm: Tiden/Arbetsmarknadsdepartementet.

Baude, Annika (1979). "Public Policy and Changing Family Patterns in Sweden: 1930–1977." In Jean Lipmen-Blumen and Jessie Bernard, eds., *Sex Roles and Social Policy.* Beverly Hills, Calif.: Sage Publications.

Belsky, Jay (1979). "Mother–Father–Infant Interaction: A Naturalistic Observational Study." *Developmental Psychology* 15: 601–7.

Bronfenbrenner, Urie (1986). "A Generation in Jeopardy: America's Hidden Family Policy." Testimony prepared for a hearing of the Senate Committee on Rules and Administration.

Calleman, Catharine, Lena Lazercrantz, Ann Petersson, and Karin Widerberg (1984). *Kvinnoreformer på mannens villkor* [Women's reforms on men's conditions]. Lund: Studentlitteratur.

Catalyst (1986). *Report on a National Study of Parental Leave.* New York: Catalyst.

Childs, Marquis (1980). *Sweden: The Middle Way on Trial.* New Haven: Yale University Press.

Clarke-Stewart, K. Alison (1978). "And Daddy Makes Three: The Father's Impact on Mother and Child." *Child Development* 49: 466–78.

Clay, William, and Frederick Feinstein (1987). "The Family and Medical Leave Act: A New Labor Standard." *Industrial and Labor Relations Report* 25: 28–33.

Dahlström, Edmund (1971). "An Analysis of the Debate on Sex Roles." In Edmund Dahlström, ed., *The Changing Roles of Men and Women.* Boston: Beacon Press.

Ericsson, Ylva, and Ranveis Jacobsson (1985). *Side by Side: A Report on Equality Between Women and Men in Sweden.* Stockholm: Gotab.

Familjepolitiska Kommittén [Family Policy Committee] (1969). *Jämställdhet mellan män och kvinnor inom sjukförsäkringen* [Equality between men and women within the social insurance system]. Stockholm: Socialdepartementet.

Field, Tiffany (1978). "Interaction Behaviors of Primary vs. Secondary Caretaker Fathers." *Developmental Psychology* 14: 183–84.

Försäkringskassan [Social Insurance Office] (1987). *Föräldraförsäkring* [Parental insurance]. Stockholm: Försäkringskasseförbundet.

Forsberg, Mats (1984). *The Evolution of Social Welfare Policy in Sweden.* Stockholm: Swedish Institute.

Gustafsson, Siv, and Petra Lantz (1985). *Arbete och löner: Ekonomiska teorier och fakta omkring skillnader mellan kvinnor och män* [Work and pay: Economic theories and facts concerning differences between women and men]. Stockholm: Almqvist & Wiksell.

Haas, Linda L. (1981). "Domestic Role Sharing in Sweden." *Journal of Marriage and the Family* 43: 957–67.

——— (1982). "Parental Sharing of Childcare Tasks in Sweden." *Journal of Family Issues* 3: 389–412.

——— (forthcoming). *Equal Parenthood and Social Policy—A Study of Parental Leave in Sweden.* Albany: State University of New York Press.

Hadenius, Stig (1985). *Swedish Politics During the Twentieth Century.* Stockholm: Swedish Institute.

Hamrin, Björn, Agheta Nilsson, and Clnes-Otto Sörman (1983). *Att dela på föräldraledigheten* [Sharing parental leave]. Stockholm: Socialstyrelsen.

Hedvall, Barbro (1975). *Kvinnan i politiken* [The woman in politics]. Stockholm: Trevi.

Hwang, C. Philip (1985). "Smäbarnspappor" [Fathers of small children]. In C. P. Hwang, ed., *Faderskap* [Fatherhood]. Stockholm: Natur och Kultur.

Hwang, C. Philip, Göran Eldén, and Christer Fransson (1984). "Arbetsgivares och Arbetskamraters Attityder till Pappaledighet" [Employers' and co-workers' attitudes toward paternal leave]. Gothenburg: Psychology Department, Gothenburg University.

Jalmert, Lars (1980). *Små barns sociala utveckling: En granskning av forskning om spädbarn, mammor, pappor, könsroller och daghem* [The social development of small children: A Review of research on infants, mothers, fathers, sex roles, and day care]. Kristianstad: Tiden/Folksam.

―――― (1983). *Om svenska män* [About Swedish men]. Stockholm: Arbetsmarknadepartementet.

―――― (1984). *Den svenske mannen* [The Swedish man]. Stockholm: Tiden.

Kagan, Sharon, Edgar Klugman, and Edward F. Zigler (1983). "Shaping Child and Family Policies." In Edward F. Zigler, ed., *Children, Families, and Government.* New York: Cambridge University Press.

Kamerman, Sheila B. (1988). "Maternity and Parenting Benefits: An International Overview." In Edward F. Zigler and Meryl Frank, eds., *The Parental Leave Crisis: Toward a National Policy.* New Haven: Yale University Press.

Kamerman, Sheila B., and Alfred J. Kahn (1980). *Child Care, Family Benefits, and Working Parents: A Study in Comparative Policy.* New York: Columbia University Press.

―――― (1987). *The Responsive Workplace: Employers and a Changing Labor Force.* New York: Columbia University Press.

Katz, Mary, and Melvin Konner (1981). "The Role of the Father: An Anthropological Perspective." In M. E. Lamb, ed., *The Role of the Father in Child Development.* New York: John Wiley.

Konsumentverket [Consumer Affairs Agency] (1982). *Svenska folkets tidsanvändning 1981* [Time use of the Swedish population 1981]. Stockholm: Almänna byråan/Liber.

Lamb, Michael E. (1981). "Fathers and Child Development: An Integrative Review." In Michael E. Lamb, ed., *The Role of the Father in Child Development.* New York: John Wiley.

―――― (1986). "The Changing Roles of Fathers." In Michael E. Lamb, ed., *The Father's Role: Applied Perspectives.* New York: John Wiley.

Lamb, Michael E., Joseph Pleck, Eric Charnow, and James A. Levine (1985). "Paternal Behavior in Humans." *American Zoologist* 25: 883–94.

Lamb, Michael, Graeme Russell, and Abraham Sagi (1983). "Summary and Recommendations for Public Policy." In M. E. Lamb and A. Sagi, eds., *Fatherhood and Family Policy.* Hillsdale, N.J.: Erlbaum.

Landsorganisationen [Blue-collar trade union federation] (1976). *Fac-*

kföreningsrörelsen och familjepolitiken [The trade union movement and family policy]. Stockholm: Prisma.

Lein, Laura (1979). "Male Participation in Home Life: Impact of Social Supports and Breadwinner Responsibility on the Allocation of Tasks." *Family Coordinator* 28: 389–496.

Lyle, Guhhilp, and Gunnar Qvist (1974). *Kvinnorna i mannens samhälle* [Women in a male society]. Stockholm: Esselte Studium.

Malo, Annemarie, and Mary Anne Murray (1986). "HR 4300—Maternity Leave: Helping or Hurting the Viability of the Family?" *Family Policy Insights* 4: 1–8.

Moberg, Eva (1962). *Kvinnor och män* [Women and men]. Stockholm: Bonnier.

Morgan, Robin (1984). *Sisterhood Is Global.* Garden City, N.Y.: Anchor.

Myrdal, Alva, and Gunnar Myrdal (1934). *Kris i befolkningsfrågan* [Crisis in the population question]. Stockholm: Trevi.

Näsman, Elisabet (1986). "Work and Family: A Combination Made Possible by Part-Time Work and Parental Leaves?" Stockholm: Arbetslivcentrum.

Nettelbladt, Per (1984). *Men pappa då?* [What about daddy?] Lund: Studentlitteratur.

Parke, Ross, and Barbara Tinsley (1981). "The Father's Role in Infancy: Determinants of Involvement in Caregiving and Play." In Michael E. Lamb, ed., *The Role of the Father in Child Development.* New York: John Wiley.

Pleck, Joseph H. (1985). *Working Wives/Working Husbands.* Beverly Hills, Calif.: Sage Publications.

―――― (1986). "Employment and Fatherhood: Issues and Innovative Policies." In Michael E. Lamb, ed., *The Father's Role: Applied Perspectives.* New York: John Wiley.

―――― (1988). "Fathers and Infant Care Leave." In Edward F. Zigler and Meryl Frank, eds., *The Parental Leave Crisis: Toward a National Policy.* New Haven: Yale University Press.

Press, Aric (1987). "A New Family Issue." *Newsweek,* January 26, pp. 22–24.

Quarfort, Anne-Marie, Joan McCrae, and Pauline Kolenda (1988). "Sweden's National Policy of Equality Between Men and Women." In P. Kolenda, ed., *Cultural Constructions of "Woman."* Salem, Wis.: Sheffield.

Qvist, Gunnar, Joan Acker, and Val R. Lorwin (1984). "Sweden." In Alice H. Cook, Val R. Lorwin, and Arlene Kaplan Daniels, eds., *Women and Trade Unionism in Eleven Industrialized Countries.* Philadelphia: Temple University Press.

Riksförsäkringsverket [National Social Insurance Board] (1979). "Föräldraförsäkring 1978" [Parental leave in 1978]. Stockholm: Matematiskstatistiska byrån.

―――― (1984). "Föräldrapenning för tillfällig vård av barn 1983" [Parental leave for temporary care of children 1983]. Statistisk rapport no. 12. Stockholm: Matematisk-statistiska byrån.

——— (1985). "Föräldraledighet i samband med bars födelse, barn födda 1978–1982" [Parental leave in connection with childbirth, for children born 1978–1982]. Statistisk rapport no. 4. Stockholm: Matematisk-statistiska byrån.

Sandberg, Elisabet (1975). *Equality is the Goal: A Swedish Report.* Stockholm: Swedish Institute.

Sandlund, Maj-Britt (1971). "The Status of Women in Sweden: Report to the United Nations 1968." In Edmund Dahlström, ed., *The Changing Roles of Men and Women.* Boston: Beacon Press.

Sandqvist, Karin (1987a). *Fathers and Family Work in Two Cultures.* Stockholm: Almqvist & Wiksell International.

——— (1987b). "Swedish Family Policy and the Attempt to Change Paternal Roles." In Charlie Lewis and Margaret O'Brien, eds., *Reassessing Fatherhood: New Observations on Fathers and the Modern Family.* London: Sage.

Schönnesson, Lena Nilsson (1986). Föräldraskap—Delad föräldra ledighet—Jämställdhet [Parenthood—shared parental leave—equality]. Stockholm: Delegationen för Jämställdhetsforskning.

Schorr, Alvin (1979). "Views of Family Policy." *Journal of Marriage and the Family* 41: 465–67.

Scott, Hilda (1982). *Sweden's "Right to Be Human"—Sex Role Equality: The Goal and the Reality.* Boston: Beacon Press.

Sharman, Liz (1987). "News from Overseas." *Family Matters Newsletter* (Australian Institute of Family Studies, Melbourne), October, p. 26.

Sidel, Ruth (1986). *Women and Children Last.* New York: Viking.

Statens Offentliga Utredningar [Government Official Reports] (1978). *Föräldraförsäkring: Betankande av familjestödsutredningen* [Parental insurance: thoughts of the commission for the support of families]. Rapport no. 39. Stockholm: Gotab.

——— (1982). *Enklare föraldraförsäkring: Betankande av föräldraförsäkringsutredningen* [Simpler parental leave: thoughts of the commission on parental insurance]. Rapport no. 36. Stockholm: Gotab.

Statistiska Centralbyrån [Central Bureau of Statistics] (1980). *Levnadsförhållanden: Hur jämställda är vi?* [Living conditions: How equal are we?]. Rapport no. 20. Stockholm: SCB/Modintryck.

——— (1986). *Kvinno- och mans världen* [The world of women and men]. Stockholm: SCB.

Swedish Institute (1987). "Childcare in Sweden." Fact Sheets on Sweden. Stockholm: Swedish Institute.

Trost, Jan (1983). "Mäns åsikter om ledighet från arbete [Men's view concerning work leaves]. *Familjerapporter,* no. 3. Uppsala: Uppsala University.

Wistrand, Birgitta (1981). *Swedish Women on the Move.* Stockholm: Swedish Institute.

23 | The Political History of Parental Leave Policy

Dorothy McBride Stetson

For over a hundred years, American feminists have been concerned about conflicts faced by women trying to reconcile work and family responsibilities. Policymakers have periodically responded to feminist demands, yet women workers here still receive less assistance than their counterparts in many other countries. Only recently has national debate included solutions that treat work and family equally. This chapter traces the history of the debates in the United States over policies affecting women, work, and family and the role of feminists in their elaboration. It builds on the work of those who view the policymaking process as a series of recurring conflicts over the definition of public problems (Edelman, 1977; Edner, 1976; Elder and Cobb, 1983; Fainstein and Fainstein, 1974; Graber, 1976; Kingdon, 1984; Schattschneider, 1975; Scheingold, 1974; Schelling, 1968; Spencer, 1970; Steinberger, 1980).

What is ultimately decided by government depends on the terms of the debate over particular problems and the way issues are defined in that debate. The participants seek to gain acceptance for their view of the problem. For recurring policy problems, such as labor, finance, health, commerce, and civil rights, participants form policy communities. These are networks of individuals in interest groups, political parties, and government who settle into patterns of response to issues, complete with their own terms of debate, ideology, language, and balance of interests. New policy proposals are usually absorbed into one of these existing policy communities (Heclo, 1978; Walker, 1981).

Work–family issues present special problems because they do not fit readily into any policy community. For policymakers to reconcile motherhood with work, they must look at work in new ways, breaking down widely accepted dichotomies separating the public world of employment from the private world of the family. Currently, an inadequate policy framework is accompanied by widespread social

406

disagreement about what sex roles are or should be and ambivalence about women's place in the workforce. Feminists' collective ambivalence about motherhood and women's status has limited their ability to present a clear set of demands. Not only must work–family issues surmount all these barriers, but they require a resolution of the tension between equality and difference—in this case biological differences between the sexes in reproduction.

U.S. policy responses to problems of pregnancy and childbirth, women's rights, and employment can been divided into three phases for comparison: maternity protection (1890s–1950s); pregnancy leave (1950s–1970s); and maternity/parental leave (1980s). For each of these phases, similar questions will be examined. How is the issue of motherhood and work defined? What is the theoretical foundation underlying the debate? Why has a particular definition of the issue prevailed, and how does it relate to existing policy communities? What is the effect of that definition on policy outcomes? Have feminists been successful in changing the terms of debate on the issue?

Maternity Protection

The problems produced by conflicts between childbirth and work came to the public agenda in the 1890s,[1] part of the larger reform movement that produced protective labor legislation for women. Many of those who promoted women's causes, including the social feminists led by the National Consumers' League (NCL), considered work to be harmful to woman, especially in her maternal function. Womanhood and motherhood were inseparable; motherhood and work were incompatible. Thus, work was the problem, not motherhood. The onerous conditions of factories and sweatshops threatened women's health and their ability to have healthy children. Laws were necessary to prevent employers from hurting women and potential offspring.

The theoretical basis of this view of women and work bridged the traditional public and private spheres of work and home. Woman's natural function was motherhood, and motherhood was a public concern. The health of society was at stake in the birth of the next generation. The morality of society was at stake in its rearing. These important social duties were incompatible with work outside the home. When circumstances drew women into factories and offices, they needed protection to assert their real rights. The policy solution, protective laws limiting hours of work and access to dangerous jobs for women, is well documented (Baer, 1978, pp. 14–41; Kessler-Harris, 1982, pp. 180–214). Well known too is the primary legal justification in *Muller* v. *Oregon* (108 U.S. 412 [1908]) for these laws: woman needs special help, especially when "burdens of motherhood are upon her. . . . Differentiated by these matters from the other sex, she is properly placed in a class by herself, and legislation designed for her protection may be sustained, even when like legislation is not necessary for men and could not be sustained" (p. 421). Few of these reforms addressed employment policy affecting pregnancy and childbirth per se. It was widely agreed that most women would leave the workforce forever either after they married or as a result of their first confinement. The idea of job security itself was alien to the labor market for the very poor. Women in sweated labor had little to lose by dropping out and later returning to work. With the victory in *Muller* v. *Oregon*, the NCL and the progressives had succeeded in dominating the policy debate on behalf of women (Collins and Friesen, 1983).

After World War I, the International Labor Organization adopted a convention urging maternity leave, and most European countries enacted some sort of policy.[2] In the United States, the ILO proposals were alien to a public debate that divorced maternal protection from labor policy altogether. After women gained the vote, the NCL, the foremost advocate of early protective laws, continued to control the debate and joined with other social feminists in the Women's Joint Coordinating Committee to pass the Sheppard–Towner Maternal Health Act of 1921. The goal of this legislation was to reduce infant and maternal death rates and had little relation to the issue of work.

Some of the sharpest critics of protective policies were equal rights advocates who challenged the social feminist definition of the issue of work and family. Led by the National Woman's Party (NWP), the opponents denounced treating women as a special class based on their maternal functions and argued that not all women are or become mothers. These drafters of the first Equal Rights Amendment wanted laws to treat workers equally and extend protections to all. The equal rights advocates failed to weaken the social feminists' grip on all matters pertaining to work and women. Instead, the social feminists institutionalized their ideology of women's work through the establishment of the Women's Bureau in the Department of Labor in 1920.

The assumption of the incompatibility of motherhood and work continued to frame the issue until the 1950s. Officially the Women's Bureau had two goals: the protection of potential mothers and the economic advancement of women workers. When these goals proved contradictory, protection prevailed. The bureau staunchly defended protective laws and opposed the Equal Rights Amendment. Even the major changes in the labor force brought about by the mobilization of women in World War II did little to dislodge this preoccupation. Nevertheless, some ideas of women's rights as workers began to seep into the bureau's overwhelming concern with maternal and child health. In 1942 it joined with the Children's Bureau and recommended maternal health standards for employed women: prenatal care, limited hours of work, rest periods, 6 weeks of prenatal leave, and 2 months of postnatal leave (no pay was mentioned). Although still mainly interested in health, the bureau added that childbirth leave should not jeopardize employment or seniority.[3]

Changes in its base of support finally brought the Women's Bureau around to supporting maternity leave. From 1920 on, the bureau had acted as an advocate for middle-class social feminists and the leaders of the National Trade Union League. By 1950 these groups had all but disappeared, replaced by women active in mainline labor unions. Women representatives of the AFL and CIO had met at the Women's Bureau in 1944 to make a formal proposal for maternity leave that became the bureau's most pro-worker statement to that date.[4] It was too little, too late. These proposals for maternity leave did not make their way to the legislative agenda because a redefinition of the issue of work and childbirth was already under way.

Pregnancy as Disability

From the 1940s until the 1970s a new definition of the issue of motherhood and work emerged, culminating in the Pregnancy Discrimination Act of 1978. It was best stated in the proposal of the Citizens Advisory Council on the Status of Women (CACSW):

> Childbirth and complications of pregnancy are, for all *job related purposes*, temporary disabilities and should be treated as such under any health insurance, temporary disability insurance or sick leave plan of an employer, union, or fraternal society. Any policies or practices of an employer or union, written or unwritten, applied to instances of temporary disability other than pregnancy should be applied to incapacity due to pregnancy or childbirth including policies or practices relating to leave of absence, restoration or recall to duty and seniority. No additional or different benefits or restrictions should be applied to disability

because of pregnancy or childbirth, and no pregnant woman employee should be in a better position in relation to job-related practices or benefits than an employee similarly situated suffering from any other disability. (U.S. Citizens Advisory Council on the Status of Women, 1971, p. 4, emphasis in original)

This definition has several important elements. It separates the functions of childbirth and childrearing. Only childbirth has any relevance to employment policy, thus eliminating the concept of motherhood from discussion altogether. Pregnancy and childbirth are seen in terms of their effect on the ability of women to work, and thus are categorized among a number of possible physical disabilities. Employers need concern themselves with pregnancy and childbirth only if they are concerned with other disabilities; then they should give the same leave and benefits as for any other disability, no more, no less. Less-than-equal treatment would be discriminatory against women workers, and better-than-equal treatment would be divisive and increase the relative cost of hiring women. Disability leave is a worker's right. Therefore, leave for pregnancy-related disability is a worker's right as well. The emphasis is on the worker and the workplace, with no reference to the family, children, or mothering, which are separated from the policy discussion.

The definition of pregnancy as a job-related temporary disability is based on theories of antidiscrimination and individualism. Advocates of women's rights who were successful in influencing the terms of debate on this issue were proponents of liberal feminism, the spiritual daughters of the NWP, the authors of the Equal Rights Amendment. For women to have equality, the idea of their separate domestic sphere had to be destroyed and women's issues separated from those of children and family. Women were members of the labor force and entitled to fair treatment and nondiscrimination. This meant no special classification, regardless of motivation. Fair treatment and individualism meant antidiscrimination. Forget race and sex; concentrate on ability, opportunity, and fitness to work. The focus on the individual right to work was a way of simplifying the complex social phenomena of pregnancy, childbirth, and their social consequences. Quite simply, this framework excluded concerns of motherhood, children, family, and health, and looked only at the physical fitness of women as full members of the labor force.

How did this definition come to dominate the policy debate in the 1970s? The idea of treating pregnancy as a temporary disability had been in the public policy arena for decades.[5] Postwar labor legislation began to provide temporary disability insurance (TDI) and leave for workers. The first such law (passed in Rhode Island in 1942) included pregnancy as one of the covered disabilities and became the test as women claimed disability leave and benefits.[6] Since women made up a relatively large portion of the state's labor force, the costs grew, and the legislature acted to restrict coverage of pregnancy. On the basis of Rhode Island's experience, other states formally excluded pregnancy from the outset. In contrast, the 1946 Federal Railroad Unemployment Insurance Act included pregnancy as a temporary disability. Because fewer than 10 percent of rail employees were women, pregnancy remained covered by the act. Opposition to the inclusion of pregnancy as a temporary disability in these early test cases came to be based on cost, compounded by traditional attitudes about women as workers. It was still widely believed that most of those who took disability benefits for maternity did not return to work: "These benefits also frequently represent a 'termination benefit,' since many women do not return to work after delivery. Many believe that benefits to non-permanent members of the labor force does not further the purpose of this program and should be prohibited" (Osborn, 1958, p. 111).

Demands that pregnancy be treated as a temporary disability came from feminists in the government, and specifically the Women's Bureau. Its role as an advocate for social feminists and labor unions declined as it merged into the mainstream of the Labor Department in the 1950s (Sealander, 1983). As part of a more activist stance toward economic planning and manpower development, the department began to encourage women to join the workforce. "The Women's Bureau crept incrementally toward equal rights for women by trying to understand the factors that discouraged wage work among them and to increase opportunities for work" (Kessler-Harris, 1982, p. 313).

The bureau worked closely with President Kennedy's Commission on the Status of Women (CSW) and its descendant, the Citizens Advisory Council on the Status of Women. Although the CSW report made only passing reference to the need for some sort of maternity benefits, the CACSW made specific policy recommendations. It was its report (U.S. Citizens Advisory Council, 1971) that separated childbirth from childrearing and defined pregnancy and childbirth as job-related disabilities.

The CACSW's proposal (issued in 1970) had wide impact. In the 1960s, the Equal Employment Opportunity Commission (EEOC) had told employers that excluded pregnancy benefits was not sex discrimination, since pregnancy was a disability "unique to the female sex" (Kamerman, Kahn, and Kingston, 1983, pp. 39–40). In

1971, Women's Bureau director Elizabeth Duncan Koontz argued that failure to treat pregnancy as a temporary disability *was* sex discrimination, prohibited under Title VII and the equal protection clause of the Fourteenth Amendment: "It seems certain that the courts, after full consideration, will adopt the obvious conclusion that pregnancy is a temporary disability and that women are entitled to the same autonomy and economic benefits in dealing with it that employees have in dealing with other temporary disabilities" (Koontz, 1971, p. 501). EEOC was convinced and adopted the CACSW proposal in its 1972 guidelines.[7]

Opponents of defining pregnancy as a job-related disability protected by anti-sex discrimination law responded to several parts of the CACSW argument. First, they maintained that pregnancy is not a disability but a natural function—a "normal physiological condition"—that is private and usually voluntary. No standard employment practice gives leave and benefits for such natural functions. Second, some opponents pointed to Rhode Island's experience with TDI legislation, claiming that pregnancy leave is just too costly. This view was bolstered by evidence that women do not return to work after pregnancy, an effect quite different from that of "real" disabilities due to illness or accident. Finally, they contended that although pregnancy does have the effect of disabling an employee, it is not sex or class discrimination to exclude this disability.

The most famous articulation of this last point of view is found in the Supreme Court opinions in *Geduldig* v. *Aiello* (1974), which dealt with sex discrimination under the Fourteenth Amendment, and *General Electric* v. *Gilbert* (429 U.S. 125 [1976]), which interpreted Title VII of the Civil Rights Act. In both cases the Supreme Court sided with the opponents and ruled that failure to include pregnancy under temporary disability benefit plans was not sex discrimination and therefore not prohibited by the Fourteenth Amendment or Title VII. Although they agreed in other cases that mandatory maternity leave is a violation of due process (*Cleveland Board of Education* v. *La Fleur*, 414 U.S. 632 [1973]),[8] and that denial of seniority after leave for childbirth was a discriminatory burden prohibited by Title VII (*Nashville Gas Co.* v. *Satty*, 434 U.S. 136 [1977]), the Court reasoned in the *Geduldig* case that employment practices removing pregnancy from a list of disabilities would affect only a subclass of women, not all women: "There is no risk from which men are protected and women are not. Likewise, there is no risk from which women are protected and men are not" (417 U.S. 484, 496–97).

The matter of Title VII was finally settled with the Pregnancy Discrimination Act (PDA) of 1978. A coalition of representatives from unions, civil rights groups, and feminist organizations, especially the National Organization for Women (NOW) and the Women's Equity Action League (WEAL), formed the Campaign to End Discrimination Against Pregnant Workers and convinced Congress that, as the CACSW had defined it, pregnancy is a temporary disability, and failure to include it on a list of covered disabilities is prohibited sex discrimination under Title VII (Gelb and Palley, 1987, pp. 162–74). The PDA constitutes the first national policy on employment and motherhood.

Defining pregnancy as a temporary disability signaled the official acceptance of women as part of the labor force. For the first time, women workers who had children could expect reinstatement and unemployment benefits, and many could receive pay through sick leave, vacation time, or disability benefit programs. Feminists had succeeded in making pregnancy an issue of sex discrimination.

Employment benefits for many women workers, however, were still far from adequate. A substantial number had no guaranteed leave for pregnancy, since the PDA applied only to those employers covered by Title VII who already had disability plans. Only five states required employers to have TDI plans—California, Hawaii, New Jersey, New York, and Rhode Island. Otherwise, it was in precisely those situations without disability plans—part-time positions, small companies not covered by Title VII—that women were most likely to be found. As many as 60 percent of women workers may have no income-protected leave for pregnancy (Kamerman, Kahn, and Kingston, 1983, pp. 39–40).

Current equal opportunity policy treats the newer entrants to the workforce, women, the same way as "regular workers," namely men. Accordingly, the benefits and rights that male workers have are extended to women. Only in those areas where they are like men do anti–sex discrimination laws work for women. Since pregnancy and childbirth are not functions of men, the courts at first did not include them as part of sex discrimination. The triumph of the feminists in the 1970s was to find a way to relate pregnancy and childbirth to something that happened to men—namely, job-related disability. Thus, the language and culture of the workplace were free of reference to maternity, mothering, children, and family.

In the 1970s there seemed to be little dissent among feminist groups over the PDA, which represented one of their major legislative victories. Joyce Gelb and Marian Lief Palley credit this victory to the fact that the issue was a "narrow role equity issue" and within the mainstream of thinking on the relation of women to the workforce (1987, p. 162). It was a triumph for the national liberal feminist leadership and fitted within the existing policy definitions of anti-discrimination in labor rights. Amid the rejoicing, however, the seeds of a new definition of the issue were taking root.

Maternity/Parental Leave

The PDA provoked a renewal of the debate over equality and difference and the problem of achieving equality in the workforce in the face of the biological differences of the sexes. This "equal treatment/special treatment" debate has been posed as a choice between a standard of equality that ignores sex as a relevant factor in policy and one that requires that women's special reproductive burdens be recognized and receive special treatment and consideration.

The vicissitudes of this debate are reflected both in scholarly journals (Baron, 1987; Finley, 1986; Kay, 1985; Krieger and Cooney, 1983; Williams, 1984–85) and in ongoing conflicts in the American political system. Continuing the long search for a definition of the issue of children and work and their relation to the status of women in the workplace, one approach is embodied in recent state maternity leave legislation, and another in the Family and Medical Leave Act in Congress.

While liberal feminists were getting Congress to treat pregnancy as a job-related temporary disability, other advocates of women's rights had begun formulating a new definition of the issue of work and children. The liberals had worked to separate women from family issues. The dissenters sought to unite them, arguing that a recognition of women's right to work did not always mean relegating pregnancy to disability and childrearing to a sphere completely apart from the workplace. For the first time feminists sought to reconcile women's two roles, at home and at work, without sacrificing one for the other.[9] This theme was developed by Betty Friedan in her dissent from mainstream feminist reform, *The Second Stage* (1981). The contemporary feminist movement had succeeded in breaking down legal barriers to equality. Friedan called for a second stage to restructure family and work relations to enable women to live in equality without the artificial sacrifice of either work or family life. She advocated maternity and paternity leaves as part of comprehensive changes to increase choice and flexibility and permit everyone to succeed in work and to rear children.

The Montana Maternity Leave Act (MMLA) represents a legislative response to this "two roles" definition. In 1972 Montana added an ERA to its constitution, prohibiting private as well as public sex discrimination. The legislature convened a subcommittee to review state statutes and bring them into compliance. "The subcommittee was aware of the most common criticism of equal rights legislation: that equal rights for men and women would destroy the family and bring chaos to an orderly society and government. Because of this awareness, the overriding concern of the subcommittee was to draft legislation that would accomplish real sexual equality while encouraging stable and workable family and societal relationships" (Montana Legislative Council, 1974, p. 3).

One of the solutions was the MMLA, which made it unlawful for an employer to terminate a woman's employment because of pregnancy and to refuse to grant a reasonable leave of absence for pregnancy. Both the Montana Supreme Court and the federal district court upheld the statute. In doing so, the courts affirmed a definition of equality that would be consistent with special leaves for childbirth: "The MMLA would protect the right of husband and wife, man and woman alike to procreate and raise a family without sacrificing the right of the wife to work and help support the family after her pregnancy. The MMLA would ensure that both men and women could choose together to raise a family without permanently relinquishing the necessary income of the working wife" (*Miller–Wohl* v. *Commissioner of Labor and Industry of Montana*, 515 F. Supp. 1266–67 [D. Mont. 1981]).

A similar argument for the equal right to work and procreate was made by supporters of the California special disability statute. The California law of 1978 was enacted in the wake of the Supreme Court's *Gilbert* and *Geduldig* decisions. Under the California statute, employers are required to provide pregnancy leave for up to 4 months, longer than for other disabilities. Employers' challenges to his law wound up in the U.S. Supreme Court. The *Cal Fed* case (*California Federal Savings & Loan* v. *Guerra*, 479 U.S. 272 [1987]) illustrated the division in the women's movement over the definition of the issue of maternity leave. Both sides argued for equality and charged that their opponents' solution would hurt women.

The Supreme Court upheld the California law, and Justice Marshall's majority opinion made references to the "two roles" argument: "By 'taking pregnancy into account' California's pregnancy disability statute allows women as well as men to have families without losing their jobs" (p. 283). It is not like the protective legislation of the past, because it "does not reflect archaic or stereotypical notions about pregnancy and the abilities of pregnant workers" (p. 283). Despite these comments, the Court chose not to base its decision on the issue of equality in work and reproduction. Rather, the plaintiffs portrayed the problem as a conflict between the California law and Title VII's ban on discrimination with respect to pregnancy in the PDA. California Federal argued that it could not comply because Title VII preempted the state law. The Court's decision rested on the interpretation of Congress's intent with respect to preemption. The Court majority ruled against California Federal, saying that the PDA was intended to end discrimination against pregnant workers and did not prohibit added benefits to them. Since the California law did not require employers to discriminate against anyone, they could comply with both laws. The Court ruled that Congress was aware of laws such as the one in Montana and other states and expected such laws to continue to be in force under the PDA.

The feminist critics of state maternity leave acts are promoting another solution in Congress. The Family and Medical Leave Act (FMLA) offers yet another definition of this issue, distinguishing leave for medical disability (including pregnancy) from leave for child care. The act as originally drafted would require large employers to have "medical leave" for up to 26 weeks and "family leave" for up to 18 weeks over two years for the care of a newborn, an adopted infant, or a sick child.[10] The act guarantees job protection, so that after medical or family leave an employee would be restored to his or her former job or an equivalent one with no loss of pay or seniority. There is no requirement that the leave be paid.

The authors of the legislation represent mainstream feminist organizations and the Congressional Caucus for Women's Issues. Fearing detrimental effects from the *Cal Fed* case, they seek to accommodate women's two roles by recognizing two roles for men as well, making childrearing a concern of all workers and employers. They have formed a coalition with labor unions, including the American Federation of State, County and Municipal Employees (AFSCME) and Service Employees International, which have a large percentage of women members. As the FMLA made its way through the congressional maze, the coalition grew, the feminists lost control of the debate, and the act lost a clear identity. As a woman's measure, it offers leave as a means of helping women keep both their jobs and their families. As a family measure, it suggests that leave for both parents will strengthen parent–child relationships and ease family burdens. As a labor measure, the FMLA extends job-protected leave to whole classes of employees not yet covered. Less and less a women's issue, family leave is more frequently presented as a family or a labor issue.

Opponents of the FMLA, led by the Chamber of Commerce, prefer to describe a proposal for a national parental leave policy as a labor issue rather than as a family or women's issue. Opponents are reluctant to argue against support for mothers, families, and children. As a matter of labor legislation, however, they can confront the issue within an existing policy community and use typical business arguments to defeat or weaken it: high cost, the danger of excessive federal regulation and interference, and the tradition of determining benefits through management–labor contract negotiations.[11] The small business interests wail to their representatives about heavy government regulations driving them to bankruptcy. Parental leave is a worthwhile benefit, they concede, but it should not be imposed on employers.

Cost has always been an effective argument when used by business groups against any benefit laws. A concern of the 1980s—U.S. competitiveness—has been added to the debate. To the criticism that the United States is the only industrial country without maternity leave, they respond that America should not be concerned—those countries with more generous family leave also have more state control and less success in job creation. Cost has also often been invoked to exclude medium-sized and small businesses from any federal labor legislation. Small firms are exempt from Title VII anti-discrimination regulations; they demand to be exempt from required family and medical leave as well. In late 1987 they wrested a compromise from the House Labor Committee to exempt firms with fewer than 50 employees for the first three years, and firms with fewer than 35 employees after that. This would mean that a large percentage of women workers would not be covered by FMLA should it go into effect. The compromise also reduced the time for medical leave and family leave to 15 weeks and 10 weeks respectively.

Before the 1988 presidential election, opponents of the FMLA prevailed. They succeeded, as noted, in defining it as labor legislation, and the bill had to compete for floor time with several other labor and health bills long delayed by "Reaganomics." Finally, along with major child care and antipornography bills, the FMLA failed to overcome a filibuster by Senate opponents in the last days of the 100th Congress.[12]

Conclusion

So far, women with children and jobs have coped with the tensions between the two responsibilities with little help from the government. In the three phases of policy development I have described, definitions of the issue have changed, as has the relationship of feminists to the existing policy communities. Although the problem has been on the public agenda for decades, public policy has failed to provide a way to accommodate the need and the right to work with continuing family responsibilities.

The third stage of policy debate is still in process. Some changes from previous debates are already clear. Work and family are reunited in this new debate, with full recognition of women's roles both in the family and on the job. What is not settled is the relation of these to the government's responsibility. One solution offered by some states and accepted by the Supreme Court is a new definition of equality: the right to procreate without losing job status, guaranteed by special policies for women workers. The other solution, represented by the FMLA, is to extend the concept of two roles to all workers and require employers to alleviate tensions between the two for men as well as women.

Feminists have been central to the policymaking process in all these stages. But we find unsatisfying results when the strategy of feminists with respect to existing policy communities is considered. The social feminists of the Progressive movement gained control of the definition of the issue and won a new set of state policies protecting women workers because of their role as mothers. They formed a small policy community with the Women's Bureau at the center to promote the needs of mothers in the workforce. The result, however, was the isolation of women workers and their advocates at the Women's Bureau from mainstream employment practice and policy. The inadequacy of this solution became overwhelmingly obvious with the increase of women in the workforce after World War II.

In the second stage, feminists opted to work within the existing policy communities, a strategy consistent with their goal of integrating the sexes. They used the framework, ideology, and language of labor and civil rights policy communities and were eventually successful in including pregnancy as a job-related disability. Yet that policy has proved inadequate for dealing with the real special needs of women workers.

Will the third time be the charm or the strikeout? Feminist proposals have implications for transforming the political discourse in labor policy communities. There have been some successes. The *Cal Fed* opinion defined maternity leave as a way of achieving real equality, not enshrining the role of mother, as had been done by the maternity protection laws. At the same time, the *Cal Fed* solution could lead to the isolation of women from the mainstream of the labor force once again. Proposals for parental leave carry the potential for a dramatic shift in public definitions of work, family, and sex roles. The potential will be unrealized if this new issue, like so many before, becomes absorbed into an existing policy community, making it little more than a symbol of partial and limited direct help to a minority of workers.

NOTES

1. The idea of maternity leave and benefits for women originated in Germany in the 1880s and received added support from the International Labor Organization in 1919. There were few advocates in the United States. Only six states adopted statutes prohibiting the employment of women immediately before and after childbirth: Connecticut, Massachusetts, Missouri, New York, Vermont, and Washington. These laws were framed as restrictions on employers rather than as rights for workers.

2. The ILO convention defined maternity protection as follows: (1) an employed woman has the right to leave work for 6 weeks before and 6 weeks after confinement; and (2) the employee will receive benefits for full and healthy maintenance of herself and her child.

3. Some states adopted laws preventing employers from employing women before and after childbirth, but few offered job protection. Private employers' policies varied, but it was "generally understood" that most women would quit working to care for a newborn child (Kamerman, Kahn, and Kingston, 1983, pp. 33–38).

4. The Women's Bureau proposed that (1) pregnancy should not be grounds for dismissal; (2) pregnant workers could be transferred to other duties if physicians agreed; (3) maternity leave must be at least 6 weeks before and 2 months after birth, extendable to one year if necessary; (4) there should be no loss of seniority; (5) sick and vacation leave could be used (at the employee's option) for maternity leave; (6) the employee could return to her former job or one at comparable pay.

5. Pro-ERA/NWP feminists in the 1920s reconciled maternity leave with equal rights philosophy by equating pregnant workers with maimed workers and disabled soldiers.

6. Four others followed: California (1946); New Jersey (1948); New York (1949); and Washington (1949).

7. Some scholars say that EEOC members were influenced by debates on Title VII amendments in Congress that same year (Kamerman, Kahn, and Kingston, 1983).

8. In *Crawford* v. *Cushman* (531 F.2d 114, 2d Cir. [1976]), the federal circuit court ruled that mandatory discharge of pregnant women from the military violated the Fifth Amendment. The armed services now accommo-

date pregnancy and childbirth along with military employment (Holm, 1982).

9. Alva Myrdal and Viola Klein's *Women's Two Roles* (1956) forecast the impact on family life and children of women's increasing entry into the labor force and argued that employers must adopt practices to answer the special needs of women trying to juggle home and family responsibilities.

10. A House version of the bill would also permit leave to care for a seriously ill parent.

11. To counteract the Chamber's claim that parental leave will cost business billions of dollars, the Institute for Women's Policy Research has presented data showing that it would in fact shift costs now borne exclusively by women workers and their families to the larger business community (Spalter-Roth and Hartmann, 1988, and Chapter 3).

12. A few policy reform efforts have taken place at the state level. Minnesota, Oregon, and Rhode Island have parental leave only, while Connecticut, Maine, and Wisconsin have passed medical and family leave acts.

REFERENCES

Adams, C. T., and K. T. Winston (1980). *Mothers at Work.* New York: Longman.

Baer, Judith (1978). *The Chains of Protection.* Westport, Conn.: Greenwood Press.

Baron, Ava (1987). "Feminist Legal Strategies: The Powers of Difference." In Beth Hess and M. M. Ferree, eds., *Analyzing Gender.* Newbury Park, Calif.: Sage Publications.

Bernard, Jessie (1971). *Women and the Public Interest.* Chicago: Aldine.

Boneparth, Ellen, and Emily Stoper (1988). *Women, Power, and Policy* (2d ed.). New·York: Pergamon Press.

Brazelton, T. Berry (1985). *Working and Caring.* Reading, Mass.: Addison-Wesley.

Collins, Ronald and Jennifer Friesen (1983). "Looking Back on Muller v. Oregon." *American Bar Association Journal* 69: 295–98, 472–77.

Edelman, Murray (1977). *Political Language.* New York: Academic Press.

Edner, Sheldon (1976). "Intergovernmental Policy Development: The Importance of Problem Definition." In C. O. Jones and R. D. Thomas, eds., *Public Policy Making in a Federal System.* Beverly Hills, Calif.: Sage Publications.

Elder, C. D., and R. W. Cobb (1983). *The Political Use of Symbols.* New York: Longman.

Erickson, Nancy (1979). "Pregnancy Discrimination: An Analytical Approach." *Women's Rights Law Reporter* 5: 83–105.

Fainstein, N. I., and S. S. Fainstein (1974). *Urban Political Movements.* Englewood Cliffs, N.J.: Prentice-Hall.

Finley, Lucinda M. (1986). "Transcending Equality Theory: A Way Out of the Maternity and Workplace Debate." *Columbia Law Review* 86: 1118–82.

Freeman, Jo (1975). *The Politics of Women's Liberation.* New York: Longman.

Friedan, Betty (1981). *The Second Stage.* New York: Summit Books.

Gelb, Joyce, and Marian Lief Palley, eds. (1987). *Women and Public Policies* (rev. ed.). Princeton: Princeton University Press.

Gladstone, Leslie (1986). "Parental Leave: The Family and Medical Leave Act." Washington, D.C.: Library of Congress, Congressional Research Service.

Gladstone, Leslie W., Jennifer D. Williams, and Richard S. Belous (1985). *Maternity and Parental Leave Policies: A Comparative Analysis.* Washington, D.C.: Library of Congress, Congressional Research Service.

Graber, Doris (1976). *Verbal Behavior and Politics.* Urbana: University of Illinois Press.

Heclo, Hugh (1978). "Issue Networks and the Executive Establishment." In Anthony King, ed., *The New American Political System.* Washington, D.C.: American Enterprise Institute.

Hess, Beth, and M. M. Ferree, eds. (1987). *Analyzing Gender.* Newbury Park, Calif.: Sage Publications.

Hewlett, Sylvia A. (1986). *A Lesser Life: The Myth of Women's Liberation in America.* New York: William Morrow.

Holm, Jeanne (1982). *Women in the Military: An Unfinished Revolution.* Novelo, Calif.: Presidio.

Kamerman, Sheila B., and Alfred J. Kahn (1981). *Child Care, Family Benefits, and Working Parents: A Study in Comparative Policy.* New York: Columbia University Press.

Kamerman, Sheila B., Alfred J. Kahn, and Paul W. Kingston (1983). *Maternity Policies and Working Women.* New York: Columbia University Press.

Kay, Herma Hill (1985). "Equality and Difference: The Case of Pregnancy." *Berkeley Women's Law Journal* 1: 1– 38.

Kessler-Harris, Alice (1982). *Out to Work.* New York: Oxford University Press.

Kingdon, John W. (1984). *Agendas, Alternatives, and Public Policies.* Boston: Little, Brown.

Koontz, Elizabeth Duncan (1971). "Childbirth and Child Rearing Leave: Job Related Benefits." *New York Law Forum* 17: 480–502.

Krieger, Linda, and Patricia Cooney (1983). "The Miller–Wohl Controversy: Equal Treatment, Positive Action, and the Meaning of Women's Equality." *Golden Gate University Law Review* 13: 513–72.

Lemons, J. S. (1973). *The Woman Citizen: Social Feminism in the 1920s.* Urbana: University of Illinois Press.

Little, Caroline (1982). "Motherhood or Overload: The Need for a National Maternity Policy." *New York University Journal of International Law and Politics* 17: 717–49.

Mead, Margaret and Frances B. Kaplan (1965). *American Women: Report of* the President's Commission on the Status of Women and Other Publications of the Commission. New York: Scribners.

Montana Legislative Council (1974). Equality of the Sexes. Interim Study by the Subcommittee on the Judiciary. Helena: Montana Legislative Council.

Myrdal, Alva, and Viola Klein (1956). Women's Two Roles: Home and Work. London: Routledge & Kegan Paul.

Olsen, Frances (1983). "The Family and the Market: A Study of Ideology and Legal Reform." Harvard Law Review 96: 1497– 578.

Osborn, Grant M. (1958). Compulsory Temporary Disability Insurance in the United States. Philadelphia: R. D. Irwin.

Radigan, A. L. (1988). Concept and Compromise: The Evolution of Family Leave Legislation in the U.S. Congress. Washington, D.C.: Women's Research and Education Institute.

Safilios-Rothchild, Constantina (1974). Women and Social Policy. Englewood Cliffs, N.J.: Prentice-Hall.

Schattschneider, E. E. (1975). The Semisovereign People. Hinsdale, Ill.: Dryden Press.

Scheingold, Stuart A. (1974). The Politics of Rights: Lawyers, Public Policy and Political Change. New Haven: Yale University Press.

Schelling, Thomas C. (1968). The Strategy of Conflict. London: Oxford University Press.

Sealander, Judith (1983). As Minority Becomes Majority: Federal Reaction to the Phenomenon of Women in the Workforce 1920–1963. Westport, Conn.: Greenwood Press.

Smirnov, S. A. (1979). "Maternity Protection: National Law and Practice in Selected European Countries." International Social Science Review 32: 420–44.

Spalter-Roth, Roberta M., and Heidi I. Hartmann (1988). Unnecessary Losses: Costs to Americans of the Lack of Family and Medical Leave. Washington, D.C.: Institute for Women's Policy Research.

Spencer, Martin E. (1970). "Politics and Rhetorics." Social Research 37: 597–623.

Steinberger, Peter J. (1980). "Typologies of Public Policy: Meaning Construction and the Policy Process." Social Science Quarterly 61: 185–97.

Tidwell, James (1985). "Equality in the Workplace: Is That Enough for Pregnant Workers?" Journal of Family Law 23: 401–18.

U.S. Citizens Advisory Council on the Status of Women (1971). Women in 1970. Washington, D.C.: Government Printing Office.

U.S. Congress, House Committee on Education and Labor (1985). Hearings on Parental and Disability Leave Act, 99th Congress, 1st Sess. Washington, D.C.: Government Printing Office.

——— (1987). Joint Hearings on the Family and Medical Leave Act of 1987. 100th Congress, 1st Sess. Washington, D.C.: Government Printing Office.

U.S. Department of Labor (1969). *Handbook on Women Workers*. Washington, D.C.: Government Printing Office.

——— (1970). *Laws on Sex Discrimination in Employment*. Washington, D.C.: Government Printing Office.

——— Women's Bureau (1952). *Maternity Protection of Employed Women*. Bulletin no. 240. Washington, D.C.: Government Printing Office.

Walker, Jack (1981). "The Diffusion of Knowledge, Policy Communities and Agenda Setting." In John Tropman, Milan J. Dluhy, and Robert Lind, eds., *New Strategic Perspectives in Social Policy*. New York: Pergamon Press.

Williams, Wendy W. (1984–85). "Equality's Riddle: Pregnancy and the Equal Treatment/Special Treatment Debate." *New York University Review of Law and Social Change* 13: 325–80.

Wolgast, Elizabeth (1980). *Equality and the Rights of Women*. Ithaca, N.Y.: Cornell University Press.

Zigler, Edward F., and Meryl Frank, eds. (1988). *The Parental Leave Crisis: Toward a National Policy*. New Haven: Yale University Press.

24 | Parental Leave and Child Care in China

Li Min

As the People's Republic of China has developed, maternity leave and child care have been given increasing attention by the government, especially in the two decades since the initiation of a new birth control policy.

After the liberation of 1949, women in both urban and rural areas went out of their homes to be factory workers and farmers. To meet their needs, new laws were written. Child care has also been developed. In 1987, there were 347,251,189 children under the age of 14 in China. Five kinds of child care facilities enroll 30 percent of the children in China. These benefits for women and children help women participate more actively in their work and contribute more to society.

Maternity Leave and Child Care: The Current Situation

A 1988 law (Legislation of Labor Protection for Female Workers) extends maternity leave from 72 days to 90 days, including 15 days prenatal leave. Women who have twins or triplets can take an additional 15 days or more. Women have a right to sue an employer who disobeys the law, and the relevant government official must make the decision within 30 days. If the woman is not satisfied with the decision, she can appeal to a higher-level official within 15 days. The law also states that any job that is suitable for women (that is, a job that is not toxic or otherwise harmful to women's health) should be open to them, and no work unit has the right to terminate a woman's basic income while she is pregnant or on maternity leave. Furthermore, beginning in the seventh month of pregnancy, a woman may not be placed on a night shift, and any pregnant woman who needs to have a prenatal examination during work hours must be treated as if she were at work. Finally, in the baby's first year of life, the mother is allowed to nurse twice a day (30 minutes each time) while she is at work. This new law gives women more legal rights than ever before. But people who disobey the "one child" birth control policy are still punished and denied these benefits.

In the last two decades, as the birth control policy has been increasingly emphasized, child care has also been improved. According to the *China Annual Statistics 1987*, there were 172,262 kindergartens and 14,797 kindergarten teachers in that year, with a teacher to child ratio of 1 to 26.9. In addition, a 1987 study of children's issues in nine provinces was conducted by the National Statistics Bureau, the Ministry of Public Health, the Ministry of Public Security, the Ministry of Civil Administration, the All-China Women's Federation, and the Central Committee of the Communist Youth League, supported by the Children's Fund of the United Nations. It found that 92.9 percent of children live with their parents, 82.5 percent of parents pay close attention to training children to be independent, and 72.3 percent of parents frequently teach their children how to study, suggesting that the family atmosphere for children is better than ever before. Of 93,100 pre-school-aged children, 22.6 percent are in day care centers (51.7 percent of children in urban areas, and 14.9 percent of children in rural areas). Two-thirds (66.4 percent) of 32,600 infants are breastfed (69.5 percent of babies in rural areas, and 53.9 percent of babies in urban areas). Of children from birth to five years of age, 82.9 percent had been inoculated against measles (91.8 percent in urban and 80.6 percent in rural areas), and 61.0 percent had been vaccinated (smallpox, 80.2 percent in urban and 55.9 percent in rural areas). Medical health services are available in 87.6 percent of rural administrative areas and urban neighborhoods, indicating that most children can easily see a doctor when they are sick.

Currently, the Coordination Committee for Children, which was organized by the All-China Women's Federation (the Chinese Communist Party organization representing all Chinese women), has set up five kinds of day care centers in China:

1. State-owned child care centers and kindergartens, financed by the government, whose teachers are treated as government employees. The facilities, teachers, and management are the best available, but there are not enough of these centers to accommodate the large population of young children, so that they can only play an exemplary role for others.
2. Child care centers organized by government departments, the army, schools, and the mining industry. The work unit allocates some money from its welfare fund to meet the center's financial needs; some work units apply for extra money from the local government. Whatever the

source of the money, each center is run by the work unit itself, and the teacher is treated the same as other employees.

3. Child care centers run by neighborhoods, villages and towns. These institutions account for a large percentage of all child care centers. Their funds come from three sources: surplus funds of the village or town; money collected from local industries and personal donations; and financial allowances from the local government. The center is under collective ownership, and the teachers are nongovernmental employees.

4. Child care centers established by a group of villagers whose economic condition is above average. In some cases, a portion of the fund is subsidized by neighborhood, village, and town governments. Teachers are selected by a committee from among the applicants.

5. Family or individual child care services. They are owned and managed by individuals, and teachers are usually nongovernmental employees, including young girls and retired kindergarten teachers.

In addition, there are private arrangements between child care users and providers. Most of them connect with each other through relatives, friends, and neighborhoods. These arrangements are particularly helpful to parents who have difficulty finding a day care center for their child.

Services and Benefits for Women and Children: The Historical Background

Before 1949, China was a feudal society in which women were seen as machines for bearing children. Many new mothers and infants died from bacterial infections.

Professional women were not guaranteed the right to a maternity leave; their jobs were not protected while they were on leave; and their cash benefits were small, if they received any benefit at all. Thus, most professional women remained single in order to keep their jobs. Women workers, especially in textiles, had a particularly miserable time when they were pregnant. Women tried to hide their pregnancies from their supervisors so that they would not be fired. Many miscarriages and stillbirths were due to the mother's harsh working conditions.

After the liberation of 1949, more and more women in both urban and rural areas went out of their homes to be factory workers and farmers. Child care arrangements were often less than ideal. Babies were sometimes tied to the bed with the doors locked, and childhood accidents such as falling into a well often occurred during busy farm seasons. Maternity leave and social child care systems became major issues in China.

New laws were formulated to meet working women's needs. In 1951, the Labor Insurance Regulations were inaugurated, and in 1953 they were expanded, giving women a 56-day maternity leave with full pay. In cases of difficult labor, a 70-day leave was available. Furthermore, in the seventh month of pregnancy, women were allowed to switch to lighter work. Medical care was free for women who worked in state-operated industry and commerce; it was one-half the regular fee for dependents of workers. Under law, *all* women should be switched to light work when they are five- to eight-months pregnant. There was considerable variation in the length of maternity leave: in some communes, women had 56 days off, the same as women in the city; in others, women returned to light work after 30 days and regular work after 4 months.

In conjunction with the new laws, there were attempts to introduce nursing rooms and caretakers for children under three. These attempts were gradually expanded to include mining enterprises, schools, and government organizations. Nurseries were usually organized by the All-China Women's Federation or the women's department of a local trade union and were subsidized by the enterprise itself. According to an annual report covering 27 provinces and cities, in October 1950 there were 390 kindergartens and nursing rooms accommodating 28,422 children. Three-quarters of them were established after 1949. In 1952, under government leadership, women's federations and neighborhood government committees established a program of neighborhood nurseries and mutual aid teams to help solve the child care dilemma without heavy cost to either the central or provincial governments. But the problem remained because more and more women were going outside the family for work, and there were more births and children than ever before. In 1956, the number of women workers, office employees, cadres, and intellectuals was 2.7 million. With only 6,900 day care facilities caring for about 192,000 children, women had great problems finding a place to leave their children.

Beginning in 1958, the "Great Leap" increased the number of women working in regular industry by 5 million and mobilized additional millions to take part in neighborhood industry, especially in the newly established neighborhood nurseries and kindergartens. In rural areas, public health work became better organized after the People's Commune was formed in 1958. "Barefoot" doctors (peasant doctors who were commune members) or midwives went to see pregnant women, talk with them about prenatal self-care and the new delivery methods, and teach them how to look after their infants. The resulting reduction in maternal mortality rates is suggested by the figures in Table 24.1.

In the 1960s, many communes instituted a cooperative system of medical care. Each member, including children, paid a yuan a year and was entitled to free medical care for that year. If a commune member was hospitalized, the cooperative or the brigade paid for the hospitalization. Pregnant women were covered under this system. Later, the same medical services were provided in urban areas. This benefit was important to people in rural areas, the unemployed, and some who worked in neighborhood nurseries and urban processing factories. It was especially important for women, since women workers are the first to be laid off when employment drops. In 1962, because of a general increase in unemployment, large numbers of women lost their jobs. Some unemployed women took on piecework from factories at home. Although they had half the benefits of regular medical insurance through their employed spouses, they had no right to full paid maternity leave—that is, cash benefits after childbirth.

The next improvements in maternity leave and child care systems came with the new birth control policy.

Benefits for Women and Children Under the New Birth Control Policy

During the 1950s, the Chinese government encouraged families to have many children. This resulted in a population boom in China in the early 1970s, especially once those born in the 1950s married and had children.

A Public Letter on the Increasing Population in China to All Members of the Chinese Communist Party and League (September 25, 1980) stated that 600 million people were born during the 30 years between 1949 and 1979, compared with 130 million born between 1840 and 1949. The peak birth rate occurred between 1963 and 1970, when about 65 percent of the population was under the age of 30. On the average, 20 million young people have married each year since then. At the same time, improvements in welfare and medical care systems have enabled people to live longer and decreased the number of deaths during childbirth. In other words, China's population was out of control. As a result, it was hard for the Chinese government to develop the economy. Without control of the birth rate, the quality

TABLE 24.1
Mortality Rates, 1936 and 1957 (As Percentage of Population)

| | Rural Population, 1936 | | Population, 1957 | |
Age	Male	Female	Male	Female
15–19	9.1	12.0	2.07	2.60
20–24	9.7	11.8	2.79	3.74
25–29	9.8	11.6	2.97	4.14
30–34	7.3	11.7	3.70	4.73
35–39	10.9	13.5	5.31	6.06
40–44	13.7	14.0	7.96	8.10

Sources: See Note on Sources on page 434.

of life would decrease and shortages of clothing, food, housing, and transportation would be unavoidable.

Around 1970 the Chinese government started to pay attention to population control and to advocate late marriage and family planning. The new birth control policy was established, and contraceptive methods were introduced to couples of childbearing age. In the mid-1970s, "one couple, two children" was regarded as acceptable for both the family and the development of society. In the later 1970s, the government stated "one child per couple is no longer considered to be too few for a family," although having a second was not yet illegal. In the New Marriage Law of 1980, "one couple, one child" became government policy, confirmed in 1982 by the Constitution of the People's Republic of China. People who disobey the family planning policy are subject to fines and other disciplinary measures.

To encourage acceptance of the new policy, the government created incentives for women and families. "Late marriage, late family planning, less childbirth, healthy child" is the prescribed pattern, and maternity leave and child care systems have become more and more important.

Under the new policies, a couple agreeing to have only one child would receive 5 yuan (equivalent $1 U.S.) per month (about 5 percent of monthly income for the majority of couples with a single child) until the child was 16 years old. This money, along with any day care fees, is provided by the work units of both parents.

From the beginning of the seventh month of pregnancy, a woman is allowed one hour of leave per day from her regular work hours. After giving birth, she has a 72-day maternity leave, provided that she was not married before the age of 25. In cases of difficult childbirth, a 3-month leave is available. All maternity leave is fully paid. Furthermore, women who want to nurse their babies can apply for an extended leave, up to two years, depending on the woman's needs and her particular work situation. This is a job-protected leave, with 70 percent of her regular wages in the first year and 60 percent in the second year. Some more profitable work units often give women who are on leave a subsidy to help them cope with reduced income.

In 1980, the Lead Group of the State Council for Birth Control as well as province and city groups were set up to guarantee the success of the birth control policy. That same year the National Leadership Group for Child Day Care was established by the Central Committee of the Communist Party of China. This special institute works on child care policy and mobilizes each work unit to set up its own day care center. It reorganizes day care centers and kindergartens directed by departments of public health and education and by industry/mining enterprises, government departments, schools, and army units; it supports the development of town and neighborhood day care; and it assists individual child care centers.

In this period maternity leave and child care gained importance in Chinese society. Chinese women and children receive more benefits than ever before.

Problems During the Current Reform

In many ways China's current economic reform offers people a chance to realize their own potential and aspirations. The more work people do, the more pay they get. This ensures progress in developing the social economy, but for some people, especially women who cannot work a great deal, it provides a challenge.

Moreover, many leaders of work units see women as a problem because maternity leave and child care increase the costs of the enterprise. Some see a crisis in women's and children's benefits as some enterprises refuse to employ female workers, some nursing rooms and nurseries are eliminated, some overstaffed work units ask women to stay home longer than they need to after childbirth, at 60 percent of their normal wages, and some village and town enterprises base decisions on profit and ignore women's legal right to lighter work during her menstrual period, pregnancy, maternity leave, the period when her child is nursing, and menopause.

Social welfare facilities that meet people's needs generate no profit. Unfortunately, some government officials cut the financial allocation for child care and even use some kindergarten and nursery space to open businesses. In addition, teachers' wages in kindergartens and nurseries are not commensurate with the responsibility of teaching, so that many kindergarten and nursery teachers choose to change occupations. The quality of service in some kindergartens and nurseries is declining. Although the government has paid more attention to training kindergarten teachers, many well-educated people reject the job. Only 56.6 percent of all kindergarten teachers have completed their middle school education. Negative effects include accidents due to poor training and negligence.

Several factors affect the current status of maternity leave and child care. First, when the idea that "Class Struggle Is the Key to Everything" prevailed, the welfare service was considered antipolitical, even contrary to "Chairman Mao's Thought," making it impossible to develop welfare projects. Second, the economic situation in China is still undeveloped. Finally, women's organizations have not historically been strong enough to push the government to promote women's and children's legal rights. The development of the Chinese women's movement has been very slow, really beginning anew only a few years ago. It will take time to become a powerful force.

The Coordinating Role of Women's Federations

In the 1980s the All-China Women's Federation played a major coordinating role in women's affairs. A new department of women's and children's rights and interests in each local women's federation carries out publicity and education work concerning relevant laws and policies, monitors their implementation, investigates and appropriates legislative proposals and suggestions for improvements, attends to women's personal visits or letters of complaint, offers the complainers legal advice when necessary, and cooperates with other departments to ensure labor protection for the female workforce. Women's federations in provinces, autonomous regions, centrally administered municipalities, and some cities and counties have set up legal advisory and public liaison services to help women solve a variety of problems.

These activities have fostered a considerable amount of local legislation to protect women's and children's legal rights, such as maternity leave, child care, and the legal equality of husband and wife. This legislation has guaranteed the status of women and children under the Marriage Law and the Constitution of the People's Republic of China.

Women's federations have solved many problems concerning women's legal rights by using these local laws. For example, a woman in Shanghai went to the Shanghai Women's Federation for advice. It would be very difficult for her to rear her newborn baby if she had to return to her job after her guaranteed 70-day maternity leave because she had no extended family living with her and her husband was frequently away from home on official business. Considering her special situation, the department of women's and children's rights asked the leaders to make an exception for her. Later, the women's federation arranged for her to place her baby in a boarding nursery, a situation that is difficult to obtain. She was very relieved to be able to work again without child care problems.

Child care has, as noted above, been part of federation work since the 1950s. By the 1980s, the All-China Women's Federation had taken the lead in coordinating the work of various children-oriented departments, a task entrusted to it by the Central Committee of the Chinese Communist Party. Child welfare departments ensure the healthy growth of children, publicize scientific childrearing methods, give advice to parents on improving family education, and motivate and assist social service departments in setting up various types of child care facilities and public catering services.

The Coordination Committee for Children is composed of people from the Chinese Communist Party's Central Committee, government ministries, national mass organizations, and individuals. It is supported by the China Children's Fund, which solicits donations from various sources. It has many branches led by local women's federations. The main task of the committee is to raise the quality of child care by setting up teacher–parent–child educational organizations. It encourages teachers to gain more education, offers them classes in child care, and conducts routine checks of their work. It also organizes the system of day care management and the health care network, makes new policies to benefit factories and companies that produce articles for children's daily use, and encourages government offices and departments to set up after-school child care centers, playgrounds, and children's palaces. It relates the educational work of day care center and family, and, finally, it carries on research on child care and publishes teaching materials and magazines for children.

In the 1980s, as the population continued to grow, the women's federations tried to enroll every child who needed day care in a nursery or kindergarten. The Coordination Committee for Children held conferences on child care and coordinated all efforts to increase the number of day care centers.

Because 70 percent of pre-school-aged children are cared for at home, it is now recognized that family education is an important part of child care. The women's federations raise the quality of family education by setting up associations for childrearing and socialization, offering classes, and publishing materials on practical and psychological aspects of childrearing. A major improvement, especially in cities and among young couples, is that more and more husbands are sharing in child care.

In the 1980s, the research departments of women's federations identified and investigated the problems facing women and children and presented policy suggestions to relevant departments. In addition, they considered new work opportunities for women, promoted theoretical research in women's studies, and influenced the government to issue new policies on women's and children's rights and benefits. An exciting development was the 1986 second national conference organized by the Policy Research Department of the All-China Women's Federation, which discussed the reproduction of the population and urged the government to set up a birth fund to subsidize work units with more female employees. After the conference, the Policy Research Department proposed a birth foundation. That proposal, which has been submitted to the Central Committee of the Communist Party, suggested that each work unit contribute some part of its profits to the government for distribution to the birth foundation; the birth foundation would then distribute money to work units for the benefit of their pregnant women and to offset the cost of maternity leave benefits after child birth. If implemented, this proposal will greatly benefit women in the Chinese labor force in the future.

Conclusion

The attention paid to maternity leave and child care in China in recent decades suggests that these issues have become much more serious than ever before, primarily because the government has recognized their importance to the birth control policy.

Unfortunately, because of overpopulation and economic underdevelopment, 70 percent of Chinese children still cannot be enrolled in the social day care system. Even for the 30 percent who are in that system, problems exist. The opening time of neighborhood day care centers is the same as the starting time of many workplaces, so that parents have difficulty dropping off and picking up their children. In factory nurseries and kindergartens, this is not a problem, since parents can leave their children there when they arrive for work. However, the buses in many cities are so crowded that it is dangerous for parents to bring a baby to their workplace.

Although maternity leave has been improved considerably by the Legislation of Labor Protection for Female Workers, the traditional idea that child care is women's duty is reflected in the absence of policy giving both husband and wife parental leave benefits. If the current reform succeeds in developing Chinese economics and politics, child care systems would be greatly expanded, enabling many more children to get good care. A parental leave law would alter traditional ideas on maternity leave and eliminate discrimination against women by employers worried about the disruptive effects of childbirth and maternity leave.

Gaps remain in China's maternity and family policy, but China's working mothers and their children have good reason to expect more benefits and to have more legal rights in the future.

NOTE ON SOURCES

The citations for specific statistics and other information in this chapter are taken from documents published by the Chinese government. Unfortunately, the author, who is now in the United States, is no longer able to obtain direct access to these documents so that complete citations cannot be provided.

25 | Cultural Values, Child Care, and Parenting: The Italian Experience in Anthropological Perspective

George R. Saunders

Except perhaps in the most autocratic political regimes, public policy both reflects cultural values and shapes the further development of popular sentiment. Intelligent public policy thus depends in part on the recognition of the ways in which people's behavior is embedded in historically derived consciousness. Legislation and its practical realization must be grounded in some understanding of the ways in which people will "use" the instruments established by public policy and of the ways in which that policy will support, modify, or interfere with their values and behavior.

Few anthropological studies have paid direct attention to public policy issues, but many have examined the connections between the structural contexts in which children are raised and cultural values about children and parenting. Indeed, attitudes about children and the family are core features of culture everywhere. Their logic is derived from wider systems—ecological, economic and political—and integrated as well into aesthetics, religion, and other symbolic forms. Ever since Margaret Mead's classic 1928 study, *Coming of Age in Samoa*, anthropologists have focused ethnographic attention on cultural variations in the ideals and realities of family life, parenting, and the experience of the child. Mead noted, for example, that the Samoan personality evinced a "casualness" and emotional evenness that stood in sharp contrast to common American patterns, and she suggested that this personality characteristic was rooted in child care arrangements in which many people—especially older siblings—tended to an infant. "From the first months of its life, when the child is handed carelessly from one woman's hands to another's, the lesson is learned of not caring for one person greatly, not setting high hopes on any one relationship" (Mead, 1949, p. 118). (Incidentally, although these comments may sound critical, Mead went on to compare the Samoan experience favorably with the rather intense and exclusive relationship of the American child to her or his parents.)

Subsequent anthropological work on the relationship between cultural context and childhood experience has taken several directions. One important line has been the attempt to relate socialization styles to ecological adaptation and economic structure. For example, Barry, Child, and Bacon (1959) used the cross-cultural correlational method to demonstrate that agricultural societies were more likely to socialize their children for obedience and responsibility and that hunting and fishing societies were more likely to emphasize independence, self-reliance, and achievement. Other studies have refined this line of analysis, and Robert Edgerton (1971), working in East Africa, and Charlene Bolton and associates (1976), in the Andes of Latin America, have confirmed significant differences between pastoralists (shepherds) and farmers in socialization styles, the degree of supervision of children by adults, and the encouragement of independence in children. Still others have studied variables less directly derived from economic factors but nonetheless "ecological" in the broad sense. For example, Ruth and Robert Munroe (1971) related household density to patterns of infant care in western Kenya and found that infants are more indulged in large households but also develop less intense attachments to the mother in particular. The Gilmores (1979) related class differences in a rural Spanish town to the structure of relationships between men and women in the family and the consequent development of gender identity in boys.

Another direction of investigation has concerned the sharpness of the division of labor by sex in various societies, a factor clearly relevant to understanding how "parental" (as opposed to "maternal") leave policies might function in particular cultural contexts. Roy D'Andrade's (1966) review of sex differences in relation to cultural institutions, for example, found the division of labor by sex to be related in systematic ways to descent systems (patrilineal, matrilineal, bilateral, and so forth), residence rules (patrilocal, matrilocal, neolocal), sexual behavior, and patterns of authority, deference, aggression, identity, and even fantasy and cognition. Many anthropologists have used hunter–gatherer societies as a kind of baseline case for the analysis of division of labor by sex, and have particularly attempted to locate the assignment to women of primary responsibility for child care in its adaptive advantages in a foraging economy. As Ernestine Friedl (1984), Jane Lancaster (1976), and others have argued, there is no need to postulate any gender differences in innate motivational factors in order to understand why foragers have typically assigned child care primarily to women. Since "child-care responsibilities are only compatible with activities which do not demand long trips from home; with tasks which do not require rapt concentration; and with work which is not dangerous, can be performed in spite of interruptions, and is easily resumed once interrupted" (Lancaster, 1976, p. 47), it makes sense that in a foraging economy child care is usually the responsibility of women, who are often pregnant or lactating. "There is no need to posit special 'killer' or 'maternal' instincts in males and females to explain the assignment of these roles" (Lancaster, 1976, p. 47). Consequently, when the ecological and economic adaptations change, we should assume that parenting arrangements can also be transformed. Interestingly, societies in which the ideological separation of men and women and the division of labor by sex are most rigid seem also to be those in which men experience the most ambiguity in gender identity and the most ambivalence about women and children (Chodorow, 1974; Gregor, 1985; Herdt, 1981; Whiting, Kluckhohn, and Anthony, 1958). These findings would indicate that policy which makes it possible to break down such a division of labor might have salutary effects both psychologically and socially.

This brief survey of anthropological studies suggests that ecological adaptations and economic factors, the division of labor by sex, parenting behavior, the child's experience, and cultural values all form a more or less coherent system. The most obvious characteristic of such a system, of course, is its complexity. Though there are no simple formulae for success, then, it is apparent that public policy that attempts to effect changes in one area of the system must contend as well with other areas. The body of this chapter will illustrate some of the complex historical and economic factors that have influenced attitudes toward child care in Italy, demonstrate the cultural embeddedness of parental leave policies there, and perhaps, by contrast, suggest solutions to such problems in other societies. Italy is here treated as an ethnographic example of the cross-cultural variability of the ideology of child care and as an illustration of the ways in which parental leave policy reflects, reproduces, and yet modifies that ideology.

Gender, Family, and Work Life in Italy: Images and Realities

In many respects, legislation and social programming in Italy reflect considerably greater attention to the needs of women, men, and children in their familial roles than does U.S. policy. However, particular ideological and economic features of Italian family life have also made the realization of such progressive programs problematic and idiosyncratic. In particular, the prevalent ideology of motherhood and the continuing division of labor in the family demonstrate, as Chiara Saraceno has put it, "how far a society can go to assist women and even to acknowledge some of their demands without fundamentally changing its sex/gender system" (1984a, p. 24).

In the last century, the politics of work and family life in Italy has reflected multiple contradictions and tensions: between the Church and lay interests, between the Church and the Italian state, between both Church and state and the organized left, and between the mainstream leftist parties and organized feminists. Some of these tensions have been the product of an immediate historical moment, such as the unification of Italy in the 1860s and the realization of a liberal state in part through the seizure of papal territories. Others, however, reflect enduring features of Italian life. Let us look first at the former.

In the nineteenth century, most of Italy was still primarily agrarian. In the Po Valley in the north, however, industrialization was well under way by the time Vittorio Emanuele II of Piedmont became the first king of unified Italy in 1861. Women's labor is almost always important in agriculture, of course, but—despite the stereotype of the home-bound Italian mother—women early became a major component of the Italian industrial labor force as well. As early as 1881, for example, an estimated 43 percent of all workers were women, and 32 percent of all women were employed outside the home (Beccalli, 1985, p. 155). Women's high participation rate led to early politicization of the relationship between family life and work, with social programs in the late nineteenth and early twentieth centuries generally shaped by a strong and well-organized left, closely identified with the labor movement (Barkan, 1984).

Activist feminism in Italy developed along with this strong leftist industrial labor movement, and women such as Anna Maria Mozzoni in the 1890s and later Teresa Noce—a Turin factory worker and union activist—were articulate spokespersons on women's issues. As Judith Adler Hellman has pointed out, however, the history of Italian feminism in fact reflects a persistent tension with the organized parties of the left. The "protection of women workers" was an important issue for the early Italian Socialist party (PSI), for example, but mainly because of the threat "that women were thought to represent as a source of unorganized, unpoliticized, cheap labor" (Hellman, 1987, p. 28). Thus, the PSI campaigned in the 1890s for legislation to reduce working hours for women and children, improve factory conditions, and provide for maternity leave, but did so in large part in order to protect the interests of working men, and the party did little to challenge the general division of labor in society. Later, Communist party (PCI) theoretician Antonio Gramsci, as an aspect of his analysis of ideological and cultural problems, directed considerable attention to the *questione femminile*, as did party secretary Palmiro Togliatti, who actively supported the formation and development of the Unione donne italiane (the Union of Italian Women) (Hellman, 1984). Nonetheless, the ambivalence of the parties of the left inhibited the full development of a women's movement and of a gender-fair social policy. As Annarita Buttafuoco puts it, "the PCI has often wound up sacrificing the deepest needs of women in favor of more 'general' political issues, 'broader' strategies, and mediations that have sometimes been disastrous for the advance of the masses of Italian women" (1980, p. 198). In addition, the leftist parties and the labor movement have often seemed to fear the politicization of women precisely because women have been regarded, accurately or not, as "more traditional than Italian men in their attitudes; . . . more conservative, more apathetic, and less informed" (Zariski, 1972, p. 105), and as "almost always attracted to the panoply and social snobbery of monarchy and aristocracy, and generally susceptible to the inflence of the priests" (Kogan, 1983, p. 24; see also Saunders, 1988a).

The high participation rate of women in the labor force declined after the turn of the century, in any case, especially during the fascist period (1926–1944), when both government and Church policies (such as those enunciated in the 1930 encyclical *Casti connubi*) combined to discourage women's work outside the home (Birnbaum, 1986, p. 36). The pro-natalist ideology of the Mussolini government, indeed, led to the development of systematic and comprehensive policies for the restriction of women's rights and the reinforcement of maximal gender differentiation. Hellman points out that "fascist doctrine celebrated womanhood, but only with respect to women's reproductive capacity. *Femminilità* was understood as maternity, sacrifice and the rejection of all involvement in social life" (1984, p. 61). Mussolini suggested that 12 children was the ideal number for a family, contraceptive devices and abortion were outlawed, and severe penalties were imposed for their use (Birnbaum, 1986, p. 37). Employers in both public and private sectors were ordered to discriminate against women, and in 1927 women's salaries were cut to one-half those of men (Hellman, 1987, p. 32). Educational opportunities for women were restricted, and Italian women did not gain the right to vote until after World War II. In general, fascism reaffirmed and strengthened men's authority in family relations and also shored up the rigid boundary between public and private spheres as gender domains (despite the considerable intrusion by the state into the private sphere). Indeed, what is now regarded as the "traditional" division of labor and power in Italian family life might to some degree be seen as a reconstruction of the fascist period. While both the ideology and the reality of such gender differentiation certainly existed prior to fascism, and have long been reflected in the official doctrine of the Catholic Church, fascism effectively erased from legislative and cultural memory the considerably greater equality of women and men that had been developing in the early 1920s.

Following World War II, then, Italy faced the problems of recovering not only from the physical and human devastation of the war itself, but also from the regressive policies of twenty years of fascism. The economic boom of the early 1950s and again of 1959 to 1963 accompanied a major restructuring of Italian society, with mass movements of workers out of agriculture and into industry, and out of the South and into the industrial North (see Kogan, 1983, pp. 129–46), as well as the reentry of significant numbers of women into the labor force. This period saw a distinct political shift to the left, especially in regional and municipal government, and presaged an increase in progressive legislation on family life and the workplace.

The postwar period also brought the renewed development of an activist feminist movement and a more general politicization of women. The Unione donne italiane (UDI), for example, was formed immediately after World War II as a feminist flanking organization for the PCI (Hellman, 1987, p. 34), and reached its peak membership by about 1950. The organization and political socialization of women again increased dramatically during the 1960s and 1970s. The Movimento di liberazione della donna (MLD) was formed in 1971 in Rome to raise women's consciousness and lobby for women's interests. It had close ties to the Radical party (a rather eclectic and intellectualist party that has supported disarmament and ecological causes as well as feminist issues, and recently confounded many Italians by electing a pornographic film star to Parliament). The rapid radicalization of the women's movement during this period also led to a number of splinter groups, such as Rivolta femminile (Women's Revolt), Collettivo di lotta femminista (Collective of Feminist Struggle), and Collettivo femminista communista (Feminist Communist Collective) (Dodds, 1982). Some of these groups were born also out of the more general radical struggles of the period, though many women became feminists precisely because their treatment in the leftist student groups often seemed to replicate the gender distinctions of the wider society.

Legislation on Work and Family Life

Divorce, Marital Property, and Family Planning

Prior to the 1970s, when the feminist movement began to make itself felt in progressive legislation, much of Italy's family law was particularly anachronistic. Divorce was first legalized in 1970, for example, although even then it was still highly restricted and in most cases required a five-year waiting period. The legalization of divorce was strongly contested by the Catholic Church and the Christian Democratic party (the dominant party in the postwar period, which has usually represented official Church policy in Italian politics). The Christian Democrats forced a referendum in an attempt to repeal the bill in 1974; the vote emphatically reaffirmed the right to divorce. Though divorce is now possible, however, cultural values and legal complications continue to discourage it. Indeed, as of 1985 less than 0.8 percent of the population was divorced or legally separated, and only 25 percent of divorced women have remarried (Istituto Centrale di Statistica, 1985a, pp. 57, 106). By contrast, the 1980 U.S. census listed 6.3 percent of the U.S. population over the age of 15 as divorced, with another 2.3 percent separated (U.S. Department of Commerce, 1980).

In 1975, there were major revisions of the entire legal corpus as it applied to "the rights of the family." Earlier legislation had expressly supported men's power and authority in family relations. For example, adultery had been a crime only for women; women were required to have their husband's or father's formal permission in order to get a passport or a job; a husband had usufruct rights over his wife's property, and dowries were legally required (Dodds, 1982, p. 150; Hellman, 1987, p. 51). The 1975 law gave women equal rights with respect to children, property, citizenship, and place of residence, and in general strengthened women's legal position in relation to their husbands.

Legislation on abortion, contraception, and family planning also underwent dramatic changes during the 1970s. In the fascist period, it had been illegal to sell contraceptive devices or to disseminate information about birth control, and abortion was punished by imprisonment for two to five years for both the woman and the person performing the abortion (Caldwell, 1986, p. 106). These restrictions reflected the pro-natalist policies of the fascist regime, but also represented the position of the Catholic Church, which was reconciled with the Italian state (after a long period of opposition following the unification of Italy) in the Concordat of 1929. In general, during the fascist period Church and state policies on the family were quite congruent, both actively opposing birth control and abortion and upholding male authority in family affairs (see Porter and Venning, 1976). After the war, the Church's conception of the "Catholic family" was called into question by feminists and challenged as well by ordinary women and the lay political parties. In 1971, the restrictions on birth control devices were repealed, and a 1975 law provided for the establishment of family-planning clinics (Hellman, 1987, p. 51).

The struggle to decriminalize abortion was considerably more difficult, as in other areas of the West. Bills to legalize therapeutic abortion were introduced in Parliament as early as 1971, but none was passed until 1978. The resultant law is one of the most liberal anywhere, allowing free abortion in state-provided clinics and hospitals for women over 18 years of age, restricted only by a seven-day waiting period after application (Caldwell, 1986, p. 109). Despite the progressive legislation, however, abortions are often difficult to obtain. Among other things, the law allowed doctors to declare themselves "conscientious objectors" and to decline to perform abortions. Within the first two years of legalization, it was estimated that 80 percent of Italy's gynecologists had done so (Dodds, 1982, p. 153). Accordingly, long waiting lists developed at the clinics, and often the procedure could not be scheduled within the legal period. Dinah Dodds notes that in much of the South it has remained virtually impossible for a woman to get an abortion in a public hospital, and many are forced either to have the child, to seek inexpensive illegal abortions, or to pay high fees at private clinics.

Abortion has also remained a politically problematic issue. Almost immediately after its legalization, the Italian Right to Life Movement, supported by the Church and the Christian Democratic party, introduced a referendum to overturn the law. Though this attempt was defeated in 1981, the issue continues to resurface. Indeed, in 1988, following the publication of a study by the Istituto Ricerche Studi Economici e Sociali on rates of abortion since legalization, Minister of Health Carlo Donat Cattin joined the prominent leader of the new-right religious–political movement Comunione e liberazione, Robert Formigoni, in calling for reconsideration and possible repeal of the law (Gandus, 1989, p. 62).

Parental Leave

Maternity leave legislation was considerably less problematic, in large part because it is consistent with cultural values about mothers and infants. The first law providing for maternity leave was passed in 1950, and the benefits were improved through the new legislation of 1971. The current law provides women with 2 months of employer-paid leave prior to the birth of a baby and 3 months after, at 70 percent of salary, with an additional 6 months of leave at 30 percent of salary paid by the national social insurance system, all with guaranteed job security and seniority (Saraceno, 1984b, p. 356; cf. Beccalli, 1985, p. 159, and Dodds, 1982, p. 150). After returning to work, women were also given the right to two hours off each day for nursing the child. In 1977 a "parity law" was passed. In addition to guaranteeing women equal pay and access to jobs and providing special protection for women's health and safety in the workplace (Hellman, 1987, p. 53), this law made the supplementary maternity leave (after the first 3 months) into parental leave, available to either parent for 6 months with full job protection. Furthermore, it gave fathers the right to take days off to care for a sick child (Kamerman, 1988, p. 241). The law did not create fully symmetrical treatment for women and men, however, as fathers are given these rights only if their wives are employed (Saraceno, 1984b, p. 356).

A further problem is brought into relief by the parental leave issue. The provision of parental leave obviously applies only in jobs that are legal in other respects (that is, where employers pay social security and other taxes, where employees pay income taxes and have minimal guarantees of job security and the right to union representation, and so forth). In fact, a formidable portion of Italy's economy is "underground," and a great deal of Italian labor is *lavoro nero* ("black work") contracted surreptitiously between employers who want to avoid such obligations and employees willing to forego the other benefits in order to find immediate work and income. And as Joanne Barkan points out, the underground economy draws particularly on the social groups marginal to the regular labor market, including women (1984, p. 154). Women employed in such unfavorable circumstances clearly have little recourse in the event of pregnancy. The Italian government is increasingly efficient at prosecuting the employers of *lavoro nero*, but its continued prevalence demonstrates the pitfalls of progressive legislation in a society that lacks the infrastructure to enforce it.

Day Care

Day care is another area in which the legislative ideals and the reality are less than completely congruent. In 1971, UDI pushed through Parliament a law providing for state-supported community day care centers, which were to provide free day care for children (primarily children of working mothers) up to the age of three (Dodds, 1982, p. 149). The funding and organization of the day care centers were left to regional and local governments, however, and the implementation of the law has been very spotty. Bologna, one of the most progressive cities in Italy's "red belt" (where the parties of the left have been in control of local government for most of the postwar period), had centers available for 25 percent of the eligible children by 1983, but in Sicily there was virtually no coverage (Saraceno, 1984b, p. 353). By 1985, according to a national study of Italian families, 9 percent of children from birth through two years in urban areas (cities with populations of over 100,000) were attending day care centers. A center for these younger children is referred to as an *asilo nido* ("nest"), and the limited funding and generally poor availability reflect an ideology that children of this age ought to be in the care of family members (Saraceno, 1984b, p. 353).

For three- to five-year-old children, the picture is different. There is a dramatic increase in attendance in this age group, where children attend a *scuola per l'infanzia*, earlier officially referred to as a *scuola materna* ("maternal school") and still commonly called that by many Italians. These centers are also locally funded, but are much more widely available and utilized. The 1985 study indicated, in fact, that 74.1 percent of three- to five-year-olds attend these schools (IS-TAT, 1985a, p. 65). The differences in services and attendance rates strongly suggest that whereas the *asilo nido* is regarded as a kind of emergency shelter for children who simply have nowhere else to go, the *scuola per l'infanzia* is seen more as the beginning of "school" for all children. This is reflected also in the relative professionalization of the staff at the *scuola per l'infanzia* as compared with the minimal training required for the attendants of the younger children (Saraceno, 1984b, p. 354).

This relative lack of day care for infants reflects an ideal of mother-infant relations that is a practical impossibility for many women. According to the 1985 survey, women constitute 35 percent of the active labor force and well above half of the unemployed in search of work (ISTAT, 1985b). Furthermore, 35.1 percent of the households with children include a working mother, and the rate goes up to 44.9 percent in families where the average age of the couple is between 30 and 34 years (ISTAT, 1985a, p. 50). In addition, despite the low divorce rates, almost 9 percent of households are single-parent families, the vast majority headed by women. If, as noted above, less than 9 percent of the children under 3 are in day care centers, many are clearly being cared for in some other way. We will return to this issue in the following section.

In general, this review suggests some of the complexity of the relationship between public policy and its realization, between political pronouncements and cultural values. As far as legislation goes, Italy seems to have recovered well from the sexual discrimination of the fascist period and has provided on paper a fair opportunity structure for women, men, and children in familial roles. Nominally, legal parity for women and men has been approximated, and institutional support for the children of working and single parents is assured. Indeed, Italian legislation in some ways places it among the leaders of the West in assuring fair treatment of women as both mothers and workers. On the other hand, as Hellman notes, "some of the most progressive legislation affecting women's lives could not be implemented not only because the funds, facilities, and administrative apparatus were lacking, but also because popular understanding lagged behind the spirit of the reforms" (1987, p. 53). Cultural values do change along with economic and social realities, but—as in other Western societies—class relations, religious ideology, and other factors continue to inhibit the development of full parity for women, particularly with respect to division of labor.

The Division of Labor and the Two Spheres in Italy

Italian family life is the subject of a number of popular stereotypes, and, indeed, the image of the Italian mother is almost as mystified as that of the Jewish mother. The reality of family and motherhood is, of course, considerably more complex, in some ways conforming to stereotypes and in other ways directly contradicting them (see Saunders, 1981, 1985).[1] Indeed, general characterizations, such as Marzio Barbagli's recent description of the earlier (fifteenth- to eighteenth-century) Italian family as "patriarchal" (Barbagli, 1984, p. 16 et passim; cf. Bravo, 1980, p. 67), are sure to provoke polemical responses (Kertzer, 1987; Saraceno, 1987). In addition, Italy is like any other complex modern society in encompassing tremendous regional differences, urban–rural differences, and a formidable class structure, all of which affect the differential realization of cultural images and valued behaviors. Even within the same rural community, one can find considerable diversity in both the ideology and the reality of family life. "Countercultural" ideas and values are an integral feature of any cultural system, even in those communities and social groups that seem most homogeneous and "traditional," and such contradictory ideas about family and motherhood are certainly evident in Italian life. Indeed, such countercultural values help explain the rather sudden development of a radical feminist movement in an Italy where women have long been regarded as the guardians of tradition and of the values of the Church. On the other hand, the values and beliefs developed over the long sweep of history in the Mediterranean have a certain resilience, and notwithstanding the contemporary ideological and practical circumstances, remain a formidable foundation for family life.

Thus, despite these cautions about cultural complexity and internal contradictions, it seems reasonable to attempt a general characterization of Italian family life. Many of the key features are shared with other southern European cultures and reflect a common ecology and history (Braudel, 1972). As noted earlier, ecological and economic systems have been linked by anthropologists to a variety of structural and psychological features of family life. The Mediterranean pattern combines mountainous land with arid soil and an extensive seacoast, and though agriculture was established early in Europe and—in contrast to north Africa, where pastoralism prevailed—became the dominant economic adaptation, most areas of Mediterranean Europe did not develop stable peasant societies. Indeed, the Mediterranean reflects dramatic social contrasts. An urban civilization developed over two thousand years ago, and urban centers have long set the cultural standards, and yet communication of this culture until recently took place primarily across water, with inland, mountainous villages sometimes demonstrating a profound isolation. Even in the preindustrial cities themselves, the majority of the people were day-laborers on nearby farms, and land ownership was frequently concentrated in the hands of the wealthy. At some places and times, a rich agriculture has developed, and yet much of the land has been given over rather to eroded and overgrazed sheep and goat pastures. The wealth of both urban and country elites has stood out sharply against the misery of the many.

The "symbiotic competition" between pastoralism and agriculture, the extreme social stratification of an urban-focused agrarian society, and the inability of the state in much of the Mediterranean over much of its history to monopolize the use of violence and to protect the rights of individuals encouraged the development of family loyalty, integrity, and honor as key resources in a system of social relations frequently described as "agonistic" (Blok, 1974, 1981; Davis, 1977, 1987; Schneider, 1971; Schneider and Schneider, 1976). The family became the primary unit of economic and social competition and was forced to use its own strength to defend its interests. Though elites have always managed to maintain family honor and integrity better than the poor, the understanding that family was the key to success became an ideology that crossed class boundaries.

Mediterranean peoples are also regarded—at least in Anglo-Saxon stereotypes—as deeply emotional. This cultural predisposition to the experience and display of deep emotion, as well as the reluctance to dichotomize emotion and reason as has been done in much of the West (Lutz, 1986), reflects the importance of attaching individuals to the family, securing their loyalty, and ensuring their willingness to act—if need be with dire consequences—in support of family interests. The evolutionary adaptiveness of emotion is well understood, and differential development of affective depth and display may also have material advantages in particular cultural contexts (cf. Bailey, 1983; De Sousa, 1980; Medick and Sabean, 1984). That is, sometimes strong emotion is an extremely "reasonable" response to a situation, and in Italy strong emotion serves very practical ends: historically, it has been essential to social reproduction and to defense of family interests (Saunders, 1988b).

Women have had a critical role to play in this process, particularly in the recreation of family unity and loyalty. As Schneider (1971), Campbell (1964), and many others have argued, women's sexuality has long been a key symbol for family unity and honor, and women have been well socialized to bear the burden of monitoring their behavior so as not to compromise that honor. The Church's role in this socialization process has been extremely important, and the emphasis on women's chastity, reproductive behavior, and mothering are exquisitely symbolized in the behavior of the Madonna, particularly in the virgin birth. The Madonna functions as a positive model for women, and there are corresponding negative models, such as the prostitute (Giovannini, 1981). Again, the official pronouncements of the Church have consistently reinforced the role of women as mothers and have subordinated women to the authority of men (Goody, 1983, p. 212). This doctrinal emphasis has not abated even in this century: Pius XII said that "woman is the home-maker; man can never replace her in this task," and even the relatively liberal John XXIII reiterated that "the end to which the Creator has ordained [women's] whole being is maternity" (cited in Porter and Venning, 1976, p. 83). A good woman, then, is one who stays at home as an obedient and virginal daughter until marriage and as an attentive and fertile mother and wife after. In either case, she accepts the authority of the men, and her behavior supports their claims to honor.

As in other ares of southern Europe, the emphasis on women's sexuality has also meant a symbolic fortification of the boundaries between public and private domains and the relegation of women substantially to the private (see Dubisch, 1986a; Pitt-Rivers, 1977; Reiter, 1975). Similar and perhaps more extreme forms of this process, such as veiling (a complex symbol not amenable to monolithic interpretations, but surely involving at least in part the creation of a mobile private sphere), can be found in the north African and Middle Eastern areas of the Mediterranean. In both areas, as Jane Schneider has so cogently argued, women's sexuality early became a resource in the competition for honor (or family reputation), and that honor in turn was a major ideological and practical asset in the economic and political struggles of everyday life—that is, in competition for scarce grazing land, for access to jobs, water rights, and even bureaucratic favors. A woman who could be violated by outsiders symbolized the lack of unity and strength of her own men; a woman who failed in her role as mother symbolized a loss of family continuity and thus both economic and moral vulnerability. Indeed, as in other cultures, women's sexual behavior is paradoxically often a central element in a system of political economy oriented primarily to the establishment of hierarchies among men (Rubin, 1975).

Aside from the symbolic significance of their sexuality, however, women have also had an active role to play in the creation of a loyal and unified family. As mothers, women are key agents in the process of social reproduction, which Muriel Dimen (following Rapp, Ross, and Bridenthal, 1979) has defined as the "reproduction of social relations through the creation of the new generation and the daily biological and psychological renewal of the present one" (1986, p. 59). Women not only nurture children and take care of their physical needs, but also train them for their own future roles in society. As Dimen further points out, this process may be fraught with contradictions and ambiguities, as women may have the responsibility of transmitting to their children a respect for hierarchy (including gender hierarchy) while yet teaching them to have self-respect—that is, to struggle against such hierarchy.

In the division of labor, then, women in Italy have been given nearly complete responsibility for the care and socialization of children. One of their primary tasks has been the reproduction of ideological and emotional commitment to the family itself, a question of quality, style, and depth of interaction with children. Contemporary observations provide some sense of this quality. While American culture tends to glorify individualism and encourage early independence from the family, Italian mothering has tended to encourage centripetality, continuing interdependence of family members, and commitment to the welfare of the family as a whole.[2] Mothering is in many respects defined as service to the children, and mothers tend to encourage their children to rely on them for satisfaction of both material and emotional needs. For example, it is not unusual to see mothers spoon-feeding three- or four-year-old children and helping them dress themselves (cf. New, 1988, p. 59), and there is relatively little encouragement of children to be emotionally independent. Children are allowed to cry when upset, allowed to be angry, and generally treated with sympathy when expressing dependency.[3] Angelomichele De Spirito, for example, in describing the southern Italian family, notes "the mother–infant symbiosis . . . that particular physical and emotional fusion of mother and child . . . which in consequence will determine a strong dependence of the individual on the group and a prevalent importance of the group in the life of the individual" (1983, p. 11; my translation).

The interaction of Italian mothers with their children tends to be emotionally intense in all respects, in marked contrast to parenting styles recorded by anthropologists in cultures where family unity is of less significance. For example, the casualness that Mead noted in Samoan parenting is echoed in Robert Levy's description of the Tahitian tendency to minimize emotionality, and his notes on infant care likewise include references to handing the baby around to a wide variety of caretakers. Levy also indicates that "the most common way of holding the baby now is with two hands, one underneath its buttocks and the other supporting its upper back and head. It is held as a separate individual, often at some distance from the mother's body, and clinging, blending, and cuddling are infrequently seen" (Levy, 1973, p. 438). Where the Italian baby is merged with its mother, the Tahitian baby is separate from the beginning. In another contrast, Walter Goldschmidt has described the process of "socialization for low affect" among the Sebei of eastern Africa.

Goldschmidt finds a common "psychological disengagement" in the social relations of the Sebei, and traces it to the "absent eyes and idle hands" of women who seem hardly to notice their children even as they tend them (Goldschmidt, 1976, pp. 65–66). If this description is accurate, it contrasts dramatically with the Italian pattern, in which children are held tightly, with close and intense eye contact, and noticed in all their particularity. Mother–child interactions in Italy are often accompanied as well by a noisy commentary on the significance of the relationship and on the emotional interconnectedness of mother and child.

The loyalty of Italian mothers to their children and of children, even as adults, to their mothers is striking. Anthropologist Thomas Belmonte notes that during his fieldwork in Naples he was frequently asked, "*C'è l'hai la Mamma?*" ("Do you still have your mother?"), as a kind of primary locating datum (1979, p. 90). That is, people with mothers always have a support system, a moral and practical foundation in life. Without a mother, a person is alone, and the object of pity. I would argue that the closeness of the mother–child tie is also the basis of the cultural approval of deep emotional experience, of passion, kindness, and sympathy as well as "righteous" anger.

Food has long been a central symbol of maternal love, though it can certainly also symbolize other things, such as the power relationships implicit in "hospitality" (see Herzfeld, 1987). Psychoanalysis has, of course, emphasized the connection between feeding and dependency, and feminist psychoanalysis in recent years has noted the significance of the pre-Oedipal identification of infant and mother that reflects the emotional closeness of the nursing experience. Throughout the Mediterranean, the preparation of meals and the presentation of wholesome and delicious food to their families has been a significant source of identity and pride for women, a symbol of their centrality in the family domain, their importance in protecting the home from the pollution of the outside world, and, again, the recreation of the unity and integrity of the family (Dubisch, 1986b). As Carole Counihan notes in describing the significance of home-baked bread in Sardinia, "Consumption of bread reaffirmed the complementarity of men and women and the nuclear family social structure, the basis of society and locus of individual identity" (1984, p. 53). And in my own fieldwork, during a discussion about the high rate of emigration from the mountain village of Valbella to the provincial capital some 30 kilometers down the valley, one woman commented that she was afraid that her family would have to move soon: her husband was already working in the capital, and one of her children would soon begin high school there, and thus both of them would have to eat their noon meal away from the family. In this woman's eyes at least, their absence from the meal was the critical factor. On the other hand, the current urban trend toward simple and quick noon meals near the workplace clearly indicates that food is losing its centrality in family relations and that eating is becoming an individualized and less patently symbolic activity.

Other domestic labor (besides cooking) has also been defined as women's work, as in other areas of the world, and Italian women are generally fastidious house-cleaners. This division of labor is both an aspect of the subordination of women and a reflection of the fact that in such a system of gender hierarchy women's only acceptable route to status, power, and honor is through proper action in that sphere. Resistance to such hierarchy is readily evident in the counterculture, but the reality of everyday family life suggests the continuing hegemony of the ideology of separate spheres. The 1985 study of the Italian family, for example, included self-report data on domestic labor. In households where the wife did not have outside employment, women reported an average of 51.5 hours per week of housework, and men averaged 6.1 hours. Where the wife was employed, women's hours of domestic labor declined to 31.7, but men's increased only to 6.3 hours, or a mere 12 minutes more than when the wife was not working (ISTAT, 1985a, p. 74). The continuing assignment of domestic labor to women is integral to the reproduction of gender inequality, since, as Friedl (1978) has argued, anthropological evidence strongly suggests that power and prestige in any socioeconomic system are allocated primarily to those who control resources valued for exchange in extradomestic spheres. Assuming that women's work time is limited, the more exclusive their responsibility for domestic labor, the less opportunity they have to participate in extradomestic systems of exchange.

The ideological aspects of the division of labor are also reflected in the extradomestic work of women. Women's employment is overwhelmingly (64 percent) concentrated in the tertiary or service sector, and, indeed, women's employment in both industry and agriculture has declined rather than increased in recent years (ISTAT, 1985b). As Saraceno puts it, more and more women "perform professionally the work traditionally accomplished by women in the family—taking care of children and the sick, counseling, and so forth" (1984a, p. 7). In fact, a number of apparently unrelated social reforms of recent years assume and depend on the continuing provision of such services by women. For example, the antipsychiatric movement emptied out mental hospitals all over the country, returning to the family (meaning, to women) the responsibility for the care of the mentally ill. Other hospital reforms and the restructuring of schools have also required greater participation of families (read "women") in service activities outside the home (Saraceno, 1984a, p. 10). There is clearly some culture change under way, and men will undoubtedly eventually assume more of the domestic labor, but—as in other countries—the short-run consequence of women's employment outside the home is almost certainly an even greater burden for women themselves, and in some ways a reinforcement of rather than a liberation from gender difference.

The burden of child care is probably diminishing, however, in part because of the declining birth rate and in part because of the lowered age of near-universal school attendance. Italy appears to be approaching (if not already at) a below-zero population growth rate. In the 1985 study, the median household size was 4 persons, and the median number of children born to women currently between 15 and 64 years of age was 2. Women born between 1945 and 1949 had had an average of only 1.8 children by the time they were 34 years of age, and the average for all women born between 1919 and 1934 for their entire period of fertility was only 2.3 children. Declining birth rates are always difficult to analyze, but they may in part reflect the ambivalence of women and men about managing both family roles and work life. They certainly reflect the diminished material advantages of large families and the difficulties families have in providing adequately for many children. In my field research in Valbella, women frequently commented on their perception that children (particularly "too many" children) were a serious economic burden and that they negatively affected the quality of life, especially for women.

The issue of providing day care for very young children brings out all of the contradictions, ambiguities, and potential identity crises inherent in women's roles in Italy today. As in other parts of the world, women are caught in the bind of needing the income from outside employment, recognizing that personal worth in capitalist and postcapitalist society is measured primarily by the status of that employment, and yet being expected to perform adequately in time-consuming and emotionally intense familial roles. In Italy, such contradictions are perhaps more salient than in other areas, precisely because of the cultural emphasis on and idealization of both family and mothering. Such conflicts surely engage men as well, but "since leaving their children for many hours during the day has long been part of the experience, if not the definition, of being a father, leaving them among 'strangers' or in a daycare center rather than with their mothers is generally a less agonizing choice. It is not a question that involves their personal identity as fathers" (Saraceno, 1984a, p. 23).

Indeed, the connection between child care and "mothering" remains a central ideological component of Italian culture and continues to structure the division of labor in the family. In a recent study, Rebecca Staples New noted the "social density" of households in her field site in Città Fantera, where infants spent less than 5 percent of their time alone and were usually in the company of at least two other people. Nevertheless, mothers still performed virtually all of the infant-care tasks (New, 1988, p. 59). Indeed, "mothering" is so definitively connected to gender and to the experience of bearing and nursing a child that Italian familes are very reluctant to separate mother and infant. If they must, they usually prefer to use other women of the family—grandmothers, aunts, and older sisters—as caretakers. Recall that only 9 percent of the children from birth to two years old in urban areas, and 6.1 percent of such children in smaller communities, are in either public or private day care centers. The 1985 survey also noted that when these children were not in the care of their parents or in day care centers, they were left with their grandparents (45.5 percent) or other relatives (9.1 percent). Only in 4.5 percent of the cases were they left with paid nonfamily caretakers.[4] Grandmothers, particularly the mother's mother, are often regarded as ideal caretakers. They are experienced as mothers, and they are "family" in the closest and most significant sense of the word.

The use of relatives for child care may also reflect the fact that extended family households have been relatively prevalent in Mediterranean Europe, as compared with northern Europe and the United States (Kertzer and Brettell, 1987, p. 251; Saunders, 1979). While only 2.6 percent of the households in the 1985 government survey are shown as "extended" (ISTAT, 1985a, p. 45), the rate is understated because of the definitions, which, for example, count "a married couple with children living with the widowed mother of one of the couple" as "a single nucleus with another isolated person" (ISTAT, 1985a, p. 43). (Unfortunately, the presentation of the data makes it impossible to sort out these from other "nuclear" families.) In addition, as other studies (Berkner, 1972; Saunders, 1979; see also Kertzer, 1984) have demonstrated, the statistics taken at any one moment automatically understate the proportion of households that at *some* time in the domestic cycle include three generations. In Italy, the ideology of familism has meant that even though newly married couples may set up residence apart from their parents, they are likely to reincorporate one or more elderly parent into their household when the parent is widowed or infirm. This is especially likely if there can be some mutual benefit, such as the sharing of child care. In addition, even when parents and their adult children do not share the same residence, they frequently reside in the same neighborhood, visit each other daily, and in other ways act rather like an extended family.

Despite the ready availability of parental leave from work and of other family members who will help with child care, however, many women resign their employment when they have children. In the government census, women between 15 and 64 years of age were asked about the effects of marriage and childbearing on their decisions about work life. Of these women, 16.8 percent indicated that they had renounced their search for work, resigned their job, reduced their hours, or interrupted their career for an extended period when they married; an additional 22.6 percent did so on the birth of their first child, and another 20.2 percent on the birth of their second child (ISTAT, l985a, p. 102). Many of these women do know how to use the system, retaining their rights to the job and their leave pay for as long as possible, but in the end they often drop out of the labor market for a prolonged period. In addition, of course, those women who work in the underground economy have no protection in the first place. Finally, though I have not been able to obtain statistical corroboration, my impression is that few men have made use of the parental leave provisions.

Conclusion

Socialization has sometimes been referred to as a form of cultural communication (Schwartz, 1976), transmitting in both literal and symbolic ways the kinds of information that individuals need in order to function in their own society and to understand their experiences—even those experiences that are "universal" and "natural"—as "meaningful." As an aspect of our common evolutionary heritage, all humans are born helpless and depend on care and nurturance from parents and other caretakers in the early stages of life. The prolonged period of dependency of human infants is indeed a primary experience, one that evinces in more ways than even Freud or Piaget imagined the significance of the arrangements through which children are nurtured and educated. In this period, children learn things far more fundamental than reading, writing, and arithmetic. They learn to express or control emotions; they learn styles of attachment to adults; they learn culturally appropriate gender roles; and they form attitudes toward family, work, and social relations. In short, they learn to reproduce the patterns that their culture deems right and proper. Modification or interruption of those patterns through social policy is thus a weighty responsibility and one that demands sensitivity and knowledge. Above all, it is incumbent on policymakers to understand how social policy both reflects traditional cultural patterns and may shape them for the future.

The Italian culture-history presented here illustrates some of the problematic aspects of social policy related to work and family life. The feminist movement, the exigencies of life in a consumerist industrial society, the strong leftist political parties, and other factors have effected tremendous change in many aspects of Italian society. Among these changes have been several varieties of progressive legislation, which have provided women with considerable protection and parity. Nonetheless, the essential patterns of division of labor, of gender hierarchy, and of separate spheres of status and responsibility for men and women continue to reflect the historical significance of family in the Mediterranean and the centrality of women in maintaining family unity and loyalty. There is no doubt that proper action within those family roles gives women a great deal of covert power and moral authority, and also makes them active agents in their own gender socialization. There may be benefits for both men and women in the system; for example, I would argue that the kind of dependency encouraged in Italian families ultimately provides people with a strong sense of social connectedness and a capacity for deep and empathetic emotion. The restriction of women to the domestic domain, however, limits them in other important ways. As Friedl (1984, p. 8) and others have argued, without control of significant (economic) resources in the extradomestic realm, women are unlikely to achieve full equality of opportunity. Though legislation has facilitated movement in that direction, the contradictory processes of social reproduction and social change depend also on ideological factors, on cultural beliefs and values, and in Italy these continue to focus on motherhood. In both public and private spheres, tasks related to nurturing and the care of dependent persons are still defined primarily as women's work, and men have been brought into these roles only minimally and reluctantly.

The relations among gender, family, and work life in Italy find both analogues and contrasts in other societies. Gender inequalities and the sexual division of labor are aspects of ecological and economic systems, and values about family life change only as those wider systems change. Perhaps the moral of the story is that parental leave and day care legislation are only two of the many steps of progressive change toward gender equity. They are extremely important elements in the program, but they must be supported by other, more fundamental and more radical economic and cultural movements.

NOTES

1. This section is in part a review of historical and ethnographic work by other scholars and in part based on my own field research in the alpine village of Valbella (a pseudonym) in the Piedmont region of northwestern Italy. I conducted research in this village during the summer of 1972, during 1974 and 1975, and again in the summers of 1979, 1980, and 1985. The research has been supported at various times by a National Institute of Mental Health Traineeship administered by the Department of Anthropology at the University of California in San Diego, a Fulbright Scholarship, and several grants from Lawrence University. In addition, some of the general observations derive from a year spent in Florence as director of the Associated Colleges of the Midwest program there and from two months spent as a visiting scholar at the University of Rome through the gracious invitation of Professor Tullio Tentori. I gratefully acknowledge all of these sources of support. I also appreciate the advise and friendship of Marilyn Essex, who solicited this paper and provided valuable help toward its completion.

2. For an excellent recent ethnography describing this centripetality in the history of a single family, see Pitkin, 1985.

3. Independence is such a cherished value in U.S. culture that it is essential to point out that satisfied dependency needs may have very positive psychological and social consequences, especially by contrast with a kind of independence born of early and forced separation from secure nurturing relationships.

4. A somewhat enigmatic response in 30.2 percent of the cases was that the child was "not entrusted to any adult" (ISTAT, 1985a, p. 97). This may suggest either a reluctance to use day care facilities or their unavailability. In many cases, it may be that infants are left in the care of older (but still juvenile) siblings.

REFERENCES

Bailey, F. G. (1983). *The Tactical Uses of Passion*. Ithaca, N.Y.: Cornell University Press.
Barbagli, Marzio (1984). *Sotto lo stesso tetto*. Bologna: Il Mulino.

Barkan, Joanne (1984). *Visions of Emancipation: The Italian Workers' Movement Since 1945*. New York: Praeger.

Barry, Herbert III, Irvin L. Child, and Margaret K. Bacon (1959). "Relation of Child Training to Subsistence Economy." *American Anthropologist* 61: 51–63.

Beccalli, Bianca (1985). "Italy." In Jennie Farley, ed., *Women Workers in Fifteen Countries*. Ithaca, N.Y.: ILR Press.

Belmonte, Thomas (1979). *The Broken Fountain*. New York: Columbia University Press.

Berkner, Lutz (1972). "The Stem Family and the Developmental Cycle of the Peasant Household: An Eighteenth Century Austrian Example." *American Historical Review* 78: 398–418.

Birnbaum, Lucia Chiavola (1986). *Liberazione della donna: Feminism in Italy*. Middletown, Conn.: Wesleyan University Press.

Blok, Anton (1974). *The Mafia of a Sicilian Village, 1860–1960*. New York: Harper.

———— (1981). "Rams and Billy-Goats: A Key to the Mediterranean Code of Honour." *Man* 16: 427–40.

Bolton, Charlene, Ralph Bolton, Lorraine Gross, Amy Koel, Carol Michelson, Robert L. Munroe, and Ruth H. Munroe (1976). "Pastoralism and Personality: An Andean Replication." *Ethos* 4: 463–81.

Braudel, Fernand (1972). *The Mediterranean and the Mediterranean World in the Age of Philip II*. New York: Harper & Row.

Bravo, Gian Luigi (1980). *Donna e lavoro contadino*. Cuneo: L'Arciere.

Buttafuoco, Annarita (1980). "Italy: The Feminist Challenge." In Carl Boggs and David Plotke, eds., *The Politics of Eurocommunism: Socialism in Transition*. Montreal: Black Rose Press.

Caldwell, Lesley (1986). "Feminism and Abortion Politics in Italy." In Joni Lovenduski and Joyce Outshoorn, eds., *The New Politics of Abortion*. London: Sage Publications.

Campbell, J. K. (1964). *Honour, Family, and Patronage*. Oxford: Oxford University Press.

Chodorow, Nancy (1974). "Family Structure and Feminine Personality." In Michele Zimbalist Rosaldo and Louise Lamphere, eds., *Woman, Culture, and Society*. Stanford, Calif.: Stanford University Press.

Counihan, Carole M. (1984). "Bread as World: Food Habits and Social Relations in Modernizing Sardinia." *Anthropological Quarterly* 57: 47–59.

D'Andrade, Roy G. (1966). "Sex Differences and Cultural Institutions." In E. E. Maccoby, ed., *The Development of Sex Differences*. Stanford, Calif.: Stanford University Press.

Davis, John (1977). *People of the Mediterranean*. London: Routledge & Kegan Paul.

———— (1987). "Family and State in the Mediterranean." In D. D. Gilmore, ed., *Honor and Shame and the Unity of the Mediterranean*. Washington, D.C.: American Anthropological Association.

De Sousa, Ronald (1980). "The Rationality of Emotions." In Amelie Oksenberg Rorty, ed., *Explaining Emotions*. Berkeley: University of California Press.

De Spirito, Angelomichele (1983). *Antropologia della famiglia meridionale*. Rome: Editrice Ianua.

Dimen, Muriel (1986). "Servants and Sentries: Women, Power, and Social Reproduction in Kriovrisi." In Jill Dubisch, ed., *Gender and Power in Rural Greece*. Princeton: Princeton University Press.

Dodds, Dinah (1982). "Extra-Parliamentary Feminism and Social Change in Italy, 1971–1980." *International Journal of Women's Studies* 5: 148–60.

Dubisch, Jill, ed. (1986a). *Gender and Power in Rural Greece*. Princeton: Princeton University Press.

——— (1986b). "Culture Enters Through the Kitchen: Women, Food, and Social Boundaries in Rural Greece." In Jill Dubisch, ed., *Gender and Power in Rural Greece*. Princeton: Princeton University Press.

Edgerton, Robert B. (1971). *The Individual in Cultural Adaptation: A Study of Four East African Peoples*. Berkeley: University of California Press.

Friedl, Ernestine (1978). "Society and Sex Roles," *Human Nature* 1: 68–75.

——— (1984). *Women and Men: An Anthropologist's View*. Prospect Heights, Ill.: Waveland Press.

Gandus, V. (1989). "Aborti in giallo." *Panorama* 27, no. 1189, p. 62.

Gilmore, Margaret, M., and David D. Gilmore (1979). "'Machismo': A Psychodynamic Approach (Spain)." *Journal of Psychological Anthropology* 2: 281–300.

Giovannini, Maureen J. (1981). "Woman: A Dominant Symbol Within the Cultural System of a Sicilian Town." *Man* 16: 408–26.

Goldschmidt, Walter (1976). "Absent Eyes and Idle Hands: Socialization for Low Affect Among the Sebei." In Theodore Schwartz, ed., *Socialization as Cultural Communication*. Berkeley: University of California Press.

Goody, Jack (1983). *The Development of the Family and Marriage in Europe*. Cambridge: Cambridge University Press.

Gregor, Thomas (1985). *Anxious Pleasures: The Sexual Lives of an Amazonian People*. Chicago: University of Chicago Press.

Hellman, Judith Adler (1984). "The Italian Communists, the Women's Question and the Challenge of Feminism." *Studies in Political Economy* 13: 57–82.

——— (1987). *Journeys Among Women: Feminism in Five Italian Cities*. New York: Oxford University Press.

Herdt, Gilbert (1981). *Guardians of the Flutes: Idioms of Masculinity*. New York: McGraw-Hill.

Herzfeld, Michael (1987). "'As in Your Own House': Hospitality, Ethnography, and the Stereotype of Mediterranean Society." In David D. Gilmore, ed., *Honor and Shame and the Unity of the Mediterranean*. Washington, D.C.: American Anthropological Association.

Istituto Centrale di Statistica (1985a). *Indagine sulle strutture ed i comportamenti familiari*. Rome: ISTAT.

——— (1985b). *Le donne italiane e il lavoro*. Rome: ISTAT.

Kamerman, Sheila B. (1988). "Maternity and Parenting Benefits: An International Overview." In Edward F. Zigler and Meryl Frank, eds., *The Parental Leave Crisis: Toward a National Policy*. New Haven, Conn.: Yale University Press.

Kertzer, David I. (1984). *Family Life in Central Italy, 1880–1910: Sharecropping, Wage Labor and Coresidence*. New Brunswick, N. J.: Rutgers University Press.

—— (1987). "L'analisi della famiglia italiana diventa maggiorenne." *Rassegna italiana di sociologia* 28: 135–39.

Kertzer, David I., and Cardine B. Brettell (1987). "Recenti sviluppi nella storia della famiglia italiana e iberica." *Rassegna italiana di sociologia* 28: 249–89.

Kogan, Norman (1983). *A Political History of Italy: The Postwar Years*. New York: Praeger.

Lancaster, Jane B. (1976). "Sex Roles in Primate Societies." In M. S. Teitelbaum, ed., *Sex Differences: Social and Biological Perspectives*. Garden City, N. Y.: Anchor.

Levy, Robert I. (1973). *Tahitians: Mind and Experience in the Society Islands*. Chicago: University of Chicago Press.

Lutz, Catherine (1986). "Emotion, Thought, and Estrangement: Emotion as a Cultural Category." *Cultural Anthropology* 1: 287–309.

Mead, Margaret (1949). *Coming of Age in Samoa*. New York: Mentor [1928].

Medick, Hans, and David Warren Sabean, eds. (1984). *Interest and Emotion: Essays on the Study of Family and Kinship*. Cambridge: Cambridge University Press.

Munroe, Ruth H., and Robert L. Munroe (1971). "Household Density and Infant Care in an East African Society." *Journal of Social Psychology* 83:3–13.

New, Rebecca Staples (1988). "Parental Goals and Italian Infant Care." In Robert A. LeVine, Patricia M. Miller, and Mary Maxwell West, eds., *Parental Behavior in Diverse Societies*. San Francisco: Jossey-Bass.

Pitkin, Donald S. (1985). *The House that Giacomo Built: History of an Italian Family, 1898–1978*. Cambridge: Cambridge University Press.

Pitt-Rivers, Julian (1977). *The Fate of Shechem, or the Politics of Sex: Essays in the Anthropology of the Mediterranean*. Cambridge: Cambridge University Press.

Porter, Mary Cornelia, and Corey Venning (1976). "Catholicism and Women's Role in Italy and Ireland." In Lynne B. Iglitzin and Ruth Ross, eds., *Women in the World: A Comparative Study*. Santa Barbara, Calif.: American Bibliographical Center—Clio Press.

Rapp, Rayna, E. Ross, and Renate Bridenthal (1979). "Examining Family History." *Feminist Studies* 5: 174–200.

Reiter, Rayna R. (1975). "Men and Women in the South of France: Public and Private Domains." In Rayna R. Reiter, ed., *Toward an Anthropology of Women*. New York: Monthly Review Press.

Rubin, Gayle (1975). "The Traffic in Women: Notes on the 'Political Econ-

omy' of Sex." In Rayna R. Reiter, ed., *Toward an Anthropology of Women.*
New York: Monthly Review Press.

Saraceno, Chiara (1984a). "Shifts in Public and Private Boundaries: Women
as Mothers and Service Workers in Italian Daycare." *Feminist Studies* 10:
7–29.

———— (1984b). "The Social Construction of Childhood: Child Care and Education Policies in Italy and the United States." *Social Problems* 31: 351–
63.

———— (1987). "Tra storia e sociologia, un contributo importante allo studio
della famiglia." *Rassegna italiana di sociologia* 28: 127–34.

Saunders, George R. (1979). "Social Change and Psychocultural Continuity
in an Alpine Italian Village." *Ethos* 7: 206–31.

———— (1981). "Men and Women in Southern Europe: An Analysis of Some
Aspects of Cultural Complexity." *Journal of Psychoanalytic Anthropology* 4:
435–66.

———— (1985). "Silence and Noise as Emotion Management Styles: An Italian Case." In Deborah Tannen and Muriel Saville-Troike, eds., *Perspectives on Silence.* Norwood, N. J.: Ablex.

———— (1988a). "Political Religion and Religious Politics in an Alpine Italian
Village." In George R. Saunders, ed., *Culture and Christianity: The Dialectics of Transformation.* Westport, Conn.: Greenwood Press.

———— (1988b). "Family Feelings: The Political Economy of Emotion in
Mediterranean Europe." Paper read at the annual meeting of the
American Anthropological Association, Phoenix, Arizona, November
20–25.

Schneider, Jane (1971). "Of Vigilance and Virgins: Honor, Shame and Access to Resources in Mediterranean Societies." *Ethnology* 10: 1–24.

Schneider, Jane, and Peter Schneider (1976). *Culture and Political Economy in
Western Sicily.* New York: Academic Press.

Schwartz, Theodore, ed. (1976). *Socialization as Cultural Communication.*
Berkeley: University of California Press.

Whiting, John W. M., Richard Kluckhohn, and Albert S. Anthony (1958).
"The Function of Male Initiation Ceremonies at Puberty." In E. E. Maccoby, T. M. Newcomb, and E. L. Hartley, eds., *Readings in Social Psychology.* New York: Holt.

Zariski, Raphael (1972). *Italy: The Politics of Uneven Development.* Hinsdale,
Ill.: Dryden Press.

*Appendixes, The
Contributors, and Index*

Appendix A

Task Force Recommendations on Parental Leave and Child Care

THE GROUP of experts who gathered on September 15–17, 1988, in Racine, Wisconsin, for the Wingspread Conference on Parental Leave and Child Care formed themselves into four task forces, each assigned to thrash out an agenda for a specific area. The products were then reworked and evaluated against similar recommendations made by other bodies. The result was four sets of recommendations, covering both research and policy and both parental leave and child care. Authors of chapters in this volume have elaborated on many of the issues involved. We include these research and policy agendas as an appendix so that readers can find, in compact form, the opinions of experts on research and policymaking priorities. Appendix B provides a current listing of parental leave legislation by state.

Recommendations of the Task Force on
Parental Leave Research

In general, a need exists for longitudinal studies that identify the relationship between policies and the population with respect to sociodemographic variables, especially race, total family income, and gender. Specific areas that warrant investigation include the following:

1. The effect of leave policies on the entire family, with the introduction of additional variables such as complications in maternal or child health, type of infant care, and infant–parent attachment.

2. Development of a national data base that describes current family leave policies across the population by organizational variables such as the type, size, and nature of industry, level of profitability, and job type. This data base would also document the effects of family and medical leave policies on the workforce, especially women. For example, how many people lose jobs because of the lack of family leave policies?

3. Alternative strategies for funding paid family leave:
   a. Investigate the relationship of parental leave to medical leave, and

whether using one type of leave affects an individual's ability to use the other.
  b. Consider alternative ways to fund and structure TDI so that medical leave coverage can be extended to all states.
  c. Consider how TDI programs specific to medical leave can be extended to cover family leaves.
  d. Examine the Canadian experience with medical and family leave: advantages and disadvantages, and applicability to the United States.

4. Strategies for increasing men's contributions to child care:
  a. Consider how pay equity affects who takes leave.
  b. Consider how flexible scheduling (part-time, gradual return to work after the birth or adoption of a baby) affects the ability of men and women to reenter the workforce.

5. The implications of family leave policies on business:
  a. Identify the benefits of family leave policy to the employer.
  b. Investigate whether firms really do relocate as a result of mandated leave policies.

6. The influence of corporate culture on work–family conflict.

Recommendations of the Task Force on
Parental Leave Policy

There is a serious need in the United States for a national family policy. The recommendations of the Task Force on Parental Leave Policy are as follows:

1. All employees should have a right to up to 26 weeks of job-guaranteed *medical leave*[1] in any one year if they are temporarily disabled. Disability due to pregnancy, childbirth, and recuperation from childbirth should be included in this category.

2. All employees should have a right to up to 26 weeks of job-guaranteed *family leave* in any one year for the purpose of caring for a newborn or adopted child or a seriously ill child, spouse, or parent.

3. Employees should have a right to use both family and medical leave consecutively or nonconsecutively, with a possibility of 52 weeks of leave in total.

4. All benefits, including health insurance, life insurance, and retirement contributions should be maintained during leave, in the same manner as during the period prior to the leave. Seniority should be maintained.

5. Employees should receive income replacement during medical leave and family leave at a rate of 75 percent of the individual's weekly wage, up to a maximum rate of 150 percent of the median individual income in the United States that year.[2]

6. Research should be conducted to determine the best manner in which to finance income replacement during medical leave and family leave.

There are various existing models that might be incorporated. Two likely possibilities are to extend existing temporary disability insurance (TDI) programs or unemployment insurance programs. Models of employer/employee contributions should be investigated. For example, in New Jersey the employer and employee make equal contributions, whereas in California the employee pays the entire amount.

7. These family and medical leave policies should be mandated by federal law and administered by states.

8. All employers participating in unemployment insurance must participate, and there should be some sanction or consequence for noncompliance, as with state unemployment insurance programs.

Recommendations of the Task Force on Child Care Research

A need exists for study designs that address the interface of child care and parental leave policy and research issues. Some child care issues (for example, quality, type, and availability) should inform parental leave research and require further research in themselves. Specific issues that should be considered include the following:

1. Integration of child care and parenting issues into surveys and other areas of research, including economic, demographic, social science, and census studies:
   a. Include the needs, contributions, and impact of policy on fathers in research questions.
   b. Look at the supply of child care available to workers as a variable in research.

2. The range of child care options available to families:
   a. Develop a clear terminology for characterizing child care arrangements.
   b. Examine the options for families and employers.
   c. Measure the average length of time needed to locate adequate child care—post partum and during illness or emergencies.
   d. Conduct needs assessments regarding parents' preference for type and location of child care (home-, center-, or work-based). These surveys (by employers and policy researchers) should include open-ended questions to allow individual differences in needs to emerge.

3. The interface between parental needs and the needs of children in our society (e.g., what each needs, wants, and receives):
   a. Recognize changes in the parent–child relationship over time and their influence on parental needs and satisfaction with child care arrangements. Conceptualize family needs from both a developmental and a systems perspective.

b. Consider how the timing or onset of care by someone other than parent affects child and family functioning, and particularly the individual child's mental health.

c. Include amount and sources of family stress and social support.

4. The quality of care and interactions that children experience:
   a. Devise clearer definitions leading to more meaningful and specific assessments of "quality child care."
   b. Assess the quality of parent–child–caregiver relationships.
   c. Consider how relationships between caregiver and child and between caregiver and parent can be supported and enhanced.
   d. Include many child and family process and outcome measures in study designs, not only attachment measures.
   e. Take a longitudinal perspective in process and outcome studies.

5. Professionalizing the caregiver role:
   a. Consider approaches to enhancing the professional development of caregivers that go beyond increases in salaries and benefits to include training and consultation.
   b. Implement studies to evaluate the effectiveness of increased professionalization on caregiver–child interactions, caregiver–parent relations, and the satisfaction and self-respect of workers.

In addition to the above recommendations, which were informed in part by the Research Facilitation Committee of the National Center for Clinical Infant Programs (NCCIP),[3] the Task Force on Child Care Research also supports the additional recommendations of the NCCIP committee. This committee's recommendations focused on the importance of the quality of care and emphasized that child care must be viewed as support to the entire family and that a comfortable relationship between caregivers and parents can help to promote the well-being of children and their parents. Additionally, the NCCIP committee suggested two major areas of study for child care researchers: (1) family processes prior to supplementary care (for example, demographic variables, stress, support, parental feelings and attitudes towards separation and child care, and individual differences in infants), and (2) the quality of care provided to infants by both parents and caregivers (for example, stability and continuity of care, temperament and education of caregivers, and other physical and social characteristics of the caregiving environment).

Recommendations of the Task Force on Child Care Policy

A national family agenda should, at a minimum, include a coordinated national child care policy and a strategy to obtain adequate income supports for families with children. The national child care policy will need to address the following issues:

1. The quality of child care should be improved through:
   a. Training of personnel
   b. Regulations and standards
   c. Parent education about what constitutes quality child care
   d. Incorporation of such important principles as gender and race equity into curricula.

2. The supply and variety of child care options should be increased for:
   a. Children of all ages, infants through early adolescents
   b. Sick children
   c. Children with special needs
   d. All parts of the country—urban, suburban, and rural areas
   e. Evening and night shifts.

3. Child care should be made affordable through:
   a. A substantial investment of federal dollars in child care subsidies
   b. A minimum universal benefit to all, with special assistance to those in need.

4. Wages and benefits for child care workers should be improved, to reduce staff turnover and improve the quality and continuity of child care arrangements. This objective will increase the potential cost of child care, making the affordability strategies discussed above even more salient.

NOTES

1. We make a distinction between "medical leave," which refers to leaves that are necessary because of an individual's temporary medical disability (for example, disability due to surgery, serious illness, or childbirth and post-partum recovery), and "family leave," which refers to leave for the purpose of caring for a family member (see item 2).

2. Paid leaves were judged to be essential for two reasons. First, unpaid leaves discriminate against those with low incomes, who may not be able to afford the leave. Second, it is essential for fathers to be more involved in the rearing of children; most families cannot afford to have a father take an unpaid leave of any substantial length.

3. *Infants, Families and Child Care: Toward a Research Agenda.* Report to the field from a meeting of infant day care researchers convened by the Research Facilitation Committee of the National Center for Clinical Infant Programs (1988). National Center for Clinical Infant Programs, 733 15th Street, N.W., Suite 912, Washington, D.C. 20005. Telephone: (202) 347–0308.

Appendix B

State Laws and Regulations
Guaranteeing Employees Their Jobs
After Family and Medical Leaves

What the Chart Covers

THIS CHART, prepared by the Women's Legal Defense Fund, summarizes the laws and regulations of the 25 states and Puerto Rico that guarantee state or private employees their jobs if they must be out of work temporarily because of family or personal medical needs. State legislative activity in this area is intense; 32 states considered some form of family or medical leave legislation in the first seven months of 1989 alone.

Of the 20 jurisdictions that cover private employees,

3 (Connecticut, Maine, and Wisconsin) guarantee jobs after family *and* medical leaves.

1 (New Jersey) guarantees jobs after family leave.

4 (Minnesota, Oregon, Rhode Island, and Washington) guarantee jobs only after parental leaves.

1 (Kentucky) guarantees jobs only after leave for adoption.

11 (California, Hawaii, Iowa, Kansas, Louisiana, Massachusetts, Montana, New Hampshire, Puerto Rico, Tennessee, and Vermont) guarantee jobs during periods of pregnancy- and childbirth-related disability and, for women only, after childbirth.

The remaining 6 jurisdictions (Florida, North Carolina, North Dakota, Oklahoma, Pennsylvania, and West Virginia) provide some form of job-guaranteed family or medical leave for state employees only.

Categories Shown on the Chart

Family Leave

Leave for employees of both sexes to care for family members: a new-born child; a newly adopted child; a child placed with the employee for

468

foster care; or a seriously ill child, spouse, or parent. If the leave is for only one of these purposes, this is stated. If the leave is limited to female employees, this is stated; otherwise employees of both sexes are covered. Leave is unpaid unless otherwise noted.

Medical Leave

Leave because of an employee's own serious health condition (of any kind), including as a subcategory leave limited to that period during which a female employee is disabled by pregnancy, childbirth, or a related medical condition. Leave is unpaid unless otherwise noted.

Employers Covered

The threshold number of employees an employer must have in order to be covered by the applicable legislation.

Eligibility Requirement

The length of time an employee must have worked for an employer in order to be eligible for family or medical leave; this category also shows whether coverage is provided for part-time workers.

Notice Provision

Requirements that the employee give advance notice of the time and duration of family and medical leave or notice of intent to return to the job; requirements that the employee provide some form of medical certification.

Reinstatement Provision

Specific requirements for protection of the employee's job (and accrued leave, seniority, pension rights, and the like) upon return from family or medical leave.

Leave Benefits

Provisions regarding insurance and other benefits during leave: whether the legislation requires the employer to continue medical coverage for an employee on leave, or whether the employee is permitted or required to pay for continued coverage.

Source

Citation of state statutory and/or regulatory provisions on family and medical leave.

Enforcement Agency

The agency responsible for enforcement of the statute or regulation requiring family and medical leave. This agency generally provides information to employers and employees and accepts complaints of violations of the law or regulation. The length of time a plaintiff has to file a complaint with the agency is shown.

What the Chart Does Not Cover

State laws or regulations that deal with some form of family or medical leave, but do not *require* employers to guarantee employees their jobs while the employees are out on family or medical leave, are not covered on this chart. Thus, the following types of laws are not included: antidiscrimination statutes or regulations that provide that the lack of a "maternity leave" policy is unlawful if it has a disparate impact on women; statutes that provide that employees may take family or medical leave at the discretion of their employers or supervisors; and statutes that require employers to extend to adoptive parents the same leave benefits they provide to biological parents.

Also not covered on the chart are state temporary disability insurance (TDI) laws. Under these laws—which are in effect in 5 states (California, Hawaii, New Jersey, New York, and Rhode Island) and Puerto Rico—the state TDI programs pay salary replacement benefits during periods when employees are temporarily disabled from working, including periods of disability due to pregnancy, childbirth, and related medical conditions. *The existence of a state TDI program does not necessarily guarantee an employee the right to return to her or his job, however.* In Puerto Rico, in addition to the TDI system, an employer must pay half of a pregnant woman's salary, wages, or other compensation during pre- and postnatal leave; however, the law does not require payment during extended postnatal leave due to complications.

Finally, although not a state law, the federal Pregnancy Discrimination Act (PDA), which was passed by Congress in 1978 as an amendment to Title VII of the Civil Rights Act of 1964, provides important protections for many employees, especially those whose employers provide some leave benefits. The PDA provides that if an employer chooses to make leave available to employees, it must be made available on a nondiscriminatory basis; that is, that employers must treat employees affected by pregnancy, childbirth, and related medical conditions the same as other temporarily disabled employees.

In practical terms, this means that a woman cannot be fired, denied a job, or denied a promotion because of her pregnancy. She cannot be forced by her employer to take "maternity" leave; that determination is to be based on her ability to perform her job. Leave must be provided for pregnancy, childbirth, and related medical conditions to the same extent as it is provided for other temporary medical conditions such as cancer or surgery. When a woman does take a pregnancy disability leave, her job and employment benefits are protected to the same extent as when leaves are taken for other temporary disabilities. Health insurance coverage must be provided for pregnancy, childbirth, and related medical conditions to the same extent as for other medical conditions. When an employer provides leave to care for a new or ill child, as distinguished from leave for the period of disability related to pregnancy and childbirth, that leave must be made available to both fathers and mothers.

The requirements of the federal law apply to all employers of 15 or more employees. Many states have almost identical laws that apply to smaller employers in the state. The United States Equal Employment Opportunity Commission (EEOC), 2401 E Street, N.W., Room 412, Washington, D.C. 20507, (202) 634–6922, enforces the federal law. Information about state antidiscrimination laws can be obtained from the state civil rights or fair employment agency or commission; the name, address, and telephone number of this agency can be obtained from the federal EEOC or from the state enforcement agency listed on this chart.

Additional legal protection may also be available through collective bargaining agreements, employment contracts, and employer personnel policies.

State	Family Leave	Medical Leave	Employers Covered	Eligibility Requirement
CALIFORNIA (Effective date: 1/20/80)	Not addressed.	Pregnancy disability—reasonable leave up to 4 months.	Employers with 5 or more employees.	Not addressed.
CONNECTICUT (Effective date for Stat. 1: 7/1/88)	Stat. 1: Family leave for birth or adoption of a child, or for serious illness of a child, spouse, or parent.	Stat. 1: General disability.	Stat. 1: The state and agencies.	Stat. 1 & 2: Not addressed.
(Effective date for Stat. 2: 1973)		Stat. 2: Pregnancy disability—reasonable leave.	Stat. 2: Employers with 3 or more employees, certain family businesses exempted.	

Reinstatement Provision	Notice Provision	Leave Benefits	Statutory or Regulatory Provision	Enforcement Agency
mployee must e reinstated to riginal or sub-antially similar osition unless ie job has eased to exist or legitimate usiness reasons nrelated to the mployee's preg-ancy or because ich means of reserving the ob would under-iine the em-loyer's ability to perate the busi-ess safely and fficiently.	Employer may require notice; may require medical certifica-tion if required of other disabled employees.	None required; must be the same as those pro-vided for other temporarily dis-abled workers.	Stat.: Cal. Gov't Code secs. 12945 (1)–(2), 12960–75 (West 1980 and Supp. 1988). Reg.: Cal. Admin. Code tit. 2, secs. 7286.9, 7420–7466 (1985).	Dist. Administra-tor Dept. of Fair Employment & Housing 1201 I Street, #214 Sacramento, CA 95814 (916) 445–9918 1 year to file complaint.
tat. 1 & 2: Em-loyee must be einstated to riginal position r to an equiva-nt position with quivalent pay nd accumulated eniority, retire-ient, fringe enefits, and ther service redits. However, 1 the case of a rivate em-loyer, the em-loyer is not equired to rein-tate the em-loyee if the mployer's cir-umstances have o changed that t is impossible or nreasonable to lo so.	Stat. 1: Medical certification re-quired for med-ical leave; notice required for family leave. Stat. 2: Not ad-dressed.	Stat. 1: The state must pay for the continuation of health insurance benefits for the public employee during the leave of absence. Stat. 2: Not ad-dressed.	Stat. 1: State Per-sonnel Act, Conn. Gen. Stat. Ann. sec. 5–193 et seq. (West 1988 and 1989 Supp.) Stat. 2: Conn. Gen. Stat. secs. 46a–60(a)(7)(B) to (D), 46a–82 to –96 (1986).	Stat. 1: Dept. of Administrative Services 165 Capital Ave. Hartford, CT 06106 (203) 566–4720 Stat. 2: Com'n. on Human Rights & Oppor-tunities 90 Washington Street Hartford, CT 06101 (203) 566–3350 180 days to file complaint.

State	Family Leave	Medical Leave	Employers Covered	Eligibility Requirement
(Effective date for Stat. 3: 7/1/90)	Stat. 3: Family leave for birth or adoption, or for serious illness of child, spouse, or parent. Stat. 1: Total of 24 weeks in 2 years for family and medical leave combined. Stat. 3: Total of 12 weeks in 2 years for family and medical leave combined; to be raised to 16 weeks by 1993.	Stat. 3: General disability.	Stat. 3: Employers with 250 or more employees; to be reduced in stages to 75 by 1993.	Stat. 3: Employee must have been employed 12 months or more and for 1,000 or more hours in the 12-month period preceding the first day of leave
FLORIDA (Effective date, Stat.: 1979)	Stat.: Up to 6 months leave for women after birth (including pregnancy disability). Reg.: Up to 4 months leave for adoptive parents. (No provision for biological fathers.)	Not addressed.	State agencies: service, select exempt, and senior management employees.	Not addressed.
HAWAII (Effective date: 11/15/82)	Not addressed.	Pregnancy disability—reasonable leave.	Employers with 1 or more employee(s).	Not addressed.

Reinstatement Provision	Notice Provision	Leave Benefits	Statutory or Regulatory Provision	Enforcement Agency
Stat. 3: Employee must be reinstated to same or equivalent position and pay with retention of seniority, retirement, fringe benefits, and other service credits. If employee's physical condition mandates a different position, employer must transfer employee if a suitable position is available.	Stat. 3: 2 weeks advance notice, if possible, and physician's certification. Employee must submit to examination by physician selected by employer upon request. If leave is for nonemergency medical treatment, employee must, subject to physician's approval, avoid disrupting business operations.	Stat. 3: None required.	Stat. 3: 1989 Conn. Public Act 89–382.	Dept. of Labor 200 Folly Brook Blvd. Wethersfield, CT 06109 (203) 566–4550
Stat.: Employee must be reinstated to same or equivalent position and pay, with retention of seniority, retirement, fringe benefits, other service credit accumulated before leave.	Notification in writing prior to leave.	None required.	Stat.: Fl. Stat. 110.221 Reg.: Fl. Admin. Code 22A–8.016.	Dept. of Administration 435 Carlton Bldg. Tallahassee, FL 32399–1550 (904) 488–4116
Employee must be reinstated to original job or to position of comparable status and pay without loss of accumulated service credits and privileges.	Employer may require medical certification.	None required.	Reg.: Hawaii Dept. of Industrial and Labor Relations; Sex and Marital Status Discrimination Regulations, 12–23–1 to –22, 12–23–58, Fair Empl. Prac. Manual (BNA) 453: 2301 to 2308, 453:2328 (1983).	Dept. of Labor, Enforcement Div. Fair Empl. Practices 830 Punchbowl Street Room 340 Honolulu, HI 96813 (808) 548–3976 90 days to file complaint.

475

State	Family Leave	Medical Leave	Employers Covered	Eligibility Requirement
IOWA (Effective date: 7/1/87)	Not addressed.	Pregnancy disability—up to 8 weeks.	Employers with 4 or more employees.	Not addressed.
KANSAS (Effective date: 1/1/74)	Not addressed.	Pregnancy disability ("childbearing")—reasonable period.	Employers with 4 or more employees.	Not addressed.
KENTUCKY (Effective date: 7/15/82)	6 weeks for adoption of a child under age 7.	Not addressed.	Employers with 1 employee or more.	Not addressed.
LOUISIANA (Effective date: 9/1/87)	Not addressed.	Pregnancy disability—reasonable leave up to 4 months; only 6 weeks of disability leave required	Employers with 26 or more employees.	Not addressed.

476

Reinstatement Provision	Notice Provision	Leave Benefits	Statutory or Regulatory Provision	Enforcement Agency
Must be the same as those provided for other temporarily disabled workers.	Notice required; employer may require medical certification.	None required; must be the same as those provided for other temporarily disabled workers.	Stat.: Iowa Code secs. 601A.6(2), 601A.15–.17 (1988).	Iowa Civil Rights Com'n. 211 E. Maple Street 2d Floor c/o Grimes State Office Bldg. Des Moines, IA 50319 (515) 281–4121 (800) 457–4416 (toll-free, Iowa only) 180 days to file complaint
Employee must be reinstated to original job or to position of comparable status and pay without loss of service credits, seniority, or other benefits.	Employee must signify intent to return to work within a reasonable time.	None required; must be the same as those provided for other temporarily disabled workers.	Reg.: Kansas Commission on Civil Rights, Guidelines on Discrimination Because of Sex, secs. 21–32–6(D), 21–41–1 to 45–25, Fair Empl. Prac. Manual (BNA) 453:3311, 453:3318 to 3337 (1977).	Com'n. on Civil Rights Landon St. Ofc. Bldg. 8th Floor 9100 S.W. Jackson St. Suite 851 South Topeka, KS 66612–125 (913) 296–3206 6 months to file complaint.
Not addressed.	Notice required.	None required.	Stat.: Ky. Rev. Stat. Ann. sec. 337.015 (Michie/Bobbs-Merrill 1983).	Ky. Labor Cabinet Div. of Employment Standards & Mediation 1049 US #127 South Frankfort, KY 40601 (502) 564–2784
Not addressed.	Employer may require notice.	None required; must be the same as those provided for other temporarily disabled workers.	Stat.: La. Rev. Stat. Ann. sec. 23:1007 (West 1988).	None; enforcement by civil action.

State	Family Leave	Medical Leave	Employers Covered	Eligibility Requirement
		for normal pregnancy or childbirth.		
MAINE (Effective date: 8/4/88)	Family leave for birth or adoption, or the serious illness of a parent, spouse, or child. Total of 8 weeks in 2 years for family and medical leave combined.	General disability.	Employers with 25 or more employees.	Employee must be employed by same employer for 12 consecutive months.
MASSACHU-SETTS (Effective date: 10/17/72)	8 weeks for female employee for birth or adoption of a child under age 3.	Not addressed.	Employers with 6 or more employees.	Completion of employee's initial probationary period of employment or 3 consecutive months as a full-time employee.
MINNESOTA (Effective date: 8/1/87)	6 weeks for birth or adoption of a child.	Not addressed.	Employers with 21 or more employees.	12 months employment at 20 or more hours per week.

Reinstatement Provision	Notice Provision	Leave Benefits	Statutory or Regulatory Provision	Enforcement Agency
mployee must e reinstated to riginal job or to osition of comarable status, eniority, emloyment beneits, pay, and ther terms and onditions of emloyment.	30 days notice required except in emergency; employers may require medical certification of serious illness.	Employer is required to make available during leave all benefits such as group life, health, and disability insurance and pensions, with all expenses borne by the employee.	Stat.: Me. Rev. Stat. Ann. tit. 26, sec. 843–49 (1988).	None; enforcement by civil action.
mployee must e reinstated to riginal position r to a similar osition with the ime status, pay, ngth of service redit, and seiority unless ere is a layoff; etains existing reference for ther positions.	2 weeks notice required.	Must be the same as those provided for other temporarily disabled workers.	Stat.: Mass. Gen. Laws Ann. ch. 149, sec. 105 D (West Supp. 1988) and ch. 151B, secs. 1(5), 4(11A) (West 1982). Reg.: Mass. Regs. Code tit. 804, sec. 8.01, 1.03(1) to −.18 (1983).	Mass. Com'n. Against Discrim. 1 Ashburn Place Boston, MA 02108 (617) 727–3990 6 months to file complaint.
mployee must e reinstated to riginal job or to osition of comarable duties, umber of ours, and pay nless there is a ayoff. Employee etains prior pay ate and all ccrued preleave enefits and senrity. Employee etains all rights nder the layoff /stem.	Employer may require notice.	Employer must continue to make health insurance coverage available to the employee on leave; employer is not required to pay costs of insurance during the leave.	Stat.: Minn. Stat. Ann. secs. 181.93–.98 (West Supp. 1988).	None; enforcement by civil action.

State	Family Leave	Medical Leave	Employers Covered	Eligibility Requirement
MONTANA (Effective date: 9/14/84)	Not addressed.	Pregnancy disability—reasonable leave.	Employers with 1 or more employees.	Not addressed.
NEW HAMPSHIRE (Effective date: 11/15/84)	Not addressed.	Pregnancy disability (for the period of physical disability).	Employers with 6 or more employees.	Not addressed.
NEW JERSEY (Effective date: 1990)	12 weeks over a 24-month period for birth or adoption or the serious illness of a child, parent, or spouse.	Not addressed.	Employers of 100 or more for first year after enactment; employers of 75 or more for second and third years; employers of 50 or more thereafter.	12 months of employment for not less than 1,000 hours during the immediately preceding 12 months.
NORTH CAROLINA (Effective date: 2/1/88)	Not addressed.	Pregnancy disability (for period of physical disability).	State agencies.	Permanent full-time, part-time, trainee, and probationary employees.

480

Reinstatement Provision	Notice Provision	Leave Benefits	Statutory or Regulatory Provision	Enforcement Agency
Employee must be reinstated to original job or to position of comparable pay, and accumulated seniority, retirement, fringe benefits, and other service credits are retained. A private employer is exempt from the reinstatement requirement if the employer's circumstances have so changed as to make it impossible or unreasonable to reinstate.	Employee must signify her intent to return at the end of the leave of absence.	None required; must be the same as those provided for other temporarily disabled workers.	Stat.: Mont. Code Ann. secs. 49–2–310 to –311, 49–2–501 to –509 (1987) Reg: Montana Human Rights Com'n., Maternity Leave Rules secs. 24.9.202–.264, 24.9.1201–.1207, Fair Empl. Prac. Manual (BNA) 455:1903–.1925, 455:1932–1934 (1988).	Human Rights Com'n. Montana Dept. of Labor & Industry 1236 6th Ave. Helena, MT 59624 (406) 444–2884 180 days to file complaint.
Employee must be reinstated to original job or comparable position unless business necessity makes this impossible or unreasonable.	Not addressed.	None required; must be the same as those provided for other temporarily disabled workers.	Stat.: NH Rev. Stat. Ann. secs. 354-A: 9–10 (Supp. 1987). Reg.: NH Code Admin. R. Hum. 402.03, 201.01–212.06 (1988).	Com'n. for Human Rights 163 Loudon Rd. Concord, NH 03301 (603) 271–2767 180 days to file complaint.
Employee must be reinstated to original position or to an equivalent position unless there is a layoff.	Notice required where need for leave is foreseeable; employer may require medical certification.	Employer is required to maintain health insurance during leave period; employer must maintain other benefits as it would for other employees on temporary leave.	Not yet codified.	Div. on Civil Rights, Dept. of Law & Public Safety 383 W. State Street Trenton, NJ 08625 (609) 292–4605
Employee must be reinstated to same or compa-	Employee must apply in writing.	Sick leave and vacation must be continued;	NC State Personnel Manual sec. 8, pp. 19.2–19.3.	Not addressed.

State	Family Leave	Medical Leave	Employers Covered	Eligibility Requirement
NORTH DAKOTA (Effective date: 1/1/90)	4 months per year for full-time employees for birth or adoption, or illness of spouse, child, or parent; prorated for part-time employees.	Not addressed.	State and its agencies.	1 year minimum employment for an average of 20 hours a week.
OKLAHOMA (Effective date: 8/20/89)	Family leave for birth or adoption, or care of terminally or critically ill child or dependent adult. Length to be specified by regulation.	Not addressed.	State agencies.	6 months minimum employment time.
OREGON (Effective date for Stat. 1: 1/1/88) (Effective date for Stat. 2: 10/3/89)	Stat. 1: 12 weeks per child for birth or adoption (under age 6).	Stat. 1: Not addressed.	Stat. 1 & 2: Employers with 25 or more employees.	Stat. 1: 90 days of employment. Employer not required to grant family leave to a worker hired on a seasonal or temporary basis for a period defined at the time of hire to be less than 6 months.
	Stat. 2: Not addressed.	Stat. 2: Pregnancy disability—for a reasonable period if such leave can be reasonably accommodated.		Stat. 2: Not addressed.

Reinstatement Provision	Notice Provision	Leave Benefits	Statutory or Regulatory Provision	Enforcement Agency
able position. tatus, pay, and eniority are etained unless ther arrange- nents are made n writing.		health coverage will continue if employee pays full premium cost.		
mployee must be reinstated to ame or compa- able position nless there is a ayoff.	Employer may require notice.	Health coverage continues, but employee may be required to bear costs.	ND Cent. Code sec. 54-52.4.	Employees may bring a civil action.
Employee must be reinstated to original position.	Employee must give reasonable notice, if possi- ble. If leave is foreseeable, it should be scheduled to ac- commodate em- ployer, if pos- sible.	Group health and life insur- ance benefits continue at em- ployee's expense.	Okla. Stat. sec. 840.7C of Title 74.	Office of Person- nel Management Jim Thorpe Bldg. 2101 N. Lincoln Blvd. Oklahoma City, OK 73150 (405) 521–2177
Stat. 1 & 2: Em- ployee must be reinstated to original job or equivalent posi- tion. However, if circumstances have so changed that the same or equivalent job no longer exists, the employee must be reinstated in any other posi- tion that is avail- able and suitable.	Stat. 1: 30 days notice required unless there is an emergency. Stat. 2: Medical certification may be required in advance.	Stat. 1 & 2: Benefits are not required to accrue during leave unless re- quired by an agreement with the employer, a collective bar- gaining agree- ment, or an em- ployer policy. Employee retains earned seniority, vacation or sick leave, pension benefits, and any other employee rights or bene- fits.	Stat. 1: Oreg. Rev. Stat. secs. 659.010–.121, 659.360–.370 (1987). Stat. 2: Oreg. Rev. Stat. sec. 659.340 (1989).	Stat. 1 & 2: Comn'er, Bureau of Labor & In- dustries Civil Rights Div. State Office Bldg. 1400 SW 5th Ave. Portland, OR 97201 (800) 452–7813 (toll-free in Oregon) (503) 229–5841 1 year to file complaint.

State	Family Leave	Medical Leave	Employers Covered	Eligibility Requirement
PENNSYL-VANIA (Effective date: 12/15/86)	6 months parental leave for birth or adoption.	Sick leave for employee's own illness (includes pregnancy disability).	State and its agencies.	Must be a permanent employee.
PUERTO RICO (Effective date: 6/11/42)	Not addressed.	Pregnancy disability—8 weeks leave, which may be divided as employee desires, from 4 weeks before and 4 weeks after childbirth to 1 week before and 7 weeks after; must be extended an additional 12 weeks in the event of complications.	Employers with 1 or more employees.	All employees are eligible.
RHODE ISLAND (Effective date: 7/1/87)	13 weeks within a 2-year period for birth, adoption, or the serious illness of a child.	Not addressed.	Private employers with 50 or more employees; any city, town, or municipal agency with 30 or more employees; the state and state agencies.	Employee must be employeed for 30 or more hours per week; must have been employed by same employer for 12 consecutive months.
TENNESSEE (Effective date: 1/1/88)	Not addressed.	Pregnancy disability and nursing—up to 4 months.	Employers with 100 or more employees.	12 consecutive months as a full-time employee.

Reinstatement Provision	Notice Provision	Leave Benefits	Statutory or Regulatory Provision	Enforcement Agency
Employee must be reinstated to same or equivalent position and pay. Seniority and benefit rights are retained, but do not accrue during leave.	2 weeks advance notice, if possible; medical certification required.	Not addressed.	Reg.: Pa. Management Directive 505.7 secs. 30.101–30.115.	Not addressed.
Employee must be reinstated to the same position.	Medical certification required.	Employee is entitled to receive half-pay during leave period.	Stat.: PR Laws Ann. tit. 29, secs. 467–72 (1985).	Dept. of Labor & Human Resources Anti-Discrimination Unit 505 Munoz Riveria Ave. Hato Rey, PR 00918 (809) 754–5292
Employee must be reinstated to original job or to a position with equivalent seniority, status, employment benefits, pay, and other terms and conditions of employment.	Notice required.	Employer must continue to maintain any existing health benefits of the employee for the duration of the leave. Employee pays employer sum equal to premium prior to commencing leave; employer refunds payment on employee's return.	Stat.: RI Gen. Laws secs. 28–48–1 to 9 (Supp. 1987).	Administrator, Div. of Labor Standards R.I. Dept. of Labor 220 Elmwood Ave. Providence, RI 02907 (401) 457–1808
Employee must be reinstated to original job or to position with	Notice required.	Employer must continue to provide benefits, plans, or pro-	Stat.: Tenn. Code Ann. secs. 50–1–501 to 50–1–505 (Supp.	Tennessee Human Rights Com'n. Suite 602

485

State	Family Leave	Medical Leave	Employers Covered	Eligibility Requirement
VERMONT (Effective date: 7/1/89)	Parental leave for women after childbirth.	Pregnancy disability.	Employers with 10 or more employees; government employees not explicitly covered.	1 year of employment for an average of 30 hours per week.
	Total of 12 weeks for parental and pregnancy disability leave for women.			
WASHINGTON (Effective date for reg.: 10/28/73)	Not addressed.	Reg.: Pregnancy disability—reasonable period.	Reg.: Employers with 8 or more employees.	Reg.: Not addressed.
(Effective date for stat.: 9/1/89)	Stat.: 12 weeks within 24 months for birth, adoption, or terminal illness of child.	Not addressed.	Stat.: Employers with 100 or more employees.	Stat.: Employee must have been employed 52 weeks at 35 or more hours per week.

Reinstatement Provision	Notice Provision	Leave Benefits	Statutory or Regulatory Provision	Enforcement Agency
comparable pay, status, length of service credit, and seniority unless the job is so unique that an employer cannot, after reasonable efforts, fill the position temporarily. Employee retains previously earned benefits. Employee may lose reinstatement rights if she works or seeks work elsewhere.		grams during leave that an employee is eligible for incident to her employment; employee may be required to pay the cost of such programs during leave, unless an employer pays the costs for all employees on leaves of absence.	1987) (as amended by 1988 Tenn. Pub. Acts 607).	225 Capitol Blvd. Nashville, TN 37129 (615) 741–5825
Employee must be reinstated to same or comparable job with same level of seniority, benefits, and compensation.	Reasonable written notice must be given, including date leave begins and expected duration.	Employer must continue benefits, though employee may be required to pay full cost at employer's rate.	Stat.: Vt. State. Ann. secs. 471 et seq.	Employee may bring civil action.
Reg.: Employee must be reinstated to same or similar job with same pay.	Reg.: Employer may require notice.	Reg.: None required; must be the same as those provided for other temporarily disabled workers.	Reg.: Wash. Admin. Code secs. 162–08–011 to –700, 162–30–020 (1977).	Reg.: Wash. State Human Rights Com'n. 402 Evergreen Plaza Bldg. FJ-41 711 S. Capitol Way Olympia, WA (206) 753–6770 Reg.: 6 months to file complaint. Stat.: Wash. State Dept. of Labor & Industries 925 Plum St. HC 710 Olympia, WA

State	Family Leave	Medical Leave	Employers Covered	Eligibility Requirement
WEST VIR-GINIA (Effective date: 7/7/89)	12 weeks per 12-month period for birth or adoption, or illness of spouse, child, or parent.	Not addressed.	State employers, schools.	12 consec weeks of ment.
WISCONSIN (Effective date: 4/26/88)	6 weeks in a 12-month period for birth or adoption of a child. 2 weeks in a 12-month period for serious illness of a child, spouse, or parent. Total of 8 weeks in a 12-month period for any combination of these reasons.	General disability—2 weeks in a 12-month period.	Employers with 50 or more employees.	Employee have been ployed by employer more than consecutiv weeks and have work least 1,000 during the ceding 52

488

Reinstatement Provision	Notice Provision	Leave Benefits	Statutory or Regulatory Provision	Enforcement Agency
				98504 (206) 753–3475
Stat.: Employee must be reinstated to same or equivalent position with retention of benefits, seniority, and pension rights accrued before leave unless there is a layoff.	Stat.: 30 days written advance notice for new child; 14 days notice for terminally ill child.	Stat.: Employer must allow continued coverage at employee's expense.	Stat.: Wash. Rev. Code Ch. 49.12, secs. 1–12.	Stat.: 90 days to file complaint.
Employee must be reinstated to same position. Benefits accrued prior to leave are retained.	Employer may require medical certification; 2 weeks notice required if leave is foreseeable.	Employer must continue group health insurance, but employee must pay premium costs.	Stat.: Code of WV, 1981 Ch. 21, Art. 5D.	Dept. of Labor, Wages & Hours Div. Capital Complex Bldg. 3 Charleston, WV 25305 (304) 348–7890
Employee must be reinstated to the same job or to a job equivalent in compensation, benefits, working shift, hours, and other terms of employment.	Notice required; employer may require medical certification regarding a serious health condition.	Employer shall maintain group health insurance coverage during leave under the conditions that applied immediately before the leave began; employee may be required to continue prior contribution; employee may be required to escrow funds for premiums pending return to job.	Sec. 103.10, Stats.	Dept. of Industry, Labor, & Human Relations Equal Rights Div. P.O. Box 8928 Madison, WI 53708 (608) 266–6860 30 days to file complaint.

The Contributors

ANN BOOKMAN is Director of a new Center for Children, Families and Public Policy at Lesley College in Cambridge, Massachusetts. As an anthropologist she has conducted research on work and family issues in East Africa and the United States and is co-editor of a book on workplace and community organizing, *Women and the Politics of Empowerment* (Temple University Press, 1988).

DEANNE BONNAR is assistant professor of social welfare at Boston University School of Social Work. Prior to assuming that position in 1989 she was director of the Massachusetts Office for Children, Boston Region.

ELLEN BRAVO is Associate Director of 9to5, the National Association of Working Women, and Executive Director of the group's Milwaukee Chapter, which she helped found in 1982. 9to5 is a membership organization of low-wage workers. In 1988 members helped lead the successful fight for a family leave law in Wisconsin.

ROSEANNE CLARK is assistant professor of psychiatry at the University of Wisconsin-Madison and director of the Parent–Infant Development Program and Clinic. In collaboration with colleagues, she developed the Parent–Child Early Relational Assessment (ERA), which is used to assess the quality of parent–child relationships. Professor Clark is also co-investigator on the Wisconsin Parental Leave Study.

LINDA M. CLIFFORD is a partner with the law firm of LaFollette & Sinykin, Madison, Wisconsin, where she chairs the firm's family leave committee. She is a graduate of Beloit College and the University of Wisconsin Law School and a former Assistant Attorney General of the State of Wisconsin. She is married and has two daughters.

MITZI (MARY E.) DUNN is manager of benefits and human resource information systems at Time Insurance Company in Milwaukee, Wisconsin. She is currently a member of a corporate day care task force committed to involving the private sector in the development of day care solutions, and she was previously a board member of the Women's Crisis Line, a United Way agency in Milwaukee.

MARILYN J. ESSEX is a senior scientist at Women's Studies and Psychiatry at the University of Wisconsin-Madison and author of numerous articles on women's health and family issues and mental health. She also is co-principal investigator, with Janet S. Hyde and Marjorie H. Klein, of the Wisconsin Parental Leave Study, currently underway.

JACQUELINE FAWCETT, Ph.D., R.N., is a professor and chair, Division of Science and Role Development at the University of Pennsylvania School of Nursing. She is co-investigator on the study of functional status and health during pregnancy and the postpartum period.

LUCINDA M. FINLEY is a professor of law at the State University of New York at Buffalo, and Co-Director of the Graduate Group in Feminist Studies. She has written extensively on employment equity for women and work and family issues.

PATRICIA GARRETT is a senior investigator at the Frank Porter Graham Child Development Center at the University of North Carolina at Chapel Hill. She has written extensively on family policy, especially as it relates to economic development and maternal employment.

LINDA HAAS is an associate professor of sociology and women's studies at the Indiana University-Indianapolis. She has studied parental leave in Sweden extensively, and her book on that topic is forthcoming.

HEIDI I. HARTMANN is currently Director of the Washington-based Institute for Women's Policy Research, a scientific research organization that conducts and disseminates research on policy issues of importance to women. She is an economist with a B.A. from Swarthmore College and M.Phil. and Ph.D. degrees from Yale University. She writes and lectures widely on women's employment and related issues.

JANET SHIBLEY HYDE is professor of psychology and Director of the Women's Studies Research Center at the University of Wisconsin-Madison. She is the author of two textbooks, *Half the Human Experience: the Psychology of Women* and *Understanding Human Sexuality*. She is principal investigator on the Wisconsin Parental Leave Study, working with Marilyn J. Essex, Marjorie H. Klein, and Roseanne Clark.

ELIZABETH JAEGER is a doctoral candidate in developmental psychology at Temple University. She is also serving as Study Coordinator on the National Study of Young Children's Lives.

SHEILA B. KAMERMAN is professor of social policy and planning at Columbia University School of Social Work, where she also co-directs the Cross-National Studies Research Program. Her teaching and research areas are the United States and Comparative Social and Family Policies. Her most recent books, co-authored with Alfred J. Kahn, are *Mothers Alone: Strategies for Times of Change* and *Child Care: Facing the Hard Choices*. One current project concerns new developments in European parenting policies.

MARJORIE H. KLEIN is professor of psychiatry and women's studies at the University of Wisconsin-Madison. Her research has focused on depression in women, assessment of depression, personality disorders, and outcome research in psychotherapy. She is a co-investigator in the Wisconsin Parental Leave Study.

LYNNE SANFORD KOESTER is a Research Scientist at the Gallaudet Research Institute, Washington, D.C., currently studying the early development of deaf infants. She previously taught at the University of North Carolina at Greensboro, and spent several years as a postdoctoral fellow at the Max-Planck-Institute for Psychiatry in Munich, Federal Republic of Germany.

SALLY LUBECK is a senior investigator at the Frank Porter Graham Child Development Center and clinical assistant professor in the School of Education at the University of North Carolina at Chapel Hill. Her work focuses on maternal employment, families, schools, and public policy.

JULES M. MARQUART is a research associate at the Foundation for Human Service Studies in Ithaca, New York, and she has been a UNDP consultant to the government of Singapore. Her research and consulting are in the areas of program evaluation, child care, and work and family linkages.

LI MIN is a doctoral student in sociology at the University of Wisconsin-Madison. Her B.A. degree in Chinese Language and Literature was awarded by Fudan University, Shanghai. Her books include *Chinese Women's Studies* (JiangXa People's Press) and *Research on Women's Issues* (Shanghai Women's Federation).

MARGARET K. NELSON is director of the Women's Studies Program and professor of sociology at Middlebury College. She is co-editor (with Emily K. Abel) of *Circles of Care: Work and Identity in Women's Lives* (State University of New York Press, 1990) and author of *Negotiated Care: The Experience of Family Day Care Providers* (Temple University Press, 1990).

JOHN R. PLEWA is a Milwaukee Democrat who has served in the Wisconsin Legislature since 1973 when he took office as a State Representative. He was elected to the State Senate in 1984. Plewa is the author of Wisconsin's Family and Medical Leave Act. He and his wife Susan are the parents of two young sons.

SUSAN DELLER ROSS is a professor of law at Georgetown University Law Center and director of the Women's Law and Public Policy Fellowship Program. She has written or co-authored books and articles on gender and the law, including *Sex Discrimination and the Law: Causes and Remedies* and *The Rights of Women*.

GEORGE R. SAUNDERS is associate professor of anthropology at Lawrence University in Appleton, Wisconsin. He has done extensive field research in Italy on gender and family and on popular religion, and he is editor of *Culture and Christianity: The Dialectics of Transformation*.

FREYA L. SONENSTEIN is a senior research associate at the Urban Institute in Washington, D.C. She directed the Child Care and Self Sufficiency Study, which was funded by the Rockefeller Foundation and the U.S. Department of Health and Human Services. She was formerly co-director of the Family and Children's Policy Program at the Florence Heller School, Brandeis University.

ROBERTA M. SPALTER-ROTH is currently Deputy Director for Research and Director for Research on Work and Family Policies at the Washington-based Institute for Women's Policy Research. Dr. Spalter-Roth is also adjunct associate professor in the Women's Studies Program at George Washington University, where she directs the graduate Women and Public Policy Program. She holds the B.A. degree from the University of Indiana and the Ph.D. from American University, both in sociology.

DOROTHY MCBRIDE STETSON is a professor of political science and a member of the women's studies faculty at Florida Atlantic University. She is author of *A Women's Issue: The Politics of Family Law Reform in England* (1982), *Women's Rights in France* (1987), *Women's Rights in the USA: Policy Debates and Gender Roles* (1991), and several articles on comparative public policy.

EILEEN TRZCINSKI is an assistant professor in the department of consumer economics and housing at Cornell University. She has conducted numerous projects on leave policies, including a study for the U.S. Small Business Administration on the prevalence and costs of leaves and on how firms manage when employees take leaves.

LORRAINE TULMAN, D.N.Sc., R.N., is an assistant professor at the University of Pennsylvania School of Nursing. She is currently the principal investigator on a three-year study funded by the National Center for Nursing Research of the National Institutes of Health on functional status and health during pregnancy and the postpartum period.

MARSHA WEINRAUB is a professor of psychology at Temple University and has written extensively on various aspects of early socioemotional development. She is a principal investigator in the National Study of Young Children's Lives.

DEEANN WENK is currently assistant professor in the department of sociology at the University of Oklahoma at Norman. She was formerly a Fellow at the Carolina Population Center at the University of North Carolina at Chapel Hill. Her research concerns female labor force participation, labor markets, and child care.

CAROLYN YORK is currently a labor economist for the American Federation of State, County and Municipal Employees (AFSCME). At the time this article was written, she was working as a research analyst for the Service Employees International Union (SEIU).

Index